Contents

Part three
Reframing the social policy of old age

Preface

In looking back over the fifty years of our existence 1947–1997, first as the National Corporation for the Care of Old People and more recently as the Centre for Policy on Ageing (CPA), it quickly becomes evident that we have been supported during that time by an impressively long line of illustrious benefactors and supporters. Although it would be impossible to acknowledge by name the contribution of all, we wish to take this opportunity to thank some, mainly members, who have been particularly closely associated with the Centre. For our very existence we are indebted to the social conscience of William Morris, Lord Nuffield, and the generosity not only of the Nuffield Foundation but also of the Lord Mayor of the City of London through the Air Raid Distress Fund and of the South Africa Gift. The Nuffield Foundation – its past and present Trustees, Directors and staff – have been a constant source of support over the years, with representatives sitting on our own Board of Governors. Other Foundations have also been generous in their sponsoring of our work – in particular the Hayward Foundation, the May Fund and the Marjorie Warren Fund – dedicated as most readers will know to the memory of one of the 'founding mothers' of British gerontology. From our earliest years, the Department of Health (and Social Security, until 1988) and other government departments have supported our work, looking to us for innovative ideas and 'new attitudes to old age'.

Throughout the years, we have been honoured by the presence of leading figures in the field of gerontology on our Boards of Governors and Advisory Councils, which oversaw our work for many years. Since the beginning, we have been blessed with loyal and forthright members who have supported us through good and bad times. Our reputation as leaders in the field was in no small way established by Mike Simson, Secretary from 1947 to 1973 and by Hugh Mellor, Assistant Secretary from 1951 who took over as Secretary from 1973 until 1980. Seminal studies on many subjects including mental illness, residential care, social work, meals on wheels, alarm systems and retirement – to name but a few – were either undertaken by us or were commissioned by us during this time.

Since 1980, when we became the Centre for Policy on Ageing, our influence as an imaginative and innovative 'think tank' has continued to grow. The leadership of key figures during the 1980s – Eric Midwinter, who was Director, and Deputy Directors, Alison Norman and Deirdre Wynne-Harley – has been crucial in the development of current attitudes within gerontological research, information and practice. The year of our name change, 1980, also saw the launching of our journal *Ageing and Society* which is jointly sponsored by CPA and the British Society of Gerontology. The early editors, Malcolm Johnson and Peter Coleman, are both members of the Centre. In 1984, a CPA Working Party chaired by Kina, Lady Avebury produced the code of practice *Home Life*, to accompany the Registered Homes Act; this has proved to be the most influential publication in the field of residential care ever published.

During all these years, we have developed fruitful relationships with many organisations in the field of ageing, both at home and abroad. Notable amongst these are the Dementia Services Development Centre, University of Stirling directed by Mary Marshall, a CPA Governor, the Age Concern Institute of Gerontology, directed by one of our past Governors, Anthea Tinker and Age Action Ireland, led by Robin Webster, another CPA member. We value greatly the benefits of these and all our many other collaborative relationships.

The Centre has always been fortunate in being served by impressive and committed staff working as a small but extremely productive team. Our current Board of Governors, under the chairmanship of Christopher Bourne, is a source of great support and sound advice, as indeed are our past Board members and Chairmen. As Director and Deputy Director under their leadership, we both wish to express our thanks to them. It was with their encouragement that the decision was made to commission this book to mark our fiftieth anniversary.

In this respect we wish to record our special thanks to the contributors to this volume and in particular to the editors, Miriam Bernard and Judith Phillips, who have freely given untold amounts of time to bring the book to completion, while at the same time making an original and very demanding contribution to the substance of the book – as those responsible for the management and direction of the Centre, we hope that we shall be able to respond to the challenges set out in their final chapter! We are grateful to Angela Clark, our Publications Officer, and Jeremy Austen who both laboured long and hard in preparing the text for publication.

In conclusion, there is one outstanding person who we should especially like to thank and acknowledge in this preface – Margot Jefferys. For many years – as an Advisory Council member 1973–1977, as a Governor from 1978, Chairman of the Board of Governors from 1980–1988 and current member of the Futures Group, she has been, and remains, an extraordinary source of support and wisdom to governors, members, directors and staff. We are greatly indebted to her constancy and vision over the years.

The editors of this publication, Miriam Bernard and Judith Phillips, wish to express special thanks to their parents, Cyril and Margaret Bernard and Bill and Bridget Phillips. Through them, they have come to a better understanding of what living through the last fifty years has been like; from them they have learnt the value of so many things expressed in these pages – the importance of continued education and learning throughout life; the development of political sensibility; a belief in social justice and in our rights and responsibilities towards each other; and the recognition that we all have a part to play in the creation of a better and more egalitarian society.

These sentiments indeed underscore the whole CPA enterprise. It is a privilege and a pleasure for the two of us, as the present directorial incumbents, to carry that enterprise on into the next fifty years.

Gillian Dalley   Gillian Crosby
Director   Deputy Director

November 1997

1 Social policy and the challenge of old age

Miriam Bernard and Judith Phillips

> There is no place, therefore, for either dark pessimism or sunny optimism in the creation of a social policy for older age in British society. What is required is a robust, commonsensical appreciation of the benefits and disbenefits of living through and out the last third of life, and a critical appraisal both of what is similar to other parts of the life-cycle, and what, for good or ill, is specific to that latter part.
>
> *Eric Midwinter (1987) Redefining Old Age: a review of CPA's recent contribution to social policy, pp. 1–2*

Introduction

This commemorative volume celebrates and acknowledges the half century of work carried out by the Centre for Policy on Ageing (CPA). The primary aim of this opening chapter is to provide the reader with an indication of the contributions which CPA has made to the development of social policy as it affects the lives of older people in Britain. We attempt to do this by locating and interweaving the Centre's work with the dramatic social and policy changes of the last fifty years. In what ways, we ask, have older people featured in or been targets of, British social policy? What impact have changing conceptualisations and images of older people and old age had on the shaping of those policies? And, most importantly, where does this leave us now in terms of developing policies which will move us into the twenty-first century?

Our purpose then is to trace the major shifts which have occurred since the euphoric beginnings of the welfare state, the creation of the National Health Service, and the birth on 1 August 1947, of what was initially called the National Corporation for the Care of Old People (NCCOP). Nurtured in the fertile soil of the welfare state, sponsored by the Nuffield Foundation and housed in premises in Regent's Park, London, the Corporation can be seen as a prime example of a long-established British social philanthropic tradition. We therefore begin this chapter by sketching in the background to post-war welfarism, reviewing the major policy concerns of the time and the ways this was reflected in the work of the embryonic Corporation. This is followed, in the second part of the chapter, by an evaluation of developments from the 1950s to the 1970s: a period during which issues of accommodation (both institutional forms and community-based alternatives) were to dominate the social policy agenda where older people (and the NCCOP) were concerned.

The oil crisis of the early 1970s, global recession and continuing inflation at home, together marked the end of the post-war boom period. With the return of a Conservative government in 1979, and the rising panic about population ageing, the welfare state came under increasing attack. In the third and fourth sections, we chart this changing policy agenda which, for older people, has meant a breaking of the 'welfare compact' between the generations; an emphasis on market solutions; the unregulated growth and expansion of the private and independent sectors; and the discovery (in the 1980s) of informal carers. In response to these turbulent times, the maturing and flourishing NCCOP broadened its concerns and expertise and, in 1980, officially changed its name to the Centre for Policy on Ageing (CPA) – a title more in keeping with its independent policy role and its increasing gerontological orientation. In 1986, it finally uprooted from Nuffield Lodge and replanted itself in its present premises in Ironmonger Row.

The last ten years or so have also proved to be difficult times for the development and implementation of social policies affecting older people. We have witnessed the coming together of demographic changes with a growing social and political awareness of the widening disparities which exist amongst older people themselves, and between them and other sectors of the population. Policy in the 1990s has been characterised by increasing tensions and contested ground over issues such as pensions, poverty, health and social welfare, leisure and education, with politicians using older people in ways which reflect and magnify particular images they wish to portray. In the fifth section of this chapter, we bring the fifty-year story full circle from the paternalistic post-war portrayal of older people as 'social casualties' to present day images of a more pluralistic and diverse nature.

Finally, we draw together the threads of our review and consider what the contributors to this volume have to say about the themes on which we have been reflecting, and the implications this has for moving forward the debates about social policy and old age at this important crossroads in our history.

Warfare, welfare and the creation of the National Corporation for the Care of Old People

It is always difficult, in any review such as this, to know precisely where to begin the story. A fifty-year time-frame may seem somewhat arbitrary, especially since social policy – the major perspective with which we are concerned here – has origins dating back at least to the turn of this century and to the work of notable social reformers such as Charles Booth and Octavia Hill. Social policy and social welfare, therefore, have an intimate and reciprocal relationship. Put simply, those working within social policy not only aim to contribute to, and encourage debate on policy formation, but also to inform and influence those responsible for the provision of welfare services. Moreover, as Alan Walker (1997) also argues, the development of social policy as a field of teaching and research over the last fifty years, has undoubtedly made a substantial contribution to the advancement of knowledge within social gerontology and to the ranks of those regarded as social gerontologists. It is here, at the confluence of social policy and social gerontology, that we can now clearly locate the work of the Centre for Policy on Ageing.

How though have we arrived at this point, both in the historical development of British social policy and social welfare, and in the organisation whose achievements we celebrate in this volume? And, perhaps more importantly, what has that journey been like and what lessons can we learn from it?

Many observers on the scene point to the period from about 1870 to 1940 as a time of 'creeping collectivism' (Midwinter, 1994; Sullivan, 1996), marked out by increasing state intervention, support for large-scale institutional solutions to social needs, and partnerships between central and local government. Society had become increasingly urbanised and industrialised, underpinned by a large working class. Means-tested state pensions for those over the age of 70 were introduced in 1909, with contributory pension schemes operating from the 1920s for particular sectors of the population. National insurance cover had begun to address problems associated with unemployment and, by the outbreak of the Second World War, there were already other policies and provisions in place which were to directly and indirectly affect the lives of older people: public health measures, housing legislation and illness insurance, in addition to the old age pension. These then were the immediate forerunners of the welfare state whose arrival, both during and immediately after the war years, was to herald radical changes for British society in general, and older people in particular.

The Beveridge Report of 1942 signalled this critical period of social change and emerged from a growing consensus about the inadequacy and irrationality of the existing health and social welfare system. Beveridge's proposals were regarded as a blueprint for post-war social reconstruction in which services were to be comprehensive, and not subject simply to whether people could afford to pay for them or not. In order to tackle his 'Five Giants' (want, idleness, squalor, ignorance and disease), Beveridge recommended the reform and extension of the social security system and the creation of a national health service. That selfsame year, the British Medical Association also advocated increased state involvement in health provision, and suggested that health insurance should be extended to cover most of the population.

At this juncture, it is worth reminding ourselves of two things: first, that the British population has in fact aged rapidly since Beveridge's time and, second, that his original proposals were predicated on a number of assumptions, many of which no longer hold true fifty years later. In 1931 there were 3,316,000 people in Britain over the age of 65, representing 7.4 per cent of the population (there was no census in 1941). Life expectancy at birth, for men, was nearly 58 years, and for women 62 years. Today, by contrast, the numbers of people aged 65 and over have trebled to over nine million (or 15.5 per cent), with life expectancy increasing to 73 for men and 79 for women (ONS, 1996). This means that Britain, in common with many other developed nations, has experienced a rapid ageing of its population in a relatively short time. We also need to remind ourselves of some of the assumptions underlying Beveridge's proposals. The most important of these were that fewer than 10 per cent of the population were aged 65 or over, and that widowhood was regarded as the main contingency to be faced within marriage. Furthermore, his model was constructed on a vision of stable families where children would be born to, and looked after by, two legally married parents. In peacetime, seven out of eight women would be following 'no gainful employment', supported by full-time male breadwinners. Employment levels would be high, unemployment of over six months would be a 'rare thing', and poverty would be dealt with through the proposed national insurance system with very few people requiring means-tested top-ups. Today, such a vision seems nothing short of quaint!

Whilst older people have always featured in social policy debates (Walker and Phillipson, 1986), particularly in demographic terms, in other respects they can be seen at this time as being increasingly marginalised and excluded, sometimes literally so. We have to remember for example that many elderly patients were being discharged wholesale from hospitals to make way for war casualties. In addition, large numbers of elderly people in the cities were being left homeless by the air raids. Together, these factors meant that the existing Public Assistance Institutions (the workhouses) were becoming seriously overcrowded (in fact, nearly 400 of them still existed, accommodating more residents than they had done at the start of the century). Even with the Health White Paper in 1944 and the passing of the National Health Services Act in 1946, reforms were slow in coming. The pervasive issues where social policy and older people were concerned, remained those of poverty and destitution (Parker, 1990).

It was against this background that the Nuffield Foundation was to carry out its seminal inquiry, under the Chairmanship of B. Seebohm Rowntree, into the conditions in which old people were living (Rowntree, 1947). Research for the inquiry was undertaken in England and Wales and revealed that very many old people were living in extremely poor housing with few amenities. Outside lavatories, lack of water, poor cooking facilities and few, if any, bathrooms, were commonplace. For those old people in the Public Assistance Institutions, conditions were often appalling with regimented regimes, lack of privacy and few amenities being the order of the day. So concerned was the committee of inquiry at what it found, that it made far-reaching recommendations for improving the conditions of older people. Amongst these recommendations, it called for the establishment of a body which would engage in research and the dissemination of information – and thus, the National Corporation for the Care of Older People (later to become the Centre for Policy on Ageing) was born on 1 August 1947.

The Corporation was financially underpinned by both the Nuffield Foundation and the Lord Mayor's National Air Raid Distress Fund, both of whom nominated members to serve on the Board of Governors of the new organisation. Three main objectives were formulated,[1] an Advisory Council was set up to oversee the day-to-day work, and Mike Simson was appointed Secretary (a position he was to hold for twenty-six years, until 1973). Poor housing, exacerbated by wartime destruction, and the parlous state of residential care, meant that 'hands-on' help for older people, in the form of grant aid, was a high priority for the new organisation. In its first year, over a quarter of a million pounds was distributed, chiefly to provide places for 'able-bodied' older people in residential homes. With the formal end of the old Poor Law arrangements, and the broad division of services between hospital boards and local authorities, NCCOP's role can best be viewed at the time as complementing state provision for older people.

However, alongside what was understandably a very practical early orientation, it was evident too that the Corporation also intended its role to be one of information dissemination. It is primarily in this role that the Corporation has ventured beyond its grant making remit, to examine, down through the years, a whole host of social policy issues affecting the lives of older people. Together, this body of work has, as we shall see throughout the remainder of this chapter, both helped to shape social policy for older people in this arena, as well as offering critical comment on some of the key legislative changes and their implications.

The 'new literature on old age': policy from the 1950s to the 1970s

The Labour party, after its landslide victory in the general election of 1945, and subsequent government between then and 1951, was faced with the task of developing social policies and building a welfare state, against a background profoundly influenced by the economic difficulties attendant on post-war reconstruction (Sullivan, 1996). As a result, the emergent welfare state has variously been seen as, and indeed criticised for, combining both radical and conservative threads and leading to a 'mosaic of reform' (Morgan, 1985: 179). With regard to the situation of older people, it is evident that despite the optimism embodied in the 1948 National Assistance Act, the reality fell some way short of this. Although the three Conservative administrations from 1951 until 1964 were apparently committed to furthering the development of the welfare state, the 1950s and 1960s can be seen as at best low key, and at worst, a failure in social policy terms. Indeed, as Robin Means (1986: 88) has argued, 'few social policy academics have had a kind word to say about the 1948 Act', and its effect on the subsequent development of welfare services for elderly people. Thus, social policy during the 1950s and 1960s effectively became divorced from the range of needs of older people. We can identify several reasons for this.

First, provision for the welfare of older people lacked a conceptual framework. There was no clear direction for social policy, with the legacies of the Poor Law system persisting well into the 1960s. Despite the 'reforms' embodied in the 1948 Act, there continued to be complete reliance on residential care as the solution to the needs of older people, even though community care had been around as a concept since the 1940s. In reality, there was a lack of political commitment to its development, even given the growing critique of policy from people like Crosland (1956), Marshall (1965) and Titmuss (1968). This critique, together with the emergent research evidence, suggested that families, and in particular daughters, would not in fact abandon care of their older parents if the state switched its focus to community care (Townsend, 1963). But, the impetus for developing alternatives was slow.

Second, despite the lack of a coherent rationale for residential care, there was an inbuilt inability to move to community care, because of the huge resources already committed to its perpetuation. Substantial capital investment in buildings deterred flexibility, and a strong residential care lobby ensured that resources were not diverted elsewhere. Such factors guaranteed that residential care for older people would dominate the history of welfare provision and social policy for most of this century.

Third, and in contrast to more recent years which have been characterised by debates on the future of long term care, there was comparatively little research attention given to older people living in residential care in the 1950s. Even when the graphic and highly negative accounts of Townsend in *The Last Refuge* (1962) and Robb's *Sans Everything* (1967) surfaced in the public domain, action was directed at the institutions and their building regulations, rather than at the situations of individuals and standards of care. Residential care therefore continued to maintain people who could not look after themselves but were not considered ill enough to go into hospital.

Following on from this point, the final reason we can identify concerns the (continuing) lack of clear boundaries between health and social care. One consequence of this was that during the 1950s and 1960s, many older people suffered inappropriate admission to hospital or residential care, whilst others who needed residential care remained at home. Local authority procedures for admission to residential care reflected a service-led rather than needs-led approach, with older people exercising no choice whatsoever. The hotel simile embodied in the Nuffield Report (Nuffield Foundation, 1947) which recommended smaller institutions, and the 1948 Act promising freedom of choice despite financial resources had, by the 1960s, proved woefully unrealistic.

In summary, social policy as it affected older people at this time, can be seen as heavily focused on residential care, with older people continuing to receive a 'Cinderella' service (Means and Smith, 1985). One of the main criticisms of this period, therefore, is the lack of vision among many social policy analysts and sociologists who reframed residential care as 'the last resort' without suggesting any realistic alternatives in its place.

This lack of co-ordination and strategic planning with other sectors of welfare continued on into the 1970s. There were, however, signs that the appropriateness of residential care for older people was being questioned. Several additional factors contributed to this, the most dominant being the effects of the 1973/74 oil crisis on welfare expenditure. Amongst the consequences were restrictions in local authority building and the development of rationing systems which excluded active older people. Institutional care was increasingly portrayed in a harsh light, deterring entry and thus helping to persuade people to accept inadequate community services, which were often seen as cheaper since they relied on the family rather than the state. Furthermore, the negative images of older people as dependent and disabled led many professionals, such as social workers, to develop their interests in other groups in society. Indeed, work with older people was regarded in certain quarters as a form of professional suicide (Phillipson, 1982).

Progress towards community care in the 1970s was therefore painfully slow, as social policy attempted to move from a position of maintenance to one of prevention – enabling people to live at home as long as possible through the expansion of domiciliary services, such as home helps and meals-on-wheels. Although several policy documents stressed the importance of community care, initially there was little widespread impact on services. Even with the reorganisation of personal social services in the 1971 Seebohm reforms, when work with older people was brought into the mainstream of social work activity, public sector residential care still remained the major provision for older people. Means and Smith (1985) argue that this was due to three factors: trade union and professional self interest, the symbolic importance of institutions, and the continuing concern about hospital costs.

As a result, most domiciliary initiatives such as the Kent Community Care schemes remained localised, in part because there was still an assumption that such services would undermine the willingness of families to care. In addition, there was a belief amongst many professionals that domiciliary care would not in fact be cost effective (Means, 1986). Combined with the adverse economic climate of the 1970s, domiciliary provision was unable to expand sufficiently to replace residential care. In essence, no substantive financial commitment was made to a realistic community care alternative, whilst a continuing lack of co-ordination was to dog the development of services for older people. It was only when economic and demographic imperatives re-surfaced, fuelling a moral panic about the growing burden of dependency older people represented, that social policy debates were driven forward again into the 1980s. This was encapsulated in the 1978 discussion document, *A Happier Old Age* (DHSS, 1978), which predicted that by 1986 there would be 24 per cent more older people over the age of 75, and that public expenditure on this group was already at unacceptably high levels.

What becomes clear by the end of the 1970s, then, is that despite the growth of research and critical debate, older people were still seen, in policy terms, as primarily a dependent group in need of care. Their own views and voices were unheard, and issues about autonomy, privacy and dignity in residential care, together with ideas about what older people at home might need to bolster their independence, had yet to be addressed in policy debates.

It is also equally clear, from reviewing the NCCOP's early decades and its associated reports and publications (see Appendix 1), that the bulk of its work was focused, not surprisingly, on issues concerning residential care and accommodation for older people. Moreover, this accommodation and residential care orientation, is perhaps the one continuous thread traceable throughout its fifty year history. As an organisation, it has funded practical initiatives in this field (initially through financing things like boarding-out schemes and short-stay homes, and subsequently through establishing Britain's first sheltered housing association: the Hanover Housing Association in 1963 and then, since 1974, through administering Hayward Foundation grants for improvements to voluntary residential care homes); overseen the running of the Homes Advisory Service; published its highly influential *Home Life: a code of practice for residential care*; as well as producing policy reports, manuals and critiques of various dimensions including design issues, staffing practices and policies, and quality of life issues for residents. Under the Directorship of Hugh Mellor (from 1973 to 1980), the Corporation also began to move away from some of its more practical schemes, towards a greater information and policy oriented role, paving the way for a change of name in 1980. The library and information service, which began as a small unit in 1972, has been integral to these developments and continued to grow and expand throughout the 1980s and up to the present day.

'10 years before the mast': the stormy seas of policy in the 1980s

With the advent of the 1980s, we were to see the beginnings of the negative stereotypes of old age being challenged, and the emergence of ageing issues taking centre stage on the political agenda and in policy and practice debates. Symbolically and practically, the National Corporation for the Care of Old People changed its title to the Centre for Policy on Ageing – a title, we have already noted, more in keeping with its broadening policy remit. The 1980s, therefore, can be seen as a watershed both in the development of social policy as it affected older people and, under the charismatic directorship of Eric Midwinter, in CPA as an organisation.

The restructuring of welfare in the wake of the Conservative election victory in 1979, was driven by the new right. Privatisation, competition and the development of what Le Grand (1990) calls the quasi-market, anti-state and decentralisation of services, were the order of the day. The state was left to regulate, finance and co-ordinate care for older people and other vulnerable groups. Ideologically, the influence of new right thinking on policy was substantial. Whilst there is still debate as to whether the changes in the supplementary benefit rules were a convenient mistake or a planned policy of welfare privatisation, the resultant massive growth in private residential care is a legacy with which we are still dealing today.

Alongside this, the demographic 'time bomb' again raised its head, calling into question the ability of the state to sustain a growing dependent population; ability being seen in terms of finance (economy), output (effectiveness) and value for money (efficiency). This view was encapsulated in 1983 with the appearance of *A Rising Tide* in which it was predicted that the health care system would be overrun by the projected large numbers of old people suffering with dementia (Health Advisory Service, 1983). At the same time, the traditional relationship between the state and the family was also being challenged. Policy was seen as 'rolling back the frontiers of the state' with increasing reliance being placed on the private sector and the family to provide care for older people. Although the government had set out its stall towards what it called a 'mixed economy of welfare' in *Growing Older* (1981), in reality one sector of welfare was to be promoted throughout the 1980s – the independent sector.

As the decade progressed, however, there were increasingly vocal debates about the extent of choice in the private sector. Documentary evidence began to expose some of the poor standards of care and exploitation of older residents, and led to the Registered Homes Act (1984) and the introduction of an advisory code of practice produced by CPA, *Home Life* (1984). The Act in fact placed the state in a contradictory position: it was required to 'police' the private sector whilst, at the same time, being urged to develop a partnership approach with the very same people. Ironically, this situation contributed to a gradual reviewing and re-framing of old age, which began to take hold on the welfare agenda. Social policy itself was increasingly vacillating between seeing older people as dependent social casualties, and seeing them as individuals capable of exercising choice. In the private sector, older people were viewed – in theory at least – as customers with rights, in contrast to the state sector which, its critics argued, fostered dependency, harboured abuse and was paternalistic as well as ignorant of the wishes of older people. The changes introduced by the Thatcher administrations of the 1980s revolutionised the fundamental principles which had underpinned policy since the 1940s, and began to challenge the key relationship between the state and older people.

However, whilst there was undoubtedly considerable change at this time, there were also several strands of continuity running through the decade. Amongst these, we can identify yet again the tension between residential and community care. The growth in private residential care served to highlight a perverse incentive, namely that it was easier to access residential care than to attract financial support to remain in the community. Once more, it seemed that the professed policy of community care was directly in conflict with the reality of the expansion of residential care. Spiralling costs of residential care eventually forced major policy debate around funding, management and co-ordination of welfare, and four influential reports appeared rapidly one after another. First, the Firth report (DHSS, 1987), outlined the importance of a needs-led assessment of older people seeking entry to residential care. This was followed by the Wagner report on residential care (1988) which highlighted the need for people who move into residential care to do so by positive choice. Then came the Griffiths report (1988) which, along with a report by the Audit Commission (1986), led to the White Paper and subsequent NHS and Community Care Act (1990). This, as we shall see below, has been the most influential piece of social policy legislation to affect the lives of older people in the 1990s.

Whilst the provision of welfare dominated social policy throughout the 1980s, it is important to our concerns to note that during this same period, social gerontology was also emerging as a field of research and teaching, and helping to inform debates around ageing. In particular, social gerontologists were beginning to examine the situations of older people, attempting to explain and critique, through approaches such as that of political economy, why it was that older people were such a low priority in relation to other groups. CPA at this time too was broadening its policy agenda. In 1982, it launched Policy Studies in Ageing which, along with its Reports' series, sought to address the fact that 'the whole of those in older age and not just those rendered social casualties in older age, were fit focus for social and political analysis' (Midwinter, 1988: 12).

By 1987 CPA, now in its fortieth year, had added to its numerous resources on residential care with a 'lengthy series of highly elaborate policy formulations' (Midwinter, 1987: 43). These illustrate the breadth of topics which were coming onto the social policy agenda. CPA researched and published on issues ranging from money, citizenship and civil liberties, to the situations of black and minority ethnic elders, those suffering with mental health problems and terminal illness, and concerns about the role of education and leisure in the lives of older people. With Eric Midwinter at the helm, the Centre's orientation throughout the 1980s was one which emphasised informed choice and self-determination as important concomitants in the creation of an appropriate social policy for older age. At the same time, there was an acknowledgement that a balance had to be struck between the good, and the not so good, aspects of ageing. In his 1987 review of CPA's contributions to social policy, Eric Midwinter expressed it thus:

> The thrust of CPA's policy formulation, therefore, is about the practice of active citizenship in older age, underlying its discreet balance of rights and responsibilities; seeking, pragmatically, for a reasonable saliency for individuals – or, if appropriate, their carers – as decision-makers, and looking for authentic models of self-determination which sensibly appreciate both the similarities and the differences of being old (p. 10).

Without losing sight of the continuities with the past, CPA saw its role in the 1980s as enlivening the debates about social policy and old people. It offered challenges to long-established ways of thinking, and drew attention to the need for a new and creative appraisal of the place of older people in late twentieth century Britain.

Policies on ageing: the place of old people in the society of the 1990s

Whilst the commentators of the late 1980s recognised the need for social policy to be formulated from a basis of detailed examination and analysis of the needs of older people (a call which resonates strongly with Seebohm Rowntree's original report), the reality of the 1990s has been somewhat at odds with this. With community care 'in disarray' (Audit Commission, 1986), Sir Roy Griffiths (former Chairman of Sainsburys) was charged with the task of reviewing services and making recommendations on the way forward. It is instructive to note that within the space of forty years, we moved from an inquiry into the situation of old people and associated social policy implications conducted under the auspices of a 'social investigator', to a contemporary review undertaken from the perspective of a consummate businessman (Baldwin, 1993). This in itself speaks volumes about how, at the close of the Thatcher years, social policy was still being narrowly constructed from a basis of entrepreneurialism.

The 1988 Griffiths' Report 'Agenda for Action' and the subsequent White Paper, 'Caring for People' (DoH, 1989), were the precursors to the key piece of social policy legislation affecting the lives of older people today: the National Health Service and Community Care Act of 1990. It is this Act which has been described as 'the major determinant of both the shape of services for older people and the context and philosophy within which these services are provided' (Hughes, 1995: 1). Essentially, it was attempting to distil the findings of recent critical reports and inquiries, and to lay the ground for a system which would move social policy irrevocably away from universal welfare provision, to more selective, targeted and accountable services.

What is particularly striking about these recent reforms is that despite their origins in a very different ideological perspective from that which pertained in the 1940s, they are couched in a recognition that public expenditure cannot, and should not be a bottomless pit, and that some attempt has to be made to balance the claims of different sectors of the population. In essence, this is not a million miles away from either Beveridge or Rowntree. Beveridge (1942: 92) noted for example, that:

> It is dangerous to be in any way lavish to old age until adequate provision has been assured for all other vital needs, such as prevention of disease and the adequate nutrition of the young.

For his part, Rowntree (1947: 95) commented that:

> There has been a considerable awakening of public interest in the problems of old
> age, an awakening that has manifested itself in a sympathetic attitude to old people
> and a widespread desire to be generous to them. The Committee are in full
> sympathy with this attitude but they have felt bound to take into account another
> point of view, based not on any lack of sympathy with the aged but on a
> recognition of the country's limited resources of wealth and labour and on the
> rapidly growing proportion of old people in the total population.

Almost half a century later, 'Caring for People' argues that:

> The aim of assessment should be to arrive at a decision on whether services should
> be provided and in what form... Decisions on service provision will have to take
> account of what is available and affordable (p. 20).

The Act also illustrates how social policy in the 1990s has been characterised by
the emergence of a new language with which we are now all very familiar. By this
we mean that terms such as empowerment; advocacy; user involvement and
participation; consumerism; care management; purchasers and providers; enablers
and facilitators; internal markets; and packages of care, to name but a few, have
come into everyday parlance – at least amongst those professionals charged with
responding to the needs of older people; and those whose research seeks to inform
policy directions. However, behind the rhetoric of this new language we can
discern the continuing erosion of state responsibility for the care of older people.
Alan Walker (1993), amongst others, has argued that the 'new community care',
imposed from the top down, is mainly concerned with cost containment and
management issues; that it fragments services, and is more about targeting than
rights. Indeed, Higgs (1995) shows how 'rights' all but disappear as services
withdraw still further, and older people without financial or personal resources are
faced with very little choice over their lives.

Moreover, the continuing problems over the health and social care divide
which have dogged policy for the last fifty years, have manifested themselves
again and again in the wake of the NHS and Community Care Act. In particular,
the National Health Service has effectively tried to shed any involvement in the
social care of older people (James, 1994). The decline in the numbers of long-stay
beds are by now well-documented, with older people being left largely reliant on
private, means-tested provisions (Henwood, 1992). Other contentious areas have
also begun to emerge. For example, within whose remit should responsibility for
respite care fall? If it is seen as relief of carers, some argue that it is therefore a social
provision; if it is about rehabilitation of the older person, it can be seen as a health
provision. What this means is that still, in the 1990s, social policy is bedevilled by

structural problems relating to co-ordination, boundary disputes and conflicts between local authority and health purchasers and providers (Heyman, 1995).

It seems that the goal of improving the welfare of older people via social policy reforms has always been hedged around with caveats and, some would argue, with a reluctance in recent years to commit fully adequate resources to its achievement (Baldwin, 1993; Means and Smith, 1994; Hughes, 1995; Lewis and Glennerster, 1996). Whilst the mantra of welfare pluralism continued to be heard loud and clear during the first half of the 1990s, it was increasingly evident that older people's entitlements to services were continuing to be eroded. As the state withdrew further and further from provision, unregulated services (particularly domiciliary care ones) proliferated. Needs assessment and means testing have meant that issues around older people's ability to pay for care and/or to supplement state provided services, have moved centre stage in contemporary debates. Increasingly, the focus has been on what the appropriate balance between the state and the individual might be in terms of financing care in old age. This means that in late twentieth century Britain, pension provision has again assumed a particular salience in policy terms, against an ever present background of discussion about health and social care (Walker, 1996).

These issues have also been thrown into sharp relief by the fierce debates which persistently rage around related topics such as generational equity. Hard questions continue to be asked about whether older people are, in some way, 'consuming more than their fair share of society's resources to the detriment of younger groups, particularly children' (Vincent, 1995: 140). Proponents of this position employ the arguments of 'apocalyptic demography' in an effort to justify reductions in state pension and thereby reduce government expenditure. However, because of the generalised ways in which this debate still persists in viewing older people, it is evident that certain sectors of the older population – notably older women, and black and minority ethnic elders – will continue to be disadvantaged. Indeed, looking beyond the issue of pensions, many critical commentators have argued that much contemporary social policy making actually exacerbates the inequalities which exist amongst older people, and that these inequities are likely to continue well into the future (Evandrou, 1997).

Moreover, the 1990s have also witnessed increasing concern with related policy issues such as the role of informal care of older people, health care rationing and euthanasia, the place of advocacy and empowerment in older people's lives, and political activism – all of which are addressed in this book. CPA too has played a key role here, with publications and critical commentaries which continue to tackle familiar issues around community and residential care, reflected in the publication of an updated code of practice in 1996, *A Better Home Life*, but which have also considered topics as diverse as arts and older people, the press and broadcasting, and crime; European issues; the service needs of black and minority ethnic groups; citizen advocacy; and concerns with spirituality and religion, and about older people who live, and die, alone (see Appendix 1). Again then, we can identify both continuities in terms of informing the existing social policy of old age, as well as new and developing areas which may assist us in reframing policy for the twenty-first century.

On 1 May 1997, Britain elected a new Labour government, following eighteen years of Conservative policy. It is too early to judge whether ageing will become a key issue in the government's social policy agenda. Will there be a radical shift in policy to address the needs of older people or a continuity in policy, segregating older people and making their needs invisible in major policy debates? It could be argued that the focus of policy has to change with issues such as health rationing, long term care and technology, forcing a public debate on ethical and economic issues and creating dilemmas for health and social care practice.

Undoubtedly, the last fifty years has witnessed substantial changes in the situations of older people in Britain: changes reflected in the now substantive body of work emanating from the Centre for Policy on Ageing. Whilst many of the developments we have outlined have yielded benefits for older people, others increasingly pose challenges – challenges which the contributors to this book take up in the following pages.

About the book

This book is divided into three parts. The seven chapters in Part One – Revisiting the Social Policy of Old Age – seek to document the traditional areas of social policy as they have impacted on the lives of older people. In Chapter 2, Gillian Dalley, the present Director of the Centre for Policy on Ageing, takes up some of the editors' opening themes and focuses specifically on health and social welfare policy. She examines how health and social care services have developed in light of political, organisational and administrative changes over the last fifty years. This is accompanied by a review of how health and social care policy has affected older people over the same period. This is followed in Chapter 3 by a consideration of education, in which Eric Midwinter first revisits its different roles and motivations in the lives of children and of older adults, before going on to argue the case for its central importance in the development of a future 'third age' lifestyle.

Sheila Peace and Julia Johnson then look, in Chapter 4, at policy around the living arrangements of older people, exploring both housing policy and policies for residential care. They suggest that there have been dramatic changes in policy over the last fifty years, but that more imaginative responses are still needed to meet the accommodation requirements of older people in the next century. Similar issues are discussed by Chris Phillipson in Chapter 5, but this time in the context of changing patterns of work and retirement. Having reviewed trends in the employment of older workers, he contends that major changes are needed if support for workers, and the design of the pension system, are to adequately reflect the greater flexibility now inherent in the organisation of working life. Pension policy is picked up again by Jane Falkingham in Chapter 6, when she discusses financial security in old age. Whilst present trends suggest that older age is no longer a period of financial hardship for many, she also warns against too over-optimistic a view, particularly where the situations of older women and black and minority ethnic elders are under consideration. Finally in Part One, the contributors to Chapter 7 examine the growth and development of geriatric medicine and of social work, as two distinctly professional responses to meeting the challenge of old age.

In Part Two – Reviewing the Social Policy of Old Age – our contributors concentrate on more contemporary themes and issues which have come onto the social policy agenda from the 1980s onwards. These seven chapters begin with Julia Twigg's exploration of the informal care of older people (Chapter 8) in which she concludes that far from being a peripheral subject, carers and caring have now assumed a new prominence within social policy. The gendered dimensions of such policy are developed further in Chapter 9, when Jay Ginn and Sara Arber explicitly examine the invisibility and neglect of gender. Material resources and pensions, health and social welfare, and social relations, all come under the microscope in this review. These issues are picked up again when Karl Atkin explores, in Chapter 10, what it is like to age in a multi-racial Britain. In order to help overcome the impact of structural racism, he suggests that social policy has to become informed by the perceptions of minority ethnic people themselves.

His emphasis on positive action is echoed by Joanna Bornat in Chapter 11. Here, she reviews the growth of pensioners' organisations and pensioner action, suggesting that pensioners need to seek alliances and allegiances that link across generations and identity groups; the challenge for the pensioner movement being to profit from these links. A further dimension concerned with attempts to make the voice of older people heard in the creation of social policy, is discussed by Andrew Dunning in his exploration of the development of advocacy and empowerment in Chapter 12. This draws on debates around consumerism and citizenship. Then, in Chapter 13, we turn our attention to a consideration of other groups for whom ageing represents an increasing challenge. Carole Archibald and Liz Baikie review what it is like for gay and lesbian older people, and for people suffering with dementia, and conclude that the increasing awareness of the sexual needs of older people must not only be reflected in a change in attitude but also in policy. In the final chapter of Part Two (Chapter 14), Ken Howse discusses the debates which are now raging around health care rationing, non-treatment of older people, and euthanasia. These are issues which the social policy of old age has neglected but which are increasingly moving into the public domain.

The third and final part of the book – Reframing the Social Policy of Old Age – consists of three contributions which offer different perspectives on how policy might develop in the twenty-first century. CPA, we the editors, and all our contributors would hold to the importance of hearing the voice of older people in the construction of future policy. Consequently, in Chapter 15, Margaret Simey offers us a personal politics of old age in which she makes the case for a morally and ethically sound social policy to address the inequalities which still persist in our society. In Chapter 16, Maria Evandrou conducts a research audit of what life will be like for the baby boomers as they enter old age, suggesting that they will be better educated and discerning consumers of health and welfare. Consequently, social policy in the twenty-first century needs to be coherent, involve long-term planning and be socially inclusive in nature. Finally, in Chapter 17, the editors draw together the contributions in the main body of the book, in an attempt to outline some of the directions which policy and practice might take in the future.

Focusing on the social aspects of ageing, this book is concerned both with reviewing policy developments over the five decades that the CPA has been in existence, and with addressing new and emerging themes. By so doing, it aims to take forward significant debates on ageing, but also to outline a policy agenda for moving into the twenty-first century.

Note

1   The objectives of the NCCOP (1948) were:

(i) To promote the welfare of the aged and those persons suffering from those disabilities commonly afflicting the aged (hereinafter called the aged) in any manner which constitutes the furtherance of the charitable purpose according to the laws of England for the time being.

(ii) To establish and conduct or to assist by donations loans or otherwise any other person or corporation or public authority to establish and conduct hostels, occupational centres, convalescent and holiday homes or other institutions for the benefit of the aged.

(iii) To undertake the management of property held on charitable trusts for the benefit of the aged and to undertake and execute any other trusts the undertaking of which may seem calculated to promote the objects of the Corporation either gratuitously or otherwise.

References

Audit Commission (1986) *Making a Reality of Community Care*, London: HMSO.

Baldwin, S. (1993) *The Myth of Community Care: an alternative model*, London: Chapman and Hall.

Beveridge, W. (1942) *Social Insurance and Allied Services*, Cmnd. 6404, London: HMSO.

Centre for Policy on Ageing (1984) *Home Life: a code of practice for residential care*. Report of a working party sponsored by the DHSS, under the chairmanship of Lady Kina Avebury, London: CPA.

Crosland, C. A. R. (1956) *The Future of Socialism*, London: Jonathan Cape.

Department of Health (1989) *Caring For People*, White Paper, Cmnd. 849, London: HMSO.

Department of Health and Social Security (DHSS) (1978) *A Happier Old Age: a discussion document on elderly people in our society*, London: HMSO.

Department of Health and Social Security (DHSS) (1981) *Growing Older*, Cmnd. 8173, London: HMSO.

Department of Health and Social Security (DHSS) (1987) *Public Support for Residential Care*. Report of the Joint Central and Local Government Working Party (The Firth Report), London: HMSO.

Evandrou, M. (1997) 'Introduction', Chapter 1 in Evandrou, M. (ed) (1997) *Baby Boomers: ageing into the 21st century*, London: Age Concern England.

Griffiths, R. (1988) *Community Care: agenda for action*, London: HMSO.

Health Advisory Service (1983) *The Rising Tide: developing services for mental illness in old age*, London: HMSO.

Henwood, M. (1992) *Through a Glass Darkly: community care and elderly people*, Research Report 14, London: King's Fund Institute.

Heyman, R. (ed) (1995) *Researching User Perspectives on Community Health Care*, London: Chapman Hall.

Higgs, P. (1995) 'Citizenship and old age: the end of the road?', *Ageing and Society*, 15(4): 535–50.

Hughes, B. (1995) *Older People and Community Care: critical theory and practice*, Buckingham: Open University Press.

James, A. (1994) *Managing To Care: public service and the market*, London: Longman.

Le Grand, J. (1990) 'Equity versus Efficiency: the elusive trade-off', *Ethics*, 100.

Lewis, J. and Glennerster, H. (1996) *Implementing the New Community Care*, Buckingham: Open University Press.

Means, R. (1986) 'The development of social services for elderly people: historical perspectives', Chapter 5 in Phillipson, C. and Walker, A. (eds) *Ageing and Social Policy: a critical assessment*, Aldershot: Gower.

Means, R. and Smith, R. (1985) *The Development of Welfare Services for the Elderly*, London: Croom Helm.

Means, R. and Smith, R. (1994) *Community Care: policy and practice*, London: Macmillan.

Marshall, T. H. (1965) *Social Policy*, London: Hutchinson.

Midwinter, E. (1987) *Redefining Old Age: a review of CPA's recent contributions to social policy*, CPA Papers No 1, London: Centre for Policy on Ageing.

Midwinter, E. (1988) *Annual Report 1986–87*, London: Centre for Policy on Ageing.

Midwinter, E. (1994) *The Development of Social Welfare in Britain*, Buckingham: Open University Press.

Morgan, K. O. (1985) *Labour in Power*, Oxford: Oxford University Press.

NHS and Community Care Act (1990) London: HMSO.

ONS (Office for National Statistics) (1996) *Population Trends 84*, Summer, London: HMSO.

Parker, R. (1990) 'Elderly people and community care: the policy background', pp. 5–22 in Sinclair, I., Parker, R., Leat, D. and Williams, J. (eds) *The Kaleidoscope of Care: a review of research on welfare provision for elderly people*, London: HMSO.

Phillipson, C. (1982) *Capitalism and the Construction of Old Age*, London: Macmillan.

Robb, B. (1967) *Sans Everything: a case to answer*, London: Nelson.

Rowntree, B. S. (1947) *Old People: report of a survey committee on the problems of ageing and the care of old people*, London: Oxford University Press.

Sullivan, M. (1996) *The Development of the British Welfare State*, London: Prentice Hall.

Titmuss, R. M. (1968) *Commitment to Welfare*, London: Allen and Unwin.

Townsend, P. (1962) *The Last Refuge*, London: Routledge and Kegan Paul.

Townsend, P. (1963) *The Family Life of Old People*, Harmondsworth: Penguin.

Vincent, J. A. (1995) *Inequality and Old Age*, London: UCL Press.

Wagner Report (1988) *Residential Care: a positive choice*. Report of the independent review of residential care, London: HMSO.

Walker, A. (1993) 'Community care policy: from consensus to conflict', in Bornat, J., Pereira, C., Pilgrim, D. and Williams, F. (eds) *Community Care: a reader*, London: Macmillan.

Walker, A. (1996) 'Intergenerational relations and the provision of welfare', Chapter 1 in Walker, A. (ed) (1996) *The New Generational Contract: intergenerational relations, old age and welfare*, London: UCL Press.

Walker, A. (1997) 'Social Policy and Ageing', pp. 32–9 in Phillips, J. (ed) *British Gerontology and Geriatrics: experience and innovation*, London: BSG, BGS and BSRA.

Walker, A. and Phillipson, C. (1986) 'Introduction', Chapter 1 in Phillipson, C. and Walker, A. (eds) *Ageing and Social Policy: a critical assessment*, Aldershot: Gower.

2 Health and social welfare policy

Gillian Dalley

By the time these new approaches to community care are fully worked through, applied and consolidated, it will be the 21st century. It is worth pausing to recall that some, perhaps many, of the services and agencies committed to caring for those in social and allied need were established in the 19th century. This means that some of the traditions, conventions, models and approaches are, on occasion, still tainted by the past.

CPA (1990) Community Life: a code of practice for community care, p. 42

Introduction

Older people are major recipients or consumers of health and social welfare services. A constant theme in public policy debate throughout the life of the post-war welfare state has been a concern with their high level of usage of services in contrast to the size of their overall representation in the population. In recent years, this has been compounded by the growth, both absolute and relative, in their numbers – particularly those over the age of 85, since they are seen as the heaviest consumers of all. This is not to begin on a note of gloom and doom but, rather, to assert that a chief obligation of any humane society is to ensure that the needs of all groups of citizens are catered for appropriately.

The aim of this chapter is to review post-war developments in health and social welfare as they have affected older people and to assess current trends and developments. In particular it seeks to explore the interweaving of three broad sets of issues, namely, the organisational and administrative changes and developments that have taken place within health and social welfare over the past fifty years, the ideological shifts that have accompanied them, and the matching of both these to the actual circumstances of older people themselves during the period.

Organisational and administrative developments

The immediate post-war period saw the end of the old order. New structures were established within a new legislative framework. Three landmark laws were passed: the National Health Service Act 1946, the National Insurance Act 1946 and the National Assistance Act 1948. Perhaps most significantly from the perspective of older people, the new framework meant health care free at the point of use and the formal end of the old Poor Law provision – in particular the public assistance institutions with the workhouse associations which they held for many older people reaching their declining years. Relatively limited social welfare responsibilities were allocated to local authorities, with additional powers added later in an amendment in 1962 to the National Assistance Act to develop meals on wheels services and the imposition of a general duty on local authorities to 'promote the welfare of the elderly' in the Health Service and Public Health Act 1968.

If the first decade of the welfare state was a period during which the new structures were establishing themselves and settling down, the 1960s and 1970s marked a period during which an essentially corporate culture of long-term planning was in the ascendant, particularly in the health service. A hospital plan for England and Wales was published in 1962 (Ministry of Health, 1962) forecasting over a twenty year period a planned closure of substantial numbers of hospital beds and an associated transfer of resources to community care. It set out detailed projections and norms for the numbers of in-patient beds required for different categories of patients. A further series of documents concerned with planning for a number of 'priority groups' – of whom 'the elderly' were one – followed during the 1970s (DHSS, 1971; DHSS, 1975; DHSS, 1976). During this time, there was a generalised acceptance of a dirigiste model of central control. Incremental growth, national planning based on standardised norms and resource allocation formulae which could take account nationally of local variation (such as the RAWP formula) were accepted almost without question until the 1980s.

The consensus broke down in the 1980s with the attempted application to the health and social welfare sector of a belief, held by the new right, in the superiority of the free market. This culminated in the NHS and Community Care Act 1990. The Act brought together two rather different policy strands, one managerial and one focused on patient/client care. The move towards tighter management control of the health service which had started with the introduction of general management in 1985 was transformed by the introduction of a contractual relationship at the point of purchasing and providing. Health authorities became commissioners and purchasers of health services; hospitals (acute services) and community health services were transformed into quasi-independent Trusts which were expected to compete with each other in securing business contracts from local health authorities. The language of norms and national plans was abandoned. Similar but less clear cut changes were introduced into local government although the major change was the development of a 'mixed economy' approach with the statutory authorities coming under heavy pressure from central government to withdraw entirely from their service providing role and being encouraged to develop the role of the independent (both private and not-for-profit) sector in their place.

The other aim of the Act was to impose greater control over how the care of what were known as the 'priority groups' was organised and funded. Older people, mentally ill people, and those with learning difficulties had been the subject of policy concern for many years, partly because it was recognised that the care they received was often very poor but also because they took up a large proportion of the health and welfare budget. The issue became acute during the 1980s. As the numbers of older people, particularly those over 75, grew throughout the decade, so too did demand for health and social care. Changes in the way in which access to residential care could be obtained because of unforeseen loopholes in the social security system hugely increased expenditure on residential care for older people. In the eyes of government, a cap had to be placed on that demand. In addition, the Audit Commission (1986) reported critically on the way in which community care policies (largely concerned with the care of the priority groups) were developing. The appointment of the enquiry into community care headed by Sir Roy Griffiths (architect of the earlier general management changes) which reported in 1988 made it clear that the burgeoning claims of community care clients were to be constrained. The outcome, as encoded in the 1990 Act, was to give the lead role to local authorities (already being kept on a tighter and tighter financial leash by central government) and to require them to be much more rigorous in decision-making about the provision of community care services to individuals (through the process of assessment and care management).

Ironically, though central government had avowedly eschewed direct control of local provision, there was a series of attempts to impose control by any other name. Cloaked under a rhetoric of the free market and rights to local decision-making, government attempted to exert a very tight control over the direction policy was taking. A flood of guidance emerged from the Department of Health – for example, the efficiency index, the Patient's Charter, the 85 per cent rule whereby community care transfers under the Special Transitional Grant had to be spent in the independent sector and, perhaps most significantly from older people's perspective, the guidance on the need to establish eligibility criteria for admission to NHS long-term care beds (Department of Health, 1995). Local authorities, while taking lead responsibility for community care, came under an increasingly tight budgetary regime through the setting of strict SSAs (standard spending assessments) year by year.

Ideological shifts: from hospital to community

The structural changes which have been introduced periodically over the past fifty years have largely been concerned with introducing greater organisational efficiency into the system. But they have been accompanied by other policy shifts, most notably, perhaps, by a change in the perceived balance between hospital and community. It has been widely recognised (Dalley, 1996; Lewis and Glennerster, 1996) that the development of community care pre-dates current policies by many years and the history of the growth of community care policy is a complex one.

It can be characterised first as an expression of organisational efficiency – putting an end to over-bedding and to the tying up of too many resources in costly buildings and the infrastructure supporting in-patient services (especially in the wake of medico-technological advances that enable people to be treated outside the hospital setting). Secondly, it can be seen as a shift away from an ideology of incarceration to one of human rights and the freedom of the individual to live a 'normal' life. Thirdly, it is tied into the ideological debate about the appropriate roles of family, state and voluntary sector in caring for dependent members of society.

The efficiency and medical advances argument

A number of government reports published over the past fifty years have assumed that reducing the number of hospital beds and residential care places and developing services in the community would promote cost savings. The Phillips, Guillebaud and Boucher reports, for example, all dating back to the 1950s, saw the development of domiciliary services as a way of reducing pressures on (expensive) institutional care (Means and Smith, 1985).

More recently, as a result of more advanced methods of treatment, the length of in-patient stays has been shortened and growth in day-case surgery and other treatment has meant that more patients are treated, staying for shorter and shorter periods or not entering hospital as in-patients at all (Harrison and Prentice, 1996). For example, although demographic change has meant that there are many more older people presenting with acute health needs, average lengths of stay in 'geriatric' beds have fallen from 66.1 days in 1981 to 23.5 in 1992/93. During the same period, the volume of day cases rose by over 150 per cent.

In the case of mentally ill patients, many commentators date the origins of the move towards care in the community to the more relaxed approach developed by some psychiatrists in the 1950s to the care of people with severe mental health problems, coupled with the introduction of the new benzadiopene drugs which allowed for better management of mental illness (Jones, 1972) – a mix of new attitudes to the rights of psychiatric patients and of scientific/technical advance. Forecasts in the 1960s of reductions in the numbers of hospital beds were largely related to reductions in the numbers of mentally ill people residing in hospital. Indeed, numbers of in-patients had already fallen substantially during the 1950s from 3.4 per 1,000 population in 1954 to 3.1 in 1960 (DHSS, 1976). This change, which then gathered pace, was often put down entirely to the new forms of treatment and the introduction of an 'open door' policy.

THE HUMAN RIGHTS ARGUMENT

The movement from hospital to community gained ground as a philosophical issue as the writings of Peter Townsend, Erving Goffman, RD Laing and, later, Michel Foucault (Goffman, 1961; Foucault, 1977; Jones and Fowles, 1984) became widely read. The view that institutional care of any sort meant the denial of human rights became commonly accepted. The 'mortification or curtailment of the self' which in Goffman's eyes is the central characteristic of the total institution came to be regarded as the defining criterion of all residential establishments. Thus a movement, which was partly developing as a response to increasing costs and as an outcome of improved techniques of treatment, took on an ideological mantle.

In the case of older people, there was a general recognition pre-dating the establishment of the welfare state that many of the old institutions were inhumane in the way they cared for their residents. The 1947 Rowntree report looked forward to a time when the old Poor Law institutions would finally be abolished and be replaced by humane and caring homes (Rowntree, 1947). Gradually, however, a view developed that this was not enough. The principles of independence and autonomy, regarded as fundamental human rights, should be applied to the care of older people as much as to any other social group. Institutional care, the argument proceeded, could never do this, however much the old institutions were replaced by new – 'better' – ones.

FAMILY OR STATE CARE?

By the end of the 1950s, opinion began to harden against institutional care for older people on the grounds of its poor quality. The expectation that conditions would improve with the running down of the Poor Law institutions proved to be premature. Revelations by Townsend in *The Last Refuge* (1962) that little had improved in the former Poor Law institutions influenced a generation of thinking about residential care.

But while it was largely recognition of, and concern about, these poor conditions which led to changing attitudes towards institutional care, questions about the appropriate role of the family also began to be asked. The Rowntree report itself, while acknowledging the poor quality of care sometimes experienced, was written in the belief that for a large proportion of the very old (over 85), institutional care was the appropriate form of care. While Rowntree noted that most old people (95 per cent) lived at home or in their children's homes, he believed there came a point when moving into a Home was the best option. His report concluded:

> ...excessive devotion to independence can be explained partly by the present serious lack of suitable Homes for old people and partly by the regulated life which is widely believed, not always with justice, to be the common feature of all Institutions. If sufficient Homes can be provided, and if the homelike atmosphere found in some of them is introduced into all Homes, many old people will prefer no doubt to enter them rather than to continue living in unsatisfactory conditions in private houses. This will lessen the need for extensive plans of home help, home nursing, visiting and home meals service for old people who would be better off in a Home or Institution (pp. 95–6).

He also cautioned against too great a reliance on the development of domiciliary care on the grounds of expense:

> it should be pointed out that the provision of domiciliary services of the sort considered below [domestic help, meals and home nursing], when added to the cost of old-age and supplementary pensions, may often raise the total cost of preserving the independence of old people much above the cost of caring for them in Institutions or Homes (p. 49).

But the straightforward assumption that residential care was the appropriate option started to be challenged in terms of the relative duties of family and state. In a study of the health and social conditions of old people just after the war, Sheldon (1948), although an advocate of residential care for older people, had already drawn attention very graphically to the significant part played by families in caring for their elderly relatives. He also pointed to the contribution that many older people themselves made in helping the younger generation. He concluded that these reciprocal levels of support had:

> administrative implications as a factor in the care of old age deserving the utmost encouragement. It is imperative to remember however that it is an arrangement which is essentially voluntary and is possible only when family affection is deep (p. 196).

He went on to argue strongly for improved institutional care for older people who were no longer able to remain independent in order to relieve their families of the heavy burden he had seen them bear. However, by the early 1950s, he began to call for greater preventive measures to be taken to restrict admissions to residential care

(Means and Smith, 1985). It is likely that these concerns were directly related to the unexpectedly spiralling costs of the health service in its first years. Webster (1991), the NHS's official historian, certainly argues that the policy shift towards community care which took place in the 1950s was due to this concern.

At the same time, politicians and other public voices (Means and Smith, 1985) began to make claims about the supposed decline in families' willingness to care and stressed the need to make them live up to their responsibilities. There were suggestions that the readiness of voluntary organisations to provide care services of various kinds might undermine the fragile inclination of families to care.

A decade later, however, the findings of social scientists – notably those of Peter Townsend in *The Family Life of Old People* (1957) – contradicted the pessimistic assertions about families' willingness to care. Families, they found, still provided the bulk of care for their dependent relatives and, moreover, were willing to do so. Ironically, it was both the willingness of families to care and their assumed shirking of responsibility, which fuelled the moral debate about the appropriate roles and responsibilities of state and family.

In 1975, a Canadian social policy analyst, Robert Moroney, developed the debate further. He was commissioned by the Joseph Rowntree Memorial Trust to investigate the extent of family willingness to care in the light of concern expressed by, amongst others, the UK Central Policy Review Staff that it could be declining (Moroney, 1975). In reviewing the available evidence, he looked at national studies conducted throughout the 1960s and early 1970s. He concluded that there was little evidence to show that family care was in decline but pointed out that there was a tendency for state policy to support *individuals* through community care rather than to support families in helping them to care for their infirm relatives.

Changing policy responses

The debates about community care as opposed to institutional care and the respective roles of family and state did not leave health and social care practitioners unaffected. During the 1970s the primacy of community care over institutional care became an article of faith. This view informed the series of major government documents already cited relating to the health and personal social services (DHSS, 1976) and to mental handicap (DHSS, 1971) and mental illness (DHSS, 1975). As well as laying down detailed plans for the continued development of community care, these three documents also provided a clear philosophical framework for the policy. Although there was some questioning of the progress which had been made towards community care, it was unequivocally stated that 'the main objective of services for elderly people is to help them remain in the community for as long as possible' (DHSS, 1976: 38). In passing, it also made mention of the role of the voluntary sector and stated that 'voluntary effort also plays an important part in meeting the needs of elderly people'. The discussion document, *A Happier Old Age*, published in 1978, raised a series of points for discussion, amongst them the question of whether or not family ties could be strengthened and the reciprocal exchange of help and support between the generations encouraged. Until the beginning of the 1980s, however, these provide the only indication of any belief that the family or the voluntary sector had a significant strategic role to play in community care policy.

With the change of government in 1979, a major ideological shift took place. Although the objective of enabling people to remain in the community was unchanged, the role of government and public services in ensuring this was much downplayed. The discussion document, *Growing Older*, published in 1981, stated:

> the Government sees the primary role of the public services as an enabling one,
> helping people to care for themselves and their families by providing a framework
> of support...it is essential that scarce professional skills should be reserved for the
> circumstances in which they can provide care and treatment not otherwise
> available (p. 38).

The responsibility for the care of infirm older people lay directly on the shoulders of families, friends and neighbourhoods:

> the primary sources of support and care for elderly people are informal and
> voluntary. These spring from the personal ties of kinship, friendship and
> neighbourhood. They are irreplaceable. It is the role of public authorities to sustain
> and, where necessary, develop – but never to displace – such support and care (p. 3).

It went on to borrow Michael Bayley's phrase (Bayley, 1973: 3), stating that 'care *in* the community must increasingly mean care *by* the community.' This was a major predictor of things to come: informal caring (predominantly family care) became the big growth area of the 1980s.

The 1980s saw the growth of a community care industry – in terms of health and social services, voluntary sector developments, a burgeoning private sector and academic research. There was little questioning of underlying principles apart from a feminist critique that developed during the decade which suggested that community care policies were founded on gender-based assumptions about family structures and capacities and as such placed an undue burden on women (Finch and Groves, 1980; Finch and Groves, 1983; Baldwin and Twigg, 1991; Dalley, 1996).

The Department of Health funded numerous development projects, largely to do with stimulating the voluntary and independent sectors. In the mid-80s, it supported the establishment of the *Informal Caring Programme* at the King's Fund (King's Fund, 1988) and the *Caring for People* demonstration projects (Department of Health/SSI, 1991); in the early 1990s, it funded the *Caring for People who Live at Home* initiative. Despite the plethora of this sort of activity, the extent of practical support (or alternatives to caring) being offered to carers was in all likelihood very limited. On the basis of the project reports, many of the initiatives were concerned with coordinating information and support services rather than providing direct relief.

For the most part, there was a consensus about community care as the accepted policy solution for the care of the priority groups. But community care meant different things to different people. For practitioners it meant broadly that it would secure people's independence and autonomy; for politicians it meant putting the individual and the family at the centre of responsibility, on the one hand, and developing opportunities for independent suppliers of services on the other; for managers and planners it presented the possibility that moving care out of the institutions would permit savings and greater efficiencies. For older people and their families, it meant continued reliance on personal and family resources with state support as a fluctuating back-up, although for a period in the 1980s because of the social security loophole it meant greater opportunities to move unassessed into residential care.

The role of the independent sector

In the period leading up to the establishment of the welfare state, there was an assumption by some policymakers, that the role of the voluntary sector would be superseded by state institutions taking over the social welfare role (Webb et al, 1976). Indeed, there was a tradition on the left of regarding the voluntary sector as an expression of interfering middle class moralising dating back to the nineteenth century and earlier. The expected demise of the voluntary movement did not in fact take place and over the years the sector has continued to develop and play an important part in providing health and welfare services to older people. In particular, for example, for much of the post-war period, the growth of the meals on wheels service was dependent on voluntary effort (both in terms of it being run by voluntary organisations and being staffed by volunteers) (Harris, 1961). Residential care, too, has continued to be an area where the voluntary sector has played an important role and, indeed, small homes established by voluntary organisations provided the model for the Part III homes set up by local authorities to replace the public assistance institutions (Kendall and Knapp, 1996).

But it has been in the 1980s that the role of the voluntary sector – subsumed into the wider 'independent' sector (that is, both voluntary and private) – has become even more prominent. In its pursuit of reducing the role of the state in welfare provision, the Thatcher government bestowed a key role on the independent sector. As a major player in the 'mixed economy of welfare', the sector was encouraged by government to expand and extend its activities into the provision of services which had hitherto been the province of the statutory authorities.

For the Thatcher government, support for voluntary effort was an expression of its view that social responsibility derived from individual obligation (as outlined in *Growing Older*); its parallel support for the role of the private sector in providing social welfare stemmed directly from a hostility towards state institutions playing a part in providing services. These, it was argued, should be limited to an 'enabling role'. Private initiative should be encouraged and enabled to take over from where the state was forced to withdraw. As a result, there was a substantial growth of independent sector provision during the fifteen years from 1980. Independent residential and nursing places doubled between 1984 and 1994 (House of Commons, Health Committee, 1996) and since the implementation of the community care reforms in 1993, independently provided domiciliary services also grew. Requirements on local authorities to spend community care transfer funds in the independent sector were a major spur.

An associated aspect of the radical overhaul of traditional approaches to welfare which the Thatcher government accomplished, was the changing relationship that voluntary organisations have had with local government. In the past, they tended to receive grant aid to provide services and carry on their activities. This underwrote their accepted role as both provider of services but also as catalysts and innovators. Voluntary organisations were often able to pursue new ways of thinking and doing that what the statutory sector could not. Since the reforms, this role has been compromised by the introduction of contractual relationships between voluntary organisations and local authorities in which clearly specified and delimited activities are funded – often directly replacing services which were previously provided by the local authorities themselves (Lewis, 1993; Lewis, 1994; Kendall and Knapp, 1996).

The changes which have taken place over the past decade, for older people themselves, have been profound. They can no longer expect services to be provided directly by their local authority. Even where people have 'survived' the means test and qualify for local authority purchased residential care or community care services, they can expect to receive services from an array of independent providers. Questions about quality, safety and accountability may be asked but the debate about regulation and standards has only just begun. The Centre for Policy on Ageing led the way in 1984 in publishing *Home Life* (Centre for Policy on Ageing, 1984) as a code of good practice to accompany the Registered Homes Act 1984 and again in 1990 and 1996 with *Community Life* and *A Better Home Life* (Centre for

Policy on Ageing, 1990; Centre for Policy on Ageing, 1996) respectively. More recently, the Burgner report (1996) raised the issues of regulation and national benchmark standards but so far its recommendations have not been acted upon.

Actual circumstances

How far, it may be asked, has there been any improvement in the services which older people actually receive as a result of policy shifts during the lifetime of the welfare state? At the outset, according to evidence presented in the Rowntree and Sheldon reports, there were few services and little care provided for older people outside institutions. The reports looked forward to the establishment of the NHS and its accompanying benefits. They urged the authorities to provide home helps, home nursing and meals services, although recognising it would take time for them to be set up on any widespread basis. It is worth remembering how hard domestic life was for some old people at that time. Rowntree (1947) gives one example among many:

> The husband 77 and wife 66 live in one room. To reach their room they pass through an alleyway, through a groundfloor room rented by another family and up a steep dark staircase. Their room is dirty and dilapidated. Several of the window panes are broken and stuffed with sacking. They have no cooking facilities except an open grate and no washing facilities at all. Water and coal have to be carried up, and slops and cinders down, the steep staircase (p. 33).

Charles Webster (1991) confirms this view: old people suffered hearing loss without access to hearing aids, poor sight only alleviated by glasses bought from Woolworth's, early tooth loss, second-class treatment from doctors in crowded surgeries and degrading experiences in chronic and infectious diseases hospitals. He concludes:

> the elderly were...accustomed to ill-health without anticipation of humane or effective care. Their health was poor and their expectations low (p. 168).

It is perhaps not surprising in these circumstances that residential care was regarded as the best option.

Townsend strongly advocated the development of domiciliary services as a way out of what he saw as too great a dependency on residential care (Townsend and Wedderburn, 1965). A number of important social surveys were conducted during the 1960s and 1970s revealing the extent of (and deficiencies in) domiciliary provision. In 1961, the National Corporation for the Care of Old People (later CPA), in anticipation of greater powers being given to local authorities in this field of provision in 1962, conducted a survey of meals on wheels, at that time provided by a host of voluntary organisations across the country (Harris, 1961). It found that provision was patchy and recommended greater local authority responsibility in administering and supporting the services. A study of the home help service in 1970 (Hunt, 1970) found similar patchiness in provision and extensive unmet need. It estimated that the service would have to be extended between two and three times its existing size to meet the needs of all those who were eligible. A further study in the mid-70s found that a majority of those in need of domiciliary services did not in fact receive them (Hunt, 1978).

In 1963, a white paper on the development of community care (Ministry of Health, 1963) estimated that the number of home helps stood at 0.54 per 1,000 population, forecast to rise to 0.73 per 1,000 by 1972. But it also acknowledged that there was considerable variation in levels of provision across the country. The white paper on health and personal social services published over a decade later in 1976 (DHSS, 1976), suggested that provision of home helps and meals on wheels should be increased by 2 per cent per year to make up the shortfall. Day centre places should increase by 600 places per year. It was even more generous in its estimates for the home nursing service which it recommended should be increased by 6 per cent per year. It hoped that by substantial increases of this sort, the need for residential places would be contained or reduced.

The recent growth in the residential and nursing home sector outlined above suggests that this did not happen despite policy intentions going back thirty years and more. Nevertheless, there are difficulties in drawing an accurate picture of this trend over a long period, since definitions of services change, normative guidelines are altered, and new sectors whose services do not immediately figure in government estimates appear quite suddenly (for example, the private residential and nursing home sector in the 1980s and private domiciliary services in the 1990s). In addition, eligibility criteria for services change over time so that someone who may have qualified for a particular service thirty years ago, might be excluded now. In a context where central planning is resisted, as in recent years, and norms and the formulae for setting them have been abandoned, it is particularly difficult to make comparisons over time.

Older people's experiences of other aspects of health and welfare over the past fifty years have been variable. While Charles Webster (1991) argues that the NHS, by and large, has treated older people badly, there is no doubt that advances in medical technology over the years have had their beneficial impact on older people as well as others. Joint replacements, improvements in coronary care, the treatment of cancer, the development of palliative care are all now available to the ageing population. Indeed some have argued that the availability of treatment has gone too far in terms of maintaining any acceptable quality of life (Williams, 1997) and see Chapter 14. Nevertheless, there is some doubt about how far access is available to all those who need it and arguments abound about discrimination on the grounds of age (Titley, 1997). Life expectancy has increased but this is largely due, it is argued, to the elimination of childhood illnesses and improved social and environmental conditions (McKeown, 1976).

Health trends

Future developments in the treatment of diseases associated with old age are predicted. Tallis (1994), for example, sees surgical advances in relation to joint disease such as athroscopic re-lining and re-shaping of joints and the use of new improved materials for prostheses. He predicts advances in the prevention of stroke due to the modification of risk factors, new ways of reversing neurological impairments, earlier diagnosis of Parkinson's disease which will aid treatment, and improved drug therapies. The development of 'key hole' surgery will 'improve the safety of surgical operations for frail old people' (p. 83).

The major question for those concerned with the demographics of health and ageing is whether or not increased longevity will be accompanied by an increase in 'healthy active life years' (Grimley Evans, 1993) or whether older people as they live for longer will be faced with a long drawn-out period of decline and disability (Dalley, 1997). Proponents of the first thesis, often referred to as the 'compression of morbidity' (Fries, 1980), suggest that improved socio-economic conditions, healthier lifestyles and improvements in medical treatment will enable older people to live longer and more healthily. Opponents such as Gruenberg (1977) argue that the onset of disability and its progression will remain unchanged, the only difference being that death is postponed. So far, there is little evidence to support either case although Tallis (1994) points to data which show that in the UK the trend to increased reporting of long-standing illness is less in the over-75s and in the US increased life expectancy is beginning to be associated with a decline in age-specific disability.

There is growing recognition that health promotion strategies can be beneficially directed at older people (Howse et al, 1997). Criticism was widely voiced that the national strategy for improving the nation's health, *Health of the Nation*, published in 1992, largely overlooked older people's health. Although scope for primary prevention may be limited, opportunities for early detection and the establishment of rehabilitation to prevent deterioration in some of the chronic degenerative diseases can have remarkable benefits for older people. The prevention of disability or functional loss is now beginning to be seen as a major aim of health policy. The association of health inequalities with social inequality – although rejected as a legitimate area for research by the Conservative government in 1980 when the Black report on inequalities in health was published (Black, 1980) – has now been accepted as an important area for investigation. Exploration of these factors in relation to the health status of older people, and variations between groups within the older population now and over time, may illuminate the search for effective preventive strategies.

However, whatever results from this research, it remains the case that old people in the final years of life will remain high users of health and social care. This is not something we should be surprised at (those at the beginning of life also use health care disproportionately). The challenge for society is to ensure that the need for medical and social care is met adequately irrespective of age or social category.

In terms of current social policy, this challenge, some would argue, has been addressed with insufficient commitment (Titley, 1997). There may be little evidence of overt discrimination against older people on the grounds of age, but taking the broad sweep of social policy as a whole, there is evidence that older people are disadvantaged. For example, older people are increasingly being expected to pay the costs of long-term care themselves, and social services departments are unable to provide support services in the community to the level required (Harding, 1997). In addition, little recognition is given to the economic contribution made by informal carers (often older people themselves) – estimated by some sources to be in the region of £34 billion per annum if fully costed (Nuttall et al, 1993).

The somewhat guarded support given to the welfare of old people by leading policy-makers fifty years ago (Rowntree, 1947; Beveridge, 1942), and referred to in Chapter 1, is perhaps being replicated today. While improvements have been made over the period, there have been shortfalls. The failure to develop domiciliary services throughout the past fifty years, and the current reluctance to consider funding long-term care, both already noted, are prime examples.

Passivity to empowerment?

An encouraging development however in recent years has been the changing way in which the 'patient' or 'client' has been viewed and older people themselves are beginning to play a part in pushing for this. Sociological literature has regularly described the 'medical model' of health and illness which objectifies illness, sees only its pathology and neglects looking at the needs of the individual as a whole (Stacey, 1988: 173–4). In the case of older people in particular, it has been commonplace to regard them as passive recipients of treatment and services (Townsend, 1986).

The profession of medicine itself has endeavoured to modify this approach in recent years, perhaps in response to its critics – both from within and without the profession (Illich, 1975; McKeown, 1976; Kleinman, 1978; Navarro, 1979). Medical sociology as an academic discipline developed out of critiques of the medical domination of health and illness and its approach has been listened to by most of the health and social care professions. Joint statements issued periodically by professionals working in the field of older age increasingly commit practitioners to roles which champion patients as individuals, and declare the importance of recognising and responding to their whole needs (BGS/ADSS/RCN,1993; RCN, 1995).

More generally, there has been a shift in recent years towards 'consumerism', whereby recipients of welfare are re-cast as users or consumers of services. The origins of this shift have been located in the new culture imposed on the NHS and other public services by the Thatcher government in the 1980s (Beresford and Croft, 1988; Bernard et al, 1994; Parker and Etherington, 1989) and specifically in the Griffiths report on community care (Griffiths, 1988) and the white papers (Department of Health, 1989a, 1989b) which heralded the NHS and Community Care Act, 1990. Other developments, such as the introduction of the Patient's Charter in 1993, have also fostered the concept of the recipient of services as consumer, with rights of redress if service providers fail to deliver.

The idea of older people as powerful consumers of health and welfare services is an attractive one. Certainly, the rhetoric of empowerment conveys an image of informed choice. Department of Health guidance to health and social services frequently talks of choice and empowerment (Department of Health/KPMG, 1993). A recent review of the central policy context regarding users and carers states that 'promoting choice and independence for individuals is stated to underlie all the Conservative government's proposals for community care' (Nocon and Qureshi, 1996: 19). User involvement as a way to empowerment is actively encouraged across a range of fronts (Nocon et al, 1997; Stevenson and Parsloe, 1993)

Nevertheless, the degree to which older people – particularly the frailest and most vulnerable (and therefore those most reliant on services) – can realistically be expected to exercise choice and be empowered must depend on the willingness of decision-makers to listen. Choice presupposes a variety of options. The contemporary climate of resource constraint hardly allows for this. The rhetoric, though welcome insofar as it represents a change in prevailing perceptions of older people, remains just that. However, older people's groups are in some places taking up the challenge: advocacy projects to protect the interests of vulnerable older people have been established (Dunning 1994; Ivers, 1991) run by older people themselves and peer counselling groups providing support and advice on health matters have been set up in several places (Ivers and Meade, 1994), and see Chapter 12.

Future developments

The number of older people in the population is set to grow substantially in the next fifty years. Far more individuals than ever before will be able to expect an extended period of active life ahead of them after they have retired. The impact of changed attitudes and expectations is likely to have as much significance as any objective improvement in health status on the social roles which older people take in later life. One hundred years ago, people worked until they died. The idea of retirement was foreign to most of the working population who had no pension provision and relatively short life expectancy. The view of retirement at the advent of the welfare state, half a century later, has to be seen in contrast to that: pensioned retirement was a major social advance. It has gone on to colour our contemporary views of the position that older people occupy in society – as economically inactive and therefore dependent on the rest of the working population.

In fifty years time, with the rapid changes which are taking place in styles of work, the fragmentation of the concept of the lifelong career and greater flexibility in individuals' attitudes to work, retirement may cease to be the fixed point that it is seen as today. Continuing advances in medical technology and the growing capacity for people to maintain their independence will mean that older people may wish – and be able – to retain and extend their role in the community. The idea of older people as a burden on the rest of society will have become redundant. Dependency will increasingly be confined to the last few years of life. An active third age, and the social contribution which that signifies, will more than offset the demands made in the closing years of life for health and social care.

References

Audit Commission (1986) *Making a Reality of Community Care*, London: Audit Commission.

Baldwin, S. and Twigg, J. (1991) 'Women and community care – reflections on a debate' in Maclean, M. and Groves, D. (eds) *Women's Issues in Social Policy*, London: Routledge.

Bayley, M. (1973) *Mental Handicap and Community Care*, London: Routledge and Kegan Paul.

Beresford, P. and Croft, S. (1988) 'The new paternalism', *Social Work Today*, 19(51).

Bernard, M., Johnson, N. and Waterson, J. (1994) *Monitoring and Evaluation: a key issue for voluntary groups*, Social Services Research, no 4, Department of Social Policy and Social Work, University of Birmingham.

Beveridge, W. (1942) *Social Insurance and Allied Services*, London: HMSO.

BGS/ADSS/RCN (1995) *The Discharge of Elderly Persons from Hospital for Community Care: a joint policy statement by the British Geriatrics Society, the Association of Directors of Social Services and the Royal College of Nursing*, London: BGS.

Black, D. (Chairman) (1980) *Inequalities in Health*, London: Department of Health and Social Security.

Burgner, T. (1996) *The Regulation and Inspection of Social Services*, London: Department of Health and Welsh Office.

Centre for Policy on Ageing (1984) *Home Life: a code of practice for residential care*, London: Centre for Policy on Ageing.

Centre for Policy on Ageing (1990) *Community Life: a code of practice for community care*, London: Centre for Policy on Ageing.

Centre for Policy on Ageing (1996) *A Better Home Life: a code of good practice for residential and nursing home care*, London: Centre for Policy on Ageing.

Dalley, G. (1996) *Ideologies of Caring: rethinking community and collectivism*, second edition, London: Macmillan.

Dalley, G. (1997) 'Health and health care' in Evandrou, M. (ed) *Baby Boomers: ageing in the 21st century*, London: Age Concern England.

Department of Health (1989a) *Caring for People: community care in the next decade and beyond*, London: HMSO.

Department of Health (1989b) *Working for Patients*, London: HMSO.

Department of Health (1995) *NHS Responsibilities for Meeting Continuing Health Care Needs*, Leeds: Department of Health.

Department of Health and Social Security (1971) *Better Services for the Mentally Handicapped*, Cmnd 4683, London: HMSO.

Department of Health and Social Security (1975) *Better Services for the Mentally Ill*, Cmnd 6233, London: HMSO.

Department of Health and Social Security (1976) *Priorities for Health and Personal Social Services in England*, London: HMSO.

Department of Health and Social Security (1978) *A Happier Old Age: a discussion document on elderly people in our society*, London: HMSO.

Department of Health and Social Security (1981) *Growing Older*, Cmnd 8173, London: HMSO.

Department of Health/KPMG (1993) *Implementing Community Care: informing users and carers*, London: Department of Health.

Department of Health/Social Services Inspectorate (1991) *Carer Support in the Community: evaluation of the Department of Health initiative: 'Demonstration districts for informal carers' 1986–1989*, London: HMSO.

Dunning, A. (1995) *Citizen Advocacy with Older People: a code of good practice*, London: Centre for Policy on Ageing.

Finch, J. and Groves, D. (1980) 'Community care and the family: a case for equal opportunities', *Journal of Social Policy*, 9(4).

Finch, J. and Groves, D. (eds) (1983) *A Labour of Love: women, work and caring*, London: Routledge and Kegan Paul.

Foucault, M. (1977) *Discipline and Punish: the birth of the prison*, trans. A. Sheridan, London: Allen Lane.

Fries, J. F. (1980) 'Ageing, natural death and the compression of morbidity', *New England Journal of Medicine*, 303.

Goffman, E. (1961) *Asylums: essays on the social situation of mental patients and other inmates*, Harmondsworth: Penguin Books.

Griffiths, R. (1983) *Report of the NHS Management Inquiry – A Letter to the Secretary of State*, London: Department of Health and Social Security.

Griffiths, R. (1988) *Community Care: agenda for action*, London: HMSO.

Grimley Evans, J. (1993) 'Hypothesis: healthy active life expectancy (HALE) as an index of effectiveness of health and social services for elderly people', *Age and Ageing*, 22(4).

Gruenberg, E. M. (1977) 'The failures of success', *Milbank Memorial Quarterly*, 33(1).

Harding, T. (1997) 'Confusion reigns', *Community Care*, 8–14th May.

Harris, A. (1961) *Meals on Wheels for Old People*, London: National Corporation for the Care of Old People.

Harrison, A. and Prentice, S. (1996) *Acute Futures*, London: King's Fund.

Howse, K., Dalley, G., Killoran, A. and Seal, H. (1997) *Towards a Framework for Promoting the Health of Older People*, London: Centre for Policy on Ageing/Health Education Authority.

House of Commons, Health Committee (1996) *Long-term Care: future provision and funding*. Report, together with the proceedings of the Committee, Volume 1, London: HMSO.

Hunt, A. (1970) *The Home Help Service in England and Wales*, London: HMSO.

Hunt, A. (1976) *The Elderly at Home: a study of people aged sixty five and over living in the community in England in 1976*, London: HMSO.

Illich, I. (1975) *Medical Nemesis: the expropriation of health*, London: Calder and Boyars.

Ivers, V. (1994) *Citizen Advocacy in Action: working with older people*, Stoke on Trent: Beth Johnson Foundation.

Ivers, V. and Meade, K. (1991) *Older Volunteers and Peer Health Counselling: a new approach to training and development*, Stoke on Trent: Beth Johnson Foundation.

Jones, K. (1972) *A History of the Mental Health Services*, London: Routledge and Kegan Paul.

Jones, K. and Fowles, A. J. (1984) *Ideas on Institutions: analysing the literature on long-term care and custody*, London: Routledge and Kegan Paul.

Kendall, J. and Knapp, M. (1996) *The Voluntary Sector in the United Kingdom*, Manchester: Manchester University Press.

King's Fund Informal Caring Programme (1988) *Action for Carers: a guide to multi-disciplinary support at local level*, London: King's Fund.

Kleinman, A. (1978) ' Concepts and a model for the comparison of medical systems as cultural systems', *Social Science and Medicine*, 12(2B).

Lewis, J. (1993) 'Developing the mixed economy of care', *Journal of Social Policy*, 22(2).

Lewis, J. (1994) 'Voluntary organizations in "new partnership" with local authorities: the anatomy of a contract', *Social Policy and Administration*, 28(3).

Lewis, J. and Glennerster, H. (1996) *Implementing the New Community Care*, Buckingham: Open University Press.

McGlone, F. and Cronin, N. (1994) *A Crisis in Care? The future of long term care for older people in the European Union*, London: Centre for Policy on Ageing/Family Policy Studies Centre.

McKeown, T. (1976) *The Role of Medicine: dream, mirage or nemesis*, London: Nuffield Provincial Hospitals Trust.

Means, R. and Smith, R. (1985) *The Development of Welfare Services for Elderly People*, London: Croom Helm.

Ministry of Health (1962) *A Hospital Plan for England and Wales*, Cmnd 1604, London: HMSO.

Ministry of Health (1963) *Health and Welfare: the development of community care. Plans for the health and welfare services of the local authorities in England and Wales*, Cmnd 1973, London: HMSO.

Moroney, R. M. (1976) *The Family and the State: considerations for social policy*, London: Longman.

Navarro, V. (1979) *Medicine Under Capitalism*, London: Croom Helm.

Nocon, A. and Qureshi, H. (1996) *Outcomes of Community Care for Users and Carers: a social services perspective*, Buckingham: Open University Press.

Nocon, A., Qureshi, H. and Thornton, P. (1997) *Outcomes in Community Care Practice: the perspectives of users' and carers' organisations*, York: SPRU, University of York.

Nuttall, S. (et al) (1993) *Financing Long-Term Care in Great Britain*, London: Institute of Actuaries.

Parker, C. and Etherington, S. (1989) 'Will consumers have more choice?', *Social Services Insight*, 4(15).

RCN (1995) *Nursing and Older people: 1995 report of the RCN taskforce on older people and nursing*, London: Royal College of Nursing.

Rowntree, B. S. (Chairman) (1947) *Old People: report of a survey committee on the problems of ageing and the care of old people*, London: Oxford University Press.

Sheldon, J. H. (1948) *The Social Medicine of Old Age*, London: Oxford University Press.

Stacey, M. (1988) *The Sociology of Health and Healing*, London: Unwin Hyman.

Stevenson, O. and Parsloe, P. (1993) *Community Care and Empowerment*, York: Joseph Rowntree Foundation.

Tallis, R. (1994) 'Medical advances and the future of old age' in Marinker, M. (ed)

Controversies in Health Care Policies: challenges to practice, London: BMJ Publishing Group.

Thomson, D. (1983) 'Workhouse to nursing home: residential care of elderly people in England since 1840', *Ageing and Society*, 3(1).

Titley, J. (1997) *Healthcare Rights for Older People: the ageism issue*, London: Age Concern England.

Townsend, P. (1957) *Family Life of Old People: an inquiry in East London*, London: HMSO.

Townsend, P. (1962) *The Last Refuge: a survey of residential institutions and homes for the aged in England and Wales*, London: Routledge and Kegan Paul.

Townsend, P. (1986) 'Ageism and social policy' in Phillipson, C. and Walker, A. (eds) *Ageing and Social Policy: a critical assessment*, Aldershot: Gower.

Townsend, P. and Wedderburn, D. (1965) *The Aged in the Welfare State*, London: Bell.

Webb, A., Day, L. and Weller, D. (1976) *Voluntary Social Services: management resources*, London: Personal Social Services Council.

Webster, C. (1991) 'The elderly and the early National Health Service' in Pelling, M. and Smith, R. M. (eds) *Life, Death and the Elderly: historical perspectives*, London: Routledge.

Williams, A. (1997) 'Rationing health care by age: the case for', *British Medical Journal*, 314, 15th March.

3 Age and education

Eric Midwinter

Why should we be concerned with the issue of elderly people in education? Ultimately, the object is that the life of each elderly person might be enhanced by educational provision in its broadest sense. Initially, however, it is difficult to isolate the 'elderly' from the rest of the population and 'education' from what is vaguely termed a full and active life.

Eric Midwinter (1982) Age is Opportunity: education and older people, CPA, p. 1

Introduction

Education and retirement: of all cross-generational issues, this is the pair which best manages to illustrate the similarities between younger and older age, despite the heavy flavour, as we shall remark, of irony. At first sight, education appears to have a different motive in and for each of the two age-groups, but, on closer examination, the resemblance grows. It is therefore the purpose of this chapter to review the role of education in the lives of older people. Implicit in this analysis is the view that, whereas education is universally used as a social, indeed, official format for childhood and youth, it has little part to play in older age – and, in fact, nothing does fulfil that central role in the other non-working phase of life. There is, in effect, no organising principle for retirement, although, on this view, paid work remains the salient determinant of both the younger and the older periods of life. This analysis, while noting some admirable practice, is not buoyantly optimistic about likely wholesale changes in this position.

Children and consumers

The chief call for education in older age is to provide a substitute for work and parenting, those defining elements of adult life, and to offer older people the chance of constructive intellectual activity and a renewed self-esteem which those mainstream adult tasks had previously granted. Indeed, it is often said that, in older age, it is a matter of education for education's sake, just as, in the 1930s, artists spoke of art for art's sake. Education, with no vocational or other axe to grind, may assume, in older age, an aura of purity: it is primarily pursued for reasons of personal enhancement. It is true that – the road to hell being paved with good educational intentions – enlightened commentators, anxious to procure improved learning conditions for older people, argue that continued training would enable them to remain longer in the work place. This rather misses the point, as will later be demonstrated, that the call for older workers is likely to continue to decline. In any event, it is high time we stopped judging work as the be-all and end-all of human existence. It is the insistence that work is salient and non-work peripheral, which so imperils the standing of older age. To paraphrase Oscar Wilde, 'work is the curse of the ageing classes'.

Conversely, the usual justification for education in the younger age-groups is its preparatory character. Children and youth must be schooled for that adult life of work and family raising, and trained to take their place in the economic and civic arenas vacated by the older generation. In 1994 – and again in 1996 – the governmental response to questions about the non-availability of grants to students over 50 was so very negative, pointing out the fact that older students do not have the same expectation of future earnings as younger people (Hansard, 1994). There is no sentiment in governmental circles: education is steadfastly about equipping younger people for the economy and 'future earnings'.

However, a revisionist view of educational and economic history questions this rationale. It does so in the face of a massive and dogmatic credo about the value of education in this preparatory sense. The entire political machine, every developed and developing nation, in alliance with the huge vested industry of the education industry – a business worth £10bn annually in the United Kingdom – rests the policy of the former, and the existence of the latter, on the strength of the 'economic investment' argument. Barely a week passes without a leading politician or influential commentator bemoaning the effects of poor educational standards on current economic performance.

The contrary argument suggests that this view is a misreading of the social map by as much as 180 degrees. In principal in part, if not in whole, the education system is the result, not the cause, of a sophisticated economic apparatus. It is a consumer 'good', a prize arising from technological advancement. Thus developed nations have an elaborate and expensive education system because of, not in support of, intricately developed economies. It is quite possible to argue, as one expert protagonist of this position has observed, 'that education is a consequence of national economic growth, a luxury that rich countries can afford, but that is unrelated to the process of economic development' (Walters, 1981).

Custody and control

A major element in this analysis concerns custodial care and control. It has sometimes been urged, by left-wing historians and educationists, that schools were used to gentle the masses and turn them into factory-fodder, at the same time as they stripped out the likelier specimens for subaltern roles in the professions and in management. However, a more realistic version suggests that what schools and, later, colleges did was to provide a penitentiary agency for those younger people for whom there was no longer work available.

A critical decade was the 1860s. There were thousands of younger people, typically aged between 8 and 15, with neither work to do nor schools to attend. Many had had some schooling, perhaps three or four years on average, and it has been claimed that, at this time, three-quarters of the population were elementary readers, well within the scope required to staff a primary industrial economy. What probably occasioned, as much as any issue, the seminal passage of the 1870 Education Act, the foundation of the state education service, was the fear of social dislocation. 'Street-Arab...the residuum...the dangerous and perishing classes...' these were a few of the tags of opprobrium fastened on to those children destined to 'aimless drifting'. Thus the emphasis was on 'attendance', and the 1870 Act was the first of a series which allowed for the punitive enforcement of compulsory attendance at schools. This underscoring of 'attendance', rather than a discussion of what should happen to the children while actually in attendance, has dogged the educational narrative since, with truancy still frowned upon as the venial sin (Midwinter, 1995).

It was at much the same time that the first fruits of retirement policy were being harvested, with the first cycle of professional occupational pensions. The sloughing off of older workers, often the consequence of improved technologies, was key. As the 1895 Royal Commission on the Aged Poor testified, this proclivity affected working as well as middle class occupations. As is well known, the old age pension was introduced in 1908, a national award largely replacing (while not palpably increasing) the local subventions made to older paupers by the poor law unions (Thane, 1982). At about the same time, the 1902 Education Act handed over the responsibilities for schools to the new burgeoning, multidisciplinary local authorities, and provided for a modicum of secondary education. A similar parallel may be noted in the 1940s. The 1944 Education Act provided free secondary education for all, whilst in 1948, the old age pension received one of its few boosts in real value.

What has changed – what continued and continues to change – was the world of work and, in ancillary mode, parenting. Only 150 years ago it was quite customary for children of 5 years and under to be working, and for men and women to toil until they dropped. There was precious little 'first age' of socialisation and 'third age' of retirement for them. What, gradually, has occurred is a shrinkage of the 'second age' of work and a distinct pattern emerges of longer educational provision and longer retirements, from both vocational and familial chores. In truth, the school leaving age and the state retirement age might more appropriately be dubbed the work starting and the work finishing ages. Work has collapsed and continues to do so. This is demonstrated in unemployment and structural under-employment, and also in the rapid reduction in hours, days and weeks worked, from the worker's average of 3,600 hours a year in the 1840s to 1,500 hours a year in the 1990s. But it is principally to be found fore and aft, with younger people staying on at school and college longer and then often becoming embroiled in a mesh of ever-changing training schemes, and with older people faced with a mix of early retirement and last redundancy. Indeed, at both ends, the de facto ages are, for many people, later and earlier than the de jure ages.

The pattern may be described in the following manner. Given the complexity of some and the vagueness of other figures, it would not be claimed that those in Table 3.1 are any more than crude approximations. However, by attempting to consider the 'stages' rather than more usual 'ages' of comparative populations, it is felt that a clearer guide may be proffered as to the real social divisions of British society then and now. The ordinary chronological statistics – under twenties; over sixties, and so on – while valuable, mask some of these social facts. In each case in the following formula, the 'first age' includes those under viable school age and those in regular attendance at school or college; and the 'second age' encompasses those in, or in search of, work and/or involved in familial duties. In both examples, the 'second age' necessarily includes a small number, neither young nor old, who are for various reasons dependent on private or public care. For the 1990s, the 'third age' consists of those who have completed either paid employment and/or mainline parenting. For the late 1840s/early 1850s, the 'third age' embraces those registered as 'aged paupers', that is, not deemed to be any longer 'able-bodied' and capable of work, plus a reasonable estimate of those in that category cared for privately.

Table 3.1 Stages in the life cycle; proportions of the population; 1840s and 1990s

Population	First age (%)	Second age (%)	Third age (%)
early 1850s	14	84	2
early 1990s	24	55	21

The meaning is lucid enough. Chronologically, the emergence of the 'third age' in Britain by about the 1950s has been excellently analysed, and these figures, of course, underpin that change. However, by concentrating on the social circumstances of the two populations, its general effect on the overall life-span may be judged. It demonstrates that the premier alteration in the socioeconomic fabric has been the massive decline in the 'second age' of the working population, with a corresponding growth in, so to say, the thickness of bread in the surrounding sandwich. The 'third age' is, in everyday practice, a new phenomenon, but the 'first age' has itself almost doubled in proportion. The 150 year period since the completion and stabilisation of the inaugural industrial revolution has witnessed a slowly accelerating disintegration of work. As the staple time-filler of human life, it has lost much of its momentum (Read, 1979).

One should hasten to add that the appearance of 45 per cent of the population in the 'first' and 'third ages' combined is the effect of this, and not its cause. It is the increasingly intricate and refined character of the economy which has produced this dearth in demand for human labour. It was, and it is, the force of the sustained revolutions in industrial technology which have basically fabricated the enlargement of both the 'first age' and the 'third age'. On that scenario, education for children and youth is provided on the same grounds as for older people. Technically, the 'first' and 'third ages' are at leisure: they constitute the majority of what has been called 'the first mass leisure clan'. They have no direct vocational nor familial duties to perform (Dower, 1965).

Courses and classes

In effect, Britain, like every other developed nation, has avoided having a 'retirement' policy, in the sense of a positive response – the equivalent of schooling for all children – to the challenge of a huge cohort of people without work. Partly because the phenomenon in any sizeable fashion is novel, and partly because older people do not constitute the social threat which footloose younger people pose, little has been done, except, of course, in respect of welfare pensions. Residential care homes and day centres are the nearest 'corralling' counterpart in the 'third age' to schools in the 'first age'.

Such has been the dictorial pressure of 'work' that, where there have been developments in adult education, they have studiously denied the needs of retired people. One might identify three strands in the adult education movement. The first, and largest, unequivocally engages in vocational and professional training, and this includes all manner of correspondence, as well as evening and day release courses. The second has aimed at a more civic or politicised approach but, here again, the purpose has been to alert the worker to his or her higher potential. The very title of the Workers Education Association, inaugurated in 1903 by Albert Mansbridge, himself a product of the co-operative movement, is testimony enough. Like the Mechanics' Institutes of an earlier age, there was also the twentieth century movement of education settlements – Fircroft (1909) and Coleg Harlech (1927) are illustrations – chiefly aimed at improving working class awareness. The third element, of slightly later vintage, has been the straightforwardly recreational class, typically the evening offering of origami or flower arrangement. Without being avowedly work-centred, it has largely been viewed as pleasant relief from the cares of the 'second age' of work and parenting. Few efforts have been made to address the specific requirements of the close on 12 million persons in the 'third age'. Where this has been attempted, some of the examples have been alarming – 'cooking for one', for instance, has a glum and siege-like ring about it (Kelly, 1970).

Of course, older people have attended continuing and adult education classes in the UK and elsewhere, but never in large numbers. This may, in part, be a generational function in that the current group of older people has a poor experience of school, and worked during a period when the relative proportions of what, to use now old-fashioned terms, the working and middle classes remained at about 70:30, as opposed to today's more nearer 50:50 ratio. Much of adult education is the province of those who have previously enjoyed a good experience of schooling and tends to be associated with those in professional and managerial employment. For instance, 60 per cent of those aged 50–69 have no educational qualifications at all, compared with only 18 per cent in their twenties. Only 4 per cent of those over 55 have a degree, compared with 8 per cent in the population at large. The social class figures, with that in-built determinant of educational success, show that twice as many 'white-collar' as 'skilled manual' workers are currently studying, and that the gap is widening. By the same token it is even wider between the 'white collar' workers and unskilled and unemployed people.

Thus there may, over the years, be an improved cohort effect. As the educational and working experiences of the present and coming generations of 'second agers' become more education-oriented, those habits may well carry over into the 'third age'. Nonetheless, one should not too readily discount the effects of the prevailing ethos, which habituates everyone to the notion that education is mainly for children and youth, and then, if but marginally, for workers and housewives/husbands. The insistence that education and employment are directly and automatically related – now woefully epitomised in the merging of these two responsibilities at governmental level – accentuates this belief. In the wake of the collapse of the youth job market, two-thirds of the 17–19 age group and a seventh of the 20–24 age group are currently undertaking full-time study. Little wonder that there is no spotlight available to illumine the needs of older people. It may well be that 'third agers', faced with this sustained cultural imperative, will continue to eschew education.

Statistics published in 1990 suggested that 14 per cent of those between 55 and 64 and just 9 per cent of those 65 and over had undertaken formal studies during the last three years (see Schuller and Boston, 1993). This compares with 26 per cent in the general population and, to take two instances, 45 per cent of the 17–19 population and 32 per cent of 35–44 year olds. A further 9 per cent of those aged 55–64 and 6 per cent of the 65+ group, claimed to be studying informally, giving respective totals of 23 per cent and 15 per cent. An updated survey in 1996 suggested that the figures had risen marginally, from 23 per cent to 25 per cent for recent and current learners aged 55–64, and from 15 per cent to 18 per cent for those aged over 65 (Tuckett and Sargant, 1996). In the same period, the numbers for the general population had dropped from 26 per cent to 23 per cent, although there had been a rise – 63 per cent to 86 per cent – in the 17–19 years band quoted above, while the 35–44 group had remained steady at 43 per cent. These figures include both 'formal' and the so-called 'informal' figures, and are all based on interview.

A three year window of opportunity is quite a wide one in terms of older people, and it could mean that a considerable number of those cited were not currently undertaking any study. An estimate based on that latter survey might suggest something like a half of the total figure might be 'currently' as opposed to 'recently' studying, while the amount of time and the outcome of informal learning is, of course, notoriously difficult to assess.

Other research suggests that, at any one time, relatively few older people are thus engaged in any formal sense (Midwinter, 1982; Groombridge, 1989). Government statistics suggest 1.8 per cent of those over 65 were engaged in further or higher education in 1994/95, although this excludes 'a considerable number' for whom no 'estimate is available' of people over 65 in attendance at adult education centres. If anything, that is a little worse than when similar soundings were taken in the early 1990s, and may reflect the increased pressure of rising fees, fewer concessionary favours and more straitened pensioner pockets over that period.

As always with statistics, there are those who wish, for whatever motivation, to look on either the bright or gloomy side of life and who, without of course any direct mendacity, are generous or miserly in their arithmetical interpretations. In an attempt to find an innocent path between these mathematical hedgerows, a rather generous estimate might be to opine that, at a given time, about 250,000 of those aged 55–64 and about 200,000 of those aged 65 and over are engaged in formal study. That would represent nearly 5 per cent of the total post 55 population, a proportion of whom, of course, are still working and raising families and are not strictly 'third age' personnel.

Some three quarters of such enrolments are in local authority centres and further education colleges, with other providers, such as the WEA or university extramural departments, making up the leeway. Only about four or five in every hundred of the Open University's students are over 60 (it would be nearer twenty-five in every hundred on any proportionate representation, leaving aside the greater time available to older people for study). Moreover, the number of these with first degrees is higher than for those under 60, in the ratio of two to one, despite the low baseline of older graduates in the population. This is another reminder, as the scriptures counsel, that to those who have shall more be given. That said, the Open University, compared with the conventional run of colleges, has been to the forefront of widening higher education chances for older people (Schuller and Boston, 1993).

The involvement of older people in formal educational activity across Europe is not pronounced. Even in Denmark, with its well-merited reputation for adult learning, only 6 per cent of those over pensionable age are involved in any regular fashion, while only 4 per cent of Germans over 65 enrol at their local 'people's college'. As in the United Kingdom, such figures pale into significance against the much healthier enrolments among the younger age-groups (Crosby, 1993). It would appear that Britain is not alone in not providing anything like a full coverage of attractive educational courses for older people. Indeed, the sad and curious paradox whereby 'third age' people, with twice the amount of leisure time, are much less involved in constructive non-work activity than those in the 'second age', is reflected in educational circles.

The reasons for poor take-up are both material and cultural, and reports suggest that these are common grounds across Europe. The emphasis – an increasing one of late – on vocational fare and professional qualifications, the rising costs, and the usual transport difficulties and concerns about safety are among the physical obstacles. The cultural barriers include a rigorously held societal opinion that education is about children preparing for adulthood, an aversion to the over-formalised character of conventional educational provision and, certainly in Britain, as we have seen, the low levels of attainment in the current older generation. Functional illiteracy is high among the older age-groups, higher than 30 per cent on some findings and certainly more than the average for the younger age-range – in a society which insists on bemoaning falling educational standards among its youth and children. Poor initial instruction, coupled with the inadequacy of chances in adult life to gain or sustain habits of literacy, and indeed numeracy, have probably played havoc with the confidence of the older generation.

In turn, this raises the question of the appropriateness of other aspects of access. Older age brings willy-nilly hindrances – in sight and hearing and slowness of movement, for example – which, while falling short of outright disability, require consideration. In the Universities of the Third Age and elsewhere, there has been some small scale pilot work with home-visiting and telephonic tutoring schemes. Happily, gender may be less of a problem than it was, as women properly seek a decent equity with men. The University of the Third Age movement, for example, might argue, from its ratio of three women to every one man, that the problem has been reversed, although that is, in part, a function of later male retirements and later female death ages. Ethnicity raises an interesting issue apropos education and older age. It is probably true that few older Afro-Caribbean and 'New Commonwealth' people figure on the adult educational registers, but then they are relatively under-represented currently, because the relevant post-Second World War wave of immigration has not yet made its impact in the older age echelons. Conversely, one may pleasingly find many examples of earlier migrations – principally from continental Europe during the first half of the century – engaged in adult education at an older age. When all is done and said about access, it is likely that the outstanding educational uncertainty, and one which embraces some of the other posers about access such as poverty, gender and ethnicity, is the continuing cultural and social question of social class, allied, as it is, to earlier educational and professional achievement acting as a key to involvement in older age.

Plainly then, the involvement in traditional education by older people is low enough to be regarded as negligible. That is not meant as disrespectful to either those who provide or those who benefit from such adult education, and it is worth stating that, by and large, matters have improved steadily since the 1960s. Great and noble efforts have been made to improve matters. The Forum on the Rights of Elderly People to Education (FREE) was formed, chiefly as an information exchange, in 1981, with the energetic support of several leading academics and voluntary organisations. Its work has been subsumed by its main sponsor, Age Concern England, and the reliable and helpful bulletin, 'Education and Leisure', remains the securest guide to both thinking and action in the field of education and older people. An Association of Educational Gerontology, complete with the proper accoutrements of conference and journal, has emerged and has made a significant mark. In 1996 the National Institute of Adult and Continuing Education appointed a Project Development Officer to manage its 'Older and Bolder' educational initiative and, all in all, the commitment of professional educators and social gerontologists to the notion of learning opportunities for older people has dramatically expanded.

It will be remembered, nonetheless, that the comparison being made here concerns that which is conspicuous and defining about life-styles during life's three main arcs. Only a few older people would consider that learning is the main rationale of life, to the point where they would primarily describe themselves, say, as students. It is apparent that education does not play as large a role in the 'third age' as it does even in the 'second'. Whether one indulges, like students of the American Constitution, in a 'tight' or a 'loose' interpretation of the varied sets of statistics about older people and learning, there is consistency about the ratio of overall adult to 'older age' participation: it is always about 2:1. Some 'third agers' continue the habits of the 'second age', in that they sign up for an occasional course; a few others may seek out such classes on retirement. But education has no major or dominant part to play, as schooling does in the 'first age' or work in the 'second age'.

In crude approximation, the 5–20/25 year old spends about 25 per cent of waking life in full-time education and training; the average 20/25–55/60 year old spends about 33 per cent of waking life at work; while the nearest equivalence for the 60/65 plus years olds might be the fact that they spend about 36 per cent of their waking life watching television. The comparison is assuredly not with education, nor with any grouping of constructive activities (for instance, voluntary work, the arts, physical pursuits) which might embrace education. As with learning, all those activities are more keenly pursued by working than by retired people.

Hence the irony. The 'third age' is in exactly the same need of educational and allied facilities as the 'first age', and for much the same reasons that 'third agers' are not required to undertake paid employment and family duties. But neither the public nor the private sector provides a universal series of amenities, of which education might be a principal example, for the 'third age'. Even to hint at the possibility that the 'third age' might be identified wholesale with a determining character of participative and constructive performance flies in the face of credulity, so inured are we to the sense of retirement as a literal withdrawal to the ante-chambers of society. Moreover, the increased survival rates of older people mean that they are now emulating younger people in the length of time endured in the relevant stage. The 'first age' usually lasts 18 to 25 years; the 'third age' now lasts up to 20, 30 and even 40 years.

A curio of gerontological study has been the absence of much scrutiny of the retirement process per se. The construct within which the process proceeds – the funding, the accommodation, the medical and other supports – has been exhaustively examined as a kind of 'social book-keeping', as it has been termed, but the sheer business of living through those 20, 30 or 40 years has attracted less academic and, in fact, political attention. One recalls the old jibe that, were anthropologists fish, the last thing they would discover would be water.

Participation in education is one strand, at present a slender thread, of this retirement skein. Along with other constructive leisure activities, it represents the positive face of retirement. Many commentators now accept that, as a measure of quality of life, active leisure is as significant as income, health, housing, companionship and the usual traditional yardsticks, and that the more 'participatory' the involvement, the richer the benefit. It must be accepted as a pertinent 'category of life' (Neulinger, 1979).

The public interest demands the creation of a social and cultural environment conducive to the participation of 'third agers' in education, in its broadest sense, and in allied activities, so that people might seek fresh opportunities to widen their horizons and to experiment with new interests. In a phrase, this would be the hallmark of the acknowledgement of older people as citizens and not as social casualties. Without such a policy, older people are destined to remain unoccupied in the worst sense, marginalised and banned from contributing anything like a genuine and consistent social product to the commonalty of society.

Cooperation and citizenship

A tiny, beckoning light in a dark and naughty world has been lit by the University of the Third Age, which has been mentioned, as one might say with a nod in the direction of its founding nation, en passant. For the British version was inspired by the French movement, established in Toulouse in 1972 under the splendid leadership of Pierre Vellas, and now boasting forty U3As and 60,000 members. The British U3As adopted a self-help stance, as compared with the continental model of older people contracting out tutorship from the local university. With the Australians, very vigorously, and the New Zealanders picking up the British baton, the international agency, AIUTA (Association Internationale des Universités du Troisième Age), eventually accepted that 'there are two main models of U3A in the world, the French and the British'. Spurred on by belief in recurrent education, in community education and mutual aid, the British U3As form, in brief, a social co-operative movement, consciously based on the success of the pre-school playgroups initiative.

One or two studies, chiefly localised, have already underlined the strengths, especially the social strengths, of U3As and like bodies (Soulsby, 1989). A research conundrum exists because the U3As tacitly forswear the somewhat bourgeois, value-added obsessions of much of what passes for educational evaluation. How much people learn is very much secondary to whether they attend at all and enjoy themselves, so much so that the arithmetic, to the despair of the number-crunchers, remains comparatively simple.

There are over 300 U3A groups in Britain, each autonomous in organisation, but linked together nationally and often regionally and thematically, and with a democratic structure bottom to top. With accommodation often found in members' homes and with members offering administrative and convening services on a voluntary basis, there are, in toto, over 40,000 members, with possibly 6,000 interest-groups across the nation. There are no eligibilities asked for and no qualifications sought; practically alone among British educational agencies, the membership locally decides on the programme, the only points at issue being whether some wish to take up an interest and one or more are willing to steward the group; and, above all else, there is substantial evidence of friendly social interplay. Launched in 1982, and working against the grain of a then current national mood redolent of privatism and personal enterprise, the British U3As have added considerably to the numbers of older people engaged in education. But, just as importantly, they have betokened a fresh approach to the subject. Three lessons, in particular, might be noted.

First, it defies the traditional 'apprenticeship-bound' view of education, with children and young people almost the exclusive beneficiaries. It helps to substitute for that, the concept of recurrent or lifelong education, with its message that educational support, like medical support, should be on call at all stages of life. It sighs for a national educational service, as a kind of National Health Service of the intellect. It stems from a pluralist viewpoint. It recognises that, for some older people for some of the time, educational sessions with their peer-group are almost acceptable, but it is not wedded irrevocably to generational education, and several of its protagonists are involved, for instance, with schemes which link older people with school children.

Second, it puts another gloss on pluralism by taking an anti-institutional stance. The conventional education service is deeply imbued with a didactic and tutorial approach, usually negotiated behind the walls of sometimes lavish and prestigious buildings. This operates successfully for those for whom it operates successfully, but (to borrow a coinage from the economic debate) it is a 'one club' approach and, by that token, denies access to many. By its use of, to deploy a little jargon, a dialogic, as opposed to a monologic, methodology, and by housing iself in homely settings, many have found the opportunity not only to learn more comfortably, but to help organise and lead interest-groups.

Third, and most important from the standpoint of older age itself, the membership organises its own affairs. It is a statement about citizenship. U3A members are not, like many of their fellows in the past and still today, the passive recipients of services decided for them by professional cadres. They invent their own destiny, and they constantly illustrate the resilience and confidence of older humanity, and its capacity, given half a chance, to utilise its vast store of talent and experience. In the argot of the leisure industry, U3A members are the 'origin' and not the 'pawn' in the educational game (Midwinter, 1996).

Comments and conclusion

Although this and other projects demonstrate that educational gerontologists are not recruited for Mission Impossible, it is, all in all, a bleak prospect. The basic fault is curiously like the one which marred the treatment of childhood until the late nineteenth century; namely, a refusal to accept that, within the undoubted commonalty of the human experience, there are discrete phases. Thus the impediment in the way of advancement is the insistence that, just as children were treated as little men and, resonant title, little women, 'third agers' are treated as fading 'second agers', with small recognition of their distinct post-work quality. It is in the reversal of this conception that the main hope for social policy-making lies.

In his perceptive analysis of the concept of the 'third age', Peter Laslett has asserted that, because of the unprecedented nature of the phenomenon, 'third agers' would have to formulate and pioneer new institutions suitable to their novel conditions (Laslett, 1989). The U3A is an example of this, but the cheers at its success are muted by the recognition that few other agencies have come into existence. Indeed, there has been a danger that some regard U3A as the sole answer to the question of educational opportunity in this age-bracket, and critics ask why it does not cater for this or that group among old people, with those in the inner city and some ethnic minority groups among such instances. It was, of course, never intended to be a blanket response: the hope had been that it would be one of a score or more initiatives which, package by package, would offer varying brands of positive encouragement to varying groups of older people.

That sense of cultural cohesion and appropriate agencies is still largely absent from the 'third age' in general, let alone in the particular of education. Perhaps it will shortly emerge. What is interesting is that, as first children and then adolescents were deposed from the labour markets, a diverse cult developed. The notion that the child was a 'little man' was replaced by a Rousseau-like belief in the child-likeness of children, with complementary aspects of a literary, dress, musical, recreational and other kinds, and later, that circumstance was matched by similar developments in the youth field. It is not a coincidence that the stories of Lewis Carroll, normally regarded as marking the nativity of child-oriented literature, were published around 1879, just as state schooling and the limitations on child labour were taking hold. In both the USA and Western Europe, it marked a widening or a more child-centred view of the first stage of life, characterised by more 'sentimental' and less 'instrumental' family relationships.

By the 1880s and 1890s, commentators such as G. Stanley Hall felt able to identify the psychosocial phenomenon of adolescence. It is no accident that the youth cults, formally associated with the formation of the Boys' Brigade and the Boy Scouts, and later to be the subject of widespread commercial exploitation, commenced in the late Victorian and early Edwardian period, just as further extensions in schooling and, its necessary prerequisite, reductions in the labour force were envisaged. Another gloss on this social trait might be to suggest that the 'first age' has become so extended with, for many, the onset of puberty arriving in the middle of that interval of time, that it has been found necessary to split it into two sections. Indeed, the postponement of work has, along with a variety of other reasons, opened up a widening gap between the biological and cultural aspects and the economic and social aspects of the menarche. For some commentators it has similarly been found useful to divide the later stage of life in to the independent 'third age' and the dependent 'fourth age' (Hareven, 1995).

Freed from work and its concomitant cultural and social attachments, it appears that groups then develop – or have developed for them – a more autonomous or specialised lifestyle, neither better nor worse, but different. As yet, the 'third age' has not found, except in minor degree, its cultural counterpart. It lacks its seminal educators, designers, artists and narrators, and little sense of such a cohesive life-style has yet emerged. It is difficult not to conclude that a central reason for this absence of a 'third age' fashion is precisely the lack of some defining construct. A glance, for instance, at the literature or the television aimed at or based on the 'first age' or the 'second age' reminds that, respectively, 'school' and 'work', and the associated activities of either, figure very prominently. There is a sort of hollowness or vacuum about the collective life of 'third agers', and one of the explanations for the relative 'invisibility' of older people in cultural manifestations, such as on television or in novels, is exactly this deficit of socioeconomic division (Midwinter, 1991).

A personal view would be that this challenge should become the hallmark of social planning for the future. It should form the twenty-first century agenda for organisations such as the Centre for Policy on Ageing, once memorably described as 'the model of everything a think-tank should be' and an agency admirably fitted in construct, temper and personnel for this great task. On the one hand, it grows increasingly clear that the traditional areas of social gerontology should predominantly be absorbed into cross-generational policy studies and political responses. Poverty, poor housing, insecurity, ill-health, loneliness – these are flaws running throughout society like seismic rifts. For example, the poor young person becomes the poor old person; there has yet to be recorded the first case of a rich old person dying of hypothermia; and old people are not vulnerable to crime because they are old but because they are vulnerable.

On the other hand, it is time for fish to discover water. It is time to help lead 'third agers', as the Book of Exodus puts it, 'out of the land of bondage', and to explore, with substantially more conviction than hitherto, the full nature of retirement. Education would be one of the component parts in the development of a type of lifestyle commensurate with this 'new old age', and, although it is proper to expect 'third agers' themselves to play the leading roles in such determinations, all the histories of similar cultural shifts in the past point to the need for some catalyst, such as a lively and inventive agency.

Moreover, there might be lessons for, as well as from, the 'first age'. If, as has been suggested, education in the 'first' age is only a little more 'preparatory' and a future 'investment' than education in the 'third age', then the mainline schools service for children and young people may have something to learn from what might be the relaxed, unoppressive and cooperative attitudes of a new 'third age' culture. From the viewpoint then, both of the 'first age' and the 'third age', one might educationally embrace the text of the standard lyric, which exhorted us to 'accentuate the positive' and 'eliminate the negative'.

References

Crosby, G. (ed) (1993) *The European Directory of Older Age*, London: Centre for Policy on Ageing.

Dower, M. (1965) *Fourth Wave: the challenge of leisure*, London: Civic Trust. Originally published in the *Architects' Journal*, 20 January 1965.

Groombridge, B. (1989) 'Education and later life' in Warnes, A. M. (ed) *Human Ageing and Later Life*, London: Edward Arnold.

Hansard (1994) 3 May, Col. 594.

Hareven, T. K. (1995) 'Changing images of aging and the social construction of the life course' in Featherstone, M. and Wernick, A. *Images of Aging: cultural representations of later life*, London: Routledge.

Laslett, P. (1989) *A Fresh Map of Life: the emergence of the third age*, London: Weidenfeld and Nicolson.

Kelly, T. (1970) *History of Adult Education in Great Britain*, second edition, Liverpool: Liverpool University Press.

Midwinter, E. (1982) *Age is Oppportunity: education and older people*, London: Centre for Policy on Ageing.

Midwinter, E. (1991) *Out of Focus: old age, the press and broadcasting*, London: Centre for Policy on Ageing.

Midwinter, E. (1995) *State Educator: the life and enduring times of W. E. Forster*, Coventry: Community Education Development Centre.

Midwinter, E. (1996) *Thriving People: the growth and prospects of the U3A in the UK*, London: Third Age Trust.

Neulinger, J. (1979) 'Leisure: a state of mind that all desire but few achieve' in Ruskin, H. (ed) *Leisure: towards a theory and policy*, London: Associated University Presses.

Read, D. (1979) *England 1868–1914*, London: Longman.

Schuller, T. and Boston, A. M. (1993) *Learning: education, training and information in the third age*, London: The Carnegie Enquiry into the Third Age.

Soulsby, L. J. (1989) 'Developing a model for the creation and support of self-help education groups for the retired, non-wages and older adult', unpublished dissertation for the degree of M.Ed in the University of Manchester.

Thane, P. (1982) *The Foundations of the Welfare State*, London: Longman.

Tuckett, A. and Sargant, N. (1996) *Creating Two Nations? headline findings on lifelong learning from the NIACE/Gallup Survey 1996*, Leicester: NIACE.

Walters, P. B. (1981) 'Educational change and national economic development', *Harvard Education Review*, 51(1).

4 Living arrangements of older people

Sheila Peace and Julia Johnson

A considerable number of older couples find themselves contemplating not just special forms of sheltered housing, as an ultimate protection, but the possibilities which smaller and more convenient 'retirement housing' can open up by releasing them from the tiresome responsibilities of maintenance and upkeep, thus enabling them to make the very most of their later years. It is a challenge which affects us all, both as people who must respond to this changed set of needs and expectations and also, eventually, as participants in this great social moment.

Hedley Taylor (1987) Growing Old Together: elderly owner-occupiers and their housing, CPA, p. 2

Introduction

Since the setting up of the welfare state in the 1940s, there have been radical changes in housing policy and policies for residential care. In this chapter, we consider these policies as a response to the changing nature of household and population change and their impact on the living arrangements of people in later life. Our emphasis here is on accommodation, the 'where' as opposed to the 'who with', although as we demonstrate, care or support are fundamental to the development of 'special' forms of housing targeted at older people. So, what accommodation options are available to older people now and what might they be in the future? It is important perhaps to emphasise at the outset that the vast majority of older people live in ordinary, non-specialist housing in the community and that the choices available to them, should the need for care arise, are strongly influenced by income and housing tenure. Any consideration of the present and future living arrangements of older people, therefore, needs to take account of the policy context.

The policy context

The needs of families have dominated housing policy since the Second World War with older people being labelled as under-occupiers of family space. Housing policy has been based on the idea of a 'normal' housing career trajectory which moves from the family home to accommodation for young single people, to family starter homes, to larger family home, to smaller property for the so-called 'empty-nester'. Yet the needs of families with children should not be the only model on which to base housing policy within a changing society. In Britain there is a tradition of independent living, with a preference for different generations to live in separate households. This, when coupled with major changes in household and family form throughout the twentieth century, has resulted in smaller household and family sizes and more people living alone (Haskey, 1996). Consequently, in 1961, there were 16.2 million households in Britain for a population of 51 million; in 1994 there were 23.1 million households for a population of 56.8 million. Whilst housing designed for smaller households has become more common in the latter half of the century, it has not dominated new build in either the public or private sectors.

In this section we trace some of the policy developments of the last fifty years looking first at changes within the two main forms of housing tenure – renting and owner occupation – before considering the development of 'special' housing for older people.

THE RENTED SECTOR

It seems fair to say that both Labour and Conservative administrations between 1945 and 1979 saw an increase in home ownership as the main plank of housing policy. Where they differed was in their attitude to the rented sector of housing. Broadly speaking, whereas the Conservatives favoured the privatisation of the rented sector, Labour favoured the development of subsidised public housing. Yet ironically more council houses were built in the second half of the twentieth century under Conservative than Labour governments while the private rented sector declined dramatically.

In 1939, 32 per cent of dwellings were owner occupied, 58 per cent were privately rented and 10 per cent were council properties (Hughes and Lowe, 1995: 21). Although private renting dominated, it was actually losing ground to the increase in owner occupation and in council tenancies. This changing pattern of housing tenure continued after the Second World War. The newly elected Labour government in 1945 was strongly committed to continuing the council house building programme which started in 1919. Nevertheless, it was constrained by a shortage of materials in the immediate post-war period. As Table 4.1 shows, since 1950 owner occupation as a proportion of housing tenure has steadily increased, whilst private renting has decreased. Council housing, however, increased until the late 1970s and then went into decline. Now, in the 1990s, the situation is the reverse of fifty years earlier: approximately two thirds of householders are owner occupiers and one third tenants.

Table 4.1 British housing tenure, 1950–94

	Owner-occupied (%)	Public rented (%)	Private rented (%)
1950	29.0	18.0	53.0
1961	42.3	25.0	31.9
1971	51.6	30.5	17.9
1981	57.1	30.6	12.3
1991	67.2	22.9	10.0
1994	67.6	22.2	10.1

Source: The annual housing and construction statistics of the Department of the Environment (Johnson, 1997: 61).

In line with these trends in housing tenure, the proportion of heads of households aged 60 and over who are owner occupiers has increased from 44 per cent in 1975 to 57 per cent in 1991, while the proportion in private renting has declined (Rolfe et al, 1993). Table 4.2 looks at housing tenure in relation to age, and highlights not only the number of people over retirement age who own their own home outright, but also the current parallels between older and younger people in terms of rented accommodation with the very old and the very young renting from both local authorities, housing associations and the private sector. Heads of households under 25 years are most likely to be renting privately, reflecting the tendency for private renters to be young, single and male (ONS, 1997A). In contrast, those renting privately in old age are likely to be women who are either widowed or who have never married.

As pointed out in Chapter 1, the Conservative governments of the 1980s and 1990s believed that the mechanisms of the market were the most effective and efficient way of providing welfare and of creating choice. Through a series of Housing Acts, these successive governments created radical change. Their main aim was to reduce public spending and privatise the housing market by increasing owner occupation and moving publicly rented housing outside of local authority control. First, through the 1980 Housing Act, they brought in the 'right to buy' policy which allowed and provided incentives for certain council tenants to purchase their properties. Some special housing that might be occupied by older people, however, was exempt from this, leaving older people in an increasingly residual category of housing. Second, the capital building programme was severely restricted and local authorities were forced into partnerships with housing associations or private developers. Third, through the 1985 Housing Act, local authorities were given the power to dispose of blocks of housing stock with or without tenants. Fourth, through the 1988 Housing Act, secure council tenants were given the right to transfer to a different landlord, such as a housing association. Fifth, through the same Act, the Secretary of State was given the power to designate certain run-down council estates Housing Action Trusts in order to improve facilities and give tenants a greater diversity of landlords.

Table 4.2 Tenure: by age of head of household, 1995–96 UK

	Under 25	25-29	30-44	45-59	60-64	65-79	80+	All
Owner occupied								
Owned outright	1	1	4	23	50	56	52	26
Owned with mortgage	28	55	67	56	24	7	3	42
Rented unfurnished								
Local authority/new town	25	17	15	13	18	26	29	18
Housing association	6	6	4	3	2	5	7	4
Privately	15	9	4	3	3	5	9	5
Rented furnished	22	9	3	1	1	1	-	3
Rented with job or business	2	3	3	2	2	1	0	2
All tenures	100	100	100	100	100	100	100	100

Source: ONS (1997a: 170) Table 10.3.

In addition to these measures, the system for financing housing and setting rents has changed: overall, rents have increased and eligibility for housing benefit has been reduced (Randolph, 1993). Of the 4 million people receiving Housing Benefit in Great Britain in 1991, 49 per cent were aged 60 or more and over three quarters of these were local authority tenants (Griffiths, 1995).

The 1988 Housing Act has radically changed the role of housing associations. Traditionally, housing associations were small, non-commercial and diverse, catering for those with special housing needs. These associations have been squeezed and the housing association movement is now dominated by large scale national organisations catering for more commercially viable general needs housing. One outcome of this is that since 1989, there has been a decline in the proportion of new build housing that meets established mobility and wheelchair standards (Means and Smith, 1994).

A relatively small proportion of older people live in privately rented accommodation but it is these older people, many of whom are women living alone, who are most likely to live in the worst housing conditions. While overall the housing conditions of older people have improved during the post-war period (Department of Environment, 1993), in this sector older people are disproportionately represented in pre-1919 properties and their tenancies are more likely to be long-standing and rent controlled (Rolfe et al, 1993). Only one third of older private tenants have central heating and are faced with the cost of expensive alternative forms of heating (Askham et al, 1992). Furthermore, it is particularly difficult to get repair work or improvements done and only 25 per cent of properties are accessible for disabled people (Department of Environment, 1993). The increase in rents to market levels which resulted from the 1988 Housing Act, makes new tenancies in this sector unaffordable for the majority of older people.

For those older people who are dependent on the rented sector of housing, be it public or private, all these changes have increased problems of availability, affordability and security. Recent research for the Joseph Rowntree Foundation indicates that older people are becoming one of two distinct communities within council estates:

> At one end there are the established elderly residents, who have lived in social housing all their lives and who remember a time when having a council home was a desirable goal. At the other end are the new, younger residents, frequently suffering from multiple problems: unemployment, poverty, poor work skills and perhaps mental illness and drug abuse as well... There is a clear and damaging clash between individual and community needs.
>
> *Dean, 1997: 11*

Those left behind in council housing are finding themselves in increasingly deprived and hostile environments which may exacerbate feelings of insecurity and fuel the desire to move (Means and Smith, 1994; Tinker, 1994). Yet the options for moving within the rented sector are increasingly limited and few can afford to move into owner occupation or even shared equity housing.

OWNER OCCUPATION

The case for owner occupation has long centred on the house as both an economic asset generating wealth which will 'cascade down the generations', and as a form of ontological security – ownership of one's home reinforcing a sense of self (Saunders, 1990). Here we focus on the growth of home ownership in relation to social policies which affect older people and their families. Around a half of households over retirement age own their housing outright (see Table 4.2). In contrast, the proportion of older people who own their homes with a mortgage is relatively small. Policies like 'right to buy' have made less impact on older age groups than younger age groups and yet, for those with outstanding mortgages, developing mortgage arrears can be a real issue.

Given the variation in property values throughout the country, assets held by older people in the form of housing equity vary. However, Hamnett comments that 'data from the English Housing Condition Survey (Leather, 1990) show that more than 80 per cent of owner occupied households headed by a person aged between 65 and 74 years, and nearly 70 per cent of those headed by a person aged 75 years or older, had equity worth at least £25,000 in 1986. Average levels were higher than this, and almost all households had equity of more than £10,000' (Hamnett, 1995: 166). Yet, holding housing equity may be of little benefit to older people if their income is low and they have become 'house rich, income poor' (Bull and Poole, 1989). This is especially the case for those living in conditions which do not meet their needs. For many older people, house maintenance, including garden up-keep, can become a real problem. At a time of life when people may want to 'stay put', some will contemplate a move in order to remain owner occupiers within manageable property, but, as we have already noted, the variety of suitably sized housing integrated within the wider community may be constrained leading to a move to special provision.

In addition to meeting housing needs, wealth generated through owner occupation is also being tapped to meet care needs. Since the implementation of the National Health Service and Community Care Act 1990, the use of housing equity to pay for residential and nursing home care has increased, and some local authorities have attempted to offset the costs of domiciliary care against housing equity. For example, in 1994, a recommendation was made to Hereford and Worcestershire's Social Services Committee to take powers to set a legal charge against some clients' homes as payment for domiciliary care services because they had refused to accept an assessment for residential or nursing home care (*The Guardian*, 1994). These developments make older owner occupiers vulnerable to impoverishment if care needs arise, as well as leaving them without assets to pass on to their heirs.

As we have noted home ownership also incurs costs – of property tax, repair and maintenance, and of adaptations if needed. These costs are more significant for older people because as income reduces in later life, a greater proportion is spent on housing. As we also noted above, older people in England are no more likely to be living in the worst housing conditions than any other age group and yet, as with the private rented sector, those older owner occupiers who live in the poorest conditions are most likely to be women, over the age of 75, living alone and on a low income (Rolfe et al, 1993; Bradford, 1995). Cuts in public expenditure have made renovation grants, disabled facilities grants and minor repair grants more difficult to obtain, although older people are the main beneficiaries of these grants. Furthermore, with the introduction of the disabled facilities grants, local authority social services departments have reduced or even withdrawn altogether support for adaptation work.

A variety of equity release schemes have been developed with reduced or no repayments to enable older people to undertake repairs or adaptations. On the whole, however, there has not been a widespread take up of these schemes (Mullings and Hamnett, 1992; Hamnett, 1995). During the 1980s 'Staying Put' and 'Care and Repair' services were developed to assist older people in organising and overseeing improvement or repair work, and in accessing appropriate finance. These services continue to be successful, and have been extended to other age groups, but they are not extensive enough to offer help to all those who need it and their funding remains insecure (see Randell, 1995 for a discussion of schemes run through Anchor Housing Association).

If an older person finds that their home is becoming unmanageable, unaffordable or unsuited to their changing needs, she or he may choose to move on. Rolfe et al (1993) found that older owner occupiers who do decide to move choose, in the main, to move either to another house in the owner occupied sector, or to special housing in the owner occupied or rented sector, or (and this is particularly the case for those over 80 years of age) to a residential or nursing home. Means and Smith (1994) have suggested, however, that a move to special accommodation is often prompted not as a result of special needs, but because preferred alternatives are neither affordable nor available. At present older people are faced with combinations of accommodation and care which have either evolved through housing policy in the form of sheltered housing or through social welfare and health care policy in the form of residential care homes and nursing homes. The developments in these sectors have been unco-ordinated although as we shall argue, their futures are intimately intertwined.

SPECIAL ACCOMMODATION
Sheltered housing
Townsend (1962) placed sheltered housing high on the policy agenda when he proposed that alongside the development of specially designed housing, the creation of a strong domiciliary care service to support people and their families within their home, and better medical services for older people, it was a viable alternative to residential care. While the 1960s and subsequent decades did not see the development of a coherent overarching policy framework for older people integrating health, social services and housing – it did see some clarification over the development of 'special' housing for older people within the public sector. The

publication of guidance by the Ministry of Housing and Local Government (1969) codified the beginning of sheltered housing initiatives and the familiar distinctions were made:

> **Category One** consisted of purpose-built flats or bungalows with a warden, but often with no common room or other facilities for shared use; **Category Two** was usually identified as a scheme with individual bungalows or flats linked by heated internal corridors. A common room, laundry and guest room and other facilities for shared use are normally included.
>
> *Mackintosh et al, 1990: 87*

Table 4.3 Completions of new specialised dwellings for elderly, chronically sick and disabled people, 1981–95, England and Wales

	1981	1991	1995
Sheltered housing for elderly people			
Private sector	130	1675	408
Housing associations	1929	1537	785
Local authorities	5558	1627	90
Other housing for elderly people			
Private sector	62	319	37
Housing associations	261	657	493
Local authorities	4636	333	82
Housing for chronically sick and disabled people			
Housing associations	235	466	670
Local authorities	4181	352	47
Completions of specialised dwellings as a percentage of all completions			
Private sector	0.2	1.4	0.3
Housing associations	14.0	15.0	5.8
Local authorities	24.6	27.1	21.9

Source: ONS (1997a: 176), Table 10.14.

In the 1960s and 1970s, local authority housing departments made a major investment in sheltered housing for older people, followed by a series of specialist housing associations, such as Anchor and Hanover, which enthusiastically developed this new sector of the housing market. In the 1970s, sheltered housing 'for sale' also began to take off with companies such as McCarthy and Stone being among the market leaders. However, since the early 1980s there have been dramatic changes. While local authorities still remain major providers of specialised housing, Table 4.3 indicates that there has been a dramatic decline in local authority new build. The early 1990s saw a major period of growth for private sheltered housing and the number of completions by housing associations sustained, although the completions by these two sectors declined during the early 1990s. Nevertheless, housing associations are now major providers of special housing for older people, a position facilitated by financial subsidy provided through the Housing Corporation. Over a fifth of the completions of the local authority sector remain in specialised housing, whereas the corresponding proportion for the private sector, despite the expansion in the early 1990s, has not risen above 2 per cent.

The Department of Environment survey of 'subsidised specialised housing' for older people records that in 1991 there were 641,765 units of accommodation – 51 per cent were sheltered housing units with a warden and communal facilities, and two thirds comprised one-bedded units. Local authorities were still the largest provider of subsidised specialist housing (providing 73 per cent of all units in 1991) followed by housing associations (23 per cent) (McCafferty, 1994). Only 3 per cent consisted of alternative living arrangements such as Abbeyfield Houses.

By utilising these figures, it can be estimated that subsidised specialist housing accommodated around 800,000 older people in 1991, while additional research estimates that privately owned special housing accommodated about 80,000 (Rolfe et al, 1993). Of the sample of older people interviewed in the 1994 General Household Survey, 10 per cent reported living in sheltered housing – these included 6 per cent of the 65–69 age group and 18 per cent of the 85 and over age group (ONS, 1997b).

During the early development of sheltered housing, wardens were appointed as 'good neighbours' to the schemes, but increasingly their role has changed. For some schemes the attachment of one warden to one scheme has been eroded as high-tech alarm systems have been developed. Furthermore, the 1988 Housing Act led to rent rises and problems over the financing of wardens. For others, the warden's role has become more care oriented. As social services departments have become more involved in the management of sheltered housing schemes, through allocation rights and through employing wardens and other care staff, so the tendency has been to allocate places to those 'most in need'. The resulting rise in dependency levels amongst tenants is leading some sheltered housing towards a form of residential care. Certainly there has been a gradual growth throughout the 1980s and into the 1990s of 'very sheltered housing' or 'extra care housing' which offers additional care services such as meals, care assistants, extra wardens and more communal facilities such as special bathrooms. However, there is also an acknowledgement that older people with varying levels of mental and physical health can manage to live within the environment provided by sheltered housing based on individual apartments (Kitwood et al, 1995).

Residential and nursing homes

While many older people may see their move to sheltered housing as prompted more by concerns over accommodation than care, for those making the move into residential care or nursing home care, the reverse may be true (but not always). Some older people will die in their own homes, but the majority will die in hospital or move from hospital to a residential care or nursing home (Sidell, 1993). The choice between residential care and nursing home care may well become a financial one: for those whose needs sit along the divide between residential and nursing care and who cannot afford the nursing option, the residential care home may be a cheaper alternative. Some will experience residential living which is well resourced, well designed and allows them to meet their needs for accommodation and care. Others, less well-off however, will continue to experience a less well-resourced service which may have implications for the type of care regime available leading to block treatment and other forms of institutionalisation (Peace et al, 1997).

Over thirty years ago, Townsend questioned the role of residential care:

> The role of the residential institution or Home…is uncertain. Is it to be a permanent refuge for infirm persons who cannot care for themselves in a home of their own, who cannot be supported in their homes by any practicable system of domiciliary services, and who yet are not in need of continuous nursing care and medical treatment in hospital? Is it to be a temporary refuge for frail persons recovering from illness or malnutrition or seeking to give relatives or workers in the domiciliary services a hard earned rest or perhaps a chance of improving the facilities available at home? Or is it to simply be a rescue device for the present generation of old people whose differing needs cannot be met because good housing, adequate pensions, and comprehensive local domiciliary services are not yet provided? Many of the inherent contradictions in present policy spring from a failure to explore or attempt to answer these questions.
>
> *Townsend, 1962: 388*

While these remain salient points, the ambiguity surrounding the role of residential care is currently increased by its position in relation to sheltered housing and nursing home care whose roles, it can be argued, are more firmly centred in housing and in nursing care. Yet, the investment in 'bricks and mortar' makes it highly unlikely that residential care will disappear even though the edges between these forms of provision continues to blur.

The history of residential care since Aneurin Bevan's introduction of 'hotels for the working classes' in 1948 has been well documented (Means and Smith, 1985; Mackintosh et al, 1990; Peace et al, 1997). Like other forms of welfare provision, public sector provision dominated until the election of the Conservative government in 1979. During the 1980s the private sector began to expand dramatically. Indeed, of all welfare provision, it has been residential care and nursing homes for older people which have been most successfully privatised. Table 4.4 shows the rise in private sector provision, the relative stability of the voluntary sector and the decline of public residential care. The growth of the residential sector peaked in 1991, whereas nursing home provison has grown in recent years. In 1985, the ratio of residential to nursing home places stood at 7 to 1; by 1990 this had become 3 to 1, and by 1994 1.5 to 1. The changing fortunes of the nursing home sector stand in sharp relief to the steady decline in NHS long stay beds.

Table 4.4 Nursing and residential places for elderly, chronically ill and physically disabled people, and long stay hospital places (000s), UK, 1970–95

| | Residential home | | | Nursing home (priv/vol) | Long stay geriatric hospital | Long stay psychogeriatric hospital |
	LA	Private	Vol			
1970	108.7	23.7	40.1	20.3	52.0	23.0
1975	128.3	25.8	41.0	24.0	49.0	–
1980	134.5	37.4	42.6	26.9	46.1	–
1985	137.1	85.3	45.1	38.0	46.3	–
1990	125.6	155.6	40.0	123.1	47.2	27.0
1995	80.8	167.8	52.8	208.0	33.2	18.5

Source: Laing (1996), Table 5.2 (summarised).

Explanations for the changing nature of residential and nursing home provision are various. In Figure 4.1, Peace et al (1997) chart some of the factors which have affected the demand for long-term care during the 1980s and on into the 1990s.

Concern over the enormity of the growing public subsidy of residential and nursing home care through Income Support, provided a major impetus to the community care reforms of the early 1990s. The open ended centrally administered DSS budget for residential and nursing home care was replaced by fixed, locally administered budgets, thus encouraging a reverse of the 'perverse incentive' towards residential care that was identified by the Audit Commission (1986), and the targeting of residential and nursing home care on those most in need. Since the implementation of the NHS and Community Care Act 1990, in April 1993, local authorities have been responsible for assessing the needs of older people requiring financial assistance for residential and nursing home care, and for financing their care. Between 1993 and 1995, 85 per cent of monies transferred from the DSS to social services departments to support older people had to be spent within the 'independent' sector. However, most local authorities did not use their Special Transitional Grant (STG) allocations to shift service provision towards home care at the expense of residential services (Laing, 1996: A171). Futhermore, where the money has been directed towards home care services, it has in many cases been provided only to those who need intensive packages of care at the expense of those with lesser needs. An insufficient range of flexible and affordable home care can mean that residential care becomes the only viable option for some people. Given that measures have been taken to discourage and prevent local authorities from providing their own residential care facilities, towards the end of the 1990s, virtually all residential and nursing home care will be provided by the 'independent' (but predominantly private) sector.

Figure 4.1 Factors which may affect the demand for long-term care

- Demographic: increase in the number of very old people; increased morbidity with increasing age; in particular, increase in numbers of older people suffering from dementing illnesses.

- Social: changes in the pattern of family structures and responsibilities at work and at home; increased tendency for some families to live at a distance from each other.

- Economic/consumer: improved financial position of many older people; older people making a positive choice over long term care.

- Service: increased pressure on long stay hospital beds; more effective use of acute hospital beds; closure of psychiatric hospitals.

- Political: initial stimulation through public funding of private and voluntary provision via supplementary benefit; community care legislation; attack on residential provision. Transfer of state funding to cash-limited local authority budgets since April 1993.

- Ideological: increasing popular support for a pluralist approach to welfare during the 1980s. Increasing reliance during rhe late 1980s and 1990s on the market within health and social welfare services.

Source: Peace et al (1997: 23).

The voluntary or 'not for profit' sector remained fairly static during the 1980s but, in the early 1990s, this sector of provision grew as many local authorities transfered their establishments to local Trusts. Some large chains of care homes are in the voluntary, not-for-profit sector. For example, Anchor Housing Association, which developed a form of housing with care registered as residential homes, is one of the largest providers with 77 homes and 2,630 beds in this sector (Laing, 1997).

Developments in the private sector of residential and nursing home care are similar to those in the housing association market, where smaller providers are being challenged by larger corporate players. Although a majority of residential care homes for older people are still run by the small business sector – often husband and wife teams who own a small number of establishments – corporate providers are beginning to make in-roads into the industry, especially the nursing home market where the average facility is larger than those providing residential care.[1] Laing's Directory of major providers of long-term care for elderly and physically disabled people lists twenty-five for-profit and not-for-profit companies and groups with over 1,000 beds (Laing, 1997).

The two trends in this sector of care provision, first that ownership is becoming more concentrated and second that the average size of homes is increasing, means that older people who do enter residential or nursing homes are increasingly likely to end up in a large home with all the attendant problems of size and scale. As Wistow (1995) has observed, community care is in danger of turning full circle: in place of long-term hospital provision, we are seeing the development of large institutions in the community which is a cheaper option than the provision of home care services.

Funding for individuals within residential and nursing home settings can take several forms: entirely through means-tested public finance; through a combination of means-tested public finance and private top-up money; and entirely self-financing. Figures from 1995 show that an estimated 103,000 or 28 per cent of residents in independent sector care homes were self-financing (Laing, 1996). This means that the vast majority require at least some degree of public financial support. The future funding for long-term care is subject to much debate with radical alternative models being explored. At the time of writing various forms of long-term care insurance are being discussed. The Joseph Rowntree Foundation Inquiry into Meeting the Costs of Continuing Care has come out in favour of care for older people free at the point of delivery but supported through a new National Care Insurance scheme, a system of compulsory care insurance contributions introduced in partnership with the private sector (Joseph Rowntree Foundation, 1996). The new Labour government has promised a Royal Commission on the future funding of long-term care.

Also subject to on-going debate is the question of regulation. Since the growth of the independent sector of residential and nursing home care in the early 1980s, concern has grown over the need to regulate standards of provision to protect consumers who may have little choice over their living arrangements and whose mental and physical health may make them potentially vulnerable to abuse. In contrast, a majority of sheltered housing is unregulated. The state, no longer a major provider of care, has become a regulator of care. The Registered Homes Act 1984 developed a system of registration and inspection for the independent sector which consolidated earlier regulatory frameworks. The NHS and Community Care Act 1990 later extended powers of regulation to cover public sector provision with the setting up of 'arm's length inspection units' expected to be separate from the authority. This legislation with its accompanying regulations and codes of practice has sought to set standards. However individual authorities have discretion over standard setting and this variation has formed a major plank in the argument in favour of a national inspectorate. The Burgner review into the regulation and inspection of social services (Burgner, 1996) has recommended that regulation be kept under local authority control but possibly moved to the trading standards department.

The impact of regulation on care environments means adherence to rules and regulations surrounding fit people to manage homes, fit buildings and fit care plans. In terms of the physical environment of homes, a major concern has been the support given to the provision of predominantly single bedrooms which has been encouraged through regulation but sometimes contested by proprietors (ADSS, 1995). This could lead to the development of more settings with the potential for care to centre on independent living within a group. The extent to which this is possible, given the constraints of overall care policies, is difficult to determine.

Our discussion so far indicates how the choices available to those with changing care and accommodation needs are influenced by care, housing and income policies. But these policies differentially affect the older population and we now move on to consider this.

The impact of gender and class on living arrangements

Figure 4.2, based on the 1995 General Household Survey, highlights a number of important factors which differentiate the lives of older men and women who are living in their own homes in the community. Most dramatic is the large number of older women who live alone, and the large number of older men who live only with their spouse. The past twenty years has seen the proportion living alone increase for both men and women (Haskey, 1996). Haskey comments that 'the main reason for this change has been increased longevity, but better health and economic well-being as well as a desire to remain independent for as long as possible, have, no doubt, also played a part' (p. 9). Among older people who do not live alone, men are more likely to live with their spouse and women are more likely to live with a son or daughter.

Figure 4.2 Percentages living alone by age and sex

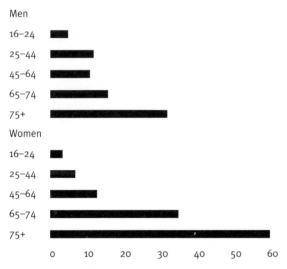

Source: ONS (1997b) table 2.14, p. 21.

Arber and Ginn (1991) have reflected upon the varied experiences of older people living in the community and have produced what they see as a hierarchy of preferred living arrangements and contexts for caring. They suggest (see Figure 4.3) that the most favoured option for older people is to look after themselves in their own homes, whilst the least would involve living in a carer's home – most likely a child or sibling – an option most likely to be experienced by older women. Such a hierarchy is based on the well-known premiss that older people prefer to live out their lives in their own homes.

As this hierarchy shows, gender is a crucial determinant of living arrangements in old age. For a majority of older married men, housing tenure and housing circumstances may remain relatively stable. Trading down to smaller property may be commonly experienced by owner occupiers, but living in accommodation specifically for older people is the preserve of the older woman. Global figures concerning living arrangements mask the diverse characteristics of the older people which lie behind them. Age, sex, marital status, health status, social class, tenure-type, ethnicity and cultural tradition may interact to influence living arrangements. The picture is complex, but data from the 1991 Census show first, that having a 'limiting long term illness in later life is a predictor of living in a residential or nursing home' (OPCS, 1993: 88). Second, they show that older people living in subsidised specialised housing are younger than those living in residential care homes (McCafferty, 1993; Peace et al, 1997). Third, they show that older women dominate all forms of special or communal settings (OPCS, 1993). Fourth, they show that older members of minority ethnic groups still form a very small proportion of residents/tenants within these settings. And finally, data from the OPCS Longitudinal study show that tenants of both genders, men of low socio-economic status, and people not living with family, were more likely to move into institutions over time, than owner occupiers and men in non-manual occupations (CSO, 1996: 23).

Figure 4.3 Proposed hierarchy of older person's preference for caring contexts

A   In older person's own home – self-care

B   In older person's own home – care provided by co-resident:

(i) Spouse

(ii) Other same generation relative

(iii) Child or non-kin

C   In older person's own home – care provided by extra-resident:

(iv) Child

(v) Other relative

(vi) Neighbour, friend, volunteer

D   In care-giver's own home – care provided by co-resident:

(vii) Unmarried child

(viii) Married child

Source: Arber and Ginn (1991: 144), Fig 8.2.

As we have already noted, those moving into specialised housing may be doing so primarily for reasons of accommodation, such as wanting a smaller home or garden, easier and cheaper maintenance, the security of warden cover, or the desire to be nearer friends and relatives (Rolfe et al, 1993). In contrast, those older people moving into residential care homes and nursing homes more commonly move from a position of poor mental and physical health, and an inability to continue to look after themselves at home. They are likely to be living alone, often already receiving home care services. The difference between these two groups is stark in terms of the degree of control that may be exerted over the change in living arrangements.

Policies and experiences

The living arrangements of people as they move into later life and on into old age are moulded by a life-time's experience of accommodation and care. People's family lives and housing histories are intimately entwined. They reflect their socio-economic circumstances at certain stages of the life course, and how the lives of particular cohorts of people can be influenced by the wider policy context of the society in which they live. People in their seventies and eighties, living at the turn of the twentieth century, have experienced dramatic changes in housing policy from the predominance of private renting, to the rise and fall of council housing, to the development of owner occupation as a preferred form of tenure. They may have also faced dramatic change within their family circumstances through marriage or non-marriage, separation/divorce, widowhood, being parents and grandparents or not being parents or grandparents. The diversity of older people's circumstances will be reflected in their living arrangements which may be:

- the older woman living alone in private rented accommodation in the inner city whose living conditions are poor and whose landlord does little;
- the couple who have lived in council housing all their lives, who have watched it change and now wonder if it's really the place for them;
- the retirement movers who thought they'd made their last move only to realise that their needs have changed again;
- the owner occupiers who strove to buy their own home in order to leave something to their children but now realising that they need the equity to purchase residential care;
- the older woman living in her own room within a residential home, who never really thought she would live in a home.

These are stereotypes, but they remind us of some of the issues which we have highlighted within this chapter. Currently, a large group of older people own their home outright with no mortgage to pay. Their home is an asset to be tapped. But what about future generations who may never pay off that mortgage? Will negative equity be so attractive to policy makers whose concern is how we pay for long-term care? For older people today, the material conditions of housing have improved. There is internal sanitation and central heating, but there is still the need for maintenance, repair and adaptation. There is also a shortage of affordable, suitably sized, accessible housing for couples or people on their own within the mainstream housing market. Policies have been developed that have separated some older people into special housing and residential care and nursing homes. Is this the inevitable consequence of the times we live in where changing communities, concerns over security, and the delivery of non-family care, mean that economies of scale determine group provision of accommodation and care for older people? Are we stuck with the bricks and mortar and the traditional household structures we inherit or should the longer term planning of Lifetime homes (Joseph Rowntree Foundation, 1997), which are adaptable across the life course, go hand in hand with more imaginative responses to care needs in later life, which make it easier for people to make choices about living alone or with others (Brenton, 1997)? What must surely be true is that the diversity of older people in Britain in the twenty-first century should be reflected in the types of accommodation and care provided.

Notes

1   In 1995 Laing reported that the average new private residential registration was 16 beds in 1994 and 36 beds for the average new nursing home registration (Laing, 1995: A222).

References

Arber, S. and Ginn, J. (1991) *Gender and Later Life*, London: Sage.

Askham, J., Barry, C., Grundy, E., Hancock, R. and Tinker, A. (1992) *Life After 60*, London: Age Concern Institute of Gerontology.

ADSS (Association of Directors of Social Services) (1995) *A Room of One's Own*, Northallerton: ADSS.

Audit Commission (1986) *Making a Reality of Community Care*, London: HMSO.

Bradford, I. (1995) *Poor Housing – Poor Health – Did You Know?* Nottingham: Care and Repair (England).

Brenton, M. (1997) 'Choice, mutual support and autonomy in old age: older women's cooperative living arrangements'. Paper presented at the Annual Conference of the British Society of Gerontology, Bristol, September 1997.

Bull, J. and Poole, L. (1989) *Not Rich, Not Poor: housing options for elderly people on middle incomes*, London: SHAC and Anchor Housing Trust.

Burgner, T. (1996) *The Regulation and Inspection of Social Services*, London: HMSO.

CSO (Central Statistical Office) (1996) *Social Trends, No. 26*, London: HMSO.

Dean, M. (1997) 'Tipping the balance', *Search*, 27(Spring): 9–12.

DoE (Department of the Environment) (1993) *1991 English House Condition Survey*, London: HMSO.

Griffiths, S. (1995) *How Housing Benefit Can Work for Community Care*, York: Rowntree Foundation/Community Care.

The Guardian (1994) 23 December.

Hamnett, C. (1995) 'Housing equity release and inheritance' in Allen, I. and Perkins, E. (eds) *The Future of Family Care for Older People*, London: HMSO, 163–80.

Haskey, J. (1996) 'Population review: (6) Families and Households in Great Britain', *Population Trends*, 85(Autumn): 7–24.

Hughes, D. and Lowe, S. (1995) *Social Housing Law and Policy*, London: Butterworths.

Johnson, J. (1997) 'Housing and income', in *Community Care: history and policy*, K259, Buckingham: Open University.

Joseph Rowntree Foundation Inquiry (1996) *Meeting the Costs of Continuing Care Recommendations*, York: Joseph Rowntree Foundation.

Joseph Rowntree Foundation (1997) *Building Lifetime Homes*, York: Joseph Rowntree Foundation.

Kitwood,T., Beckland, S. and Petre, T. (1995) *Brighter Futures*, Oxford: Anchor Housing Association.

Laing, W. (1995) *Review of Private Health Care, 1994*, London: Laing & Buisson.

Laing, W. (1996) *Review of Private Health Care, 1995*, London: Laing & Buisson.

Laing, W. (1997) *Long Term Care of Elderly and Physically Disabled People. Directory of Major Providers*, Tenth edition, London: Laing & Buisson.

Leather, P. (1990) 'The potential and implications of home equity release in old age', *Housing Studies*, 5(1): 3–13.

Mackintosh, S., Means, R. and Leather, P. (1990) *Housing in Later Life: the housing finance implications of an ageing society*, Bristol: University of Bristol, School of Advanced Urban Studies.

McCafferty, P. (1994) *Living Independently: a study of the housing needs of elderly and disabled people*, London: HMSO.

Means, R. and Smith, R. (1985) *The Development of Welfare Services for Elderly People*, London: Croom Helm.

Means, R. and Smith, R. (1994) *Community Care: policy and practice*, London: Macmillan.

Ministry of Housing and Local Government (1969) *Housing Standards and Costs: accommodation specially designed for old people*, Circular 82/69, London: HMSO.

Mullings, B. and Hamnett, C. (1992) 'Equity release schemes and equity extraction by elderly households in Britain', *Ageing and Society*, 12(Part 4): 413–42.

OPCS (Office of Population Censuses and Surveys) (1993) *1991 Census. Persons Aged 60 and Over. Great Britain*, OPCS and General Registrar Office Scotland, London: HMSO.

ONS (Office for National Statistics) (1997a) *Social Trends 27*, London: HMSO.

ONS (Office for National Statistics) (1997b) *Living in Britain: results from the 1995 General Household Survey*, London: Government Statistics Services.

Peace, S., Kellaher, L. and Willcocks, D. (1997) *Re-evaluating Residential Care*, Buckingham: Open University Press.

Randell, B. (1995) *Staying Put – The Best Move I'll Ever Make*, Oxford: Anchor Housing Association.

Randolph, B. (1993) 'The re-privatisation of housing associations' in Malpass, P. and Means, R. (eds) *Implementing Housing Policy*, Buckingham: Open University Press, 39–58.

Rolfe, S., Leather, P. and Mackintosh, S. (1993) *Available Options*, Oxford: Anchor Housing Trust.

Saunders, P. (1990) *A Nation of Home Owners*, London: Unwin Hyman.

Sidell, M. (1993) 'Death, dying and bereavment' in Bond, J., Coleman, P. and Peace, S. (eds) *Ageing in Society*, London: Sage.

Tinker, A. (1994) 'Housing' in Hobman, D. (ed) *Uniting Generations: studies in conflict and co-operation*, London: Age Concern England in association with The Nuffield Foundation.

Townsend, P. (1962) *The Last Refuge*, London: Routledge and Kegan Paul.Wistow, G. (1995) 'Community care at the crossroads', *Health and Social Care*, 3(4): 227–40.

5 Changing work and retirement

Chris Phillipson

The so-called 'collapse of work' throughout our society has been developing for some time... For instance, ever since 1973, the percentage of economically active males between the ages of 60 and 64 has zoomed down from 80% to 50%. Retirements come earlier and stay longer – already, in some cases, matching the length of the working life itself!

Eric Midwinter (1987) Redefining Old Age: a review of CPA's recent contribution to social policy, p. 5

Introduction

The period of old age is now characterised by two distinctive features: first, the growth in the proportion of the population aged 60/65 and over; second, the withdrawal of older people (men especially) from the labour market. In Britain, in the late nineteenth century, nearly three quarters of men aged 65 and over were still in employment; by the early 1950s this had fallen to one third; and by 1990 just 3 per cent of men were employed full time (the figure for women was 1 per cent).

The above trends may be found in most advanced industrialised societies (Kohli et al, 1991; Atkinson and Rein, 1993; Walker and Maltby, 1997). For example, the ratio of employment to population has fallen for older men in every Organisation of Economic Co-operation and Development (OECD) member country, and this looks set to continue into the twenty-first century (Blackwell, 1992). The situation of older women is more varied, with a mixture of experiences from country to country. However, it is the decrease in male employment that has been crucial over the past two decades, and which has led to the marked decline in labour force participation among older workers (Laczko and Phillipson, 1991; Johnson and Zimmerman, 1993; Henretta, 1994).

The emphasis of this chapter will be upon viewing work and retirement as socially constructed events shaped by a number of competing influences within society. A significant role may be attributed to economic factors, these influencing changing patterns of work and retirement (Phillipson, 1982; Laczko and Phillipson,

1991). This will be analysed with reference to the complex debate about the 'employability' of older workers conducted over the past forty years. The chapter will then review current trends in the employment of older workers summarising, in the process, literature relating to age discrimination in the workplace. Some broader questions relating to the social construction of retirement will then be analysed. Finally, a number of points will be made about the future of social policy in the field of work and retirement.

Population, productivity and the potential of older workers

The extent to which older people have been excluded from work has been established in a range of studies and surveys (Kohli et al, 1991). However, the postwar history of the older worker shows remarkable fluctuations in respect of labour and social policies. In the 1940s and 1950s, there was a vigorous debate on how to assist older people's engagement or re-engagement in the sphere of paid work (Clark and Spengler, 1980). Indeed, running parallel to the institutionalisation of retirement came the emergence of a discipline – industrial gerontology – concerned with helping the retention of older people in the labour force. The stimuli for this research were anxieties about a population imbalance between 'productive' and 'non-productive' groups within the economy. Among the non-productive, it was the threat of an ageing population that caused most concern. For the Royal Commission on Population (1949), prolonging active working life appeared the best solution to easing the burden of too many elderly people and too few workers. The immediate task, therefore, was to remove the various constraints that prompted people to withdraw from work.

A number of initiatives were taken to address this problem. In 1945 the Nuffield Foundation supported three research projects concerned with investigating the social and medical implications of an ageing population.[1] One of these examined the capacities of older people for work, and was 'inspired by the belief that the increased proportion of older people would mean that many would have to continue working beyond normal retirement age if there was not to be a serious shortage of labour' (Welford, 1976: 129).

Indeed, the mid-1940s to the mid-1950s was (in many respects) a 'golden age' for interest in older workers – men in particular. The range of interests was impressive and included investigations into: the age structure of occupations (Murrell, 1959); performance problems of older workers on conveyor-belt or assembly-line work (Brown, 1957); the difficulties of semi-skilled workers (Heron and Chown, 1967); preparation for retirement (Heron, 1962); and the relationship between skill and human ageing (Welford, 1958).

Most of these topics were discussed in articles appearing in *Occupational Psychology*, a journal which carried throughout the 1950s and into the 1960s numerous papers on experimental work relating to the position of older people in industry. Despite the limitations of this work (particularly its bias against women workers), it did reveal serious deficiencies in the way people were treated as they matured in the labour force. Heron and Chown, for example, reported on the way in which for older semi-skilled men, 'Alternative work always involves change to a relatively menial occupation – with loss of status and earnings' (Heron and Chown, 1967: 46). In addition, Murrell posed questions (in 1959) which still remain radical today given the present treatment of older workers. Amongst the questions he asked were: 'What avoidable long-term health hazards...are present in a work situation?'; 'What is the basis for discrimination against older workers in employment policies?'; 'What is the effect of bonus schemes on older men?'; 'What are determining factors in promotion, and how do they discriminate against the older man?' (Murrell, 1959: 126).

As well as raising important questions, research showed the extent to which chronological age was a poor guide for understanding work capacity and ability. Experimental research suggested that individuals could adjust to, and offset, the changes affecting them in middle age and later life (Welford, 1958). Such research also stimulated work in areas such as job redesign and retraining (Griew, 1964; Belbin, 1965).

However, we also find, running alongside work concerned with the placement of older workers in industry, a gradual appreciation that long-term trends were making permanent retirement at 65 or 60 increasingly likely. This was the message from the work of, for example, Le Gros Clark. His study *Work, Age and Leisure* was published in 1966, and had as its subtitle *Causes and consequences of the shortened working life.*

The study by Clark was prophetic. It looked ahead to the emergence of groups of older people existing outside the labour market, with an independent life-style and values and demands of their own. It was realisation of the economic and social changes described by Le Gros Clark, which was to undermine the position of industrial gerontology. According to Welford, in his review *Thirty Years of Psychological Research on Age and Work*:

> In 1955, revised population estimates made it clear that, as a result of the postwar 'baby bulge', there was unlikely to be a serious imbalance between those of working age and dependents above and below it during the next few decades.
> At the same time, automation appeared on the scene as a bogey which seemed to threaten many jobs and so to remove the need for older people to go on working – indeed, to make it undesirable that they should do so. The expected results of automation did not occur, but in Britain there was an immediate collapse of both

interest in industrial gerontology and concern for the psychological aspects of ageing which had been largely inspired by it.

Welford, 1976: 131

This 'collapse of interest' was highlighted when, in 1958, the Advisory Committee on the Employment of Older Men and Women was terminated (National Advisory Committee, 1953, 1955). The Chairman recalled that wide publicity had been given to the committee's two reports and there was evidence of 'considerable success in breaking down the traditional barriers against the employment of older workers' (Ministry of Labour and National Service, 1959: 26). It was also emphasised that the winding-up of the committee did not mean that 'the government had lost interest in the employment of older workers' (Ministry of Labour and National Service, 1959: 27). However when, at the beginning of 1959, the Minister of Labour was asked how many men had been forced into retirement as a consequence of the trade depression over the previous twelve months, the reply came: 'I regret that statistics giving the information are not available' (Hansard, vol. 599, col. 59).

The acceleration of retirement

By the 1960s and early 1970s numerous studies pointed to the employment difficulties of older workers in settings as diverse as mining (Department of Employment, 1970) and car assembly (MacKay, 1973). MacKay's work suggested that redundant car workers beyond their mid-forties stood a much lower chance than younger workers even of being re-engaged by their previous firm. Daniel's (1972) study of redundant workers at Woolwich indicated that the older the worker the greater the likelihood of lower earnings in any subsequent employment. Fogarty's comprehensive review, *40 to 60: how we waste the middle aged*, found a widespread tendency to bar middle-aged applicants from recruitment to professional and managerial jobs '[a] tendency [which] probably increased from the 1950s to the early 1970s' (Fogarty, 1975: 83).

The exclusion of older men from work gathered pace throughout the 1970s and early 1980s (Laczko and Phillipson, 1991). The striking decline in economic activity of men over pensionable age has already been mentioned. Even more remarkable is the trend towards early retirement or early exit: the percentage of men aged 60–64 economically active declining from 82.9 per cent in 1971 to 54.1 per cent in 1991. By 1996, the rate had declined to below 50 per cent (Table 5.1).

Table 5.1 Economic activity rates for older women and older men, 1971–2001

Age	1971	1975	1981	1991	1996	2001
Women						
25–34	45.5	51.8	56.4	70.0	72.3	73.9
35–44	59.7	66.1	68.0	76.8	76.4	76.7
45–54	62.0	66.3	68.0	72.8	72.3	78.7
55–59	50.9	52.4	53.4	54.6	54.7	55.2
60–64	28.8	28.6	23.3	24.0	25.7	28.7
65+	6.3	4.9	3.7	3.2	3.1	3.1
Men						
25–34	94.6	94.6	95.4	95.8	93.3	92.7
35–44	96.2	96.4	96.0	95.7	93.2	92.7
45–54	95.7	96.1	94.8	91.96	89.2	88.7
55–59	93.0	93.0	89.4	80.7	75.5	75.6
60–64	82.9	82.4	69.3	54.0	49.6	49.4
65–69	30.4	25.9	16.3	15.1	13.4	13.0
70+	10.9	8.3	6.5	4.9	4.4	4.2

Source: Employment Department, Employment Gazette (April) 1995; (February) 1997.

The trends amongst older women are more complex to assess because of inadequacies in the statistics: in particular, the failure of many women to register as unemployed or the omission of part-time workers (most of whom are women) from some labour statistics (Dex and Phillipson, 1986). Official statistics for the 1970s and 1980s showed a decline in the percentage of women 60 plus who are defined as economically active. In contrast, the rates for women aged 55–59 fluctuated between 51 per cent and 56 per cent throughout this period; for women aged 45–54 there was a gradual rise in economic activity. In the 1990s, the rates for women aged 60–64 also began to show some recovery from the period of decline in the preceding decades. In the medium-term, the retirement age for women is set to rise (from 60 to 65) over the period between 2010 and 2020. It is possible that this policy development will begin to influence activity rates.

Although the employment situation for mature women workers appears more stable than is the case for men, this is mainly because the decline in older women's activity rates has been masked by the tendency for each succeeding generation of women to have a higher activity rate than its predecessor. Trinder et al (1992) note that this effect is brought out in a comparison of the number in employment of

55–59 year old women in 1984, with that for the same cohorts who were 50–54 in 1979. This shows a drop in employment of 23 per cent.

Taking both men and women, the evidence suggests that the marginalisation of older employees gathered pace from the 1970s onwards. This arose through: first, their concentration, in many cases, in contracting industries; secondly, the operation of particular schemes to promote worker redeployment (e.g. the Redundancy Payments Act) or replacement (the Job Release Scheme); thirdly, the pressure of mass unemployment; fourthly, changing attitudes amongst government, business, trades unions and older people themselves, in respect of the older workers' right to employment in relation to other, younger age groups (Bytheway, 1986).

There is some evidence that in the move out of recession around the mid-1980s, there were increased opportunities for individuals either to delay their retirement or to find employment after they had left their main work career (Bone et al, 1992). However, the rise of unemployment (and especially long-term unemployment) in the early 1990s is likely to have produced further restrictions on the job opportunities available to older workers. At the same time, for those who remain in work there has been the emergence of greater flexibility in patterns of employment (McGregor and Sproull, 1992). In part, this reflects a marked change over the past ten years in the nature of the labour market for older workers, with the increasing importance of the self-employed, part-time workers and mature women workers. Across the British labour market as a whole there has been an increase in the proportion of people in 'nonstandard' forms of employment (Hewitt, 1993). There has been a striking increase in self-employment, from 9 per cent of the total workforce in 1980 to 15 per cent in 1990. Among older workers the increase is even greater (Laczko and Phillipson, 1991).

A higher proportion of the labour force in self-employment implies that more people approaching retirement age will not face retirement at a fixed age. Traditionally, the self-employed are more likely to work beyond state pensionable age: first, because they can adjust their hours of work more easily; secondly, for financial reasons (they are unlikely to have index-linked pensions). A higher proportion of older workers in part-time work also suggests more flexibility, with more people likely to combine elements of work and retirement.

Age discrimination in the workplace

A number of research studies published in the mid-1990s have also confirmed that discrimination in the recruitment of older workers is still relatively common (Itzin and Phillipson, 1993; McGoldrick and Arrowsmith, 1993; Taylor and Walker, 1993; Taylor and Walker, 1995). Moreover, the research evidence further suggests that older workers are a low priority when it comes to training and retraining. The 1991 British Labour Force Survey found that older workers were less likely than younger employees to have received job-related training: for example, 24 per cent of 16–19 year olds compared to only 8 per cent of 50–59 year olds had done so. Although there was an increase in job-related training between 1984 and 1991, the increase for men aged 60–64 and women aged 55–59 was below that of other age groups.

In terms of training, Article 15 of the European Charter of the Fundamental Social Rights of Workers states that every worker should have the right to vocational training, and retraining, throughout their working life. However, this is no more than a statement of intent, and few European countries have undertaken initiatives to improve the training received by older workers. Trends in industrialised countries relating to the employment and training of older workers have been reviewed in research by the International Labour Organisation (ILO). The results show that despite strong evidence regarding the training and learning potential of older workers, employers and governments have been reluctant to commit training resources to support this group (Plett 1990; Walker and Maltby, 1997).

Further evidence from research by the OECD also suggests that discrimination in the area of training is a problem in a number of countries (Blackwell, 1992). The OECD study noted that in recent years countries have put greater emphasis on programmes directed at the long-term unemployed, emphasising counselling and job-finding skills. However, the report noted that older workers have not been well-represented among those who receive these services. They also make up a small proportion of those who receive public training services. Research findings indicate an absence, in most industrialised countries, of training specifically targeted at older workers. Peter Plett, in the ILO research, summarises the situation as follows:

> There is hardly a country having a concept or even a concise policy on older people with regard to their training needs. However, there are countries, Japan, the United States, and Canada in particular, which use most of the necessary elements in hand for such a concept...nearly all countries (except Japan) are still focusing on younger people who were until recently entering the labour force in considerable numbers.

Plett, 1990: 77

Finally, although, within the European Union, there are a variety of employment regulations, there is relatively little legislation specifically targeted at older workers. Itzin and Phillipson (1993) note that there is no anti-age discrimination legislation in Belgium, Denmark, Germany, Greece, Holland, Italy, the Netherlands, Portugal, Luxembourg and the UK. Consequently, the use of age restrictions in limiting access to employment is widespread in these Member States.

The transition to retirement

The above review identifies some specific issues in relation to labour market changes and older workers. However, these also reflect more general developments in respect of the social institution of retirement. Retirement (defined in terms of entry into a public old-age pension scheme) and withdrawal or 'exit' from the workforce, no longer coincide for increasing numbers of workers (Kohli and Rein, 1992). Thus, it is misleading to view the fall in male participation rates simply as part of a trend towards earlier retirement. Retirement, as it is traditionally defined, is seen to come at a predictable point, accompanied (for most men at least) by a pension provided by the state (Laczko and Phillipson, 1991). In contrast, the retirement which emerged – in many industrialised countries – from the 1970s, did not come at the traditional stage in the life course. Moreover, many people, who are generally considered to be retired, do not receive a public pension and may not even consider themselves retired.

These developments reflect the emergence of a new phase in the history of retirement. In general terms we can distinguish between, first, the gradual consolidation of retirement from 1950 through to the mid-1960s; second, the acceleration of early exit and complete cessation of work after 60/65 in the period after 1970. The contrast between these periods is important to establish: from 1951 to 1960 the annualised labour force participation rate for 65–69 year old men was 50 per cent; for men aged 70 plus the figure was 20 per cent. The equivalent figures for the period between 1971 to 1980 were 24 and 8 per cent, and for 1981 to 1990 were 14 and 5 per cent.

The first period can best be described in terms of a steady consolidation of retirement as a social and economic institution (Phillipson, 1978; Harper and Thane, 1989), with the growth of occupational pension entitlements (Hannah, 1986; Brown, 1990), and the gradual acceptance of retirement as an accepted stage of life (Phillipson, 1990). Sociologically, this period can be identified as one in which retirement is viewed as a largely male phenomenon (and problem), a phase which is still subordinate in length and status to that of paid employment.

The second phase of retirement, from the mid-1960s onwards, is marked by a number of critical changes, these arising from the development of more flexible patterns of work and the emergence of high levels of unemployment. These produced what may be termed the reconstruction of middle and old age, with the identification of a 'third age' between the period of work (the second age) and the period of physical and mental decline (the fourth age). A characteristic feature of this new period of life is the ambiguity and flexibility of the boundaries between work at the lower end, and the period of late old age at the upper end of the life course. Both now have complex periods of transition, with the ambiguity of 'work-ending' (Schuller, 1989) in the first period, and the blurring of dependence and independence in the second (Bernard and Meade, 1993).

In the case of the retirement transition, the template of previous generations – long work, short retirement – is being dissolved (Schuller, 1989). For many (mostly male) workers, the predictability of continuous employment is being replaced by insecurity in middle and late working life – an experience shared with the majority of women workers (Itzin and Phillipson, 1993). Older workers increasingly find themselves on the margins of the labour market but with a number of years ahead of them before they reach the comparative safety of retirement. The retirement transition itself has become a period of increasing length and complexity. From the 1970s onwards there was an increase in the range of pre-retirement categories and statuses as well as an increase in the number of people entering these positions (Laczko and Phillipson, 1991). The transition has come to be organised on a much more flexible basis with a number of different pathways (e.g. unemployment, long-term sick, redundancy) which people follow before they either describe themselves or are defined within the social security system as 'wholly retired' (Kohli et al, 1992). The result of this has been increasing uncertainty as regards the position of older workers, both in their attitudes towards leaving work and in terms of their position within society (Phillipson, 1993).

Retirement and the life course

At least two interpretations may be placed upon the changes described above. One view is that they represent a fundamental break from the tripartition of the life course around one of preparation, one of 'active' work and one of retirement. Regarding the last of these, Guillemard describes the changes in the following terms:

> The retirement system has lost its central function of regulating labour force withdrawal. The other subsystems (principally unemployment compensation and disability insurance) that now do this introduce their own logic for regulating the transition from work to non-work. As a result of this replacement of retirement,

the chronological milestones that used to mark the life course are no longer visible; and functional criteria have assumed importance in organising the later years of life … The time for definitive withdrawal for the individual is no longer fixed ahead of time; it is not predictable. Since the chronological milestones of retirement are being torn up, the threefold model, which placed the individual in a foreseeable lifecourse of continuous, consecutive sequences of functions and statuses, is coming apart.

Guillemard 1989: 176–7

Another view, however, would caution against exaggerating the extent to which the sequence of education, work and retirement is breaking apart. The argument here is that whilst increasing numbers of workers experience an ambiguous status between work and retirement, there is nonetheless a clear transition between these institutions. Kohli and Rein argue that:

Life-course segmentation has become more important in relation to other lines of segmentation such as gender. The work life has been shortened, but at the same time it has become more pervasive as regards women…Thus the labour-market regime has become more exclusive and homogeneous in terms of gender, while at the same time it has become more exclusive and heterogeneous in life-course terms, with longer periods wholly outside of gainful work.

Kohli and Rein 1991: 23

Despite different points of emphasis, both the above arguments agree on certain key issues: first, that retirement is now an inevitable feature of economic and social life; second, that the point of entry into this institution is one marked by increasing insecurity for many individuals.

On the first point, we now have in place an institutionalised system of retirement which, although there may be significant developments in terms of future social policies, is unlikely to change substantially in terms of its overall shape (Schulz et al, 1991). There may be adjustments in the process of transition into this institution (i.e. there may be withdrawal from work at earlier ages and/or exit via new types of pathways), but all the evidence suggests that the institution itself will remain intact for the foreseeable future: if only because high levels of unemployment seem set to be a permanent feature of the economic landscape.

In addition, the evidence is that most industrialised economies have resisted moves towards a radical redistribution of work and leisure across the life course (e.g. to cut paid working hours to say twenty hours per week and to have later retirement ages). The impact of economic recession in the 1980s led to the abandonment of policies such as 'flexible life scheduling' (Best, 1980). Priority issues become focused around economic and employment security, and savings and investment. In this environment, for those who remained in employment, working hours stayed the same or actually increased. In the case of Britain, for example, the historical trend towards a shorter working week was reversed in the 1980s, and men in Britain work longer hours than men in almost any other European country. Within the European Union as a whole, two men in ten work an average 46 hours or more per week; in Britain, four in ten do so (Hewitt, 1993). These trends towards an intensification of work in the middle years have, of course, to be set against a major reduction in the amount of paid work both in the earlier and in the later years of life (Schultz, 1991).

The implications of these developments need to be analysed in both general and specific terms. At a general level, we are seeing the break-up of what Martin Kohli (1988: 368) has described as 'work societies'. In such societies – the industrialised societies of the western world – work (as paid employment) has traditionally been viewed as forming the basis of the economy. From a sociological perspective, work has been seen to provide not only income and opportunities for consumption, but a broader structure of individual socialisation (Kohli, 1988) as well as access to citizenship (Marshall, 1963). Such a view has always been open to criticism, omitting from consideration groups such as older people, unwaged women and children. However, such an approach has become, as Arber and Ginn (1992) suggest, even less sustainable as paid working life has itself shrunk, with the life course for men and women now being organised in equal measure around work (as paid employment) and non-paid activities (within and beyond the home). Following this, the key issue now is how to face the reality that 'being employed' is not really the normal state of affairs for the majority of people. The reality now is certainly very different.

For older people, this economic transformation conceals divergent social trends. On the one side there is the re-definition for some social groups of the period of retirement, with what Giddens (1991) describes as the 'reflexive self' developing new projects and activities independently of work-based identities. Conversely, for other groups of elders, movement from the immediate workplace may impose new types of restrictions and dependencies. Carroll Estes (1979, 1991) views some of these as arising from the social relations between older people and welfare bureaucracies. The latter constituting, she argues, the 'ageing enterprise' which contributes to the socially constructed nature of dependency in old age. According to Estes (1991):

> The dependent status of many older persons subjects them to a greater degree than younger persons to the social relations of subordination to public and private service agencies that act to reproduce capitalist culture and class relations. Analyses of class and age must be concerned with understanding how individual elders, given their unique biographies and historical moment, are made differentially dependent according to their preretirement class, gender, and racial/ethnic status.

A 'differential process of devaluation' occurs based on class and gender. Working class elderly are more rapidly devalued in the labour market and in the society as a whole than are the aged of other classes. Similarly, women, whose labour is not generally considered productive, are more devalued than men in old age

Estes 1991: 25–6

These transformations and social processes suggest radical changes will be needed to social policy itself, especially as it has been applied to groups such as older people and to the development of pensions in particular. The final part of this chapter reviews some of the key issues in terms of social policy and financial arrangements for older people facing retirement.

Social policy issues for older workers

The evidence from this review indicates that the last few decades have seen major upheavals in the lives of older workers. The 1970s and 1980s, in particular, saw a massive shake-out in second and third age workers. In consequence, many have been forced into a period of limbo in terms of their economic and social status. On the one hand, governments have been quick to use older people as a means of reducing the 'headline' level of unemployment. On the other hand, they have appeared less willing to ensure financial security in retirement and old age (see Falkingham in this volume). The reality is, however, that older workers are becoming an increasingly important group within the workforce. By the year 2020, one in four workers will be aged 50 plus, compared with one in five in 1990. Developing effective policies for work and retirement is now a major issue for governments. Individuals face the pressure of reduced years in work and increased years in retirement, thus producing diminished opportunities for acquiring savings and pensions rights. Governments face the prospect of a larger post-retirement population, but with reduced tax revenues to provide appropriate levels of support.

These developments confirm the importance of social and employment policy in the field of work and retirement. Despite the growth in popularity of retirement (especially but not exclusively) among the middle classes, a strong case is likely to be heard for encouraging employment among those in their fifties and sixties. Signs of this have already been apparent in the 1990s and reflect a number of factors. First, the longstanding interest in the United States in issues relating to older workers has coalesced in the idea of 'productive ageing', a theme that provides scope for devising new approaches to supporting mature and older people in the workplace (O'Reilly and Caro, 1994). Second, concerns over the possibility of labour and skill shortages (underpinned by demographic change) have led governments and other agencies to mount or support campaigns around the theme of 'investing in older people at work' (Employment Department Group, 1994;

Health Education Authority, 1994). Third, issues about older workers have also surfaced in campaigns around equal opportunities and discriminatory practices, with the public sector (local government especially) prominent in this activity (Itzin and Phillipson, 1993; METRA, 1994).

Over the next ten to twenty years concern about the position of older workers is likely to intensify, as the institution of retirement is further fragmented (Laczko and Phillipson, 1991; Watson, 1994). Employers and governments are beginning to recognise the costs involved in failing to utilise mature and older workers, and are beginning to construct a 'business' case for recruiting and retaining this group (Institute of Personnel Management, 1993).

A major issue in social policy – for some men and virtually all women – concerns that of financial coverage in the context of demographic change and the reorganisation of the life course. For many women there is a form of 'triple jeopardy' arising from the changes identified. First, the growth of a flexible workforce has been especially strong amongst women, but has led to significant forms of discrimination in respect of wages and career development (Itzin and Phillipson, 1993). Second, rights to employment have been significantly affected by women's role as carers. For example, a study of non-spouse carers by Glendinning (1992) found that a quarter of the carers interviewed had to give up paid work altogether; most had already had to change jobs, reduce their hours of work or lose earnings for other reasons before finishing work completely.[2] Third, low rates of pay have translated into deprivation in terms of limited access to pensions, along with high levels of poverty in late old age. Fourth, in the case of both men and women who leave employment ahead of state retirement age, the likelihood is that they will enter a financially insecure pathway in the transition from work to retirement (Atkinson and Sutherland, 1993).

In policy terms, the above trends suggest major changes are needed in the design of pensions and the support for workers when unemployed. In particular, the pension system of the future will need to be one which is detached from assumptions about continuous participation in paid work. Instead, such benefits should be attached to individual citizenship rights, reflecting the diversity of socially useful roles in which individuals engage throughout their lives. The basis for such a system must be acknowledgement of the growth of different types of paid employment, alongside greater flexibility in terms of the organisation of working life.

In general, there are major policy opportunities for securing both rights to employment for older workers, and rights to a secure and fulfilling retirement. The task of social policy in the early decades of the twenty-first century will be to ensure that a proper balance is struck between these two sides.

Notes

1   This review of research is a revised version of a section of a chapter by Dex and Phillipson (1986); see, also, Harper and Thane (1989), for a complementary perspective. More recent research in this area is reviewed in Kumashiro, 1995.

2   There is a comprehensive review of the issue of working carers in Phillips (ed) (1995).

References

Arber, S. and Ginn, J. (1992) *Gender and Later Life*, London: Sage.

Atkinson, A. B. and Rein, M. (1993) *Age, Work and Social Security*, London: Macmillan.

Atkinson, A. B. and Sutherland, H. (1993) 'Two nations in early retirement? The case of Britain' in Atkinson, A. B. and Rein, M. (1993) *Age, Work and Social Security*.

Belbin, R. M. (1965) *Training Methods for Older Workers*, Paris: OECD.

Bernard, M. and Meade, K. (1993) *Women Come of Age*, London: Edward Arnold.

Best, F. (1980) *Flexible Life Scheduling*, New York: Praeger.

Blackwell, J. (1992) 'Labour market participation and retirement of older workers' in *Employment Outlook*, Paris: OECD.

Bone, M., Gregory, J., Gill, B. and Lader, D. (1992) *Retirement and Retirement Plans*, London: OPCS Social Survey Division.

Brown, R. A. (1957) 'Age and "paced" work', *Occupational Psychology*, 31: 11–20.

Brown, J. (1990) *Social Security for Retirement*, York: Joseph Rowntree Foundation.

Bytheway, B. (1986) 'Making way: the disengagement of older workers' in Phillipson, C., Strang, P. and Bernard, M. (eds) *Dependency and Interdependency in Later Life*, London: Croom Helm.

Clark, R. and Spengler, J. (1980) *The Economics of Individual and Population Ageing*, London: Cambridge University Press.

Daniel, W. W. (1972) *Whatever Happened to the Workers At Woolwich*, London: PEP.

Department of Employment (1970) *Ryhope: a pit closes*, London: HMSO.

Dex, S. and Phillipson, C. (1986) 'Social policy and the older worker' in Phillipson, C. and Walker, A. (eds) *Ageing and Social Policy: a critical assessment*, London: Gower Books.

Employment Department Group (1994) *Getting On: the benefits of an older workforce*, London: EDG.

Estes, C. (1979) *The Aging Enterprise*, San Francisco: Josey Bass.

Estes, C. (1991) 'The new political economy of aging: introduction and critique' in Minkler, M. and Estes, C. (1991) *Critical Perspectives on Aging: the political and moral economy of growing old*, New York: Baywood Publishing Company.

Fogarty, M. (ed) (1975) *40 to 60: How We Waste the Middle Aged*, London: Centre for Studies in Social Policy/Bedford Square Press.

Giddens, A. (1991) *Modernity and Self-Identity*, Oxford: Polity Press.

Glendinning, C. (1992) 'Employment and "community care": policies for the 1990s', *Work, Employment and Society*, 6(1): 103–12.

Griew, S. (1964) *Job Re-Design*, Paris: OECD.

Guillemard, A.-M. (1989) 'The trend toward early labour force withdrawal and the re-organisation of the life course: a cross sectional analysis' in Johnson, P., Conrad, C. and Thompson, D. (eds) *Workers Versus Pensioners: international analysis in an ageing world*, Manchester. Manchester University Press.

Guillemard, A.-M. and Rein, M. (1993) 'Comparative patterns of retirement: recent trends in developing countries', *Annual Review of Sociology*, 19: 469–503.

Hannah, L. (1986) *Inventing Retirement*, Cambridge: Cambridge University Press.

Harper, S. and Thane, P. (1989) 'The consolidation of old age as a phase in life, 1945–1965' in Jefferys, M. (ed) (1989) *Growing Old in the Twentieth Century*, London: Routledge.

Health Education Authority (1994) *Investing in Older Work*, London: HEA.

Henretta, J. (1994) 'Recent trends in retirement', *Reviews in Clinical Gerontology*, 4: 71–81.

Heron, A. and Chown, S. M. (1967) 'Semi-skilled and over forty', *Occupational Psychology*, 33: 263–74.

Heron, A. (1962) 'Preparation for retirement: a new phase in occupational development', *Occupational Psychology*, 35: 1–9.

Hewitt, P. (1993) *About Time: the revolution in work and family life*, London: Rivers Oram Press.

Institute of Personnel Management (1993) *Statement on Age and Employment*, London: IPM.

Itzin, C. and Phillipson, C. (1993) *Age Barriers at Work*, Solihull: METRA.

Johnson, P. and Zimmerman, K. (1993) *Labour Markets in an Ageing Europe*, Cambridge: Cambridge University Press.

Kohli, M. (1988) 'Ageing as a challenge to sociological theory', *Ageing and Society*, 8(4): 367–95.

Kohli, M., Rein, M., Guillemard, A.-M. and Gunsteren, H. (1991) *Time for Retirement: comparative studies of early exit from the labour force*, Cambridge: Cambridge University Press.

Kohli, M. and Rein, M. (1992) 'The changing balance of work and retirement' in *Time for Retirement: comparative studies of early exit from the labour force*, Cambridge: Cambridge University Press.

Kumashiro, M. (1995) *The Paths to Productive Aging*, London: Taylor and Francis.

Laczko, F. (1990) 'New poverty and the old poor: pensioner's incomes in the European Community', *Ageing and Society*, 10: 261–77.

Laczko, F. and Phillipson, C. (1991) *Changing Work and Retirement*, Buckingham: Open University Press.

Le Gros Clark, F. (1966) *Work, Age and Leisure*, London: Michael Joseph.

Marshall, T. H. (1963) 'Citizenship and social class' in *Sociology at the Crossroads*, London: Heinemann Books.

McGoldrick, A. and Arrowsmith, J. (1993) 'Recuitment advertising: discrimination on the basis of age', *Employee Relations*, 15(5): 54–65.

McGregor, A. and Sproull, A. (1992) 'Employers and the flexible workforce', *Employment Gazette*, May, 225–34.

Mackay, D. I. (1973) 'Redundancy and re-engagement: a study of car workers', *Manchester School*, September.

Metropolitan Authorities Recruitment Agency (1994) *Lifting The Age Barrier*, Solihull: METRA.

Ministry of Labour and National Service (1959) *Annual Report for 1958*, Cmnd. 745, London: HMSO.

Murrell, K. F. H. (1959) 'Major problems of industrial gerontology', *Journal of Gerontology*, 14: 216.

National Advisory Committee on the Employment of Older Men and Women (1953) *First Report*, Cmnd 8963, London: HMSO.

National Advisory Committee on the Employment of Older Men and Women (1955) *Second Report*, Cmnd 9262, London: HMSO.

Naylor, P. (1990) *Age No Barrier*, Solihull: Metropolitan Authorities Recruitment Agency.

O'Reilly, J. and Caro, F. (1994) 'Productive aging: an overview of the literature', *Journal of Aging and Social Policy*, 6(3): 39–71.

Offe, C. and Heinze, R. (1992) *Beyond Employment*, Oxford: Policy Press.

Phillips, J. (ed) (1995) *Working Carers and Older People*, Aldershot: Avebury.

Phillipson, C. (1978) 'The experience of retirement: a sociological analysis', unpublished Phd thesis, University of Durham.

Phillipson, C. (1982) *Capitalism and the Construction of Old Age*, London: Macmillan.

Phillipson, C. (1990) 'The sociology of retirement' in Bond, J., Coleman, P. and Peace, S. (eds) *Ageing and Society*, London: Sage.

Phillipson, C. (1993) 'The sociology of retirement' in Bond, J., Coleman, P. and Peace, S. (eds) *Ageing and Society: an introduction to social gerontology*, London: Sage Books.

Phillipson, C. and Strang, P. (1983) *The Impact of Pre-Retirement Education*, University of Keele: Department of Adult Education.

Plett, P. (1990) *Training of Older Workers in Industrialised Countries*, Geneva International Labour Office.

Royal Commission on Population (1949) *Report*, London: HMSO.

Schuller, T. (1989) 'Work-ending: employment and ambiguity in later life' in Bytheway, B., Keil, T., Allat, P. and Bryman, A. (eds) *Becoming and Being Old*, London: Sage Books.

Schultz, J. (1991) 'Epilogue: the "buffer years": market incentives and evolving retirement policies' in Myles, J. and Quadagno, J. (eds) *States, Labour Markets, and the Future of Old Age Policy*, Philadelphia: Temple University Press.

Schultz, J., Borowski, A. and Crown, C. (1991) *The Economics of Population Ageing*, New York: Auburn House.

Taylor, P. and Walker, A. (1993) *Age and Employment: policies, attitudes and practice*, London: IPM.

Taylor, P. and Walker, A. (1995) 'Utilising older workers', *Employment Gazette*, April, 141–145.

Trinder, C. Hulme, G. and McCarthy, U. (1992) *Employment: the role of work in the third age*, London: Public Finance Foundation.

Turner, P., Dale, I. and Hurst, C. (1992) 'Training – a key to the future', *Employment Gazette*, August, 379–385.

Walker, A. and Maltby, T. (1997) *Ageing Europe*, Buckingham: Open University Press.

Waerness, K. (1989) 'Dependency in the welfare state' in Bulmer, M., Lewis, J. and Piachaud, D. *The Goals of Social Policy*, London: Unwin Hyman.

Watson, G. (1994) 'The flexible workforce and patterns of working hours in the UK', *Employment Gazette*, July, 239–248.

Welford, A. T. (1958) *Ageing and Human Skill*, London: Oxford University Press for the Nuffield Foundation.

Welford, A. T. (1976) 'Thirty years of psychological research on age and work, *Occupational Psychology* 49: 129–38.

6 Financial (in)security in later life

Jane Falkingham

The wage of retirement should be roughly based on what it costs the average person to lead a normal life. In 1985, this means £80 a week.
Eric Midwinter (1985) The Wage of Retirement: the case for a new pensions policy, CPA, p. 129

Introduction

Concern about financial security, or more often insecurity, in later life has a long pedigree. The plight of the 'aged poor' was highlighted by the studies of Charles Booth in the late nineteenth century and has been a recurrent theme in studies of household and family welfare ever since. In the last of his classic surveys of working class families in York in 1935-6, Seebohm Rowntree concluded that 'poverty of old age was more acute than poverty due to any other cause' (Rowntree, 1941). Prior to 1908 older people in financial need had to rely upon the Poor Law. The 1908 Old Age Pensions Act introduced a non-contributory pension, subject to a means-test, of 5s[1] a week for all persons aged 70 and over. This was raised to 10s in 1919, and a contributory pension of the same value followed in 1925. Although a welcome addition to resources in later life, the value of the new pensions was not on its own sufficient to live on, and their value was further eroded by high inflation in the late 1930s. In response to this, coupled with Rowntree's findings regarding the extent of concealed poverty among older people, the 1940 Old Age and Widow's Pension Act brought into being a system of supplementary pensions for persons whose income fell below a particular level, depending on the needs of the applicant and the number of dependants. Take-up of these new pensions, not tainted with the stigma of 'poor relief', was swift. At the beginning of 1940 around 275,000 elderly people were receiving outdoor relief under the poor law (Titmuss, 1950). By 1941, over a million elderly persons had applied and qualified for the new allowances and by July 1946 the number receiving supplementary pensions had risen to 1.5 million (Nuffield Foundation, 1947). The difference between this figure and that of only 0.25 million persons of pensionable age receiving outdoor relief six years earlier highlights the extent to which the new pensions fulfilled a hitherto unmet need. However, although they did much to relieve poverty in later life, the new supplementary pensions could only be granted to those already receiving an old age or widow's pension. They did nothing for those who were unable, or ineligible, to insure themselves and who had not yet attained the age of 70 – the qualifying age for the non-contributory pension.

Table 6.1 Chronology of pension reform

1908	Introduction of non-contributory old age pension of 5 shillings per week (25p) to all aged 70 and over, subject to income test
1925 Old Age Contributory Pensions Act	National Insurance Contributory pension
1942 Beveridge Report	Beveridge Report Social Insurance and Allied Services lays the blueprint for the post-war welfare state
1946 National Insurance Act	Established flat-rate NI retirement pension 26 shillings per week (£1.30) for those retiring after July 5th 1948
1954	Report of the Committee on the Economic and Financial Problem of the Provision for Old Age (Phillips Committee)
1959 National Insurance Act	Created the Graduated Pension Scheme, implemented in 1961
1975 Social Security Pensions Act	Established the State Earnings Related Pension (implemented in April 1978); based on 25% of the best 20 years of lifetime earnings
1984	Norman Fowler sets up the Inquiry into Provision for Retirement
1986 Social Security Act	Reform of SERPS – for those retiring from April 2009 value now 20% of lifetime average earnings; allowed individuals to contract-out by making contributions to a personal pension plan (PPP)
1991	Robert Maxwell dies. Discovery that £400 million missing from company pension funds
1993	Report of the Pension Law Review Committee (Goode Report)
July 1997	A fundamental and wide ranging review of all aspects of pension provision is announced by Harriet Harman, new Secretary of State for Social Security

The 1946 National Insurance Act and the allied 1948 National Assistance Act increased the value of the contributory pension for those that could insure themselves, and eased the qualifications for the supplementary pension for those unable to insure themselves or with no other form of income. Other welfare reforms as a result of the 1942 Beveridge Report also served to improve welfare in later life. Thus, the period with which we are concerned begins with a series of measures that, on the face of it, aimed to alleviate, if not eradicate, financial insecurity in later life. It is now over fifty years since the 1946 National Insurance Act established the basic state pension. Since then there have been significant changes in the financial circumstances of the elderly population. Rising real earnings, higher labour force participation amongst women, greater home ownership and increased occupational pension coverage have all meant that people are now retiring with higher incomes and greater security than ever before. Data from the Family Expenditure Survey shows that pensioners' income has doubled in real terms since the early 1960s (Retirement Income Inquiry, 1996). But at the same time there are still 1.8 million people aged 60 and over in receipt of means tested Income Support and an estimated further 1 million who are entitled to social assistance but fail to claim it (DSS, 1996a).

This chapter explores the change in sources, and levels, of income for older people over the last fifty years. Two key questions are addressed. Firstly, have the changes in pension provision over the last fifty years been successful in achieving greater financial security in later life? Or, is Rowntree's 'poverty of old age' still with us? Secondly, how has the distribution of income in later life changed? Have inequalities narrowed as a consequence of greater financial security? Or are they wider?

1947–1997 rising real incomes?

In 1947 there were 5.8 million persons aged over pensionable age in England and Wales, constituting around 13.6 per cent of the population. In 1997 there are an estimated 9.5 million, that is 18.3 per cent of the total population. Not only are there more persons of retirement age, but they can also expect to live longer. Table 6.2 shows the changes in some key demographic and economic indicators over the last fifty years.

Of particular importance for financial security in later life is the change in the value of the basic retirement pension across time. In 1947, the single person's pension was 26s (£1.30) and for a married couple 41s (£2.05). Twenty-five years later, in 1972, the value of a single person's and married couple's pension had increased five-fold to £6.75 and £10.90 respectively, and by April 1997 had risen nearly fifty-fold to £62.45 and £99.80. Of course such direct comparisons of absolute values are fairly meaningless as they do not take into account changes in the cost of living over time. It is estimated that £1 in 1947 would buy nearly £20 of goods in 1997. Thus even after adjusting for price inflation, we can see that the single person's pension in 1997 is worth just under *three times* as much as that in 1947.

Table 6.2 Fifty years on, 1947–97

	1947	1972	Today[1]
Population	43,050,000	49,452,000	51,820,000
Proportion of pensionable age	13.6%	16.5%	18.3%
Life expectancy at birth (years)			
men	64.4	69.0	74.2
women	69.3	74.0	79.4
Divorces	60,254	74,400	155,500
Unemployment (UK)	297,000	885,500	1,600,800
Purchasing power	£1	£2.50	£20
Retirement Pension			
single person	26s (£1.30)	135s (£6.75)	£62.45
married couple	41s (£2.05)	218s (£10.90)	£99.80
Average weekly earnings			
men (manual)	123s 5d (6.17)	716s 4d (£35.82)	£301.30
women (manual)	67s 3d (£3.36)	366s (£18.30)	£195.20
Prices			
pint of milk	5d (2p)	1s 6d (5.5p)	35p
loaf of bread	0.5d (2p)	2s 5d (10p)	53p
Swan Vesta Matches	4d (2p)	5d (2p)	10p
The Times	3d (1p)	1s (5p)	30p
Cadbury's milk chocolate (0.5 lb bar)	1s 5d (7p)	3s 6d (17.5p)	89p
beer (1 pint)	1s 4d (7p)	2s 6d (12.5p)	£1.50

1 Latest figures available, mainly 1996 and 1995
Figures are for England and Wales unless otherwise stated
Sources: ONS (1997c); Newman and Foster (1995).

Other evidence supports this trend in rising levels of real income. Table 6.3 shows average real pensioner incomes from all sources for different family types, all values being shown in January 1994 prices. Although there are marked differences in the level of income enjoyed by single female and male pensioners (a point that we will return to later), all groups witnessed at least a doubling of real income in the thirty years 1961 to 1991.

Table 6.3 Pensioner incomes by family type, 1961–91 (January 1994 prices)

	Married pensioners	Single pensioners	Single male pensioners	Single female pensioners
1961–62				
Mean (£)	106	52	65	49
Median (£)	83	40	46	39
1971–72				
Mean (£)	121	69	79	67
Median (£)	99	57	61	56
1981–82				
Mean (£)	155	87	97	84
Median (£)	127	78	82	77
1991–92				
Mean (£)	228	117	136	112
Median (£)	175	92	100	91
% change 1961–91				
Mean (£)	251%	225%	209%	228%
Median (£)	211%	214%	204%	233%

Source: Table 3.2, p. 36 in Johnson et al (1996).

However, this is not altogether surprising. Over the last fifty years the economy, as measured by the Gross Domestic Product (GDP) has grown from £11,835 million in 1948 to £742,300 million in 1996 (ONS, 1997a). After controlling for changes in prices, GDP increased by a factor of 3.2, i.e. GDP in 1996 was more than three times that, in real terms, in 1948. We would expect, and indeed it is desirable, that pensioners would have shared in the benefits of that growth. A more relevant indicator of how well the older population are fairing in retirement may therefore be the level of pensioners' incomes in relation to others in society.

Evidence from a number of sources suggests that, as well as enjoying higher real incomes, in the last fifty years pensioners have improved their position relative to the non-pensioner population. Guy Fiegehen, in an essay in 1986 in the government's flagship publication, *Social Trends*, demonstrated that the share of total disposable income 'enjoyed' by pensioners had more than doubled from 7 per cent in 1951 to 15 per cent in 1985, while over the same period the retired population had increased from around 13.5 per cent to 18 per cent of the total population (CSO, 1986). Analysis from thirty years of the Family Expenditure Survey also suggests a relative, as well as absolute, improvement in living standards. In 1961, after allowing for differences in household size and composition and housing costs, pensioners made up over 40 per cent of the bottom 10 per cent of the income distribution. By 1981 their representation in the poorest tenth of the population had fallen to around 15 per cent and by 1991 it had shrunk to just 10 per cent (Goodman and Webb, 1994). However, the decline in the proportion of elderly persons at the bottom of the income distribution does not necessarily imply increased affluence amongst the retired. Rather it may reflect the fact that families with young children and unemployed heads have now replaced pensioners as the poorest in society.

So far, we have been looking at the *average* level of income. However, as we shall see there have been, and remain, substantial inequalities *within* the pensioner population. Pensioners continue to be disproportionately represented among the poorer, if not the poorest groups in the population. Before looking in more detail at the distribution of income within the pensioner population and how it has altered, it is useful to examine the changes in the composition of income in later life.

Changes in the sources of income

Table 6.4 shows the change over time in the relative importance of the four main sources of income available to persons in later life: income from the state (from pensions and other social security benefits), private and occupational pensions, earnings, and income from savings and investments. Two features stand out: first, the continuing importance of income from the state; and second, the decline in the relative importance of income from employment, reflecting decreasing labour force participation amongst older workers.

Table 6.4 Sources of pensioners gross incomes (%)

	1951	1961	1974	1981	1986	1990–91	1993
Social security benefits	42	48	55	62	59	49	53
Occupational pensions	15	16	15	16	20	22	25
Savings and Investments	15	15	13	13	14	20	16
Employment	27	22	17	9	7	7	6

Source: Table 3.2, p. 59 in Johnson and Falkingham (1992); updated using figures from table 5.5, p. 91 in ONS (1997d).

In 1951, 49 per cent of men aged 65–69 and 21 per cent aged over 70 were economically active (Census, 1951). By 1971, these figures had fallen to 30 per cent and 11 per cent respectively and by 1994 they had halved again to 15 and 6 per cent (Employment Dept, 1996). Similarly although more women generally are working, from the 1970s onwards fewer continued to do so beyond retirement age – in 1975, 29 per cent of women aged 60–64 and 6 per cent of women aged 65 and over were in the labour force compared to 20 per cent and 3 per cent respectively a decade later (ONS, 1997b). This is despite government attempts to encourage older workers by the abolition of the earnings rule, and the fact that those over state pension age are not required to pay National Insurance (NI) contributions and have higher tax allowances than younger people.

Up to the beginning of the 1980s, the reduction in employment income was almost completely offset by increased income from social security benefits. However, since 1981 the proportion of income received from private pensions has been growing and, by 1993, occupational and personal pensions accounted for a quarter of all pensioners income.

PRIVATE PENSIONS

Membership of occupational pension schemes has grown considerably since the Second World War. Table 6.5 shows that in 1936 just over an eighth of the workforce were members of an occupational scheme. After 1945 membership grew rapidly, and by the end of the 1960s had risen to around 50 per cent of employees. Since then total membership as a share of the workforce has been steady. However the picture is different for men and women. The number of men contributing to an occupational pension has fallen steadily from a high of 9.9 million in 1967 to around 6.8 million in 1991. Meanwhile the number of women contributors has continued to rise from 2.3 million to 3.4 million.

Table 6.5 Membership of occupational pension schemes, 1936–91

	Number of members (millions)			% of workforce who are members		
	Men	Women	Total	Men	Women	Total
1936			2.6			13
1953	4.9	1.3	6.2	34	18	28
1956	6.4	1.6	8.0	43	21	35
1963	9.4	1.7	11.1	63	21	48
1967	9.9	2.3	12.2	66	28	53
1971	8.7	2.4	11.1	62	28	49
1975	8.6	2.8	11.4	63	30	49
1979	8.3	3.3	11.6	62	35	50
1983	7.8	3.3	11.1	64	37	52
1987	7.2	3.4	10.6	60	35	49
1991	6.8	3.9	10.7	57	37	48

Source: Table 2.1, p. 4 in Government Actuary (1994).

Some of the recent decline in male occupational pension membership can be explained by a switch to personal pensions. Coverage of personal pensions increased during the 1970s from 600,000 in 1974 to 1.6 million in 1979 and 4.5 million in 1985. The 1986 Social Security Act sought to extend further personal private provision by introducing tax advantages, and in the two years between 1987 and 1989, the number of personal pensions doubled. Many of those that bought pensions during that period have since been found to have been wrongly advised. It is estimated in the recent Office of Fair Trading Report that around 500,000 people are still awaiting compensation. By 1991, 10.7 million employees were in occupational pensions schemes and a further 8.1 million were in personal pension schemes (House of Commons, 1994).

Table 6.6 Number of occupational pensions in payment, 1936–91

	Private sector		Public Sector		Total
	former employees	widows and dependants	former employees	widows and dependants	
1936	0.1	–	0.1	–	0.2
1953	0.2	–	0.6	0.1	0.9
1956	0.3	–	0.7	0.1	1.1
1963	0.6	0.1	0.9	0.2	1.8
1967	0.8	0.2	1.1	0.2	2.3
1971	1.1	0.2	1.3	0.3	2.9
1975	1.1	0.2	1.7	0.4	3.4
1979	1.2	0.2	1.8	0.5	3.7
1983	1.8	0.3	2.2	0.7	5.0
1987	2.3	0.6	2.4	0.7	6.0
1991	3.0	0.8	2.5	0.7	7.0

Source: Table 3.1 in Government Actuary (1994).

The number of older people in *receipt* of an occupational pension in the early part of our period was quite low, reflecting the low rates of membership in the 1930s (Table 6.6). The majority of early recipients were former public sector employees and most of these were men. However provision expanded rapidly and, by the end of the 1950s, the number of families benefiting from an occupational pension was already over 1.5 million. A survey of the economic circumstances of older people in 1959/60, conducted by Dorothy Cole (Wedderburn) and John Utting, found that nearly 7 per cent of single (unmarried or widowed) women and 40 per cent of men and couples were receiving a pension from a former employer, trade union or charitable trust (Cole and Utting, 1962). The value of these pensions varied widely, 'stretching from the pension for the railway porter of 6s a week to the £4,000 a year of the ex-company director' (p. 74). A quarter of all those in receipt of a pension received less than £1 a week, but another quarter had more than £4 a week – at a time when the basic state pension was worth £2 10s a week for a single person and £4 for a couple. Thus, even in the late 1950s, occupational pensions were making a considerable contribution to total income for those that received them.

Throughout the 1970s and 1980s the number of retired persons drawing a private second tier pension grew rapidly as schemes matured. In 1994, nearly 60 per cent of persons aged over 65 received some income from occupational and personal pensions, and three quarters had income from savings and investments. At the same time, as the proportion of older people with occupational pensions has been increasing so too have the amounts they receive. The average for all those with any occupational pension rose by 63 per cent between 1979 and 1993, from £45 to £74 per week (in July 1993 prices) (DSS, 1995).

Receipt of private pensions varies with age and gender. Younger and more recently retired pensioners are more likely to be in receipt of income from a private pension. Women are much less likely to have an income from an occupational or personal pension, whether in their own right or via their husbands, than men. According to analysis of the 1994 General Household Survey, over two-thirds of men aged 65 and over received a private pension, with the average amount being £92 per week. In contrast, only four out of ten elderly women had a private second tier pension, averaging £51 a week. Of those women in receipt, only 60 per cent were receiving the pension through their own contributions.

SOCIAL SECURITY BENEFITS

Despite the growth in occupational pensions, state benefits continue to be the major source of income in later life, accounting for around a half of the total gross income of all pensioners. Income from the state takes three main forms: the social insurance based, flat-rate state pension, additional earnings related pensions administered by the government, and means-tested social assistance benefits. At present over 10 million people are in receipt of basic pension income from the state, at a cost of around £28 billion in 1995/96. In addition some 4 million pensioners receive SERPS, mainly in small amounts, amounting to a further £2.3 billion (DSS, 1996a: 1997). The basic state pension in 1997/78 is £62.45 per week for a single person and £99.80 for a couple.

Table 6.2 shows that there has been a small rise in the real value of the basic state pension over time. However, if we look at its value relative to the average net income in the population then the trend has been less straightforward. When the

NI scheme was introduced in 1946 there was no automatic machinery to uprate benefits. However, over the 1950s, there was a general acceptance of the principle that benefits should be adjusted in line with the growth in incomes of the working population. In the 1970s this practice was formalised, with pensions annually increased by the rise in earnings or prices – whichever was the higher. Table 6.7 shows the rise in relative value during the 1960s and 1970s.

Table 6.7 Retirement pension as a percentage of average male earnings, UK 1948–2050

	As percentage male manual earnings	As percentage male earnings
1948	19.1	–
1955	18.4	–
1961	19.1	–
1965	21.4	–
1971	19.5	17.5
1975	21.5	19.6
1981	22.9	19.8
1985	22.5	19.2
1990	–	16.0
200	–	14.0
2010	–	12.0
2020	–	10.0
2030	–	9.0
2040	–	8.0
2050	–	7.0

Note: Projections from 1990 assume the pension is uprated in line with prices and that real earnings grow at 1.5 per cent per annum.
Source: Table 4.5 in Johnson and Falkingham (1992).

The indexation of the basic flat-rate pension with earnings was abolished by the Thatcher government in 1980. This has meant that, as real earnings have continued to grow, the value of the NI pension has fallen relative to earnings. By 1997 its value has shrunk to 14 per cent of average male earnings, compared to 21 per cent in 1980. If the present indexing continues, it is predicted to fall further to, in the much quoted words of Michael Portillo (then Chief Secretary to the Treasury), a 'nugatory' 9 per cent by 2020 (*The Guardian*, 1993). Implicit in the decision to allow the basic pension to 'wither on the vine' is an assumption that people increasingly have recourse to other forms of income in retirement – most notably occupational and personal pensions. However, as we saw above, not all groups do and, equally, earnings related pensions are not suitable for everyone, particularly the low paid and those with interrupted earnings' histories. The continuing heavy reliance of many pensioners on state benefits for their income means that the level at which these benefits are paid remains crucial to the living standards of the majority of older people.

The end or endurance of poverty?

The reforms of 1946 and 1948 were designed to provide an adequate income for all in old age and to put an end to reliance on means-testing. Have the last fifty years seen the end or the endurance of poverty in old age? Several issues are pertinent here. Firstly, the Beveridge social insurance pension rested upon the basic assumptions of a working career spent in full-time and stable employment, and the model of a one-earner family with a gendered division of labour within the family between the male wage-earner and the female home-maker. These assumptions were questioned at the time and, in the fifty years since then, they have become increasingly unrealistic. The single employer working career is now very rare, even amongst men, and for women it was never the norm. The Beveridge pension was not therefore, and never has been, a universal pension. Rather it is a contributory pension and as such there have always been substantial groups that have been excluded from full 'citizenship', including married women, the civilian disabled, and many of the self-employed (Falkingham and Baldwin, 1994). For these groups at least social assistance has continued to be the safety net of last resort.

Secondly, it is questionable whether the level of the basic state pension has ever been high enough to provide an adequate income on its own. The assumption that pensioners commonly have access to income in addition to the state pension is not new. Indeed, Beveridge himself assumed that the workforce had access to private sector pensions with which to top up the state pension (Nesbitt, 1995: 8). The new pension was, however, intended to provide 'a pension on retirement which is enough for subsistence, even though the pensioner has *no other resources whatever*' (Beveridge, 1942: 92). However Beveridge also urged caution, arguing it is dangerous to be in any way lavish to old age, until adequate provision has been assured for all other vital needs (*op cit*).

In fact, even in 1948, the national insurance pension was not sufficient to guarantee on its own that people were independent of means-tested assistance. The National Assistance scale for a single person was 24s a week, plus additional housing costs. This meant that a single person receiving a NI pension of 26s, whose housing costs were higher than 2s, would have been below the National

Assistance level if he or she had no other income (Atkinson, 1991). The consequence was that the need for means-tested assistance did not die away. Rather, as Table 6.8 shows, the number of elderly people receiving National Assistance grew steadily through the 1950s and 1960s. In 1948, 63 per cent of the National Assistance Board's 1 million claimants were pensioners. By 1961, the numbers claiming means-tested benefits had doubled and pensioners share in total claimants had increased to almost three quarters. Thus, low income and financial insecurity remained an acute problem for many pensioners.

Table 6.8 Persons over pensionable age receiving means-tested social assistance 1948–96 (Thousands)

	Persons over pensionable age	Total claimants	Pensioners as a % of total claimants
National Assistance			
1948	638	1,011	63.1
1951	969	1,462	66.3
1961	1,295	1,844	70.2
1965	1,435	2,012	71.3
Supplementary Benefit			
1966	1,818	2,495	72.9
1972	1,909	2,929	65.2
1979	1,720	2,850	60.4
1986	1,724	4,940	34.9
Income Support			
1989	1,437	4,161	34.5
1991	1,413	4,487	31.5
1994	1,583	5,675	27.9
1996	1,564	5,549	28.2

Sources: 1948 to 1972 from CSo (1973) table 50; 1979 onwards from DSS (1997) table A.2.11 and 2.13 and previous equivalents.

Moreover, it became clear from a number of studies in the late 1950s and early 1960s that not all those who might have qualified for supplementation actually claimed it. Evidence from Cole and Utting's study in 1959 suggested that in addition to the quarter of all units in their sample who were already receiving National Assistance, there were more than *as many again* with incomes at or below this level but without help from the Assistance Board (Cole and Utting, 1962: 65). The great majority of both this group and of those with assistance were women.

In their now classic work, *The Poor and the Poorest*, Abel-Smith and Townsend, using a measure of 140 per cent of the standard rate of National Assistance as an indicator of poverty, found that in 1960 there were 7 million people living on incomes below the poverty level. Of these, 2.5 million were primarily dependent on pensions, and around 1 million retired people appeared to have an entitlement to assistance but were not receiving it. A further survey conducted in 1962 by Townsend and Wedderburn confirmed the finding that over half of pensioner families were living at or below the subsistence level (Townsend and Wedderburn 1965: 77). Again, a significant proportion of older people, about 11 per cent, were found to have incomes lower than the national assistance rate, but not to be in receipt of such benefit.

In response to the growing body of empirical evidence concerning continuing widespread poverty in old age, including the government's own survey in 1965 (Ministry of Pensions and NI, 1966), and in an effort to make social assistance more acceptable to the elderly population and improve take-up, in 1966 the government introduced a new Supplementary Benefits scheme to replace National Assistance (Brown, 1990). The immediate effect was an increase in claimants over retirement age. This had the effect of improving the income position of the poorest, but still meant that for a significant minority of people, old age meant living at or near subsistence level.

From 1972 onwards, the number of persons over pensionable age on social assistance has fallen. The 1970s saw the NI pension uprated in line with earnings, and a rise in its real value. Furthermore, the growth in occupational pension membership in the 1950s was now beginning to show feed through into higher numbers of people retiring with a second pension (see Table 6.6). The 1980s saw further declines in the number of elderly persons on assistance (although the drop between 1986 and 1989 in part reflects the abolition of housing benefit supplement).

However, it would be premature to claim that financial insecurity in old age has been vanquished. There remain a substantial number of persons dependant on social assistance. In 1996 approximately 1.8 million people aged 60 and over were receiving Income Support. These figures are for claimants only, and it is estimated that a further 250,000 spouses are also dependant on income support. In addition, problems associated with take-up of means-tested benefits have not gone away. In 1996 an estimated 1 million pensioners were thought to have incomes low enough to be eligible for social assistance, but were failing to claim it (DSS, 1997). Thus around 3 million elderly people are living on very low incomes today. And, just as in 1960, the majority of these are women – with over three times as many women pensioners as men dependent on income support.

As private pensions become increasingly important as a source of income in later life, are the inequalities experienced during working life – between employment and unemployment, full-time and part-time work, permanent and temporary contracts, low-paid and high-paid work – and between men and women, accentuated in retirement?

Growing inequality?

For most of the post-war period until the late 1970s there appears to have been a trend towards greater equality of incomes. Since then, this trend has been decisively reversed and the gap between the rich and poor has been growing (Hills, 1995). Growing inequality within the total population has been matched by rising inequality within the pensioner population (Hancock and Weir, 1994). Table 6.9 shows the value of median income received by pensioner households within each fifth (quintile) of the income distribution. In 1979, the median income of the richest fifth of pensioner couple households was 2.85 times that of the poorest fifth. By 1993/94 this differential had increased to 3.77 times. Although median real incomes improved for all pensioners, pensioner couples experienced better growth than single pensioners (who tend to be older and women) and the incomes of the poorest single pensioners rose by just 18 per cent compared with 50 per cent for the richest.

Table 6.9 Changes in median pensioner incomes by quintile Income after housing costs (£pw equivalised) July 1996 prices

	Bottom quintile	Second quintile	Third quintile	Fourth quintile	Top quintile	Ratio top: bottom quintile
1979						
pensioner couple	80	93	115	147	228	2.85:1
single pensioner	87	98	110	141	227	2.60:1
1993/4						
pensioner couple	103	134	172	232	388	3.77:1
single pensioner	103	121	147	208	340	3.30:1
% change 1979–93/4						
pensioner couple	+ 29%	+ 44%	+ 67%	+ 58%	+ 70%	
single pensioner	+ 18%	+ 23%	+ 34%	+ 48%	+ 50%	

Source: Derived from Table A5(AHC) p. 121, DSS (1996b).

The growing contrast between the incomes of rich and poor pensioners has its root in the changing contributions of different sources of income in later life discussed above. Figure 6.1 highlights the heterogeneity of financial circumstances amongst persons aged over 65 in Britain today. Individuals are ranked by their total family income, equivalised to take into account differences in family size and composition. The bottom decile can be thought of representing those older persons living in the poorest 10 per cent of pensioner families, whilst the top decile represents the richest 10 per cent. The most notable differences are: first, the overall levels of income from different sources; and secondly, the relative contribution that social security benefits and occupational pensions make to total gross weekly income.

Figure 6.1 Income distribution amongst those aged 65 and over, 1994[3]

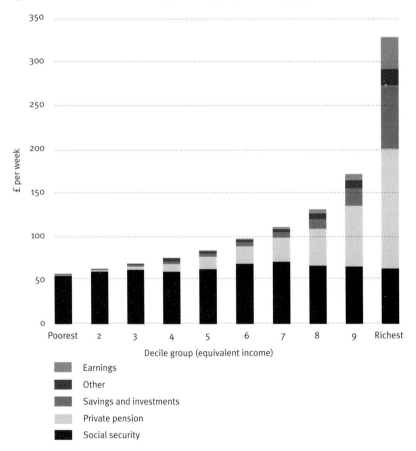

The tenth of pensioners with the highest incomes enjoy a weekly gross income over *five and a half times* the average income of those with the lowest (£328 a week, compared to £58). As noted from Table 6.3, social security benefits account for just over half of all income for those aged 65 and over. However, they are much more significant for persons with low income, accounting for over 90 per cent of income for those in the bottom three deciles. In fact, state benefits are more important than all other sources in all but the top two deciles, where they contribute 38 per cent and 19 per cent respectively. This is despite the fact that the absolute amount of benefit received by the more affluent groups is generally higher than that received by the poorest 50 per cent. One reason for this is that people with a full work history, and hence a full basic state pension, tend to be better off.

This is also reflected in the pattern of private pension income. The relative and absolute contribution of occupational and private pensions to total gross income increases as we move up the income distribution. In part this is due to the fact that the proportion of individuals aged 65 and over receiving income from occupational pensions varies across the income distribution, with only 20 per cent of the bottom two deciles receiving an income from this source compared to around half of those in the middle, and nearly 80 per cent of those in the top. However, even among individuals *in receipt* of a pension the amounts are very unevenly distributed. Those individuals in the top decile received, on average, an amount over twenty times higher (£211) than those in the bottom decile (£9.20) and nearly three times as much as the weekly average across all groups (£74.10). Thus, previous labour market experience and the ability to accrue occupational pension contributions, as well as the accumulation of savings and investments, appear to be the key determinants of a higher income stream and hence financial security in later life.

Concluding comments

The rise in occupational pensions has meant that old age is no longer a period of hardship for many. However, the increasing importance of non-state pensions in total income has also contributed to the recent growth in inequality amongst pensioners as not all people are able to share equally in this form of income. Payments of premiums for private pensions are related to the income and employment history of the individual. Unemployment, interrupted earnings histories, time out of the labour force to care for children or dependent adults, part-time work and low pay may all preclude the building up of non-state pension contributions. Inequalities established before retirement will endure beyond participation in the labour force.

In 1955, Richard Titmuss described Britain as having 'two nations in old age' – one group relatively fortunate, benefiting from occupational pensions and being able to draw on savings; the other group receiving only the basic state pension and being dependent on means-tested assistance. Given the substantial rise in the number of long term unemployed and new forms of working, with more temporary and part-time jobs, combined with the continued emphasis on private rather than public provision, it is likely that Titmuss' two nations in old age will persist well into the next century, and the gap between these two nations may continue to widen rather than narrow.

In 1942, William Beveridge remarked that old age was 'the most important, and in some ways the most difficult, of all the problems of social security' (p. 92). Little has changed over the last five decades to make the problem less difficult. Private pensions, as they currently stand, are not suitable for large sections of the working population. Some groups such as housewives, carers and the unemployed have no 'earnings' to contribute towards a second pension. Low paid workers find that nearly all their payments are eaten up in costs. Many pensions carry extortionate charges and are often inflexible. Their structure means that those who change jobs frequently, or women who take a career break to have children, are severely disadvantaged. According to the Office of Fair Trading Inquiry into Pensions published in July 1997 a worker who moved several times can find his or her pension up to 30 per cent lower than someone who stayed in the same scheme. Those groups which do not have an income high or regular enough to enable them to accumulate large private pensions, will continue to remain dependent on public pensions. But public pensions are already low, are declining in real terms, and are leading to a growing reliance on the means-test to provide top-up income (already claimed by around a fifth of all pensioners). In 1997, an estimated 3 million older persons still live on or below the subsistence minimum.

In the last fifty years income security in later life has improved, but there is still some way to go.

It remains to be seen which direction the new Labour government's pension review will take. Whatever policy reform path is chosen, care will need to be taken to ensure a decent minimum standard of living in retirement for both men and women – one which makes the best use of limited resources, but without discouraging private savings and without the stigmatising effects of means-testing. The aim of the next fifty years must surely remain 'to make want under any circumstance unnecessary' (Beveridge, 1942: 9).

Notes

1   1 shilling is equivalent to 5p.

2   Taken to be 65 for men and 60 for women.

3   Material from the General Household Survey was made available through the Office of National Statistics and the ESRC Data Archive and was used with the permission of the Controller of the Stationery Office.

References

Atkinson, A. B. (1991) 'The development of state pensions in the UK', *Welfare State Programme Discussion Paper*, London: London School of Economics.

Beveridge, W. (1942) *Social Insurance and Allied Services*, Cnmd 6404, London: HMSO.

Brown, J. (1990) *Social Security for Retirement*, York: Joseph Rowntree Foundation.

CSO (1973) *Social Trends*, London: HMSO.

CSO (1986) *Social Trends*, London: HMSO.

Census of England and Wales (1951), *Occupational Tables*, London: HMSO.

Cole, D. with Utting, J. (1962) *The Economic Circumstances of Old People*. Occasional Papers on Social Administration Number 4, Welwyn: The Codicote Press.

Department of Social Security (DSS) (1995) *The Pensioners' Incomes Series 1993*, London: DSS Analytical Services Division.

Department of Social Security (DSS) (1996a) *Social Security Statistics 1996*, London: The Stationery Office, Table B 1.03, p. 97.

Department of Social Security (DSS) (1996b) *Households Below Average Income: a statistical analysis 1979–1993/4* London: The Stationery Office.

Department of Social Security (DSS) (1997) *Social Security Statistics 1997*, London: The Stationery Office.

Employment Department (1996) 'British labour force projections: 1996–2006', *Labour Market Trends*, May, London: HMSO.

Falkingham, J. and Baldwin, S. (1994) 'Introduction' in Baldwin, S. and Falkingham, J. (eds) *Social Security and Social Change: new challenges to the Beveridge model*, Hemel Hempstead: Harvester Wheatsheaf.

Goodman, A. and Webb, S. (1994) *For Richer, For Poorer: the changing distribution of income in the United Kingdom, 1961–91*, IFS Commentary No. 42, London: Institute of Fiscal Studies.

Government Actuary (1994) *Occupational Pension Schemes*. Ninth Survey, London: HMSO.

The Guardian (1993) 8 December.

Hancock, R. and Weir, P. (1994) *More Ways than Means: a guide to pensioners' incomes in Great Britain during the 1980s*, London: Age Concern Institute of Gerontology.

Hills, J. (1995) *Joseph Rowntree Inquiry into Income and Wealth*, Volume 2, York: Joseph Rowntree Foundation.

House of Commons (1994) *Security, Equality, Choice: the future for pensions*, Volume 1, June, Cm 2594, London: HMSO.

Johnson, P. and Falkingham, J. (1992) *Ageing and Economic Welfare*, London: Sage.

Johnson, P. et al (1996) *Pensions 2000 and Beyond: The Report of the Retirement Income Inquiry*, Volume 2, Analysis of Trends and Options. London: RII.

Ministry of Pensions and National Insurance (1966) *Financial and Other Circumstances of Retirement Pensioners*, London: HMSO.

Nesbitt, S. (1995) *British Pension Policy Making in the 1980s*, Aldershot: Avebury.

Newman, O. and Foster, A. (1995) *The Value of a Pound: prices and incomes in Britain 1900–1993*, Andover: Gale Research International.

The Nuffield Foundation (1947) *Old People: report of a survey committee on the problems of ageing and the care of old people, under the chairmanship of B. Seebohm Rowntree*, London: Oxford University Press.

Office for National Statistics (ONS) (1997a) *Economic Trends 1997*, Annual Supplement, table 1.1, London: The Stationery Office.

Office for National Statistics (ONS) (1997b) *General Household Survey 1995*, London: The Stationery Office.

Office for National Statistics (ONS) (1997c) *50 Years of Vital Statistics*, London: The Stationery Office.

Office for National Statistics (ONS) (1997d) *Social Trends 27*, London: The Stationery Office.

The Retirement Income Inquiry (1996) *Pensions 2000 and Beyond*. The report of the retirement income inquiry chaired by Sir John Anson, Volume 1, London: RII.

Titmuss, R. (1950) *Problems of Social Policy*, London: HMSO/Longmans Green.

Townsend, P. and Wedderburn, D. (1965) *The Aged in the Welfare State*, Occasional papers on Social Administration No. 14. London: G. Bell & Sons, p. 77.

7 Professional responses to the challenge of old age

Contributors to the chapter are Jim Ogg, John Grimley Evans,
Margot Jefferys and Douglas G. MacMahon

The poor image of old age inevitably rubs off on those who are working in this field.
Work with old people is not a prestigious occupation and there is a vicious circle in that
jobs with low prestige tend to attract unambitious or less-skilled workers, or those
who...cannot get work elsewhere. The prestige of the work then falls still further.
There are of course many magnificent exceptions. Every profession in this field can show
splendid examples of dedication, skill, hard work, enthusiasm and good practice in both
the statutory and voluntary sectors and notable advances in skill and prestige have been
made in some fields – for example, in psychogeriatrics. But such achievements are always
made against the current and too often are the exception rather than the rule.

Alison Norman (1987) Aspects of Ageism, CPA, pp. 9–10

Introduction

The last fifty years has witnessed a growing professional interest in older people.
The relationship of older people to the 'professions', however, has moved from a
relationship based on inherent ageist assumptions to one where the empowerment
of older people is promoted. This chapter covers both health and social care
professions, which have undergone similar challenges in terms of organisational
change (purchaser/provider splits; generic versus specialism debates and moves to
locate care in the community rather than in an institutional setting); economic
change (cost containment and rationing of resources); and ethical debate (over the
rights, risks and responsibilities of patients and clients).

The social policy of old age has been dominated by health and social care issues,
yet years of experience have not bridged the divide between the two professions
as they affect older people. In terms of service provision this is seen around
hospital discharge and admission to long term care. Such dilemmas and challenges
for both professions are discussed in this chapter. Its contributors argue for the
need to move away from 'age' as a defining characteristic for resources as well as
a recognition of the major part older people play as consumers in both health and
social care arenas.

As shown in Chapter 1, the provision of social welfare services to older people and their families began to emerge in the immediate post war years as a result of the requirements of a newly formed welfare state. Social work with older people at this time was, however, recognisable only in the form of an administrative and procedural system within which specific resources were allocated. The services provided were mainly in the form of domiciliary help in the home, nutritional needs met through meals-on-wheels, help with housing matters (such as transfers and repairs), and admission to residential accommodation, all of which became the responsibility of local authority welfare departments under the two major pieces of welfare legislation of the immediate post war years.[1] In the first part of this chapter, we review the way in which social work with older people has developed over the last fifty years, and consider its future role as we approach the end of the twentieth century.

From welfare officer to social workers

Despite the early allocation of resources, the development of social work with older people evolved slowly and sporadically in comparison with other groups, particularly young children. Indeed, the priorities for social services departments have always been away from the needs of older people, regardless of the fact that in numerical terms their needs are greater than those of other groups. There are several possible explanations for this somewhat paradoxical situation.

First, the provision of social care services in the late 1940s and 1950s was divided between two distinct agencies – local authorities' health and social welfare departments (where welfare officers and domiciliary workers fulfilled statutory duties under the new legislation) on the one hand and, on the other hand, the voluntary sector. As in the medical field, the role of these respective service providers was compartmentalised and there was little coordination between the separate but related segments of social welfare. The main and often sole function of welfare officers, as far as older people were concerned, was the receipt and investigation of applications for residential care (a role which remained virtually unchanged until the 1990s) and the processing of grant applications for the voluntary sector. It would not be uncommon for welfare officers to have 'caseloads' of several hundred, and the new statutory obligations would often be fulfilled without any visits being made to assess the needs of older people. The system within which welfare officers operated did not permit the flexibility that is crucial to promoting social welfare.

The health and social welfare departments of local authorities in the immediate post war period also had a generic function which was to remain in place until the 1960s. Unlike developments in the medical field, reported in the last half of this chapter, there were no internal pressures within local authorities which could act as a catalyst for the formation of 'geriatric social workers' or their equivalent. Indeed, the winds of change within local authorities were blowing in a different direction: towards the 'general-purpose' social worker as recommended by the Younghusband report in 1959. In a review of the functions of social workers, the report stated that 'like social work with families, similar work with the elderly is not specialised but in a few areas it forms part, or all, of the duties of an almoner, or other social worker in the health department' (Younghusband, 1959: 186). Older people, unlike the psychiatrically ill or young children with needs, had to wait several more years before being recognised as a group for which there was a distinct social work role.

Outside of the statutory duties placed upon local authorities to provide residential care, the role of befriending, counselling, advocacy and supplementing domiciliary care services, fell to the voluntary sector. It is important not to underestimate the extent to which the voluntary sector provided services to older people at this time. At the end of the 1950s, for example, the National Old People's Welfare Council (the coordinating body for voluntary groups working with older people) liaised with 1,280 old people's welfare committees across England and Wales (Younghusband, 1959). The key representatives on these committees were from the British Red Cross and Womens Voluntary Service, providing a range of services to older people in the local community.

A second reason for the slow development of specific social work roles in relation to older people was that local authority services were designed to be delivered in conjunction with the new field of geriatric medicine, increasingly being adopted in hospitals throughout Britain. A key feature of geriatrics at this time (and one which has remained until the present day) was the preoccupation geriatricians had with the discharge of elderly long-stay patients who were inappropriately occupying hospital beds. This process necessitated a distinction between health and social care needs, the latter of which was deemed to be the sole responsibility of local welfare departments. The new geriatric medicine required the development of social care needs in the community, but, an unintended consequence was the 'tunnel vision' approach adopted by local authorities concerning admission criteria for residential accommodation. Residential care in effect became an administrative battleground between health and local authorities.

Furthermore, welfare officers within local authority departments were accountable to medical officers of health (i.e. doctors), for whom the dominant model of service provision in the community was one of 'social medicine'. Thus, what would later come to be defined as the role of social workers was, at this time, seen to be within the remit of the new general practitioners, who worked alongside geriatricians by treating patients in the community. Social medicine was concerned with the notion of preventing disease by focusing on the individual's social environment, something which general practitioners could never hope to fulfil in any major way given the increasing health care demands that were being placed upon them.

Despite the intentions of the new legislation to provide a more comprehensive, less institutionalised approach, which would allow older people to be supported in their own homes, it was clear by the end of the 1950s that a coordinated use of resources between health and local authorities to achieve these objectives was not taking place. Physicians rarely consulted with the new geriatricians. Geriatricians and general practitioners saw their work as competitive rather than complementary. General practitioners and social workers seldom worked together in the community and joint domiciliary visits were a rarity. Social workers had little professional contact with their colleagues in domiciliary care, and even less with the voluntary sector. It would not be uncommon for an older person in need of support to receive conflicting advice from this range of professions, and to remain suspicious of hospital care and fearful of residential accommodation. For these reasons, social work with older people in the immediate post-war period did not develop in any meaningful way other than the fulfilment of statutory obligations pertaining to residential care.

A climate of change

During the 1960s, however, it became increasingly clear that the pace of social and demographic change necessitated a radical review of the organisation and delivery of personal social services. A number of surveys (Townsend, 1957, 1964; Richardson, 1964; Tunstall, 1966) had revealed the changing structure of the family, the growing number of older people living alone, and the increase in life expectancy which had also produced a larger proportion of severely disabled older people. As these 'social problems' were identified, it was apparent that priorities for welfare provision had to be set, and moreover, that trained and qualified workers needed to be employed in the delivery of these services. The medical model of addressing social problems which had hitherto been prominent through the social medicine approach was seen as inappropriate and ineffective.

This new climate saw the demise of the medical officers of health within local authorities and the subsequent rise of the social work profession. Those individuals and groups who had previously been marginalised by the dominance of the medical profession, and its presence within social care, began to claim that they had an independent role to play in the provision of social welfare. This impetus for reform was to lead to the creation of local authority social services departments following the Seebohm recommendations in 1969, and the reorganisation of the personal social services that took place shortly after was to have further profound effects upon the ability of health and social welfare services to work together.

Despite the gradual emergence of social work as a profession (mostly in psychiatric and child care fields) throughout the 1960s, there was little development of specialist social work with older people during this period. Indeed, older people as a potential vulnerable group *per se* were not identified (apart from the continuing requirement upon local authorities to provide residential care noted above) until the 1968 Health Service and Public Health Act. This legislation aimed to provide the structures for greater collaboration between local authorities and GPs in the delivery of community care services. By the end of the 1960s, whilst the provision of services to older people accounted for much of the budget of social services departments, the bulk of social workers' caseloads were still oriented towards children and families (Goldberg, 1970).

Administratively, the establishment of local authority social services departments unified the previously fragmented structure of social work services. However, the creation of often large and bureaucratic structures had the unintentional consequence of exacerbating the divisions between health and social care further, as two monolithic structures working largely independently of each other came into being. Alongside this, a new training structure for social workers, coordinated by the newly formed Central Council for Education and Training in Social Work was created in 1971. Despite this the Certificate of Qualification in Social Work, the qualification allowing entrance to the social work profession, contained little material on the social care needs of older people other than assessment procedures for residential care (Brearley, 1975). Stereotypical images of ageing and old age were prevalent within social work training and, as a consequence, newly qualified social workers had no incentive to work with a client group for whom they believed there was little chance of effecting any change through social work intervention. Social work with older people was seen to be 'unglamorous' and the tasks that were assigned to it were in the main deemed to be administrative and procedural (Black et al, 1983). But although this was true for the majority of social workers at this time, it is arguably during the late 1970s and 1980s that the needs of older people first gained recognition. A small number of social work departments began to create structures which allowed specialist social work for older people to develop, especially in the field of psycho-geriatric social work.

From social workers to care managers

The NHS and Community Care Act (1990), together with reforms in the National Health Service, has had and continues to have profound effects upon the professions concerned with the social welfare of older people. Under the Act, care managers are increasingly replacing social workers as the key organisers of community care services to older people, although in most cases these professionals have a social work background. The role of a care manager is the organisation and delivery of 'packages of care' to enable older people (among others) to remain in their own homes, or in a homely environment within the community. The care manager is also responsible for 'multi-purpose' workers who undertake tasks that were previously the role of separate professions, for example home help, auxiliary nurse, and occupational therapist. They may be direct budget holders, but even where they are not, care managers have to work strictly within budgetary constraints when assessing older people's needs. In the first few years following implementation of the Act, care managers have found a conflict of interest between the needs of older people and the principles behind the community care reforms on the one hand, and the resources available to meet these needs on the other hand. Many care managers therefore increasingly feel that their work with older people places them in an invidious position, since they are unable to provide the very services identified in their assessments.

In this climate, the values which have underpinned the social work profession in the past (values which saw social workers as agents of empowerment, enabling individuals to take control of their lives and to help them achieve their goals), are quickly receding into the background as the bureaucratic demands of the new structures take hold. As the new culture of purchaser/provider service provision is being assimilated into welfare provision, the social care of older people has in effect become big business. Current figures suggest that there are approximately 200,000 'professional' carers employed by social services departments (DoH, 1995). The private and voluntary sector has also expanded significantly, since the community care reforms promote mixed economies of care and government requirements ensure that contracted services are purchased from private providers.

It therefore seems as though the new community care provision, which envisaged flexible packages of care being arranged for older people by health and social care agencies working together, has not materialised. Perhaps the greatest failure of the reforms is the absence of any national criteria in order for care managers to achieve some degree of parity. At present, there are wide variations in the eligibility criteria, charging policies and quality of assessments, with the result that the misplacement of older people in nursing homes still occurs, and inadequate service provision following hospital discharge is widespread (SSI, 1996).

The Social Services Inspectorate have also reported a distinct lack of a multidisciplinary approach to assessment and care management and, although it is still too early to report on whether this has been remedied, there are some encouraging examples of joint work appearing (SSI, 1994). One notable practical example of how multidisciplinary teams for older people can be operationalised is the Darlington Community Care Project (Challis et al, 1995). Here an integrated geriatric assessment team was set up with the aim of extending the principles of community care management into a geriatric multidisciplinary team.

However, these experimental schemes are in a minority and most care managers within social services departments increasingly find themselves subjecting older people to rigorous eligibility procedures in order to remain within fiscal constraints. Such a climate does little to promote multidisciplinary work since agencies in effect find themselves in competition with each other to remain within budgets, with the consequence that each tries to push responsibility on to the other.

A further important criticism of the past twenty-five years is the ineffectiveness of CCETSW (the quango which oversees social work training). This criticism is particularly relevant in relation to older people, where social work training often continues to be lacking in deference to child care. Most employees in social care, and particularly those working with older people, do not have the current Diploma in Social Work. Indeed, the majority of social care workers do not have any qualifications at all. However, the omissions of joint training which have served to enhance the divide between social and health care professions are slowly beginning to be rectified. There are now in existence joint training programmes in nursing and social work, and CCETSW intends to develop joint diplomas in social work and nursing studies aimed at working with older people in the community. In addition, this situation has prompted the call for a General Social Services Council to be created. This would cover training of the whole of the social care workforce and regulate workers within it, although the Conservative government did not accept this course of action.

For the future

Although the full effect of the new reforms has yet to be felt, the appearance of the care manager is inevitably associated with the demise of the social worker who specialises in working with older people. A move away from 'age' as the defining characteristic for resources may ostensibly prove to be a more equitable policy. But equally, in the drive for resources, the most vocal and high profile groups have an advantage over politically weaker groups (as, for example, the disability rights movement, which on the whole represents the needs of younger disabled people). Vulnerable older people run the risk of having a second rate service provision if they are not adequately represented.

It is possible that, in the future, care managers will be increasingly recruited from a variety of professions. This could include nursing, occupational therapy, and physiotherapy, or even professions which are not directly oriented towards social welfare but are more involved in management procedures and the organisation of services, such as the housing sector. Whether these new professionals will be able to empower older people, or advocate effectively on their behalf, remains to be seen.

The development of geriatric medicine

The speciality of geriatric medicine in Britain is suffering a mid-life crisis. The British Geriatrics Society is approaching its fiftieth birthday with a major paradox – four decades of success, yet marked and profoundly felt apprehension for the future. In this section of the chapter, we trace the development of what has now become the second largest specialty of hospital medicine in England and Wales and, through the recollections of some of its pioneers, consider its contributions to current and future policy affecting the care of sick and disabled older people.

THE PIONEERS OF GERIATRIC MEDICINE

In Britain we can, as noted above, date the emergence of geriatric medicine to the 1930s and 1940s, and to the pioneering work of Marjory Warren and other innovators such as Trevor Howell, Tom Wilson and Lord Amulree. Each of them applied principles adapted from the experience of the rehabilitation of injured servicemen to elderly people, and thereby challenged the then therapeutic nihilism of the medical profession. They examined the inhabitants of the Victorian workhouses – remnants of the Poor Law – and discovered hordes of elderly, largely ignored people, each of whom when appropriately assessed and treated had potential waiting to be realised. In particular, they focused attention on the taboo subjects of incontinence, dementia, falls and immobility, later described by Bernard Isaacs as the 'Geriatric Giants' (Isaacs, 1992: 1). Their attention was not only academic, but also pragmatic, since their increased attention led to laudable success rates: an early example of evidence-based practice. In addition, they were successful in building comprehensive, multidisciplinary teams, spanning health and social care. Lessons in team working were learnt, and a literature soon developed of their experiences. The services that they pioneered became the envy of the western world, where awareness was growing that the problems of elderly people were better addressed rather than ignored.

In interviews with survivors of the earliest cohort of geriatricians (those born before 1921), Margot Jefferys (1996) has shown that they mostly qualified just before or during the Second World War, and obtained consultant posts in geriatric medicine in the 1940s, 1950s and early 1960s. Their accounts of the medical arrangements which existed in the early years of the National Health Service, of the status which those working with older people and their patients could expect from fellow doctors and the public, and of the steps which were taken to establish the legitimacy of this new speciality are illuminating. It seems that part of the legacy of the Poor Law Infirmaries was a not unbenign paternalism. One Midlands interviewee commented:

> Well, the staff at the institutions were all resident, all the doctors were resident and the lay staff – clerks – were all resident, the labour masters, so-called, who would look after the able-bodied, were all residents. So, living in the place, they had their own snooker team. I played football every Saturday, but the thing is, they know the patients so that the question of the personal knowledge of the patients was possibly more in those days than later when all the resident posts went by the board.

For several of the sample, their first exposure to the chronic sick wards of the poor law infirmaries was during, or immediately after, the war. One was still a medical student at the time, and told how:

> They shoved me in charge of what they called the 'chronic sick' wards. These were mostly fairly elderly people, not always because some had MS and were younger, but they were people about whom they said 'We can do no more for him or her – she's just got to exist here until she dies.' So I saw rank upon rank of chronic sick wards in East London, with people lying in bed all the time. They never had day rooms, they had occasionally a chair beside the bed, they had minimal medical facilities, and they were just waiting for the end. Absolutely nothing going on, and no comfort and no activities and no physiotherapy – nothing of that sort.

Another from the Midlands told of his memories:

> I have some vivid memories of my early impressions of this infirmary: the gross degree of overcrowding in wards never designed for the care of the sick, and where it was not possible for a nurse with a trolley to pass another nurse with a trolley, unless the beds were pushed aside.

A further graphic picture was drawn by a Mancunian who said simply:

> Well, old people were not treated: if you were old you were regarded as sick, and if you were sick and old, you were to be nursed.

It was as a response to these kinds of conditions that Marjory Warren – the founding mother of geriatrics – began her pioneering work in the war years in West Middlesex. She was supported by Lord Amulree, a hereditary peer, and worked first as a professional civil servant in the Ministry of Health and later, as a consultant at University College Hospital. Together with a small, but growing, band of practitioners and advocates, she believed that revolutionising the care of older hospitalised patients was a feasible objective for the National Health Service on vesting day in 1948. Marjory Warren was remembered by some of Jefferys' interviewees as a charismatic personality by any standards. One regarded her as 'rigid and authoritarian', whilst another, who later became a legend in the specialty's history, had this to say:

> I was of course captivated. I think she was the sort of person whom I believe people could take a dislike to because she was very forthright; but she was a wonderful woman. She saw her way absolutely clearly; she saw no obstacle in her way; she knew what she wanted. She worked like anything on earth and inspired countless people…and I think she incurred a lot of jealousy among her fellow physicians because she was really, in my view, outstanding.

A Midlands consultant recalled one of her visits:

> She was staying in a hotel and rang me up. I was just getting out of bed about seven in the morning and she said, 'Can I come to see the hospital?' I said, 'Of course. When would you like to come?' She said, 'Now!' 'Seven in the morning!' I said, 'Give me a chance to shave Marjory and then I ll come down.' She said, 'I'll be there in twenty minutes.' No, she didn't ask permission – she gave orders. She was like a ship in full sail. She came down the corridor – master of all she surveyed – yes, with her coat tails flapping in the breeze.

In addition, an Indian doctor who worked in her department as a registrar, after a stint in the army, had this to say:

> Working with Marjory – it was almost like another regiment! She worked so hard, and worked everybody hard too…(but) she had faith in people, and enthusiasm. And she was a mother in one sense: she would say, 'Come on, calm down boys, don't be so depressed.' And in the beginning, it was very necessary… Marjory suffered two things: a) she was a woman in a jungle of men; and b) she did not have membership of the Royal Colleges. If she had been a member, she would have got an honour earlier, much earlier, and much more than what she got.

However, it was well into the 1950s before substantial changes were to come about in the rest of the country. Conditions in the first post-NHS decade were still difficult, as the pioneering consultants took gradual steps to try and improve and innovate. One appointed to a Cheshire ex-municipal hospital said:

> No patient was ever out of bed, and the first thing I had to do was to convince one nursing sister that people could get out of bed…and from then on, people got better. When people were taken out of the so-called chronic sick wards and given active treatment, they could be discharged!

Another consultant appointed to a Bradford hospital in 1953 recalls how he had to look after 750 patients in seven hospitals, single-handedly:

> When I went round they had absolutely no notes. They had a sort of card on which was written particulars for identification, and what their father had been and what their religion was. But as for medical notes, there was nothing at all.

It took quite some time, therefore, before the new departments of geriatric medicine were to fully emerge. Other consultant physicians and surgeons, whilst not overtly hostile, were disdainful or indifferent to the geriatric consultants and their plans. One interviewee spoke of this in these terms:

> A lot of general physicians were very much against it. All they wanted – I think some of them still do – was someone to take from their wards, the patients they didn't want. Simple as that. To them, geriatrics was a 'dustbin speciality'.

Another claimed that:

> The general physicians weren't interested. There was no money in it. They equated old age with poverty, and that was of no interest to them. In the beginning they were actively obstructive. Later on, they just let us be and didn't take much notice of us.

Being met with ambivalence about what they were doing was a frequent experience of this pioneer generation. There was an awareness too of the status and pecking order in the profession: geriatricians, it seemed, derived part of their low status from treating a clientele with low social status, i.e. the old and poor. However, even given this inauspicious background, the services pioneered by the new departments of geriatric medicine were eventually to become the envy of the western world.

SPECIALIST DEPARTMENTS OF GERIATRIC MEDICINE

The functions of the new departments of geriatric medicine were delineated in various ways and included initial assessment, emergency admission, rehabilitation, continuing (or long-stay) care, and terminal care. The concept was therefore essentially about progressive patient care, developed to make best use of somewhat meagre facilities. Wards became gradually more focused – each providing for one (or more) of the above functions. In addition, day hospitals providing medical and nursing care became an important feature of each department, together with outreach teams, centred on specialist nurses or health visitors. Respite care schemes also developed in various guises, providing support to the huge numbers of informal carers, and attempting to share the care between the individual and the statutory authorities.

The development of specialist geriatric departments also called for the creation of multidisciplinary teams of which the core members are the doctor, nurse, physiotherapist, occupational therapist and social worker. General practice in the early days had only the most peripheral of involvements. Indeed, many pioneers had difficulty even in negotiating for a geriatric medical slot in the GP vocational training schemes. This is despite the fact that links with other specialties have always been important. Today, the most evident links are with general medicine, with old age psychiatry and with orthopaedics.

During the 1960s and into the 1970s, the mixed pattern of provision became accentuated, with differing patterns of acute and longer term care emerging. The acute admission was often the responsibility of the acute general medicine team. This was to change in the 1970s and 1980s, with increasing acute geriatric activity in District General Hospitals (DGH), typically serving 200–500 thousand populations. By the end of the 1980s most DGHs boasted a geriatric service, headed by at least one geriatrician and with a complement of specialist staff from a range of clinical disciplines.

The academic base of geriatric medicine has also expanded over this time, with academic units springing up in all self-respecting universities. The quality, and the breadth of research expanded, and reached into the new realms of clinical medicine, science and technology. In addition, England was the birthplace of modern epidemiology and of the randomised controlled clinical trial (RCT), both of which have had a profound influence on the intellectual climate in which geriatric medicine has developed in the United Kingdom. Epidemiology has revealed important problems afflicting older people which can be underestimated by clinically based studies. These include inadequate nutrition, incontinence and other difficulties in the activities of daily living. For elderly people, RCTs have had a particularly significant impact in the field of cardiovascular disease. For example, the benefits from treating high blood pressure are now well documented up to the age of 85. Furthermore, in a review of research relevant to the needs of elderly people in the United Kingdom, the Medical Research Council has condemned the illogicality of excluding older people from research on diseases to which they are liable, or treatments from which they might benefit. British geriatricians have in fact been prominent in bringing the practical and ethical implications of ageism in medical care and research into the arena of public debate.

The interweaving of this strong tradition of clinical science with epidemiology, and the commitment to randomised trials of intervention, has helped to generate a comprehensive approach to common problems encountered by older people. However, no health care system can afford to sit on its laurels. And, by the 1980s and early 1990s, the notion of health care being free at the point of delivery had come under increasing attack from the market ethos of the Thatcherite reforms.

Geriatric medicine today

Of all medical disciplines, the specialty of geriatric medicine has felt the greatest impact of the recent reforms. The creation of a purchaser/provider system, with GP fundholders and Trusts, has splintered the traditional integrated arrangement. Geriatricians realise that, almost by definition, geriatric medicine has to be right at the interface not only between hospital and community services, but also between health and social services, and between acute and chronic care. In times of great change, this has been an uncomfortable position to hold to, and units have had to be flexible in their responses.

Having used managerial reform to kick start the changes, the managers have realised that their foot is on the accelerator with the introduction of a contract system, negotiated between putative 'purchasers' and 'providers'. The problems that are becoming apparent suggest that no-one is sure of the desirability of the present course, and still less sure of whether there is a brake or gears that can be used to control the headlong rush. Subsequently, most departments in England (in sharp contrast to Scotland), have now rushed into integration. In some, the pressure that forced integration was the (very welcome, but sometimes ill-conceived) downward pressure on junior doctor hours. In others, it was more of a managerial attempt to save money. The results have been very mixed. Attempts to produce an equitable, non-ageist service have created a lost identity for geriatric medicine. In some of the most extreme cases, integration has produced abolition of the specialist service. This has occurred where not only the admission route has been integrated, but where all the wards have been so too, and thereby lost their separate functions. Having realised their mistakes, in some cases we can now observe the re-creation of the lost specialty.

Another recent phenomenon of the last decade has been the massive expansion of private nursing homes, stimulated by the relaxation of rules allowing personal social security payments to fund placements. Whilst this dealt with the patchy problems of 'bed-blockers' in acute hospital beds, and the shortage of appropriate long term facilities, it caused a marked pressure on the Treasury, which prompted the NHS and Community Care Act (1990) (see Chapter 1). There is currently a hot debate between geriatricians and general practitioners about the appropriate organisation of medical care for such nursing home residents.

We still do not know whether the aim of the reforms to provide cost containment has been achieved. But, anecdotes about shortages of resources suggest that the cycle has revolved again, with the reappearance of 'bed-blockers'. Evidence is also mounting from clinical audit about the misplacement of people into nursing homes. This prompts a re-examination of the conflict between funding institutional placements against the cost of the rehabilitation resource required to restore an individual to the community, coupled with continued support in that environment. The contract culture that typifies the reformed health service is all pervasive, and has produced a plethora of perverse incentives. For example, because of the different funding streams for social and health care, one agency may be unwilling (or unable) to spend to help the other to save. Slower stream care has largely been lost to the health service, and health purchasers have belatedly realised that they may be guilty of throwing the baby out with the bath water. They are coming to realise that rehabilitation can not only have altruistic benefit, but that it can also be cost effective.

Approaching the new millennium

Fifty years on from the birth of geriatric medicine we should consider the needs of the future as well as the satisfactions of the past. By destiny or design, geriatricians are inheriting many of the responsibilities of the old style general physician. It is being mooted that some geriatricians may need to develop sub-specialty interests and responsibilities if older people are to have appropriate access to the best of new technologies. Some see this as a threat to the central mission of geriatrics as, it might be argued, it proved to be for general medicine. Be that as it may, in the United Kingdom, as in all western populations, older people can no longer be treated as a marginalised minority. They are major consumers of health care and a potentially formidable segment of the electorate.

As we approach the new millennium, geriatricians of the future must be equipped to occupy the high ground of medicine. Although the future is never easily predicted, the trends appear to suggest increasing specialisation within the profession, with more fragmentation, more community oriented services with fewer in-patient beds, and greater use of clinical protocols with increased emphasis on outcomes. The paradox here is that although the message of the importance of the specialty has slowly gained credence and influence within British professional and political circles, services have been increasingly fragmented and slow to recover from the inept implementation of the reforms. Such views were also expressed by the interviewees in Margot Jefferys' study (1996). In particular, they were concerned about three over-lapping issues: first, the implications of the health service reforms; second, the longer term trends – particularly the reduction in long-stay hospital facilities; and third, the controversy around the desirability or otherwise, of a separately designated geriatric specialty.

With regard to the first two of these issues, many interviewees expressed great concern over what they saw as the large-scale disgorgement of older patients from fast disappearing hospital beds into expanding private sector nursing homes. One expressed it thus:

Nursing homes, yes. That is going to compound a felony in my view, and create what we set out, in 1947, to resolve. Because, how do you ensure uniform standards of nursing and medical care and physiotherapy and so forth, from multiple little nursing homes all round the countryside?

Another remarked:

I am very worried about what will happen to longer-term rehabilitation patients and geriatric patients, because they will be thrown out of hospitals... There's no incentive on a private organisation to discharge patients who are paying good money, is there? But what still worries me is that if you have these self-governing hospitals, they will opt out of geriatrics because of its unpredictable costing.

Additional comments dealt more specifically with the future of the specialty itself, and a final telling observation encapsulates the dilemma the profession now faces at the close of the century:

I don't think there should be any geriatrics in an ideal world. I think it's a necessary evil. If you had really good GPs and really good consultants, then it doesn't matter how old a patient is or how ill they are, they would be looked after properly. But, it doesn't work out in practice. Old people, especially when they are dementing, and particularly when they are dirty, will always be neglected by the clever doctors. They are neglected by their GPs. They're neglected by the general services to be fair. So, I think you have to have a geriatric service. I think you *had* to have one. I think you *still* must have one.

When historians review the twentieth century, the story of geriatric medicine may be seen to have similarities with many other British innovations – namely that the successes tend to be overlooked in the home country, but are admired from afar, widely emulated, further developed and, finally, re-imported.

Acknowledgements

Sources for this chapter have been kindly reproduced from:

Grimley Evans, J. (1997) 'The Clinical Achievements of British Geriatrics' in Phillips, J. (ed) *British Gerontology and Geriatrics: Experience and Innovation*, London: BSG, BGS and BSRA, pp. 5-13.

MacMahon, D. (1997) 'The Development of Geriatric Services' in Phillips, J. (ed) *British Gerontology and Geriatrics: Experience and Innovation*, London: BSG, BGS and BSRA, pp. 13-19.

Jefferys, M. (1996) 'Oral histories of health and welfare'. Paper presented at the Oral History Society annual conference, Cradle to Grave: Health, Welfare and Oral History, Birkbeck College, May 1996.

Notes

1   1947 National Health Service Act and the 1948 National Assistance Act.

References

Black, J., Bow, R., Burns, D., Critcher, C. and Stockford, D. (1983) *Social Work in Context: a comparative study of three social services teams*, London: Tavistock.

Brearley (1975), *Social Work, Ageing and Society*, London: Routledge and Kegan Paul.

Challis, D., Darton, R., Johnson, L., Stone, M. and Traske, K. (1995) *Care Management and Health Care of Older People: The Darlington Community Care Project*, Aldershot: Arena.

Department of Health (1995) *Local Authority Social Services Statistics: staff of local authority social services departments at 30 September, 1994*, London: Department of Health.

Finch, J. and Groves, D. (1980) 'Community care and the family: a case for equal opportunities?', *Journal of Social Policy*, 9(4): 487–514.

Forde, A. (ed) (1969) *Penelope Hall's Social Services of England and Wales*, 7th edition, London: Routledge and Kegan Paul.

Goldberg, E. M. (1970) *Helping the Aged*, London: Allen and Unwin.

House of Commons Health Committee (1996) *Long-term Care: NHS responsibilities for meeting continuing health care needs*, Volume 1, London: HMSO.

Isaacs, B. (1992) *The Challenge of Geriatric Medicine*, Oxford: Oxford Medical Publications, Oxford University Press.

Jefferys, M. (1996) 'Oral histories of health and welfare'. Paper presented at the Oral History Society annual conference, Cradle to Grave: Health Welfare and Oral History, Birkbeck College, May 1996.

Richardson, I. M. (1964) *Age and Need: a study of old people in north-east Scotland*, Edinburgh: Livingstone.

Social Services Inspectorate and NHS Executive (1994) *Implementing Caring for People: care management*, London: Department of Health.

Social Services Inspectorate (1996) *Moving On: a further year inspection of social services department arrangements for the discharge of older people from hospital to residential or nursing home care*, London: Department of Health.

Townsend, P. (1957) *The Family Life of Old People*, London: Routledge and Kegan Paul.

Tunstall, J. (1966) *Old and Alone*, London: Routledge and Kegan Paul.

Wistow, G. (1994) 'Community care futures: interagency relationships – stability or continuing change?', in Titterton, M. (ed) *Caring for People in the Community: the new welfare*, London: Jessica Kingsley.

Younghusband, E. (1959) *Report of the working party on social workers*, Ministry of Health, London: HMSO.

8 Informal care of older people

Julia Twigg

If professional work with the elderly is seen as a low status and unrewarding occupation this is even more true of the provision of unpaid care by relatives. Again, there is a pervasive double message. On the one hand the government has woken up to the fact that, given its funding policies, health and social services are going to be less and less able to provide for the increasing number of chronically sick and disabled people in our society, so it tells us that 'Care in the Community' means 'Care by the Community' – by which is meant 'the family' or 'volunteers'. That is one message. But much lip service is also paid to the 'rights' of carers, and a good deal of research has been done to show what a heavy burden they are carrying. But the use of the word 'rights' in this connection also has a very hollow ring.

Alison Norman (1987) Aspects of Ageism, CPA, pp. 11-12

Introduction

Families have always been the main source of help to older people. But in the 1980s and 1990s, a series of studies, reports and discussion papers made this fact increasingly obvious in both the academic and policy communities. As a result, a debate on care emerged. Initially it focused on carers themselves but increasingly it widened to take in a range of issues – the role of women, the nature of carework, the rights of disabled people and the effectiveness of community care. This chapter reviews the main elements in this debate showing how it emerged and how it interacted with other social policy issues and concerns.

The rediscovery of family obligation

Through the 1950s and 1960s, the sociology of the family was caught in a narrow Parsonian functionalism that emphasised the structural affinity between the nuclear family and the nature of modern industrial society. The family was interpreted narrowly in terms of the nuclear couple and their children, and little or no attention was paid to wider kinship obligation, which was assumed to have withered away with the rise of modern society. Young and Willmot's famous study of the East End, which did chart significant transfers of support between households and generations, particularly between women, was seen as providing a dramatic contrast to the dominant account, but one that described an enclave of survival rather than a pattern that was widely current (Young and Willmot, 1957). As a result, caregiving or wider family obligation generally, were simply absent from the sociological and social policy agenda. These assumptions chimed in with popular notions that decried the selfishness of modern families and the neglect by them of their older members.

This dominant sociology of the family began to be questioned and attacked in the 1970s under the influences of feminism which sought to expose the normative assumptions that underlay it, particularly in regard to women. The black box of the family was opened up and the situation of individual members within it made subject to analysis. No longer fixated on the nuclear couple, sociologists were able to explore the range of household forms in which people increasingly lived. This included the households of older people. The conceptual separation of the household and the family made it possible to see the ways in which households were linked within a wider kin network that could involve significant transfers of help (Finch, 1989; Qureshi, 1996). During the 1980s a series of more ethnographic studies by Wenger (1984), Lewis and Meredith (1988), Qureshi and Walker (1989), Finch and Mason (1993), St Leger and Gillespie (1991), explored the nature of these transfers and their significance in the lives of older people. The earlier picture of family disengagement and neglect was shown to be wrong. The greater part of help that comes to older people continues to come from their families, and this help greatly outweighs any input from the formal sector. Estimates vary, but it is now commonly assumed that family care for older people living in the community represents between two or three times the input of the formal sector. This rediscovery of family involvement is something that has occurred across western societies, and what was true for Britain, is true also for Europe, for North America and Australasia (Biegel and Blum, 1990; Kendig, 1992; Kosberg, 1992). Caregiving has come to be recognised as an established feature of modern society.

The demographics of care

The new demographics of care were finally established in Great Britain by the 1985 General Household Survey (GHS) which included a number of questions on the subject of caregiving (Green, 1988). From this data it was possible to establish for the first time an accurate picture of the prevalence and pattern of informal care in Britain. About 6 million people, or one in seven of the adult population, were involved in caring. This figure was much larger than was popularly supposed, and its publication gave strength to the growing recognition of the carer issue among politicians and the media. Caring could no longer be seen as a marginal activity, but one that most people could expect to be involved in at some time in their lives. The definition of a carer used in the survey was an inclusive one, and caught within it some who were providing only small amounts of help, people whom Parker and Lawton term informal helpers (Parker and Lawton, 1994). For those providing more than twenty hours a week of care, the figure was 1.4 million. This still represented 3 per cent of the adult population.

The gender discrepancy in the provision of care turned out to be not as great as had been expected in the light of the earlier academic literature on carers, which had presented caring as a women's issue. Partly this was a product of the large numbers of carers of older people who are spouses, where there is no great gender imbalance (Arber and Ginn, 1991). Among intergenerational carers the difference, however, is more marked. Female carers are also slightly more likely to be involved in heavy duty caring in terms of hours and primary responsibility. They are also more likely to be giving help with personal care. Again this confirms an earlier picture of differential female involvement in intimate and bodily tending (Ungerson, 1983). Caring is thus gendered, but not in the blanket way that was initially assumed.

It is clear from the GHS data that the bulk of active caring takes place within a limited set of relationships: mostly spouses and offspring (Arber and Ginn, 1991). Where friends and neighbours are involved in caring it is usually of a limited nature – helping rather than caring – and it rarely involves personal care or extensive physical assistance. The norms of neighbourliness mean that they may be happy to help in an emergency or where they can do so without much disruption to their daily lives, but that they are wary of any stronger commitment (Wenger, 1984; Green, 1988; Hills, 1991). Typically non-kin carers are involved in activities like running errands, helping with transport, keeping an eye out for the person. These can be important in the support of older people, particularly where they bridge gaps that might otherwise result in the collapse of the person's care system, but they do not represent caring. This was a lesson that – as we shall see – policy makers and planners had to learn in the 1980s.

Friendships can be very important for many older people, indeed their significance has often been overlooked in the past by sociologists who have focused too narrowly on family relationships and on the provision of physical care (Arber and Ginn, 1991). Friends in general are not carers in this sense, but they can be important in the wellbeing of older people, many of whom prefer to confide in friends rather than family.

Assumptions made by the state about informal care

Though the state in Britain does not place legal obligations on family members to care, it does make implicit assumptions about their involvement, so that although the dominant forces that support caregiving derive from the family and from kinship obligation, the operation of this is shaped within a context of formal provision. What the state does and does not provide, affects what families do. Failing to provide alternatives, and making assumptions about involvement, represent an implicit policy by default. In practice, community care could not continue as a policy were it not for the activities of family carers. During the 1980s, this fact became increasingly visible to policy makers. Until then, little had been done overtly to encourage or support carers. The dominant approach was either to assume continued involvement or to fear that support would substitute for it. A shift in government policy did, however, occur in the late 1980s and early 1990s, and new emphasis was placed on the positive support of carers. This was largely justified on the grounds of cost effectiveness – supporting carers to support older people – but it did contain some recognition of the interests of carers themselves. This shift in policy coincided with the wider reform of community care, though the realities of the new community care have been more equivocal in relation to carers.

The debate on informal care: the linking of two problematics

The debate on care and carers that emerged in the UK in the 1980s was the product of the conjunction of two problematics: the first with its roots in community care; and the second in feminism. Neither were new in themselves, but their interconnection was, and together they created a shared territory of debate around the subject of informal care. During the 1990s, this consensus has in some degree broken up under pressure from new concerns and internal tensions.

THE COMMUNITY CARE DEBATE

The new visibility of family care in the 1980s brought carers increasingly within the view of managers and planners. The new managerialism of the 1980s emphasised the pursuit of greater effectiveness through the rationalisation of community care (Stewart, 1986). Part of this involved the incorporation of informal care into the planning and activities of the formal sector. Maximising the input of carers was seen as a cost-effective strategy. Early ideas about eliciting extra input from the informal sector were in general soon abandoned in the face of the recalcitrant and long term character of family ties. But, the argument of the cost effectiveness of small amounts of inputs from the formal sector to support the informal was widely cited, and seen as an important way to maximise the impact of limited formal inputs though a multiplier effect. The Griffiths Report, which was one of a series of influential documents that laid the foundations for the community care reforms, emphasised in particular the role of carers and the need to support them (Griffiths, 1988).

Although the 1980s were the era of the new right, the impact of its thinking was not as great as might be assumed. In general, writers in this tradition did not address the issue of informal care directly, though the subject was present obliquely in the emphasis on personal responsibility and conservative social values. Although such writing contained a general endorsement of family ties and responsibilities, its essentially individualistic and male focus, deriving from its neo-liberal roots, meant that it tended to remain focused on the nuclear family and its responsibilities. Where the new right did contribute to the debate was in a growing preoccupation with the costs of social welfare, particularly its fiscal and economic impact, and in pressure towards the privatisation of the responsibilities for old age. In this, the financing of care through the use of capital assets, such as housing, became increasingly important. As we shall see below, this has implications for families and carers through the debate on inheritance.

RESEARCH ON CARERS

Concern about carers in the 1980s was informed by a growing body of research. This explored more fully than ever before the nature of caregiving, its difficulties, tensions and burdens. Much of this literature focused on the negative aspects, exploring the ways in which carers' lives were limited by their caring role. Caring was shown to be an isolating, stressful and sometimes depressing activity (Gilhooly, 1984; Gilleard et al, 1984; Levin et al, 1989; Parker, 1990; Twigg, 1992). Some studies attempted to quantify these difficulties, pursuing a concept of carer burden. Others attempted to discover which features were hardest to bear, in which level of restriction, presence of disturbed behaviour and loss of the previous relationship were frequently identified (Levin et al, 1989).

This body of work, although very influential, was subject to certain criticisms. First, the pursuit of carer burden itself became to be seen as somewhat of a chimera. The impact of caring is complex and mediated through a range of other factors, some relating to personality, others to the nature of the relationship, and yet others to the material and social circumstances of the carer. Isolating features of caring could only lead so far in the understanding of its impact (Zarit, 1989; Parker, 1992). Secondly, it was unclear what the aim of such work was. There seemed to be an implicit policy assumption that determining the most stressful dimensions of caring would enable service managers to intervene in order to target support more effectively on the most needy carers. But this did not take into account the difficulties posed by carers to targeting (Twigg, 1993). The implicit –

indeed explicit – agenda was increasingly one of cost effectiveness, whose logic would lead to focusing solely on those carers who were on the brink of giving up. But these were not necessarily the most heavily burdened. Some carers are indeed so committed to the relationship that they will effectively never give up, what ever the costs to themselves.

The third criticism of this body of work came from carers themselves, who felt that the emphasis on burden was demeaning and at odds with how they experienced the relationship. This critique was endorsed by organisations that spoke for the cared-for person.

THE DISCOURSE OF CARE AND CARERS

The rising popularity of the term carer was itself indicative of developing perceptions in the field. The word emerged in the 1970s in an academic context and spread in popularity during the 1980s with the rise of the carer debate. In part it represented a growing recognition of the phenomenon of family care and the consequent need of a word to describe it. But its significance was never exhausted by that. To call someone a carer is to do more than simply describe the fact that they care for and support an elderly or disabled person, usually a close relative. It is also to place them in a particular discourse – a discourse of social policy in which responsibilities are recognised and to some degree assigned. Carers have become recognised as one of the building blocks of community care. Their duties and responsibilities have been acknowledged, and to some degree incorporated, into the processes of community care. Defining carers, assigning them that role, has become part of a process of co-option in which the activities of families become subject to the gaze of planners and practitioners.

The creation of the word carer has not been wholly to the detriment of carers themselves. Some carers have found that the term gives dignity and significance to what they do. Adopting a conscious carer identity has also enabled some to press more effectively for support (Twigg and Atkin, 1994). Above all it has opened up conceptual space for the recognition of carers' needs in their own right, and not simply instrumentally as a means to the end of supporting older and disabled people. We shall explore this further below when we discuss the tensions raised by the disability critique.

THE FEMINIST CRITIQUE

The initial feminist critique of community care rested on a sense of injustice. Family obligation was seen to fall unequally on men and women. Women had little option but to care, while men could discharge their family obligations through the labour of their wives and sisters. The pattern of inequality was further reinforced by the assumptions made by the state. Invalid Care Allowance (ICA), a benefit provided for carers of working age who are out of the labour market, was originally only awarded to men and unmarried women, with the assumption that married women were always available to care and did not therefore merit any compensation. This gender bias was later removed after a judgment in the European Court, but the lobbying preceeding this provided an important focus for the emerging feminist concern over informal care in the late 1970s and early 1980s (Finch and Groves, 1983; McLaughlin, 1991).

The feminist concern over informal care, however, never stood alone. It was always part of a larger project of making conceptually visible the unpaid work of women. In the 1970s this had applied to housework and child care, but in the1980s it was extended to the responsibilities for elder care that many feminists of the second wave were starting to experience in their own lives. In this approach, caring was conceptualised as labour, often hard physical labour, undertaken in unrewarding circumstances with little public recognition. Making unpaid work visible also involved giving it value and attempts were, and are, being made to develop conceptual means whereby the informal and formal economies could be linked (Joshi, 1987; Netton, 1993). Feminist writers were also concerned about caring because of its wider impact on women's lives. Caring was seen, along with other obligations and activities in the family, as restricting women's access to socially valued roles in the public sphere, and thus underlining their secondary social status (Finch and Groves, 1983; Waerness, 1984; Ungerson, 1987, 1990; Dalley, 1988; Hooyman, 1990; Baldwin and Twigg, 1991).

Lastly, caring raised questions about the meaning of care itself. Though earlier feminist work had conceptualised caring as labour, the aspect of love was never absent from the analysis. Caring could never be simply a matter of physical tasks; it always involved feelings, both in that caring takes place in the context of intimate relationships which themselves involve strong feelings, and in that the activity of caring requires the direct deployment of feelings. During the 1980s feminists were increasingly interested in the ways women's work involved emotional labour. The concept was developed by Hochschild in relation to flight attendants and extended by James in relation to hospice work (Hochschild, 1983; James, 1989). Emotional labour involves close personal attention to the needs of another in which feelings are manipulated and used to support and maintain the wellbeing of that person. Emotional labour seemed to characterise much of woman's work whether in the paid sector of the formal economy – typically the service sector – or the unpaid world of the family. Caring, whether informal and located in family relationships or formal and paid, was clearly part of this.

The feminist analysis of caring has proved very influential. One place it has met opposition and challenge, however, is within the disability movement.

The disability critique

The disability movement rests on a civil rights approach. It emphasises the ways in which disability is socially constructed, and it repudiates the oppression inherent in the medical model or the lay emphasis on disability as personal tragedy (Oliver, 1990; Morris, 1991). The social creation of disability and caring are seen as linked: all the factors which transform an impairment into a disability also tend to transform family members and friends into informal carers (Parker 1992: 70s). Out of these perceptions developed a critique of the debate on informal carers, which argued that policy should not underwrite dependence through an emphasis on supporting carers, but encourage the independence of the people they care for. People with disabilities should be able to have personal and family relationships without their becoming the basis of caring. The emphasis on the needs of carers that developed in the 1980s threatened, in this view, to divert attention and resources away from the real issue which was the needs of disabled people. Morris has, in addition, criticised early feminist work for its failure to incorporate the subjective experiences of the recipients of care – in many cases themselves women – and this in a literature that emphasised the ways in which the personal was political. She argued that feminists constituted their subject – women – in ways that excluded disabled women (Morris, 1991).

The disability movement has its roots in the experiences of younger, physically disabled people. This is not to say that its arguments do not also apply to older people. Indeed, the impact of these ideas forged in relation to younger people has had much to contribute to the debate on community care for older people, particularly in relation to user empowerment and the articulation of choice. There are however some ways in which these arguments need to be modified in relation to the circumstances of older people. The situation of people with dementia, for example, is not easily encompassed within this framework. Far from transcending the need for a carer, having one offers the best chance for people with dementia to remain living in the community. It is also not the case that all disabled people wish to be freed of caring relationships. Some disabled and older people want, and indeed require, that they be looked after by family members. Caring takes place in a relationship, often one of long duration. The dynamics of family and personal life are complex. Though some disabled people may indeed be oppressed by their carers, forced into a secondary position in relation to service providers, the reverse can also be true, and the needs of carers can sometimes be obscured behind those they care for. So long as carers feel that they are under an obligation to care, whether enforced by the cared-for person or deriving from internalised social norms, so long should there be some recognition of their needs in their own right. It is the fact that carers are obligated by family relationships that means that caring is not simply a voluntary matter. Many carers care against their own interests and are not able to give up at will. In these cases it is proper to have some regard for their needs in their own right.

The break up of consensus

During the 1990s the field of informal care began to fragment under pressure from developments in each of the two problematics. What had been identified as a remarkable consensus about caring began to be challenged. Feminist writers like Ungerson and Graham were dissatisfied with conceptions of caring that were confined to the unpaid and domestic spheres (Graham, 1991; Thomas, 1993; Ungerson, 1993). Increasingly they wanted to analyse care in the wider context of gendered labour across the public/private divide. This suggested a concept of caring that was not confined to the informal sector, thus undermining the earlier shared interpretation of caring in terms of an unpaid activity within the family, negotiated through kinship obligations.

From the perspective of those interested in community care, the realisation of the large numbers of men who were involved in care undermined the previously unquestioned identification of the issue as a woman's one (Green, 1988; Arber and Gilbert, 1989). The rediscovery of spouse carers also altered the agenda, since it refocused the debate away from intergenerational care which was more clearly gendered and related to the biographical concerns of some feminist writers. The realities of the new community care also brought home the limited nature of the leeway that was possible. The hiatus around community care in the late 1980s had allowed ideas about user-led services, carers' needs and empowerment to flourish. These were, in some degree, incorporated into the new legislation and its associated guidance, but the actual implementation was narrower in spirit. In a climate where resources were quite severely limited, wider concerns over gender equality tended to go by the board.

The new community care

Ushered in by the NHS and Community Care Act 1990, the core of its purpose was financial, to cap the escalating residential care budget and to control and rationalise spending on community care (Lewis and Glennerster, 1996). Its central mechanisms were care management, the purchaser/provider split and the stimulation of the mixed economy. As we have seen during the 1980s, a head of steam had built up behind the carer issue, and support for carers featured strongly in the associated guidance for the 1990 Act, which repeatedly referred to users and carers in the same breath.

It is hard, even at this stage, to evaluate the impact of the new arrangements on the lives of carers. The implementation of the Act was delayed, and most of the early research inevitably focused on the processes of change. Various small scale studies have attempted to assess how carers have fared, but even the best of these still describe a world in flux where the new arrangements are barely in place (Baldock and Ungerson, 1994). Research undertaken at the behest of various interest groups and charities, on the success or otherwise of the reforms, tends to be simply a vehicle for general concerns. There is, as yet, no systematic data on outcomes or on the ways the pattern of allocation may have shifted. As a result it is hard to say how carers – and indeed users – have fared.

It is likely, however, that many of the processes that applied under the old community care continue to do so. Indeed by some interpretation, the new community care is essentially the old arrangements dressed up in new guise. Service provision, despite the introduction of care management, is still in the hands of a range of actors: hospital consultants, GPs, community nurses, specialist social workers. Twigg and Atkin (1995) in their study of the responses of service providers to carers found that what really mattered was how far and in what ways mainstream service providers incorporated the interests of carers in their decision making. The degree to which they did – or did not – do so was heavily affected by who the service provider was, and by features of the carer and the case. It is likely that such systematic patterns of response, rooted in professional assumptive worlds, continue to have their effect.

The debate about inheritance

Just as English law lays no formal obligation on individuals to support their families financially, so too it leaves them free to bequeath their property as they wish. This is in contrast with some continental traditions particularly those that descend from the Napoleonic code, where inheritance is secured within the direct line. In France, for example, offspring must inherit between half and three quarters of the estate. This security of inheritance is linked with the legal obligation to support financially (though the existence of old age pensions and the minimum income for older people has done away with the substance of this obligation) (Twigg and Grand, forthcoming). The reality of English will-making however is such that the great majority of property passes to spouses and children. Finch and Wallis (1994) in their study of will-making within families, found no evidence to support the idea of care bargains or the differential use of inheritance to reward or underwrite caregiving. The dominant norm in Britain is one of equality between offspring, in which children can expect to inherit but where it is regarded as presumptuous to rely on doing so.

Inheritance and care have been increasingly linked by policy makers in the 1990s, in the context of what is seen as the growing crisis in the funding of long-term care. The reality of the crisis has been questioned. Walker and others argue that it has been exaggerated as part of a wider political strategy to restructure the welfare state and privatise its obligations (Walker, 1996). Whether the argument is correct – and it is persuasive – it remains the case that policy makers are increasingly drawn to explore the use of the assets of older people to fund their long-term care. The chief of these assets is the value of the house. This has obvious implications for offspring, and politicians have moved only cautiously in this area. The expansion of home ownership through public subsidies in the 1980s was predicated on an understanding that most people, and not just the well off, would now be able to pass on significant sums to their children and that wealth would cascade down the generations. This is clearly in conflict with the use of assets to fund care. Work by Parker and Clarke (1997) on public attitudes suggests that there is wide support for the primacy of passing on wealth as opposed to using it to fund care. The Conservative government responded to these feelings by increasing the capital amount (from £8,000 to £16,000) that older people are allowed to retain while still receiving state support for residential care. This sum is implicitly seen as allowing for some measure of inheritance.

Thus, although care and inheritance are not formally linked, they are implicitly so, in that money spent on care is in practice lost to children. The transfer into institutional care funded by personal assets has financial implications for the family. This was always so in relation to residential care, which has historically been means tested but, in the past it was not so in relation to nursing homes or long-term care in hospitals. Increasingly such care has been transferred out of the free-at-the-point-of-use health sector, and into that of the means-tested social care sector. Although there has always been anecdotal evidence suggesting that some families were aware of these differences and adjusted the situation to their advantage, there is no systematic research evidence to support or deny this. Similarly, there is little evidence in the research on caring of families making trade-offs between direct involvement in care as against the – for them implicit – costs of institutional care. This is a difficult area to research, where answers in interviews veer towards the normative and away from motivations that might appear mercenary. Systematic data on behaviour is similarly difficult to obtain. In general the research on caring does not support a view that such calculations are widespread.

Conclusion

From being a fairly peripheral subject, carers and caring have assumed a new prominence within social policy. It is no longer possible to discuss community care without acknowledging the central role played in it by carers. Though support for their involvement may wax and wane, and be subject to critique, the central significance of informal carers within social policy is no longer in dispute. This is not to say that care and caring are uncontentious. Rather, they lie at the heart of a series of wider debates concerning the nature of the welfare state, the character of carework, the relationship of the paid and unpaid economies, and the future of intergenerational relations.

References

Arber, S. and Gilbert, N. (1989) 'Men, the forgotten carers', *Sociology*, 23(1): 111–18.

Arber, S. and Ginn J. (1991) *Gender and Later Life: a sociological analysis of resources and constraints*, London: Sage.

Baldock, J. and Ungerson, C. (1994) 'Money, care and consumption: families in the new mixed economy of social care' in Millar, J. and Jones, H. (eds) *The Politics of the Family*, Aldershot: Avebury.

Baldwin, S. and Twigg, J. (1991) 'Women and community care: reflections on a debate' in Maclean M. and Groves D. (eds) *Women's Issues in Social Policy*, London: Routledge

Biegel, D. E. and Blum, A. (eds) (1990) *Aging and Caregiving: theory, research and policy*, London: Sage.

Dalley, G. (1988) *Ideologies of Caring: rethinking community and collectivism*, London: Macmillan.

Gilhooly, M. L. M. (1984) 'The impact of caregiving on caregivers: factors associated with the psychological well being of people supporting a dementing relative in the community', *British Journal of Medical Psychology*, 57: 34–44.

Gilleard, C. J. (1984) *Living with Dementia: community care of the elderly mentally infirm*, Beckenham: Croom Helm.

Graham, H. (1991) 'The concept of caring in feminist research: the case of domestic service', *Sociology*, 25(1): 61–78.

Green, H. (1988) *General Household Survey 1985: informal carers*, London: HMSO.

Griffiths, R. (1988) *Community Care: an agenda for action*, London: HMSO.

Finch, J. (1989) *Family Obligations and Social Change*, Cambridge: Polity Press.

Finch, J. and Groves, D. (eds) (1983) *A Labour of Love: women, work and caring*, London: Routledge.

Finch, J. and Mason, J. (1993) *Negotiating Family Responsibilities*, London: Routledge.

Finch, J. and Wallis, L. (1994) 'Inheritance, care bargains, and elderly people's relationships with their children' in Challis, D., Davies, B. and Traske, K. (eds) *Health and Community Care: UK and international perspectives*, Aldershot: Gower.

Hills, D. (1991) *Carer Support in the Community: evaluation of the Department of Health Initiative: demonstration districts for informal carers 1986–1989*, London: HMSO.

Hochschild, A. (1983) *The Managed Heart: the commercialisation of human feelings*, Berkeley, CA: University of California.

Hooyman, N. R. (1990) 'Women as caregivers of the elderly', in Biegel, D.E. and Blum, A. (eds) *Aging and Caregiving: theory, research and policy*, London: Sage.

James, N. (1989) 'Emotional labour: skill and work in the social regulation of feelings', *Sociological Review*, 37(1): 15–42.

Joshi, H. (1987) 'The cost of caring', in Glendinning, C. and Millar, J. (eds) *Women and Poverty in Britain*, Brighton: Wheatsheaf.

Kendig et al (eds) (1992) *Family Support for the Elderly: the international experience*, Oxford: OUP for WHO.

Kosberg, J. I. (ed) (1992) *Family Care of the Elderly: social and cultural changes*, London: Sage.

Levin, E., Sinclair, I. and Gorbach, P. (1989), *Families, Services and Confusion in Old Age*, Aldershot: Gower.

Lewis, J. and Meredith, B. (1988) *Daughters Who Care: daughters caring for mothers at home*, London: Routledge.

Lewis, J. and Glennerster, H. (1996) *Implementing the New Community Care*, Buckingham: Open University Press

McLaughlin, E. (1991) *Social Security and Community Care: the case of the invalid care allowance*, London: HMSO.

Morris J. (1991) *Pride Against Prejudice: transforming attitudes to disability*, London: Women's Press.

Netton, A. (1993) 'The costs of informal care', in Netton, A. and Beecham, J. (eds) *Costing Informal Care: theory and practice*, Aldershot: Ashgate.

Oliver, M. (1990) *The Politics of Disablement*, London: Macmillan.

OECD (1996) *Caring for Frail Elderly People: policies in evolution*, Paris: OECD.

Parker, G. (1990) *With Due Care and Attention: a review of research on informal care*, London: Family Policy Studies Centre.

Parker, G. (1992) 'Counting care: numbers and types of informal carers' in Twigg, J. (ed) *Carers: research and practice*, London: HMSO.

Parker, G. and Lawton, D. (1994) *Different Types of Care: Different Types of Carer: Evidence from the General Household Survey*, London: HMSO

Parker, G. and Clarke, H. (1997) 'Will you still need me, will you still feed me – paying for care in old age', *Social Policy and Administration*, 31(2).

Qureshi, H. (1996) 'Obligations and support within families', in Walker, A. (ed) *The New Generational Contract: intergenerational relations, old age and welfare*, London: UCL Press.

Qureshi, H. and Walker, A. (1989) *The Caring Relationship: elderly people and their families*, Basingstoke: Macmillan.

St Leger, F. and Gillespie, N. (1991) *Informal Welfare in Three Belfast Communities*, Belfast: DHSS

Stewart, J. (1986) *The New Management of Local Government*, London: Allen and Unwin.

Thomas, C. (1993) 'De-constructing concepts of care', *Sociology*, 27(4): 649–69.

Twigg, J. (ed) (1992) *Carers: research and practice*, London: HMSO.

Twigg, J. (1993) 'Integrating carers into the service system: six strategic responses', *Ageing and Society*, 13(2): 141–70.

Twigg, J. and Atkin, K. (1994) *Carers Perceived: policy and practice in informal care*, Buckingham: Open University Press.

Twigg, J. and Atkin, K. (1995) 'Carers and services: factors mediating service provision', *Journal of Social Policy*, 24(1): 5–30.

Twigg, J. and Grand, A. L. (forthcoming) 'Contrasting legal conceptions of family obligation and reciprocity in the support of older people: France and England', *Ageing and Society*.

Ungerson, C. (1983) 'Women and caring: skills, tasks and taboos' in Gamarnikow, D. et al (eds) *The Public and the Private*, London: Heineman

Ungerson, C. (1987) *Policy is Personal: sex, gender and informal care*, London: Tavistock.

Ungerson, C. (ed) (1990) *Gender and Caring: work and welfare in Britain and Scandinavia*, London: Harvester.

Ungerson, C. (1993) 'Payment for caring: mapping a territory' in Deakin, N. and Page, R. (eds) *The Costs of Welfare*, Aldershot: Avebury.

Waerness, K. (1984) 'The rationality of caring', *Economic and Industrial Democracy*, 5.

Walker, A. (1996) 'Intergenerational relations and the provision of welfare' in Walker, A. (ed) *The New Generational Contract: intergenerational relations, old age and welfare*, London: UCL Press.

Wenger, C. (1984) *The Supportive Network: coping with old age*, London: Allen & Unwin.

Young, M. and Willmot, P. (1957) *Family and Kinship in East London*, London: Routledge and Kegan Paul.

Zarit, S. H. (1989) 'Do we need another "stress and caregiving" study?', *Gerontologist*, 29(2).

9 Gender and older age

Jay Ginn and Sara Arber

Inequality and subordination can have two outcomes: those subordinated may perceive their state of inequality and dissent either openly in active resistance or in passive non-cooperation. On the other hand, they may fail to recognise their oppressed position, accepting it perhaps as different from their masters – different yet equal. Having internalised the values of those who dominate, their own status becomes unremarkable. They may even recognise their inequality but accept it as just, according to the tenets of an explicit ideology.

Gillian Dalley (1996) Ideologies of Caring: rethinking community and collectivism, second edition Macmillan/CPA, p. 89

Introduction

Age and gender are intimately linked in social life; gender roles and relations shift with age, while the process of ageing unfolds in different ways for women and men (Arber and Ginn, 1995a). Until the 1980s, social gerontology, sociology and social policy analysis were largely gender-blind, ignoring the influence of earlier gender roles on the material, health and caring resources on which wellbeing in later life depend. There has been even less attention to how ageism combines with sexism to devalue older women (Arber and Ginn, 1991). Older women were invisible, their voices unheard (Bernard and Meade, 1993).

This chapter first examines the neglect of gender in social policy thinking. The next section outlines the gendered effects of British social policy on ageing since the establishment of the welfare state, focusing on income and health care. Finally, trends and policy issues for the future of older people are highlighted in terms of their gender impact.

Invisibility of gender in theories of ageing

The development of ideas about ageing has encompassed a variety of theoretical frameworks. Early theories such as disengagement theory (Cumming and Henry, 1961) and activity theory (Havighurst, 1954), which emphasised psychological aspects of ageing, gave way to theories more concerned with how the social status of older people is constructed in western societies. These included exchange theory (Dowd, 1975), age stratification theory (Riley, 1971), and more recently a political economy perspective on ageing, including structured dependency theory. The latter approach emphasises how the state and economy devalue and impoverish most older people while enabling a minority to perpetuate their power and advantage into later life (Walker, 1980; 1981; Estes et al, 1982; Olson, 1982; Phillipson, 1982). Thus:

> The political economy perspective is not concerned with old age as a biological and/or psychological problem. It is interested in old age as a problem for societies characterised by major inequalities in the distribution of power, income and property.
>
> *Kart, 1987: 79*

The concern with social structural differentiation should have brought gender to centre stage, given the concentration of poverty among older women and their low social status (Arber and Ginn, 1991). However, political economy approaches, because of their debt to Marxism, were initially concerned primarily with class relationships, paying little attention to gender and race, even less to sexual orientation.

Sociology's lack of attention to post-retirement life, like the neglect of gender in 'malestream' sociology, originated in early theorists' preoccupation with waged work, class formation and class conflict (Kohli, 1988; Arber and Ginn, 1991). This tradition was firmly androcentric (Stacey and Thorne, 1985); the lives of pensioners, homemaker women and children were of little relevance to sociology's core concerns, while employed women were rendered invisible in a 'unisex' workforce (for example, Goldthorpe et al, 1969). Yet when feminist scholars began to attack the masculine bias of sociology, highlighting the importance of unpaid work and how this shaped women's participation in paid work, an implicit ageism in feminism marginalised older women (Macdonald and Rich, 1984). As McMullin (1995) has pointed out, theoretical construction tends to reflect power imbalances in society; those who are least powerful in economic terms, such as older women, attract the least theoretical attention.

In social policy, in contrast, old age has had a consistently high profile, but mainly as a social problem (see Chapter 1). Older people have been seen in terms of poverty, ill health, bereavement and isolation – a 'compassionate ageism' (Binstock, 1985). Use of terms like 'the elderly' have served to construct older people as 'other', denying their agency, their voice and their positive contributions to society, as well as obscuring their gender and other dimensions of diversity.

Thus, the connections between gender and ageing have been undeveloped, in spite of women's numerical predominance in later life: thinking on ageing and older people tended to be gender-blind, while feminist sociologists focused on issues affecting younger women.

From the mid-1980s, writers began to point to the parallels between ageism and sexism (for example, Reinharz, 1986): the social construction of old age as dependency has matched the construction of women as the weaker sex, exclusion from paid work often justified as protective yet accompanied by social invisibility and low income. Feminist writers began to explore how and why ageing differed for women and men, both in North America (Minkler and Stone, 1985; Olson, 1985; Gee and Kimball, 1987; Quadagno, 1988; McDaniel, 1989) and in Britain (Peace, 1986; Groves, 1983; 1987; Ford and Sinclair, 1987; Land, 1989; Arber and Ginn, 1991; 1994; 1995a; Lewis, 1992; Joshi and Davies, 1994). Such work, which is considered in the next section, has contributed to a growing understanding of the gendered effects of social policy on wellbeing in later life.

Gender, wellbeing and resources in later life

As noted earlier, gender and ageing are intertwined in social life: social ageing, or the socially created changes in behavioural norms and in self-perceived age, differs according to gender. Thus, women's lives are influenced by a socially constructed 'female chronology' (Itzin, 1990) in which the timing and sequencing of life course transitions are related to gendered cultural norms. In the female chronology, ageing is more negatively evaluated than for men. Women are seen as 'over the hill' or past their 'sell-by date' as partners at an earlier age than men leading to a double standard of ageing (Sontag, 1978). A similar process occurs in the labour market, where women's opportunities are jeopardised by employers' and managers' prejudices. Bernard et al (1995) have shown how such gendered ageism operates to women's disadvantage in their employment and diminishes women's chance of accumulating an adequate pension. In this way, gender differences in social ageing contribute to women's material disadvantage in later life as well as to their devalued social status (Arber and Ginn, 1991; 1995a).

Gender roles may become less sharply defined in later life, as the material basis of the gender division of labour diminishes (Sinnott, 1977; Rossi, 1986; Wilson, 1995), although gender inequality of power in marriage seems to persist (Rose and Bruce, 1995; Wilson, 1995). The experience of widowhood is likely to differ for women and men. Women are more likely than men to suffer a substantial drop in income when widowed and they also have less opportunity to remarry. However, Wilson's (1995) research suggests that in spite of regret at loss of their partner, widows often value their new freedom from a tiresome domestic routine.

Social ageing, and the associated gendered chronologies of the life course, varies according to birth cohort. Wars, the achievement of women's suffrage, the introduction of the welfare state, advances in reproductive technology, the expansion of women's opportunities in education and employment and so on have been experienced at varying stages in the life course by successive cohorts, affecting social attitudes and expectations as to the female chronology. Thus women born after the Second World War are less likely than their mothers to cease employment at marriage or to be widowed before age 60, but more likely to cohabit, to divorce, to be educated and to expect gender equality in employment and in sharing of domestic tasks.

Some have argued that social age has become more fluid over time and gender roles and chronologies more flexible for later cohorts (Featherstone and Hepworth, 1989; Handy, 1991). The notion of a Third Age of choice and personal growth, interposed between retirement and the onset of frailty (Laslett, 1987), seems to offer opportunities to develop identities which are free from earlier constraints of reproduction or production, with engagement in education, voluntary activities and leisure pursuits. Women may find this a time of liberation: '...when our web of family and work obligations is shrinking, we can seize the opportunity to actualise what we were only able to dream during years of self-denial' (Hen Coop, 1993: 106). However, most women continue to be more occupied than men with domestic and family obligations, especially if they are married, so that they have less 'free' time than men (Bernard and Meade, 1993; Bernard et al, 1995). Laslett's approach neglects structural inequality and the way material and cultural factors influence the experience of life transitions (Bury, 1995). A Third Age of self-development, autonomy and active leisure is less likely for those with low incomes, poor health or caring responsibilities.

Older people's ability to live independently in their own home, and to preserve dignity, self-respect and reciprocity in social relationships, is a major prerequisite for a sense of wellbeing; but a certain level of resources is necessary for independence, especially material resources – income, financial assets, car ownership and good quality housing – and health resources, including mobility and capacity to perform routine tasks of daily living (Arber and Ginn, 1991). Thus wellbeing depends on position in the social hierarchy, a position which varies according to gender as well as class. The way social policy has influenced gender differences in the material and health resources of older people is considered next.

MATERIAL RESOURCES

In most welfare states older women are materially disadvantaged relative to older men (Walker and Maltby, 1997). The extent of inequality depends on the gender ideology shaping welfare policy development (Langan and Ostner, 1991; Lewis,

1992; Ginn and Arber, 1992; 1994a; Orloff, 1993) and in particular on whether women were conceptualised as mothers, workers or citizens (Lister, 1994).

Common concerns for British feminists have been the gender assumptions underlying the social security system introduced in 1948 (Land, 1989; 1994; Lister, 1992; 1994; Lewis, 1992), the consequences for women in later life (Peace, 1986; Groves, 1987; Ginn and Arber, 1994b), and the growing divergence between the prevailing model of the family in the 1940s and the reality of women's lives half a century later.

The Beveridge system of National Insurance (NI) contributions and benefits assumed a gendered division of labour in lifelong marriage, childbearing confined to marriage, and full employment of men. It was not considered necessary to enable women with caring responsibilities to obtain a pension independently of a husband. Instead, older married women were expected to rely on a (reduced) NI pension derived from their husband's contributions and, if widowed, a pension equal to their deceased husband's. Thus obstacles to married women's employment and pension acquisition were 'compensated' by derived benefits.

Even at the time, this means of allocating state pensions was flawed in attaching women's non-contributory entitlements to marriage rather than to caring responsibilities or to citizenship. First, single or divorced women who had cared for children or others for many years would receive very little state pension. Second, derived benefits raise issues of equity (Cuvillier, 1979); married men's contributions cover a couple, irrespective of the wife's childrearing or employment, and married women who are employed most of their life may receive no more state pension than wives who cease employment on marriage. Married women were discouraged from seeking an independent state pension by the 'half-test', whereby *all* their contributions were void unless covering at least half their married life (Groves, 1993), and by the right to pay reduced NI contributions without the pension component. Thus the post-war welfare state served 'to reduce most married women to the status of appendages in the social security scheme' (Joshi and Davies, 1994: 236). The assumption that married women have no need of an independent income because married couples share money equally is challenged by a growing body of evidence (Brannen and Wilson, 1987; Millar and Glendinning, 1989; Vogler, 1989; Pahl, 1983; Davies and Joshi, 1994). Having an independent pension income, instead of sharing a spouse's income, also has implications for personal autonomy.

Beveridge expected men (but apparently not women) to add an occupational pension to the NI pension:

the state...should leave room and encouragement for voluntary action by each individual to provide more than that minimum for *himself and his family.*

Beveridge, 1942: 6–7, author's emphasis

Generous fiscal relief for occupational pensions, with a low state pension, encouraged their expansion (Shragge, 1984; Hannah, 1986), a development largely responsible for gender inequality of income in later life. Designed for middle class men's pattern of employment, occupational pensions translate women's labour market disadvantages into low personal income in later life (Groves, 1987; Ginn and Arber, 1991; 1993).

The gendered effects of the British pension system can be seen from analysis of the 1991 General Household Survey. Among those over 65, men's median personal income was £106 per week, women's only £61 (Arber and Ginn, 1994), a difference due largely to lower income from occupational or personal pensions: 66 per cent of men, but only 37 per cent of women, had a non-state pension (including widows' pensions). Older women's occupational pension income varies markedly according to marital status, single women having the highest average income from this source, comparable with men's, due to longer full time employment. Widows receive much less, even including pensions based on their deceased husband's occupational pension, while married and divorced women receive very low occupational pension income (Ginn and Arber, 1991; 1994b).

Older women are twice as likely as men to have incomes below the poverty level and in 1993–94 three quarters of older people on Income Support (IS) were women (General Household Surveys, 1993 and 1994, authors' analysis). These estimates of poverty exclude the one in five pensioners eligible for means-tested benefit who fail to claim (Atkinson, 1991), and the married women with low personal income who are ineligible for IS due to their husband's income.

The British pension system has undergone many changes since 1948, some affecting gender inequality of income. Women's opportunity to build independent state pensions was significantly advanced by the Social Security Act of 1975. The 'half-test' and reduced contribution option were removed, while Home Responsibilities Protection (HRP) for periods of caring, as well as the new State Earnings Related Pension Scheme (SERPS) based on the best twenty years earnings, minimised the adverse effect of childrearing on state pensions. SERPS was redistributive towards the low paid, providing, with the basic state pension, a maximum replacement rate of 50 per cent for a female full-time manual worker, with lower rates for the higher paid (Groves, 1991). Widows could expect to receive all their husband's SERPS pension.

The advance for women, who rely more heavily than men on state pensions, has been reversed by social security cuts since 1979. Indexing the basic state pension to prices, instead of national average earnings, has eroded its value since 1980 from 20 per cent of average male earnings to 14 per cent by 1993 (Commission on Social Justice, 1994), well below the level of means-tested benefits. The 1986

Social Security Act cut the accrual rate of SERPS, changed the basis of calculating average earnings from the best twenty years to the whole working life and reduced the SERPS widows' pension to half from the year 2000.

These cuts were accompanied by financial incentives to switch from SERPS to personal pensions, which provide poorer value than SERPS for most women and for the low paid (Davies and Ward, 1992; Waine, 1995). Although portable between jobs, personal pensions' charging structure penalises the low paid and those with breaks in employment, reducing the pension by up to 30 per cent (Ward, 1993). The cost of an annuity at retirement is higher for women than men, due to women's longer life expectancy. This practice of applying sex-based actuarial tables is lawful in the UK but not in the US (Allan, 1993).

The Conservative government's pension reforms escalated the public subsidy to private pensions while reducing the NI fund, a process of 'reverse targeting' (Sinfield, 1993: 39). Tax relief for private pensions grew from £1,200 milion in 1979 to £8,200 million in 1991 (Wilkinson, 1993), while the total net cost to the NI fund of incentives to transfer from SERPS to personal pensions was estimated as £6,000 million (1988 prices) from 1988–93 (National Audit Office, 1990). This shift in resources undermines state pensions economically and politically, and in doing so worsens women's pension prospects relative to men's.

Women's lower income in later life is likely to constrain their lives, increasing their dependence on others. Older women are less likely than men to drive or be able to afford to run a car (Arber and Ginn, 1991), limiting their opportunities to travel for leisure, shopping, hospital visits, kinkeeping and social activities, especially if public transport is infrequent and unreliable (Land, 1989). The effect of lack of private transport is exacerbated by the trend to closure of local hospitals and shops, together with privatisation and deregulation of bus services.

For home owners, low income makes it difficult to maintain the home, to purchase aids and adaptations or to move to more suitable accommodation. Low income is detrimental to health through restricting ability to afford heating and an adequate diet.

HEALTH AND ACCESS TO CARE

Most writing on gender issues in relation to health care has centred on reproduction, with debate and campaigning about women's needs for improved access to abortion, fertility treatment and woman-centred obstetric practices (Roberts, 1990). Among older people, gender differences in the need for care arising from medical conditions are related to the different illnesses of older women and men, and to women's greater longevity.

The majority of older people are healthy, living independently in the community. However, a major concern of older people is that they may develop a chronic illness or disability which makes them dependent on others for daily help with domestic tasks or personal care. An even greater fear is the loss of autonomy associated with admission to a residential or nursing home. Although the statutory obligations of the NHS and of local authority social services departments are formally gender-neutral, policy as to the provision of care (whether in the community or in an institution), is more salient for older women than for older men for several reasons.

First, older women are more likely than older men to suffer from chronic illness or functional disability. For example, in 1985 women aged over 65 were twice as likely as men to suffer from disabilities serious enough to require daily help in order to remain living in the community, 14 per cent compared with 7 per cent of men (Arber and Ginn, 1991). The gender difference in disability was confirmed in the 1994 General Household Survey (Bennett et al, 1996). Among those aged over 85, nearly half of women were unable to go out and walk down the road, compared with less than a fifth of men, while 29 per cent of women could not manage stairs compared with less than 10 per cent of men. Inability to carry out personal selfcare, such as bathing and washing unaided, was more common among older women than men. Self assessed health was also slightly poorer for women than men, at all ages over 65 (Arber and Ginn, 1991).

The greater prevalence of chronic illness and disability among women is related to women's higher life expectancy (Manton, 1988). At all levels of disability, older men have higher mortality than older women because their disabilities tend to be associated with life threatening conditions such as heart disease and cancer, while women are more likely to be disabled by less lethal conditions such as diabetes or arthritis (Manton, 1988).

Second, women's greater longevity, combined with the fact that men tend to marry women younger than themselves, means that most married women outlive their husbands. Half of women over 65 are widowed, while nearly three quarters of older men are married. Thus older men are more likely than women to have a spouse to provide help should they need it and to care for them in their last illness, whereas older women more often live alone. Older disabled women are twice as likely as men with a comparable level of disability to live alone – 43 per cent compared with 21 per cent (Arber and Ginn, 1991) – and therefore are more reliant than men on family members and friends or on statutory domiciliary services. For an older person's autonomy and self esteem, spouse care is generally preferable to informal care in a child's home or to state domiciliary services.

Third, having a spouse at home protects the sick or disabled person from admission to institutional care (Arber and Ginn, 1991). In each age group, older people who are married are least likely to live in a communal establishment (Arber and Ginn, 1991; Arber, forthcoming). In 1991, older women were over twice as likely as men to live in a communal establishment, 6.4 per cent compared with 3 per cent (OPCS, 1993). The gender differential in communal residence is most pronounced over age 85, when 26 per cent of women and 15 per cent of men are residents. Because of these gender differences in the need for domiciliary and institutional care, changes since 1948 in the provision and funding of care affect older women more than men.

Since the foundation of the NHS in 1948, a distinction has been made between free (tax funded) health care provided by the NHS and means-tested social care provided by local authority social services departments under the National Assistance Act 1948, although both types of care could be provided either in the community or in a residential setting. For those with chronic illness or disability, including dementia, long stay wards and geriatric hospitals were available within the NHS but local authority residential homes, with means-tested charges, were specified as for 'the elderly infirm', to distinguish their purpose from that of hospitals.

Under the Conservative government since 1979, the thrust of policy was to reduce the role of the state in welfare and to increase private sector provision. This had the effect of shifting the blurred boundary between what was defined as health care and what was deemed social care and, significantly, between free and means-tested care.

The 1980 Social Security Act fuelled the rapid growth of private and voluntary places in residential and nursing homes by allowing charges for those on supplementary pensions to be paid in full by social security. This set up 'perverse incentives': health authorities reduced the number of NHS beds designated for older people by a third between 1976 and 1994 (Harding et al, 1996), while social services departments increasingly recommended entry to residential care where domiciliary services could have enabled a person to remain at home. The costs to social security rose steeply, from £39 million in 1982 to £2,575 million in 1993 (Laing and Buisson, 1995).

From April 1993, the cost of new admissions to institutional care was no longer met by Income Support. Instead, local authorities became responsible for care home fees and for recouping part of the cost through means-tested charges. Under Clause 37 of the Act, the target population group for care in residential homes was changed from 'elderly infirm' to 'elderly ill and disabled', signifying the shunting of the chronically sick and disabled out of the NHS and into means-tested care. At the same time, local authorities were discouraged from direct provision of residential care.

The main effect of these changes has been that older people needing long term care are more likely than in the past to have to pay for long term institutional care which they had expected to be free under the NHS. Local authorities, faced with an insufficient transfer of central funds to meet their new liabilities and with more highly dependent people living in the community than before, have found it necessary to cut domiciliary services.

Older women have suffered particularly acutely from these developments. Older women are more likely than men to need both domiciliary and institutional care, but have less income from which to meet charges. Moreover, until recently, older married women faced a substantial loss of family income if their husband required institutional care, since local authorities were entitled to take the whole of his occupational or personal pension to pay fees. An amendment to the 1995 Pensions Act, achieved after campaigning by pensioners' organisations, improved wives' position somewhat by allowing them to keep half their husband's pension. The reverse situation, where a husband loses income due to his wife's admission to care, is far less likely.

The gender implications of charging the individual for long term care in a residential or nursing home have been generally overlooked. Where a lone older person requires such care, the value of their own home is included, as well as income and savings, in the means test for charges. Since fees ranged, in 1993/4, from £13,000 to £18,000 each year (Netten, 1994), becoming chronically ill can cost a fortune, often requiring sale of the older person's home (Hamnett and Mullings, 1992; Groves, 1995). Home has 'a profound symbolic and personal significance' for older people (Gurney and Means, 1993: 128) and ownership usually represents the result of many years effort justified in part by the expectation of passing on the value to children and grandchildren. The devastating psychological effect of facing (or fearing) loss of their home in this way affects more older women than men, due to their greater longevity and higher chance of needing long term institutional care. Private insurance against long term care costs is unaffordable for the majority of people but especially so for women: Commercial Union in 1991 quoted a single premium insurance policy, purchased at 60, at £22,000 for a man but £41,000 for a woman.

In sum, older women have borne the brunt of the changes in policy towards state welfare over the last two decades. Cuts in state pensions, in public transport, in the NHS and in domiciliary care have disproportionately disadvantaged older women, because of their lesser ability to accumulate material resources of their own, and their greater health care needs due to living longer.

Gender differences in later life: the future

The progress made by women since 1948, in terms of increased education, control of their own fertility and participation in employment, might be expected to diminish gender inequality in later life. For example, while men's time in paid employment occupies a diminishing fraction of the life course (see Chapter 5), women's childbearing has been compressed and their years of employment extended. However, such advances have been accompanied by other trends reinforcing older women's disadvantage and raising new issues of concern. Trends both in social relations and in policy on pensions and health care, especially the privatisation of welfare, are considered.

SOCIAL RELATIONS

Kinship ties, in Victorian times typically the horizontal intragenerational ties of large families and uncertain longevity, have become more commonly vertical, or intergenerational. This change, combined with a reluctance to share accommodation with younger generations, has contributed to an unprecedented rate of solo living in later life (Wall, 1992). Between 1962 and 1986 the proportion of older men living alone increased from 11 per cent to 20 per cent, while for older women solo living rose from 30 per cent to 48 per cent (Arber and Ginn, 1991). The trend to solo living may represent older women's preference, compared with moving to live with children or in a communal setting. It may, however, bring difficulties for them in maintaining and repairing their home, in fears of burglary and attack, in lack of access to private transport, in meeting the costs of utilities on one income and, in the event of illness, lack of readily available informal care. The trend to solo living also has implications for housing policy as discussed in Chapter 4.

Care for older people by family members, mainly daughters, shows no sign of diminishing. Yet, there are tensions between this response to family obligations and the individualistic orientation needed to secure an adequate pension income (see Chapter 8). Women in midlife are the group most likely to provide informal care (Arber and Ginn, 1990) and for some carers this affects their own employment and pension entitlements.

The increase in divorce has implications for future informal care by women for the older generation. Among informal carers, women provide more hours of care than men for parents-in-law as well as for their own parents (Arber and Ginn, 1991). Divorced women, especially if struggling to support children on a single wage, may not feel able to help their own parents, even less their ex-parents-in-law (McGlone and Cronin, 1994).

The link between marriage and childbearing, once very close, is increasingly tenuous. Divorce has replaced widowhood as the main reason for a family's loss of a husband's wage, while widowhood is now typically associated with later life.

The impact of divorce on women's pensions is emerging as an urgent issue and has been the subject of research and campaigning (Joshi and Davies, 1991). Since it is the demands of childcare, more than being female or married, which handicap women in the labour market (Joshi, 1990), the rise in divorce and in motherhood among single or cohabiting women is likely to leave a growing proportion of older women in the future with neither an adequate pension income of their own, nor benefits derived from a husband. Although the Pensions Act 1995 allowed divorce courts to earmark part of an occupational or personal pension for the other spouse, until the pension scheme member decides to draw the pension, usually at age 65, the other spouse cannot receive their share. Pension splitting at divorce, which would transfer funds between spouses, is planned for the future. However, a drawback of both an earmarked pension or funds transferred at divorce is that the amount of pension is likely to reflect the years of marriage rather than the years in which a woman's employment and ability to accumulate pension entitlements is constrained by caring for the children of the marriage. Nor is there provision for sharing non-state pension entitlements between cohabiting partners who separate, even though the pension loss will be no less than for a divorced spouse.

POLICY ON PENSIONS AND HEALTH CARE

The Conservative government, in its project to cut welfare provision, attempted to use demographic change to legitimate this policy, paralleling similar developments in the US. The ageing of populations, due as much to declining fertility as to increased longevity, has been accompanied by doom-laden portrayals of older people as an increasingly unaffordable burden on society through the cost of pensions and health care. Such accounts are ageist, insofar as they scapegoat older people for current and projected economic difficulties which have multiple causes (Minkler, 1991; Street and Quadagno, 1993) and are also sexist. First, the majority of older people are women, especially among those aged over 75; second, the focus is on intergenerational equity in narrow monetary terms, leaving out of the equation the massive donation of unpaid work by women to the younger generation, at the expense of their own earnings and pensions (Joshi, 1990); third, the shifts from state to private welfare, and from redistributive to earnings-related benefits, which are legitimated by these views, are mainly to the detriment of women.

A notable example of this process can be seen in the 1995 Pensions Act, which raises women's state pension age from 60 to 65, phasing in the change from the year 2010. This change was justified by the government as necessary to stem the rise in public expenditure resulting from a declining ratio of workers to pensioners and as reflecting gender equality in employment participation (DSS, 1993). The argument concerning the continued affordability of welfare has been contested

(Hills, 1993), as has the extent of gender equality in opportunity to acquire occupational pension income (Ginn and Arber, 1995a). For women born after 1950, especially if they are unable to work full time from age 60 until age 65, raising the state pension age will reduce the amount of both basic and SERPS pensions (Ginn and Arber, 1995a; Hutton et al, 1995). It has also influenced managers of most occupational pension schemes to equalise the normal pensionable age at 65 rather than 60, worsening women members' benefits.

Raising the pension age for women may appear to promote gender equality and offer opportunities for women to work longer. However, the trend towards earlier exit from the labour market for men may apply also to women. British research on the timing and reasons for retirement and early exit from the labour market was, until recently, mainly concerned with men (for example see Casey, 1992). But, the timing and manner of women's exit from paid work are equally important (Szinovacz, 1982; Arber and Ginn, 1995b). Although an increasing proportion of women are employed in midlife (from 45 to 59), the rate of employment falls from age 50 onwards in each birth cohort from 1897–1901 until 1937–41, the latest for which data is available (Ginn and Arber, 1996a). In 1992 only 23 per cent of women aged 60–64 were employed, most of them part time (CSO, 1994). There are indications that age discrimination by employers contributes to the decline in employment participation with age, after controlling for factors such as educational level, class and household circumstances (Ginn and Arber, 1995b; 1996a).

In spite of formal sex equality and women's increasing employment, the proportion of women contributing to a non-state pension scheme is rising only very slowly. The notorious lack of child care facilities in Britain contributes to a high rate of part time, instead of full time, employment among British women, compared with other countries (Joshi and Davies, 1992). Part time work and low occupational level associated with breaks in employment seriously impair women's ability to acquire good non-state pension entitlements (Ginn and Arber, 1993; 1996b; forthcoming). Thus a substantial gender gap in pension income is likely to persist as long as women shoulder the bulk of society's unpaid caring.

As more people retire with personal pensions in the future, other issues of importance to women, in addition to the poor and uncertain return on contributions, are likely to emerge. The requirement to provide a minimal survivors' benefit applies only to the part of pensions replacing SERPS; contributors to personal pensions may choose not to include this benefit in any additional pension provision, thereby obtaining a larger pension for a given contribution level. Their wives may be unaware of this until they are widowed and find how little they are entitled to as a survivor of the contributor. Women who are contributing to their own personal pension may be unaware, until they retire, of the discriminatory effect of differential annuity prices.

Little is known about the pension income of ethnic minority women, mainly because the numbers of older people from minorities has so far been small. As these minority groups age, the extent of gender inequality of pension income will become evident. It is likely to be much higher among older women of Pakistani or Bangladeshi origin than among those of Afro-Caribbean, Indian or Chinese descent, due to the different patterns of employment followed by women in these groups (Dale and Holdsworth, forthcoming).

The debate on long term care has considered several options for future funding: collective insurance (as in Germany), individual insurance, partnership schemes whereby those with insurance may protect a proportion of their assets from means testing, or maintaining the present lottery in which chronic illness can bring catastrophic loss of assets (Harding et al, 1996). It has also been argued that nursing care for the chronically ill should be funded by the NHS, irrespective of the location of care. This issue, which is likely to become increasingly pressing, is of particular relevance for older women.

Conclusion

Social policies which assumed women's financial dependency in marriage reinforced their financial disadvantage in later life. Yet policies which appear to be evenhanded between women and men are not gender-neutral: equal treatment, by ignoring women's caring roles through the life course, their lower lifetime earnings and greater longevity, leaves older women multiply disadvantaged. Briefly, in the 1970s, legislation on pay, employment rights and pensions gave hope of improving gender equality in later life. However, policy since then appears to have been driven by City financial interests and anticollectivist ideology, to the detriment of older people and especially older women.

If women (and men) who devote time and energy to caring for others are not to be penalised in later life, policy on pensions needs to recognise unpaid work and the constraint it places on employment and earnings. Using resources to restore and improve state pensions, instead of to boost the private pensions industry, would greatly reduce women's financial dependency in later life.

Women's pension disadvantage could be alleviated by redistributive state pensions supported from taxation, as in Denmark, but the trend is in the opposite direction: in Britain and in most other OECD countries, concern at the rising cost of public pensions as the population ages, has prompted governments to consider shifting the balance of pension provision from state to private (OECD, 1988; Johnson et al, 1989; Gillion, 1991). Unless the trend towards privatisation of pensions in the UK is reversed, gender inequality of personal income in later life is likely to increase in the future.

The ageism manifested in frequent references to older people as a burden, and in their stereotyping as socially redundant, is often linked with sexism. Coping with these ageist attitudes, reasserting and valuing their diversity, creativity, resilience and skills in building and maintaining social relationships, compounds the challenge to older women posed by lack of material and health resources. The invisibility of older people's contribution to society – grandparenting, caring for spouses, activity in voluntary organisations, and transfer of resources to the younger generation – parallels the treatment of working age women's unpaid work as nonproductive. There is reason for feminists to make common cause with pensioner organisations in campaigning for a pension and health care system which reduces the disadvantages of women in later life.

References

Allan, H. (1993) 'A question of mortality', *Pensions World*, May: 53–5.

Arber, S. (forthcoming) 'Health, ageing and older women' in Doyal, L., Harrison, L. and Charlwood, P. (eds) *Women and the NHS: a case for change*, Buckingham: Open University Press.

Arber, S. and Ginn, J. (1990) 'The meaning of informal care: gender and the contribution of elderly people', *Ageing and Society*, 10(4): 429–54.

Arber, S. and Ginn, J. (1991) *Gender and Later Life: a sociological analysis of resources and constraints*, London: Sage.

Arber, S. and Ginn, J. (1994) 'Women and Ageing', *Reviews in Clinical Gerontology*, 4(4): 93–102.

Arber, S. and Ginn, J. (eds) (1995a) *Connecting Gender and Ageing: a sociological approach*, Buckingham: Open University Press.

Arber, S. and Ginn, J. (1995b) 'Choice and constraint in the retirement decisions of older married women', chapter 7 in Arber, S. and Ginn, J. (eds) *op cit*.

Atkinson, A. (1991) *The development of state pensions in the United Kingdom*, Welfare State Programme no. 58, London: Suntory Toyota International Centre for Economics and Related Disciplines.

Audit Commission (1986) *Making a Reality of Community Care*, London: HMSO.

Baldwin, S. and Falkingham, J. (eds.) (1994) *Social Security and Social Change: new challenges to the Beveridge model*, Hemel Hempstead: Harvester Wheatsheaf.

Bennett, N. et al (1996) *Living in Britain: results of the 1994 General Household Survey*, OPCS, London: HMSO.

Bernard, M. and Meade, K. (1993) *Women Come of Age*, London: Edward Arnold.

Bernard, M., Itzin, C., Phillipson, C. and Skucha, J. (1995) 'Gendered work, gendered retirement', chapter 5 in S. Arber and J. Ginn (eds) *op. cit*.

Beveridge (1942) *Social Insurance and Allied Services*, Cmnd 6404, London: HMSO.

Binstock, R. (1985) 'The oldest old: a fresh perspective, or compassionate ageism revisited', *Milbank Memorial Fund Quarterly*, 63(2): 420–51.

Brannen, J. and Wilson, G. (eds) (1987) *Give and Take in Families*, London: Allen and Unwin.

Bury, M. (1995) 'Ageing, gender and sociological theory', chapter 2 in S. Arber and J. Ginn (eds) *op. cit.*

Casey, B. (1992) 'Paying for early retirement', *Journal of Social Policy*, 21: 303–23.

CSO (1994) *Social Trends 24*, London: HMSO.

Commission on Social Justice (1994) *Social Justice: strategies for national renewal*, London: Institute for Public Policy Research.

Cumming, E. and Henry, W. (1961) *Growing old: the process of disengagement*, New York: Basic Books.

Cuvillier, F. (1979) 'The housewife: an unjustifiable burden on the community', *Journal of Social Policy*, 8(1): 1–26.

Dale, A. and Holdsworth, C. (forthcoming) 'Why don't black women work part time?', in O'Reilly, J. and Fagan, C. (eds) *Part Time Prospects*, London: Routledge.

Davies, H. and Ward, S. (1992) *Women and Personal Pensions*, London: HMSO.

Davies, H. and Joshi, H. (1994) 'Sex, sharing and the distribution of income', *Journal of Social Policy* 23(3): 301–40.

Department of Social Security (1993) *Equality in State Pension Age*, London: HMSO.

Dowd, J. (1975) 'Aging as exchange: a preface to theory', *Journal of Gerontology*, 30: 584–94.

Estes, C., Swan, J. and Gerard, L. (1982) 'Dominant and competing paradigms in gerontology: towards a political economy of aging', *Ageing and Society*, 2(2): 151–64.

Featherstone, M. and Hepworth, M. (1989) 'Ageing and old age: reflections on the postmodern life course', pp. 143–57 in Bytheway, B., Keil, T., Allatt , P. and Bryman, A. (eds) *Becoming and Being Old: sociological approaches to later life*, London: Sage.

Ford, J. and Sinclair, R. (1987) *Sixty Years On: women talk about old age*, London: Womens Press.

Gee, E. and Kimball, M. (1987) *Women and Aging*, Toronto: Butterworths.

General Household Survey 1993/4 and 1994/5, computer files held at the Manchester Computing Centre.

Gillion, C. (1991) 'Ageing populations: spreading the cost', *Journal of European Social Policy*, 1(2): 107–28.

Ginn, J. and Arber, S. (1991) 'Gender, class and income inequalities in later life', *British Journal of Sociology*, 42(3): 369–96.

Ginn, J. and Arber, S. (1992) 'Towards womens independence: pension systems in three contrasting European welfare states', *Journal of European Social Policy*, 2(4): 255–77.

Ginn, J. and Arber, S. (1993) 'Pension penalties: the gendered division of occupational welfare', *Work Employment and Society*, 7(1): 47–70.

Ginn, J. and Arber, S. (1994a) 'Gender and pensions in Europe: current trends in womens pension acquisition' in Brown, P. and Crompton, R. (eds) *A New Europe: economic restructuring and social exclusion*, London: UCL Press.

Ginn, J. and Arber, S. (1994b) 'Heading for hardship: how the British pension system has failed women', chapter 13 in Baldwin, S. and Falkingham, J. (eds) *op. cit.*

Ginn, J. and Arber, S. (1995a) 'Moving the goalposts: the impact on British women of raising their state pension age to 65', chapter 11 in Baldock, J. and May, M. (eds) *Social Policy Review No. 7*, London: Social Policy Association.

Ginn, J. and Arber, S. (1995b) 'Exploring mid-life womens employment', *Sociology*, 29(1): 1–22.

Ginn, J. and Arber, S. (1996a) 'Age, gender and attitudes to reirement in mid-life', *Ageing and Society*, 16: 27–55.

Ginn, J. and Arber, S. (1996b) Patterns of employment, pensions and gender: the effect of work history on older women's non-state pensions, *Work Employment and Society*, 10(3): 469–90.

Ginn, J. and Arber, S. (forthcoming) 'How does part time work lead to low pensions?' chapter in O'Reilly, J. and Fagan, C. (eds) *op. cit.*

Goldthorpe, J., Lockwood, D., Bechhofer, F. and Platt, J. (1969) *The Affluent Worker in the Class Structure*, London: Cambridge University Press.

Groves, D. (1983) 'Members and survivors: women and retirement pensions legislation' in Lewis, J. (ed.) *Women's Welfare, Women's Rights*, London: Croom Helm.

Groves, D. (1987) 'Occupational pension provision and women's poverty in old age', pp. 199–217 in Glendinning, C. and Millar, J. (eds) *Women and Poverty in Britain*, Brighton: Wheatsheaf.

Groves, D. (1991) 'Women and financial provision for old age', pp. 38–60 in Maclean, M. and Groves, D. (eds) *Women's Issues in Social Policy*, London: Routledge.

Groves, D. (1993) 'Work, poverty and older women', pp. 43–62 in Bernard, M. and Meade, K. (eds) *op. cit.*

Groves, D. (1995) 'Costing a fortune? Pensioners' financial resoources in the context of community care', pp. 141–62 in Allen, I. and Perkins, E. (eds) *The Future of Family Care for Older People*, London: HMSO.

Gurney, G. and Means, R. (1993) 'The meaning of home in later life' in Arber, S. and Evandrou, M. (eds), *Ageing, Independence and the Life Course*, London: Jessica Kingsley, pp. 119–31.

Hamnett, C. and Mullings, B. (1992) 'A new consumption cleavage? The case of residential care for the elderly', *Environment and Planning*, 24: 807–20.

Hannah (1986) *Inventing Retirement: the development of occupational pensions in Britain*, Cambridge: Cambridge University Press.

Handy, C. (1991) *The Age of Unreason*, London: Century Business.

Harding, T., Meredith, B. and Wistow, G. (eds) (1996) *Options for Long Term Care: economic, social and ethical choices*, London: HMSO.

Havighurst, R. (1954) 'Flexibility and the social roles of the retired', *American Journal of Sociology*, 59: 309–11.

Hen Co-op (1993) *Growing Old Disgracefully*, London: Piatkus.

Hills, J. (1993) *The Future of Welfare: a guide to the debate*, York: Joseph Rowntree Foundation.

Hutton, S., Kennedy, S. and Whiteford, P. (1995) *Equalisation of State Pension Ages: the gender impact*, Manchester: Equal Opportunities Commission.

Itzin, C. (1990) Age and sexual divisions: a study of opportunity and identity in women, unpublished PhD thesis, University of Kent.

Johnson, P., Conrad, C. and Thomson, D. (1989) *Workers versus Pensioners: intergenerational conflict in an ageing world*, Manchester: Manchester University Press.

Joshi, H. (1990) 'The cash opportunity cost of childbearing: an approach to estimation using British evidence', *Population Studies*, 44, March: 41–60.

Joshi, H. and Davies, H. (1991) *The Pension Consequences of Divorce*, CEPR Discussion Paper 550, London: Centre for Economic Policy.

Joshi, H. and Davies, H. (1992) *Childcare and Mothers' Lifetime Earnings: some European contrasts*, CEPR Discussion Paper 600, London: Centre for Economic Policy.

Joshi, H. and Davies, H. (1994) 'The paid and unpaid roles of women: how should social security adapt?' pp. 235–54 in Baldwin, S. and Falkingham, J. (eds.) *op. cit.*

Kart, C. (1987) 'The end of conventional gerontology', *Sociology of Health and Illness*, 9(1): 76–87.

Kohli, M. (1988) 'Ageing as a challenge for sociological theory', *Ageing and Society*, 8(4): 367–94.

Laing and Buisson (1995) *Care of Elderly People: a market survey*, London: Laing and Buisson.

Land, H. (1989) 'The construction of dependency', pp. 141–59 in Bulmer, M., Lewis, J. and Piachaud, D. (eds) *The Goals of Social Policy*, London: Unwin Hyman.

Land, H. (1994) 'The demise of the male breadwinner – in practice but not in theory: a challenge for social security systems', chapter 6 in Baldwin, S. and Falkingham, J. (eds.) *op. cit.*

Langan, M. and Ostner, I. (1991) 'Gender and welfare' in Room, G. (ed) *Towards a European Welfare State?*, Bristol: School for Advanced Urban Studies.

Laslett, P. (1987) 'The emergence of the Third Age', *Ageing and Society*, 7(2): 133–60.

Lewis, J. (1992) 'Gender and the development of welfare regimes', *Journal of European Social Policy*, 2(3): 159–73.

Lister, R. (1992) *Women's Economic Dependency and Social Security*, Manchester: Equal Opportunities Commission.

Lister, R. (1994) '"She has other duties" – Women, citizenship and social security', pp. 31–44 in Baldwin, S. and Falkingham, J. (eds) *op. cit.*

McDaniel, S. (1989) 'Women and ageing: a sociological perspective', *Journal of Women and Ageing*, 1: 47–67.

Macdonald, B. and Rich, C. (1984) *Look Me in the Eye: old women, ageing and ageism*, San Francisco: Spinsters Ink.

McGlone, F. and Cronin, N. (1994) *A Crisis in Care? The future of family and state care for older people in the European Union*, London: CPA/Family Policy Studies Centre.

McMullin, J. (1995) 'Theorizing age and gender relations', chapter 3 in Arber, S. and Ginn, J. (eds) *op. cit.*

Manton, K. (1988) 'A longitudinal study of functional change and mortality in the United States', *Journal of Gerontology*, 43(5): 153–61.

Millar, J. and Glendinning, C. (1989) 'Gender and poverty', *Journal of Social Policy*, 18(3): 363–81.

Minkler, M. (1991) 'Generational equity and the new victim blaming' in Minkler, M. and Estes, C. (eds) *Critical Perspectives on Gerontology: the political and moral economy of growing old*, New York: Baywood.

Minkler, M. and Stone, R. (1985) 'The feminization of poverty and older women', *The Gerontologist*, 25(4): 351–7.

National Audit Office (1990) *The Elderly: information requirements for supporting the elderly and implications of personal pensions for the National Insurance Fund*, London: HMSO.

Netten, A. (1994) *Unit Costs of Community Care 1994*, PSSRU, Canterbury: University of Kent.

OECD (1988) *Reforming Public Pensions*, Social Policy Studies No. 5, Paris: OECD.

Olson, L. (1982) *The Political Economy of Aging*, New York: Columbia University Press.

Olson, L. (1985) 'Older women: longevity, dependency and public policy', pp. 157–75 in Sapiro, V. (ed) *Women, Biology and Public Policy*, London: Sage.

OPCS (1993) *Communal Establishments*, 1991 Census, London: HMSO.

Orloff, S. (1993) 'Gender and the social rights of citizenship: the comparative analysis of gender relations and the welfare state', *American Sociological Review*, 58(3): 303–28.

Pahl, J. (1983) 'The allocation of money and structuring of inequality within marriage', *Sociological Review*, 13(2): 237–62.

Peace, S. (1986) 'The forgotten female: social policy and older women', pp. 61–86 in Phillipson, C. and Walker, A. (eds.) *Ageing and Social Policy: a critical assessment*, Aldershot: Gower.

Phillipson, C. (1982) *Capitalism and the Construction of Old Age*, London: Macmillan.

Quadagno, J. (1988) 'Womens access to pensions and the structure of eligibility rules: Systems of production and reproduction', *The Sociological Quarterly*, 29: 541–58.

Reinharz, S. (1986) 'Friends or foes: gerontological and feminist theory', *Women's Studies International Forum*, 9(5): 503–14.

Riley, M. (1971) 'Social gerontology and the age stratification of society', *The Gerontologist*, 11: 79–87.

Roberts, H. (1990) *Womens Health Counts*, London: Routledge.

Rose, H. and Bruce, E. (1995) 'Mutual care but differential esteem: caring between older couples', chapter 9 in Arber, S. and Ginn, J. (eds) *op. cit.*

Rossi, A. (1986) 'Sex and gender in an ageing society', *Daedalus*, 115: 141–69.

Shragge, E. (1984) *Pensions Policy in Britain: a socialist analysis*, London: Routledge and Kegan Paul.

Sinfield, A. (1993) 'Reverse targetting and upside down benefits – how perverse policies perpetuate poverty', pp. 39–48 in Sinfield, A. (ed.) *Poverty, Inequality and Justice*, Edinburgh: Edinburgh University Press.

Sinnott, J. (1977) 'Sex role inconstancy, biology and successful aging', *The Gerontologist*, 17: 459–63.

Sontag, S. (1978) 'The double standard of aging', in Carver, V. and Liddiard, P. (eds) *An Ageing Population*, London: Hodder and Stoughton.

Stacey, J. and Thorne, B. (1985) 'The missing feminist revolution in sociology', *Social Problems*, 32(4): 311.

Street, D. and Quadagno, J. (1993) 'The state, the elderly and the intergenerational contract', pp. 130–50 in Warner, K. and Achenbaum, A. (eds) *Societal Impact on Aging: historical perspectives*, New York: Springer Publishing Co.

Szinovacz, M. (ed) (1982) *Women's Retirement: policy implications of recent research*, Beverly Hills: Sage.

Vogler, C. (1989) *Labour Market Change and Patterns of Financial Allocation Within Households*, SCELI Working Paper No. 12, Oxford: Nuffield College.

Waine, B. (1995) 'A disaster foretold? The case of the personal pension', *Social Policy and Administration*, 29(4): 317–34.

Walker, A. (1980) 'The social creation of poverty and dependency in old age', *Journal of Social Policy*, 9(1): 49–75.

Walker, A. (1981) 'Towards a political economy of old age', *Ageing and Society*, 1(1): 73–94.

Walker, A. and Maltby, T. (1997) *Ageing Europe*, Buckingham: Open University Press.

Wall, R. (1992) 'Relationships between the generations in British families past and present', chapter 4 in Marsh, C. and Arber, S. (eds) *Families and Households: Divisions and Change*, Basingstoke: Macmillan.

Ward, P. (1993) *The Great British Pensions Robbery*, Preston: Waterfall Books.

Wilkinson, M. (1993) 'British tax policy 1979–90: Equity and efficiency', *Policy and Politics*, 21(3): 207–17.

Wilson, G. (1995) 'Im the eyes and shes the arms: changes in gender roles in advanced old age', chapter 8 in Arber, S. and Ginn, J. (eds) *op. cit.*

10 Ageing in a multi-racial Britain: demography, policy and practice

Karl Atkin

The acuteness of the isolation of those who by reason of language, skin colour or religious beliefs find themselves unable to gain access to treatment, support and care does justify the title of this report. They are not merely in double jeopardy by reason of age and discrimination, as has often been stated, but in triple jeopardy, at risk because they are old, because of the physical conditions and hostility under which they have to live, and because services are not accessible to them... But although much has been said, very little has been done to remedy the situation.

Alison Norman (1985) Triple Jeopardy: growing old in a second homeland, CPA, pp. 1-2

Introduction

Rises in living standards and advances in health care have meant that Western European societies now have a larger proportion of people over sixty than ever before. An increasing proportion of these older people belong to minority ethnic groups[1] and unlike North America, this is a new phenomenon for many European countries (Castles and Kosack, 1985). The needs of these older people, however, are not high on either the research or policy agenda. The UK literature on ageing, for example, largely ignores the experience of ethnic minorities, while the mainstream 'race' literature neglects the difficulties facing older people. UK government policy similarly focuses on either *older people or people from ethnic minorities*, but rarely concerns itself with *older people from ethnic minorities*. Consequently, little is known about the relationship between these older people and health and social care provision, and even less about the social meaning of ageing for different ethnic minority groups (Blakemore and Boneham, 1994).

This chapter, by reviewing a mix of empirical studies and theoretical debates, explores the experience of ageing in a multi-racial Britain[2] and introduces conceptual tools, of use to social gerontology, designed to understand race and ethnicity. In doing so, the chapter is in four parts. First, it outlines the demographic profile of Britain's ethnic minority populations and discusses the relevance of this data to policy and practice. Second, the chapter goes on to investigate the experience and meaning of ageing for different ethnic groups. Third, the chapter evaluates the relationship between minority ethnic groups and health and social care agencies. Finally, the chapter concludes by exploring current theoretical debates about 'race' and ethnicity, and considers their relevance to the experience of older people from ethnic minorities.

Minority ethnic populations in Great Britain: a demographic profile

Next to economic factors, demographic changes are powerful influences on the formulation and successful implementation of social policy. However, before presenting the available demographic material on Britain's minority ethnic communities it is necessary to discuss the terminology employed in the available statistics. 'Race', as an analytical category based on notions of biologically distinct stocks of humanity, has been discredited and abandoned by biological and social scientists alike. 'Ethnicity', defined with reference to shared identity, culture, language and religion has taken its place. The concept of ethnicity is dynamic, recognising that one's identity is dependent on both historical and situational factors. Ethnicity, however, does not lend itself to being used as a rigid, externally defined 'administrative category and attempts to do so have been criticised for conceptual confusion' (Ahmad and Sheldon, 1993: 130). This conceptual confusion is especially evident in the categories employed in the 1991 Census. Here a ten-fold classification was used: white, black Caribbean, black African, black other, Indian, Pakistani, Bangladeshi, Chinese, other Asian and other. These categories are based on a mixture of colour (black, white), nationality (Indian, Bangladeshi, Pakistani, Chinese) and geographical origin (African, Asian and Caribbean). Nonetheless, many remain convinced of the importance of ethnic data as a political tool for resisting racism and racial discrimination (Anwar, 1990).

Despite the limitations of demographic statistics, they still represent a useful starting point in exploring ageing in a multi-racial Britain. As we shall see, such data illustrate general differences between minority ethnic groups and the majority population, as well as the diversity of minority ethnic groups living in the UK. The data also raise particular challenges to those planning, organising and delivering welfare services. Within this context, four general factors assume particular significance: age, gender, disability and ill health, and geographical distribution. Other more specific demographic influences, such as family structure, are considered later in the chapter, within the wider context of myths and assumptions about the availability of family caregiving in minority ethnic communities.

First, minority groups are, on average, younger than the white populations (Owen, 1993). Less than 20 per cent are aged over 45 and 3 per cent are over 65.

The comparative figures for the white population are 22 per cent and 17 per cent respectively. There are also differences in the age structure of the various ethnic minority groups, resulting from the patterns of migration from the respective countries of origin. Bangladeshi and Pakistani communities, for instance, are generally younger than Indian and Afro-Caribbean people. Fourteen per cent of Pakistani and Bangladeshi people are over 45. By comparison 30 per cent of the Black-Caribbeans are aged 45 or over. The proportion of older people from ethnic minorities, although small compared to white populations, is growing. Comparing different age cohorts between the 1981 and 1991 census suggests that the largest percentage growth for ethnic minority groups had been in those people over personable age: 167 per cent (Butt and Mirza, 1996). More generally, demographic trends indicate an imminent steep growth in the numbers of older people of Afro-Caribbean and Asian (especially of Indian origin) descent over the next ten years. Potentially this could put increasing pressure on the responsibilities of health and social care agencies. Such figures also suggest that the numbers of minority ethnic older people can no longer be dismissed as being too small to cause concern for welfare provision.

Second, gender differences are thought to affect those who need care, as well as those who take on the responsibility of family care (Parker, 1992) (see Chapters 8 and 9). At present there are significant gender differences both between the white and minority ethnic groups and within the various minority ethnic groups (Owen, 1993). Fifty-one per cent of the white population is female compared with 49 per cent within minority ethnic groups. Within the minority ethnic groups, the lowest ratio of males to females is displayed among Black-Caribbeans (949 males per 1,000 females). This figure is similar to the white population. Among South Asians there is an excess of males over females (1,013 males per 1,000 females). This is most striking among the Bangladeshi group where the male to female ration is 109: 100. For both Black-Caribbean groups and South Asian groups, the excess of males over females is greatest among those over 65 (Owen, 1993). It is difficult to know the full implications of these gender imbalances because so little is known about the organisation of care among Asian and Afro-Caribbean families (Atkin and Rollings, 1993). For the white population it is assumed that females provide the bulk of care for older or disabled relatives (Parker and Lawton, 1994). A smaller number of females, therefore, would reduce the potential population of carers. On the other side of the equation, older women are more likely to be disabled or suffer a longer standing illness than older men. A growing population of older women, by definition implies a growing population of people who potentially need care (Parker, 1992). Again it is difficult to assess the impact of this proposition for older people from ethnic minorities because so little is known about disability and chronic illness among such populations.

Third, the incidence of disability amongst older minority ethnic communities obviously affects those who are likely to need care: either from family members or from health and social care agencies. Publications of findings from a national survey of impairment have produced a supposedly comprehensive picture of the incidence and nature of disability and long standing illness in Great Britain (OPCS, 1988; Owen, 1993). There are, however, few studies describing the extent, nature or experience of disability or chronic illness among older people from ethnic minorities (May, 1983: McAvoy and Donaldson, 1990). The number of surveys assessing the incidence of disability among minority ethnic groups, however, is slowly growing (RADAR, 1984; Farrah, 1986; GLAD, 1987). Here is also a growing body of work on specific conditions, such as cardiovascular disease, stroke, diabetes and mental health problems among ethnic minorities (NHS Centre for Reviews and Dissemination, 1996). Despite this interest, significant areas of neglect remain. There is still little material, for example, on the prevalence, nature and experience of mental infirmity among older people.

Another dimension to this debate is whether the incidence of disability is greater among older ethnic minorities in comparison to the general population. Although some local studies support this view (Bhalla and Blakemore, 1981; Donaldson and Odell, 1986; Farrah 1986; Moledina, 1988), data from the national OPCS survey of physical disability (1988), showed that, when standardised for age, the prevalence of disability amongst Afro-Caribbean and Asian people, compared with those of the white population, was roughly the same. More recent data from the 1991 census suggest that people identifying themselves as Black Caribbean, Pakistani, Indian and Bangladeshi have a slightly higher incidence of long standing illness than white groups (Owen, 1993), and this relationship between ethnicity and long standing illness becomes more pronounced with age (Charlton et al, 1994). There are, however, important differences among different ethnic groups. For example, the rates of limiting long term illness were lowest for Chinese men and women and highest for Bangladeshi men and Pakistani women (Charlton et al, 1994). More generally, the incidence of disability and chronic illness across ethnic groups and its relationship with age remains an area of interesting debate where more information is required.

Finally, the distribution of Britain's ethnic minorities is fundamental to planning health and social care services: areas with high numbers of people from ethnic minorities raise different planning and service delivery issues from those areas with low numbers of minority ethnic groups (cf. Young, 1990). People from ethnic minorities are clustered in certain parts of Britain. These are usually concentrated in the larger industrial areas of Britain. Greater London, for example, contains 45 per cent of the total minority ethnic population, with the West Midlands accounting for 14 per cent (Owen, 1993). For the most part, minority ethnic communities continue to live in areas with higher than average numbers of minority ethnic people. This applies to both young and old, although there is some evidence that younger people are moving into the suburbs. Older people, on the other hand, tend to remain living in inner city wards, where service provision is most under-resourced (Butt and Mirza, 1996). Nonetheless, there are few areas in Britain where ethnic minorities do not have a presence. Even where the numbers are small, there may still be a need for service support. These groups are, however, more likely to be invisible to welfare services. This disadvantages the smaller black communities, such as Somalis (cf. Torkington, 1991) or those widely dispersed groups such as Chinese communities (cf. Liebberman and Shun Au, 1988; Haskey, 1994).

The meaning and experience of old age

There are a small number of other minority communities who have a long history of settlement in Britain. Cardiff, Liverpool and East London, for example, have long standing ethnic minority settlements (Blakemore and Boneham, 1994). Most older minority ethnic people, however, entered the UK in the 1950s and 1960s. This was in response to labour shortages which threatened the continued growth of the British economy (Patel, 1990). Other significant minority groups include refugees, such as East African Asians, who were forced to leave their homes in the early 1970s, or Vietnamese who entered the UK during the 1980s; and older parents joining families who have settled in Britain (Butt and Murza, 1996). These different patterns of migration are a further reminder that older people from ethnic minorities are not a homogenous group.

There is, therefore, considerable diversity in terms of social history, individual life history and current circumstances among Britain's ethnic minority populations. This diversity is further reflected in minorities' use of cultural resources, as they adapt to growing old in another land. To this extent, the process of growing old is not uniform and is a continuation of individual life patterns (Fennel et al, 1988). Further, one generation's experience of old age is likely to be different from succeeding generations. Older people from ethnic minorities, therefore, are not a static entity and recognising ethnic differences is fundamental to thorough understanding of the lives of older minority ethnic people. Differences, for example, occur in the patterning of gender and domestic roles, in health, and in social activities, expectations of old age as well as social disadvantage (cf. Blakemore and Boneham, 1994[3]).

More generally, much current work attempting to describe the situation and experience of minority ethnic older people uses the idea, first developed in North America, of 'double jeopardy' (cf. National Urban League, 1964). 'Double jeopardy' suggests that minority ethnic older people suffer the cumulative disadvantage of racial discrimination as well as the more general risks associated with old age (Williams, 1989). In Britain the term has been taken up and extended to one of triple jeopardy (Norman, 1985), and adds the concern that minority ethnic older people's needs are not being met by health and social care agencies. Considerable evidence demonstrates the disadvantages and inequalities faced by older people from ethnic minorities, which seems to give some credence to the idea of either 'double' or 'triple jeopardy'. It is to this evidence we now turn.

In some respects, black and white people have similar expectations of old age. Both see it as a time of restricted activity, poor mobility and increased dependency (Cameron et al, 1989). The disadvantages faced by minority ethnic older people also appear similar to those experienced by white older people. Most old people, be they black or white, face similar patterns of disadvantage including poor housing, poverty, low income, and social isolation (cf. Phillipson, 1982; Blakemore and Boneham, 1994). Minority ethnic older people, however, are further disadvantaged. Evidence on racial inequalities in income and housing, for example, is overwhelming (Skellington and Morris, 1992). Though far from homogenous, the average income of Asian (particularly Pakistani and Bangladeshi) and Afro-Caribbean older people living in the UK is well below that of 'white' older people. A recent study found that most Afro-Caribbean and Asian older people maintain themselves either on the level of income support rights or below the poverty level (Jadeja and Singh, 1993). For instance, this research reported a difference of £29.10 a week between the income of white older people (£88.20) and Asian older people (£59.10).

The financial position of minority ethnic old people is often linked to the nature of immigration into Britain. As a consequence of recent arrival, people from ethnic minorities are often ineligible for full state pensions and few have occupational pensions (Butt and Mirza, 1996). For instance, only 14 per cent of Afro-Caribbean and Asian older people had access to occupational or state pensions, compared to 98 per cent of the white older population (Jadeja and Singh, 1993). Consequently, a greater proportion of minority ethnic older people derive some or all of their income from means-tested benefits: 86 per cent of minority ethnic older people relied on income support compared to 25 per cent of white older people (Jadeja and Singh, 1993). Another financial problem facing some older people is a lack of entitlement to state benefits. Older people who have entered the country to live with their family members, are denied access to benefits and have to rely on the 'sponsorship' of their family. This can, of course, increase the likelihood that the older person and the family they live with, experience poverty.

Housing suggests further inequalities. Older minority ethnic communities are more likely to be in older, un-modernised, inner city housing which is damp and draughty, as well as lacking central heating and other household amenities such as washing machines (Skellington and Morris, 1992; Owen, 1993). Moreover, although a significant number of older people from ethnic minorities are owner occupiers (particularly older people from South Asia), they still represent a smaller proportion than their white counterparts (Butt and Mirza, 1996). As we know, home ownership is an increasingly valuable resource in old age (Oldman, 1990). Minority ethnic people, however, either do not own their homes or own the worst type of accommodation. This severely limits the wealth minority ethnic people can draw upon.

Evidence also suggests that minority ethnic old people experience greater social isolation than white older people. Many older Asian people, for example, cannot speak English and may be afraid to leave their homes because of the possibilities of racist attacks (Cameron et al, 1989). Older minority ethnic people may also have to accommodate changing family structures that question their own assumptions and expectations about old age. This has led some authors to suggest that many older people from ethnic minorities experience psychological jeopardy, as their expectations of old age are not met (Chauhan, 1989). This can result in shock, disappointment and loss (Berry et al, 1981; Barker, 1984; Moledina, 1988). Fenton (1987) described 'inescapable tensions' of some older Asian people who found it difficult to comprehend changes that had occurred in the attitudes and life styles of their sons and daughters. More generally, Cameron et al (1989: 237) observed the 'conflicting expectations of different generations of Asian and Afro-Caribbean people, and the role conflict that results'.

This evidence, therefore, would seem to support the idea of 'double jeopardy'. Nonetheless, several commentators have questioned its value in fully explaining the experience of minority ethnic people (Blakemore and Boneham, 1994). While the concept of double jeopardy is useful because it focuses on the various sources of discrimination, the idea is often used to convey distinct and separate forms of discrimination that can be added together in a mechanical way (*cf.* Stuart, 1993). The experience of discrimination, however, rarely differentiates between age or race (Butt and Mirza, 1996) and, as we shall see, a more sophisticated understanding is required. To this extent 'double jeopardy' is too simplistic and does not adequately reflect the reality of most people's lives.

Other problems also occur. By focusing on disadvantage there is a danger that double jeopardy encourages a 'victim oriented' perspective. This has two consequences. First, it portrays old age as a wholly negative experience. To counter some of these difficulties, the North American and Australian literature has begun to focus on the coping strengths of older people, particularly in the face of neglect, hardship and disadvantage (cf. Rowland, 1991; Coke and Twaite, 1995). Such an approach does not belittle the considerable disadvantages facing older people from minority groups, nor does it overstate their coping ability. It does, however, attempt to provide a more balanced account of old age and examine the strengths of specific ethnic groups. Secondly, and more specifically, the 'victim oriented' approach seems to advocate a paternalist solution to the problems faced by minority ethnic older people, while neglecting the possibility of empowerment. Minority ethnic older people are not simply passive victims of racism and disadvantage; they are active agents.

Health and social care agencies

Old age does not necessitate the need for service support. Nonetheless we do know that older people – from all ethnic groups – are more likely to have contact with health and social care agencies than any other age group (Parker, 1992). Older people from ethnic minority groups, however, face particular disadvantages resulting from inadequate and inappropriate provision, which means that their needs are not being adequately met by welfare agencies. Much of the literature, for example, demonstrates a lack of knowledge and under use of health and social services by minority ethnic older people, irrespective of age and disability (Atkin and Rollings, 1993). Lewando-Hundt and Holland (1987), for example, reported that 50 per cent of their Asian and Afro-Caribbean sample had heard of none of the social services listed. Knowledge of health services appears even poorer (Atkin et al, 1989). The under use of community services among minority ethnic older people is equally well documented (cf. Atkin and Rollings, 1993). A survey in Birmingham, for example, found that approximately 7 per cent of service users were Asian or Afro-Caribbean, although population statistics show that in the two wards covered in the survey, 50 per cent of the population lived in households where the head was born in the New Commonwealth or Pakistan (Cameron et al, 1989).

More generally empirical evidence suggests that health and social care providers experience considerable difficulties in recognising and responding to the needs of older people from ethnic minorities (Dominelli, 1989; Atkin and Rollings, 1993; Walker and Ahmad, 1994; Butt, 1994). Three key issues emerge in explaining these difficulties: structural barriers to service delivery; the neglect and misrepresentation of the needs of older people from ethnic minorities; and racism on the part of front line practitioners.[4] It is to these we now turn.

STRUCTURAL BARRIERS AND RACISM

Welfare provision's inability to recognise the structural barriers to provision facing older minority ethnic people is manifest in assumptions such as *same service to all*, irrespective of needs, equates with *equal service to all*. Consequently, services are organised according to a 'white-norm' and do not recognise difference and diversity; assuming their policies, procedures and practices are equally appropriate for everyone (Atkin and Rollings, 1993; Blakemore and Boneham, 1994). Equitable access to welfare services, in effect, presumes that the recipient is white, literate and fluent in English (Ahmad and Husband, 1993) Such practices legitimate non-recognition of the community care needs of minority ethnic communities and disregard the dietary, linguistic and caring needs of minority ethnic communities (Atkin, 1996). Straightforward examples include the inability of health and social services to provide support for people who do not speak English or, more specifically, the unavailability of vegetarian food or halal meat in day care and domiciliary services. Health and social care agencies are particularly ill-prepared to meet the needs of those who are not fluent in English – which is the majority of older Asian people. Empirical evidence suggests that the onus is often on the older person to provide an interpreter, usually from another family member (Ahmad and Walker, 1996).

Further, assuming everyone has equal access to services privileges the white population by ignoring the obstacles faced by minority ethnic people in gaining access to services (NAHA, 1988). Minority ethnic older people do not have the same opportunities as the white population; they experience greater disadvantage and suffer more barriers to service receipt (Glendenning and Pearson, 1988). As we have seen racial inequalities and poverty disadvantage minority ethnic people and create additional needs for support. Providing an equal service for all ignores the consequences of this (Atkin, 1996).

MISREPRESENTATION OF HEALTH AND SOCIAL CARE NEEDS OF MINORITY ETHNIC GROUPS

The second manifestation of institutional racism is the misrepresentation of the needs of ethnic minorities. Misrepresentation of needs can occur either through organisational practices or through the use of cultural stereotypes and myths. For example, to accommodate 'cultural difference', health and social services often establish 'specialist provision'. The idea of 'special provision' in welfare services has a long history and represents the most popular means by which mainstream services feel they are implementing equal opportunity policies (Butt, 1994).

Specialist provision is seen as particularly valuable for minority ethnic older people (Walker and Ahmad, 1994). However, the existence of 'special provision', although often beneficial, does not necessarily imply that the needs of minority ethnic people are being adequately met (Patel, 1990).

Separate provision, for instance, is too often a euphemism for short-term, inadequately funded and marginal provision (Butt, 1994). Further, mainstream services often use the existence of specialist services to absolve themselves of any responsibility for the health and social care needs of ethnic minorities. By pointing to this 'special provision' statutory provision has remained relatively static and inaccessible (Atkin and Rollings, 1993). Establishing 'special provision' has led to internal divisions within the minority ethnic communities, with groups competing with each other on the basis of 'culturally distinctive needs'. More conceptually, the use of the term 'special' to describe provision to minority ethnic older people, implies their needs are somewhat unusual. Minority ethnic people, although sometimes having different needs from the majority white population, do not necessarily have 'special needs'. To consider they do implies that a minority's 'distinctiveness' is a 'problem' requiring a 'special' response. As we have seen, older people from minority ethnic groups often experience similar difficulties to those faced by the majority white population. 'Special' classification, however, segregates minority ethnic people from the general debate about health and social care for older people, isolating them from the mainstream discussion.

Beside these organisational practices, minority ethnic groups also have to contend with inappropriate generalisations of cultural practices and the use of simplistic socio-cultural explanations to explain their behaviour. This further misrepresents their needs. Introductory notes on minority ethnic communities, present in most training material for service practitioners, often follow this pattern. A text on community nursing demonstrates the shortcomings of this approach (Karseras and Hopkins, 1987: 121). The authors suggest that, although health professionals dislike *being authoritarian and aim for reasoned persuasion*, Asian women do prefer *a blunter response* and are *not offended by imperatives*. Generally neat cultural packages, identifying key characteristics of minority ethnic older people, do not solve the problems facing health and social care services and are likely to perpetuate and reinforce cultural stereotypes and myths.

A particular spurious myth, evident in the activities of welfare services, is the assumption that Asian people, and to a lesser extent Afro-Caribbean people, live in self-supporting families. This is often used as an excuse for not making necessary changes to the existing services or expanding the level of service provision to meet the needs of ethnic minorities (Atkin and Rollings, 1993; Walker and Ahmad, 1994). This is despite substantial evidence suggesting this view of the extended family is unjustified because it does not take into account the process of immigration, as well as ignoring the diversity among ethnic minority groups.

The extended African-Caribbean family has always been rare in the UK, and a third of Afro-Caribbean people live alone (Baxter, 1988). Further, a survey in Leicester suggests that 40 per cent of Afro-Caribbean people do not have frequent family contact (Farrah, 1986). Consequently many Afro-Caribbean people are not only isolated in a household sense, but do not have frequent family support (Eribo, 1991). The extended family is more common among Asian families (Butt and Mirza, 1996). Nonetheless there are still a significant proportion of Asian people who live alone, with few relatives in this country (Fenton, 1987). In addition, economic and demographic factors – such as appropriate housing and occupation mobility – may influence the willingness and ability of Asian families to provide care, thus making the extended family less prevalent (Owen, 1993). This would have important implications for older people. There is already considerable variation between the generally larger Bangladeshi and Pakistani households and the smaller Sikh and Hindu households (Owen, 1993). This is accompanied by challenges to marriage patterns both internally and by immigration rules (Fenton, 1987). More importantly, however, it is questionable whether living in an extended family should be used as a justification for not providing service support (Butt and Mirza, 1996). The general belief is that the extended family has the material and emotional resources to meet the needs of family members, and that intervention or support from community service can lead to neglect by default (Atkin and Rollings, 1993).

RACISM AND FRONT LINE PRACTITIONERS

These attitudes of front line practitioners can deprive older people from minority ethnic communities of their rights to services, especially since health and social service professionals exercise considerable discretion in their day-to-day work (Lipsky, 1981). Racist attitudes on the part of service practitioners, although not distinct from the forms of racism discussed above, have been reported in a number of studies in health and social services (Atkin et al, 1989; Ahmad et al, 1989; Bowler, 1993). For example, practitioners working in local authorities often list minority ethnic people as 'high risk' clients, 'uncooperative' and 'difficult to work with' (Dominelli, 1989; Cameron et al, 1989; Atkin and Rollings, 1993). Similarly, evidence suggests that racism within the NHS affects virtually all ethnic minorities with common stereotypes portraying minority ethnic people as 'calling out doctors unnecessarily', 'being trivial complainers', and 'time wasters' (Glendenning and Pearson, 1988; Ahmad et al, 1989).

Racism and structural disadvantage: anti-racism and multi-culturalism

The empirical evidence above suggests that minority ethnic older people face many forms of disadvantage and inequality. Their experience, however, prompts a more theoretical discussion about how to make sense of these inequalities and improve the situation of minority ethnic people. Social gerontology and social policy have largely been insulated from such debates (*cf.* Atkin, 1996). Nonetheless, these debates have important significance for social gerontology if it is to incorporate the issues of race and ethnicity into future agendas.

The opposition between multi-culturalism and anti-racism offers a useful introduction to the theoretical issues informing current discussion about the experience of the minority ethnic populations living in the UK. Until recently, much of the work on race and ethnicity tended to emphasise the structural disadvantage facing minority ethnic people, and the importance of overcoming such disadvantage. This became known as *anti-racism.* There is no doubt that anti-racist strategies have demonstrated the subtle and embedded nature of racism in British society (*cf.* Rattansi, 1992), as well as the value of active resistance (Harrison, 1993). However, anti-racist strategies are vulnerable to the criticism of reducing the experience of ethnic minorities to a single 'disembodied voice', unable to recognise the cultural diversity of Britain's minority ethnic populations (Taylor, 1991). This can be largely explained by the origins of anti-racism.

Anti-racism arose out of opposition to the orthodoxy of *multi-culturalism.* Multi-culturalism found expression in many different policy debates during the late 1970s and 1980s, ranging from community care (Atkin, 1996) and education (Rattansi, 1992) to social security provision (Craig and Rai, 1996). According to multi-cultural approaches, diversity in language, religion, cultural norms and expectations, prevent effective communication and create misunderstanding between the majority and distinct minority (*cf.* Lawrence, 1982). This orthodoxy advocated that overcoming the linguistic and cultural barriers that cause misunderstanding, and promoing awareness of the other's culture, should result in more sensitive and responsive welfare provision.

Multi-cultural approaches, although recognising difference, did so in a way that could potentially oppress minority groups. Anti-racist strategies identified several problems with multi-culturalism, most notably that the relationship between ethnically distinct minorities and the majority white society was seen exclusively in terms of cultural practices (Gilroy, 1982). Within this largely uncritical framework, the outcome was to present 'white' culture as a norm. A group's difference was then used against them. This emphasis can potentially pathologise black cultural practices. The emphasis on cultural practices, for example, can result in welfare organisations blaming ethnic minorities for experiencing specific problems or being censured for failing to understand an organisation's aims (Atkin and Rollings, 1993). Minority ethnic older people, for example, are frequently characterised as in some way to blame for their own needs because of deviant and unsatisfactory lifestyles (Cameron et al, 1989). Indeed, there is a history of defining health problems faced by minority ethnic communities in terms of cultural deficits, where a shift towards a 'Western' life style is offered as the main solution to their problems (Williams, 1989).

More generally, multi-culturalism recognised difference to the extent that difference was accorded an inferior image, that was used to distort and oppress (Taylor, 1991). Anti-racist accounts attempted to recapture the notion of difference, and use it to illustrate the disadvantages faced by people from ethnic minorities when compared to the white population. Anti-racist approaches argue that the focus on 'cultural norms' diverts attention from the wider power relations within society, and in particular fails to recognise that the dominant 'white' culture, and the distinct minority culture, do not meet on equal terms. The situation of minority ethnic people cannot be solely understood in terms of cultural artefacts – the political, social and economic positions of minority ethnic people are equally important. From this, anti-racist approaches emphasise the importance of structural disadvantage and racism in understanding the problems facing Britain's ethnic minorities. To this extent, anti-racism has successfully demonstrated the forms of discrimination and disadvantage faced by minority ethnic groups living in the UK.

This emphasis on structural disadvantage, however, has emerged as another orthodoxy, potentially distorting the experience of people from ethnic minorities. Anti-racism presented an account of difference that did not take into account the cultural experience of people from ethnic minorities. In examining structural disadvantage, anti-racist approaches have tended to dismiss cultural descriptions as a surrogate form of racism. For reasons outlined above, this has led to a – perhaps understandable – distrust of cultural descriptions. On the other hand, however, it is impossible to ignore the importance of 'culture' and 'identity' in understanding the experience of people from ethnic minorities (Stuart, 1993). Minority ethnic people are more than a product of the racisms they experience, and this reminds us of the importance of recognising diversity and pluralism (Penna and O'Brien, 1996).

Following this, the conceptualisation of 'culture' by multi-cultural approaches is the problem, rather than the concept of 'culture' *per se*, particularly since multi-cultural approaches tend to strip culture of its dynamic social, economic and gender context (Ahmad, 1995). Consequently, 'culture' becomes a rigid and constraining concept, mechanically determining peoples' behaviour and actions. As we have seen, 'neat cultural packages' perpetuate rather than challenge myths and stereotypes. Minority ethnic cultures are not static, unitary or monolithic, but as complex as white culture (Blakemore and Boneham, 1994). Cultural generalisations, encouraged by multi-cultural approaches, fail to recognise that culture is a creative resource, combining special and temporal components (*cf.* Bourdieu, 1977).

Culture, in effect, provides a flexible resource for living and ascribing meaning to one's feelings and experience. Cultural norms provide guidelines for understanding actions that predispose individuals to certain types of response. They do not, however, determine that response. Cultural norms are open to different interpretations across people and across time, and are structured by social cleavages, previous experience, relationships, resources and priorities. Descriptions of say, Hindu, Sikh or Muslim behaviour often transpose the situation in Asia to Britain, ignoring the process of migration (Ahmad, 1996). The emergence of a 'Black British' population can, for instance, subtly remould the 'traditional' cultural norms of their community. Minority ethnic people need to reconcile two or more cultural backgrounds, thus establishing a creative tension. Cultural ties with their place of origin may still be strong, yet they become faced with situations where they have to accommodate Western ways and values. They have anchorage in two or more distinct cultures but do not fully belong to either. For minority ethnic people living in Britain it is not a matter of forsaking one culture for another, but finding the space to express both (*cf.* Chowdhury, 1989). As such, cultural identity is not fixed nor constant but flexible, operating on different levels according to situation and context. Its essence cannot be captured by simple mechanical summaries.

To be successful and overcome the impact of structural racism, welfare policy and practice has to become informed by older minority ethnic peoples' own perceptions, and this means an understanding of people's culture. Cultural differences do generate misunderstandings, but perceptions of culture should not become identified as 'inferior' and 'deviant'. Difference is not a problem in itself. The notion of 'otherness' does not address the extent to which the 'taken-for-granted' norms of the white majority are equally socially constructed. It is not that minorities are culturally different, rather we are all different culturally (Ballard, 1989). This approach, in turn, has to understand these differences in the context of the political, social and economic disadvantage faced by ethnic minorities and in particular the racism they experience.

To facilitate political resistance, anti-racist approaches tended to conceptualise minority populations as having one voice, oppressed by racism. This approach, although understandable, again fails to recognise the diversity of different minority ethnic groups. Although one would accept broad commonalities among minority ethnic groups, in terms of their experience of migration, disadvantage and general racism, one would also expect great differences. Within the British context there is no one Asian culture, but a series of South Asian cultures. There are similarities, as with European culture, but there is also great diversity. The same can be said for the different Caribbean islands (Blakemore and Boneham, 1994). We have also seen how the experience of structural disadvantage is different among Indian, Pakistani and Bangladeshi groups. Consequently it is no longer possible to speak of one racism. This criticism, however, does not negate the relevance of anti-racist accounts, but reminds us about the diversity of experience of Britain's older ethnic minority population. Recognising this diversity has important implications for social gerontology since it is no longer appropriate to assume that all minority ethnic groups have the same needs.

This leads us to the final point: the importance of positive action. Writings on 'race' and social care tend to focus on the problems of accessibility and appropriateness, as well as general disadvantage in the provision of services (Atkin and Rollings, 1993). The evaluation offered by this chapter draws on such material and highlights the unfair structuring of opportunities. The critical emphasis of the literature on 'race' and social care is perhaps understandable, and has successfully highlighted the negative consequences of racism, marginalisation and unequal treatment. Describing the disadvantage faced by different minority ethnic groups, however, is not the same as responding to their need. By highlighting the negative consequences of service provision there is a danger that little is done to advance thinking and practice (Levick, 1992). Despite the considerable problems faced by minority ethnic groups, examples of empowerment and practice do occur. Social gerontology should not lose sight of this and be overwhelmed by the many examples of disadvantage and racism.

Conclusion

For the first time, health and social care agencies in the UK are facing an older minority ethnic population. Like many other European countries, the needs of these older people are not high on either the research or policy agenda. This chapter, by reviewing a mix of empirical studies and theoretical debates, attempts to address this neglect and explore the experience of ageing in a multi-racial Britain. In doing so it demonstrates the considerable disadvantages faced by minority ethnic older people and illustrates the unfair structuring of opportunities and the negative consequences of racism. This disadvantage, however, is only one aspect of minority ethnic people's experience. The concern with structural disadvantage has tended to suppress any discussion of cultural values. There is a need to recognise the role of culture in how people make sense of their lives, albeit in a way that does not associate culture with deviance. From this, it is also important to recognise the diversity of Britain's minority populations. Ethnic minority populations do not form an homogenous group, either in terms of cultural identity or the disadvantages they face.

Social gerontology needs to incorporate these concerns and recognise the structural disadvantage faced by minority ethnic groups, their cultural identity as well as their diversity. More importantly, however, studies on ageing and ethnicity should not be overwhelmed by the problems faced by these communities. To this extent, the future lies in moving beyond describing disadvantage and discrimination, to suggesting strategies ensuring they are overcome. This is the challenge facing social gerontology as it enters the twenty-first century.

Notes

1   When discussing Britain's minority ethnic populations, terminology is a notoriously fraught issue: few terms have uniform acceptance or consistent application. This chapter will largely employ ethnic minority as a generic term encompassing all racialised minorities, distinguishable by skin colour in Britain.

2   Most of the material in this area describes the experience of older people from South East Asian and African-Caribbean communities. The material reviewed by this chapter, therefore, is generally confined to the two largest ethnic minority communities in Great Britain. The themes of discrimination and racism are of course equally relevant to the experience of other minority groups, such as Somali, Polish, Cypriot or Chinese communities. Nonetheless there is little specific material that explores their situation of these communities. Nor is there much work on older people, usually political refugees, who have recently migrated to the UK.

3   Blakemore and Boneham (1994) provide an excellent account of this diversity. For example, they discuss the different experience of old age for people from different Caribbean Islands, as well as remind the reader about the heterogeneous nature of Britain's Pakistani communities.

4   Structural barriers and the misrepresentation of the needs of minority ethnic people are often equated with the concept of institutional racism. Institutional racism occurs when the policies of an institution lead to racially discriminatory outcomes for users of minority ethnic communities irrespective of the motives of individual employees in the institution. More specifically, institutional racism has been described as camouflaged, meaning it is not open or particularly visible, and is embedded in the taken for granted assumptions informing organisation practices.

References

Ahmad, W. I. U. (1995) 'Reflections on the consanguinity and birth outcome debate', *Journal of Public Health Medicine*, 16 (4): pp 423–28.

Ahmad, W. I. U. (1996) 'Family obligations and social change in Asian families' in Ahmad, W. I. U. and Atkin, K. (eds) *Race and Community Care*, Buckingham: Open University Press.

Ahmad, W. I. U and Husband, C. (1993) 'Religious identity, citizenship and welfare; the case of Muslims in Britain', *American Journal of Islamic Social Science*, 10(2): 217–33.

Ahmad, W. I. U., Kernohan, E. E. M. and Baker, M. R. (1989) 'Health of British Asians: a research review', *Community Medicine*, 11: pp 49–56.

Ahmad, W. I. U. and Sheldon, T. (1993) 'Race and statistics' in Hammersley, M. (ed) *Social Research: philosophy, politics and practice*, London: Sage.

Ahmad, W. I. U. and Walker, R. (1996) 'Asian older people: housing, health and access to services' in *Ageing and Society* 17: 141–65.

Anwar, M. (1990) 'Ethnic classification, ethnic monitoring and the 1991 Census', *New Community*, 16 (4): 606–15.

Atkin, K. (1996) 'An opportunity for change: voluntary sector provision in a mixed economy of care' in Ahmad, W. I. U. and Atkin, K. (eds) *Race and Community Care*, Buckingham: Open University Press.

Atkin, K. and Rollings, J. (1993) *Community Care in a Multi-Racial Britain: a critical review*, London: HMSO.

Atkin, K., Cameron, E., Badger, F. and Evers, H. (1989) 'Asian elders' knowledge and future use of community social and health services', *New Community*, 15(3): 439–46.

Ballard, R. (1989) 'Social work with Black people: What's the difference' in Rojeck, C., Peacock, G. and Collins, S. (eds) *The Haunts of Misery: critical essays in social work and helping*, London: Routledge

Barker, J. (1984) *Black and Asian Old People in Britain*, Mitcham: Age Concern.

Baxter, C. (1988) 'Black carers in focus', *Cancerlink*, 4: 4–5.

Berry, S., Lee, M. and Griffiths, S. (1981) *Report on a Survey of West Indian Pensioners in Nottingham*, Nottingham: Nottingham Social Services Department.

Bhalla, A. and Blakemore, K. (1981) *Elderly of the Minority Ethnic Groups*, Birmingham: All Faiths for One Race.

Blakemore, K. and Boneham, M. (1994) *Age, Race and Ethnicity*, Buckingham: Open University Press.

Bourdieu, P. (1977) *Outline of a Theory of Practice*, Cambridge: Cambridge University Press.

Bowler, I. (1993) 'They're not the same as us: midwives stereotypes of South Asian maternity patients', *Sociology of Health and Illness*, 15: 157–78.

Butt, J. and Mirza, K. (1996) *Social Care and Black Communities*, London: HMSO.

Butt, J. (1994) *Same Service or Equal Service?* London: HMSO.

Cameron, E., Badger, F., Evers, H. and Atkin, K. (1989) 'Black old women and health carers', in Jefferys, M. (ed) *Growing Old in the Twentieth Century*, London: Routledge.

Castles, S. and Kosack, G. (1985) *Immigrant Workers and the Class Structure in Western Europe*, London: Oxford University Press.

Charlton, J., Wallace., M. and White, I. (1994) 'Long term illness: results from the 1991 census', *Population Trends*, 75: 19–25.

Chauhan, B. (1989) 'Keeping in touch with the Asian community', *Community Care*, 764: vi–vii.

Chowdhury, A. (1989) 'Cultural crossroads', *Marxism Today*, October 1989.

Coke, M. M. and Twaite, J. A. (1995) *The Black Elderly: satisfaction and quality of later life*, New York: The Haworth Press.

Craig, G. and Rai, D. (1996) 'Social Security, community care and "race": the forgotten dimension' in Ahmad, W. I. U. and Atkin, K. (ed) *Race and Community Care*, Buckingham: Open University Press.

Dominelli, L. (1989) 'An uncaring profession? An examination of racism in social work', *New Community*, 15(3): 391–403.

Donaldson, L. J. and Odell, A. (1986) 'Aspects of the health and social service needs of elderly Asians in Leicester: a community survey', *British Medical Journal*, 293: 1079–82.

Eribo, L. (1991) *The Support You Need: information for carers of Afro-Caribbean elderly people*, London: Bedford Square Press.

Farrah, M. (1986) 'Black elders in Leicester: an action research report on the needs of Black elderly people of African descent from the Caribbean', *Social Services Research*, 1: 47–9.

Fennell, G., Phillipson, C. and Evers, H. (1988) *The Sociology of Old Age*, Buckingham: Open University Press.

Fenton, S. (1987) *Ageing Minorities: Black people as they grow old in Britain*, London: Commission for Racial Equality.

Foster, M. C. (1988) 'Health visitors' perspectives on working in a multi-ethnic society', *Health Visitor*, 61: 275–78.

Gilroy, P. (1982) 'Stepping out of Babylon: race, class in autonomy', in Centre for Contemporary Cultural Studies (ed) *The Empire Strikes Back*, London: Hutchinson.

GLAD (1987) *Disability and Ethnic Minority Communities: a study in three boroughs*, London: Greater London Association for Disabled People.

Glendenning, F. and Pearson, M. (1988) *The Black and Ethnic Minority Elders in Britain Health Needs and Access to Services*, Health Education Authority in Association with the Centre for Social Gerontology, University of Keele.

Harrison, M. (1993) 'The black voluntary housing movement: pioneering pluralistic social policy in a difficult climate', *Critical Social Policy*, 13(3): 21–35.

Haskey, J. (1994) 'The size and demographic characteristics of the Chinese population in Great Britain' in Williams, S., Watt, I. and Fong, C. L. (eds) *Chinese Health Care in Britain*, Leeds: Leeds Health Promotion Service.

Jadeja, S and Singh, J. (1993) 'Life in a cold climate', *Community Care*, 22, November.

Karseras, P. and Hopkins, E. (1987) *British Asians: health in the community*, Chichester: John Wily.

Lawrence, E. (1982) 'In the abundance of water the fool is thirsty; sociology and Black pathology' in Centre for Contemporary Cultural Studies (ed) *The Empire Strikes Back*, London: Hutchinson.

Levick, P. (1992) 'The janus face of community care legislation: an opportunity for radical possibilities?', *Critical Social Policy*, 12(1): 75–92.

Lewando-Hundt, G. and Holland, B. (1986) *Coventry's Ethnic Minorities Elderly Survey*, Coventry: Coventry Social Service Department.

Lieberman, S. and Shun Au (1988) 'Catering for a Minority', *Community Care*, 20–22, November.

Lipsky, M. (1980) *Street Level Bureaucracy: dilemmas of the individual in public service*, New York: Russell Sage.

May, N. (1983) 'Elderly South Asians in Britain: a survey of relevant literature and themes for future research', *Ageing and Society*, 3: 71–97.

McAvoy, B. R. and Donaldson, L. J. (eds) (1990) *Health Care for Asians, Oxford Medical Publications*, Oxford: Oxford University Press.

Moledina, S. (1988) *Great Expectations: a review of services for Asian elders in Brent*, London: Age Concern Brent.

National Association for Health Authorities (1988) *Action Not Words: a strategy to improve health services for Black and ethnic minority groups*, London: National Association of Health Authorities.

National Urban League (1964) *Double Jeopardy: the older negro in America today*, New York: National Urban League.

Norman, A. (1985) *Triple Jeopardy: growing old in a second homeland*, Policy Studies in Ageing No 3, London: Centre for Policy on Ageing.

NHS Centre for Reviews and Dissemination (1996) *Ethnicity and Health*, York: NHS Centre for Reviews and Dissemination.

Oldman, C. (1990) *Moving in Old Age: Directions in Housing Policy*, London: HMSO.

OPCS (1988) *The Prevalence of Disability Among Adults OPCS Survey of Disability in Great Britain.*

Owen, D. (1993) *Ethnic Minorities in Britain* (Census Papers), Warwick University: Centre for Research in Ethnic Relations.

Parker, G. (1992) 'Counting care: numbers and types of carers' in Twigg, J. (ed), *Carers: research and practice*, London: HMSO.

Parker, G. and Lawton, D. (1994) *Different Types of care, Different Types of Carer: evidence from the General Household Survey*, London: HMSO.

Patel, N. (1990) *A Race Against Time, Social Services Provision to Black Elders*, London: Runnymede Trust.

Penna, S. and O'Brien, M. (1996) 'Postmodernism and social policy: a small step forwards', *Journal of Social Policy*, 25(1).

Phillipson, C. (1982) *Capitalism and the Construction of Old Age*, London: Macmillan.

RADAR (1984) *Disability and Minority Ethnic Groups: a factsheet of issues and initiatives*, London: The Royal Association for Disability and Rehabilitation.

Rattansi, A. (1992) 'Changing the subject? Racism, culture and education' in Donald, J. and Rattansi, A. (eds), *Race, Culture and Difference*, London: Sage.

Rowland, D. T. (1991) *Pioneers Again: immigrants and ageing in Australia*, Canberra: Australian Government Publishing Service.

Skellington, R. and Morris, P. (1992) *Race in Britain Today*, London: Sage.

Stuart, O. (1996) '"Yes we mean black people too." Thoughts on community care and disabled people and from black and minority communities' in Ahmad, W. I. U. and Atkin, K. (eds) *'Race' and Community Care*, Buckingham: Open University Press.

Taylor, C. (1991) *The Ethics of Authenticity*, Harvard: Harvard University Press.

Torkington, P. (1991) *Black Health: a political issue*, Liverpool: Catholic Association for Racial Justice/Liverpool Institute for Higher Education.

Walker, R. and Ahmad, W. (1994) 'Windows of opportunity in rotting frames: care providers' perspectives on community care and Black communities', *Critical Social Policy*, 40: 46–69.

Williams, F. (1989) *Social Policy: a critical introduction*, Cambridge: Polity Press.

Young, C. (1990) 'Black and ethnic minority users and carers in rural areas', *ARVAC Bulletin*, 43: 4–5.

1 Pensioners organise: hearing the voice of older people

Joanna Bornat

There has sometimes been an enthusiasm for a mobilisation of pensioner opinion, whose success would depend on the efficacy with which this collective vote was delivered. This is a chimera. With one in four voters in their Third or Fourth Age, it appears that the scope for this form of political togetherness is limited and negligible. Because of the social make-up of the older electorate, the constitutional constraints in our political process upon sectional pressure and the way in which 'old age' is presented on the political stage of the United Kingdom, it is unlikely that grey power has any chance of succeeding in the foreseeable future. So firmly is this opinion grounded that we would argue that it is best forgotten as a political notion.

Eric Midwinter and Susan Tester (1987) Polls Apart? Older voters and the 1987 general election, CPA, p. 50

Introduction

Older people organising on their own behalf with programmes detailing rights and demands, are a relatively recent feature in the political landscape of modern Britain. The first campaigns in the early decades of this century tended to speak for, rather than be the voice of, older people. A shift towards representative organisation began with new movements in the period just before the Second World War. These periods of activity featured campaigns for a universal pension claimed on the moral basis of just reward for a life's work, fuelled by the reality of poverty and dependency in old age. The search for a set of unifying claims and appeals drawing on experiences of exclusion and powerlessness has posed difficult challenges for a movement whose membership today potentially draws from a segment of society divided by inequalities of gender, income, ethnicity and health status. The term 'pensioner' may not have a broad appeal, yet 'pensioners' movement' continues to typify the campaigning style and structural characteristics of the most prominent organisations claiming to represent the interests of older people.

This chapter reviews developments in these organisations over the last fifty years and in doing so considers a number of questions. What has been the territory over which struggles have been fought? How much has changed for organisations of older people and the context in which they campaign? To what extent does the language of campaigning represent the diversity of older people? Are older people a separate political force?

Accounting for the history of the pensioner movement represents something of a challenge. In narrative terms the pensioner movement has largely been invisible and, with few exceptions, scarcely any written or recorded history has been attempted. With few exceptions (Goodman, 1987, Blaikie, 1990, Miles, 1994) this has been a neglected topic by both older and younger historians, gerontologists and policy makers. In attempting to map out chronologies and locate developments I am conscious of this lack, and hope that the account may inspire others to undertake the research and the recording of past experience which older people's organisation so vitally needs.

The emergence of mass membership organisations

In the first forty years of this century there were two periods of organisation around 'the pension'. The National Pensions Committee, campaigning for a universal non-contributory pension, saw the culmination of its efforts in the 1908 Old Age Pensions Act. The organisation was led by a coalition of trade unions, leading Liberal and Tory politicians, the churches and early labour organisations. Pensions and pensioner issues emerged again in the latter part of the First World War as poverty in old age, in contrast with high earnings amongst younger people, became a focus for agitation. The campaigners, led by the National Conference on Old Age Pensions, an alliance of trade unions, Friendly Societies, co-operative societies, the Free Church Council and members of parliament, argued against a means-tested pension, claiming that this penalised the thrifty (Blaikie, 1990). These were periods of campaigning and lobbying which were targeted at specific pieces of legislation and focusing on poverty in old age. These early organisations were short term, without broader aims, and were forced to compete with other interests taken up and represented by the organisations which provided their leadership. Movements of this type tended to be linked directly to success or failure in achieving particular goals. Success in 1908 ended one phase while failure in 1924 ended another. Hopes that the first Labour government would legislate in favour of a non-contributory pension were dashed when it became clear that the 1924 Pensions Act would bring little change to the status quo.

Independent organisation has continued to be an issue for older people right through the century as has another issue, gender. The mid 1930s saw the emergence of the first sign that older women might have their own interests. The National Spinsters' Pensions Association (NSPA) had over 150,000 members by 1939 (Smith, 1995). Arguing that older women faced discrimination in terms of age and gender, it put the case that unmarried women should be treated as 'war widows', and that single women, through their insurance contributions, were subsidising widows and married women's pensions. This position led to bitter debates within the Labour party and was opposed by leading women's organisations as divisive. Although it failed in its principal aims, the NSPA can probably be credited with securing women's inclusion in the Conservative government's 1940 Old Age and Widow's Pensions Act, and the reduction in insured women's age of eligibility for pension to 60, where it remained until 1993 (Smith, 1995).

The early years of the war and the immediate post-war period saw the emergence of two new membership based organisations. The National Federation of Old Age Pensions Associations (NFOAPA) originated in meetings held in Lancashire in 1938 and was launched at a meeting in London in March 1939. Prior to this, the first official meeting of the Scottish Old Age Pensions Associations (SOAPA) had taken place in 1937 in Edinburgh.

Both the NFOAPA and Scottish OAPA grew rapidly. By early 1944 some branches of the NFOAPA had nearly 10,000 members and by 1953 there were 1,300 branches in England and Wales (Blaikie, 1990). In analysing the reason for this success, Blaikie points out a shift in attitudes and organisational practice. The new organisations were not run by affiliations of the powerful Friendly Societies, political parties and trade unions; they were set up as politically independent structures with a branch membership which drew on grassroots energy and initiative.

Though independent in relation to national bodies, these new organisations were drawn from a new generation of older people who had developed skills of organisation through trade union structures and whose life experience included the hardship and bitterness of the First World War and the new forms of militancy around unemployment in the 1920s and 1930s. They were also a new creation: a generation of retired people outside the labour force either because of a shift towards mandatory retirement in some sectors, or because of the increasing likelihood of unemployment amongst the oldest workers (Laczko and Phillipson, 1991). The cartoons and editorial writing in the NFOAPA's *The Pensioner* conveyed a quite different mentality to the quiet petitioning and passivity of the earlier movement. Blaikie (1990) also suggests that the NFOAPA's tactic of petitioning Parliament gave it a sense of purpose and national identity (its 1940 petition was signed by 2 million people, in comparison, in 1993 half a million people signed a national petition against pit closures).

However there are also two other significant differences to the earlier pre-war period. One was the role of the press. By the late 1930s newspapers had changed dramatically. The number of papers with a circulation of a million had increased from two in 1920, to five by 1930 and by 1947 daily sales of newspapers had risen to over fifteen million (Bourke, 1994: 184). Circulation figures were not the only factor. Sections of the press had their own target audiences and writers, such as Ritchie Calder, whose journalism could catch a public mood. Papers like the *Daily Dispatch* and *The Daily Herald* championed the pensioners' cause with articles and, on one occasion, a front-page story (Blaikie, 1990: 31-32).

Though the press undoubtedly played a part in identifying the interests of a particular segment of the population, it was clear that public opinion had changed. Here perhaps is the other main reason why organisations of older people in the late 1930s and early 1940s took a different form. Taking the temperature of political views at different stages throughout the war, Mass Observation observed that by August 1942 one in three of the population said that the war had changed their opinions (Timmins, 1995: 37) War time propaganda appealed to democratic traditions and to social and economic reconstruction in a post-war era. This was a national commitment drawing in almost an entire political generation. Gains for all groups seemed possible and with events leading up to the publication of the Beveridge Report, there were many opportunities for debate and a public airing of injustices. The NFOAPA was vocal in its participation and scathing when the Beveridge Report's recommendations were published. A cartoon in *The Pensioner* read, 'Cheer up Maggie, we shall get £2 a week when we are 97' (quoted in Blaikie, 1990: 31).

Divisions and coalitions

The war years saw the emergence of new forms of organisation taking up the cause of older people and their living standards. Pratt (1993b), a US observer who has looked at the Canadian, UK and US histories of older people's organisations, argues that the-post war years were typified by the growth of lobbying organisations which resulted from government's more extensive commitment to support for older people. In Britain he suggests that this was the basis for the development of two separate and quite different coalitions in the post-war period: the 'age coalition' – organisations concentrating on lobbying around policy formation and service provision; and the 'pensions coalition' – organisations focusing on campaigning around the traditional income and subsistence issues. This separation of welfare-oriented as opposed to income-oriented campaigning continued for almost five decades and has only, towards the end of the century, begun to break down. The new organisations of the 'age coalition' differed and continue to differ in two other respects from the organisations of the 'pensions coalition'. They had access to resources beyond the 'pensions coalition' which, until the 1970s relied solely on pensioners' own membership subscriptions. Though they drew on the support of older people as volunteers at all levels, they emerged as representative rather than as lobbying organisations speaking and acting on behalf of older people rather than as older people.

The three constituents of 'the age coalition' – Age Concern England, the Centre for Policy on Ageing and Help the Aged – each emerged as a response to wartime dislocation and disruption in the lives of older people (Means and Smith, 1985; Tout 1997). Though each took a separate path: Age Concern as a federation of local voluntary organisations providing services and information to older people; the Centre for Policy on Ageing with policy making and advisory functions; and Help the Aged as a fund-raiser for projects in the UK and overseas, they continue to share common characteristics. London-based, they seek to influence national policy through direct contact and pressure on government and the main political parties. They have sources of income from government grants, charitable support and direct fund-raising which support head office staff with a full range of responsibilities, including campaigning, information and advice, and networking. As such, they present something of a contrast with 'the pensions coalition'.

In the decades immediately following the end of the Second World War, the 'pensions coalition' was represented by the National Federation of Retirement Pensions Associations (NFRPA) as NFOAPA became, with its monthly magazine *Pensioners' Voice*. Though the organisation's goal of improving the living standards of older people remained consistent, its locally based structure of branches and the location of its headquarters in Blackburn, tended to mean that it was sidelined by the larger London-based lobbying organisations of the 'age coalition'. Moreover its persistently non-partisan line, politically speaking, gave it few powerful allies nationally. The return of Labour governments in the 1960s and 1970s renewed possibilities to directly influence pensions policies. In 1972, a split in the NFRPA led to the formation of the British Pensioners and Trades Union Action Association (BPTUAA). Members of the BPTUAA sought a more politically militant alignment, targeting Labour MPs and making use of the Labour party's conference structure to publicise and press for policy changes (Miles, 1994). Twenty years later its membership is organised in 400 branches often known as Pensioners Action Groups.

The involvement of trade unions represented a new phase and led to a specific orientation for the pensioners' movement. Although trade unions had been active in establishing the movement for increased pensions at the turn of the century, any formal commitment died away after the 1920s. Jack Jones describes himself as being involved in the formation of the NFOAPA before the Second World War, but official support at a national level had not been forthcoming for several decades. It was not until the 1970s, following Jack Jones's successful appeal to the TUC and Labour party, that key unions once more became involved, developing their own retired members' sections and committing these to support for the pensioners' movement (Jones, 1992).

Jack Jones' personal history is, of course, closely entwined with the history of the Labour party and the TUC, and his commitment to the pensioner movement over a period of twenty years has been pivotal. When he describes lobbying politicians in the 1960s and 1970s he is talking about lobbying close political associates. As the leader of what was then the largest and traditionally most militant trade union in the country, the Transport and General Workers Union, he was in a powerful position to influence the direction of government policy during the Labour administrations of those years. Though, as Miles points out, too much should not be assumed about this relationship, as Barbara Castle describes herself keeping the TUC at a distance while she was drafting the 1975 pensions legislation (Miles, 1994).

Individual trade union support for the pensioner movement has remained important. For example, the BPTUAA has thirty-two national trade unions affiliations (Age Concern, 1996: 4). By the early 1990s one survey showed fifteen unions had retired members' sections organised at a national and local level (*Labour Research*, 1993: 19). As well as this, forty other unions had made special arrangements for their retired members, including special voting rights, advisory committees, local branches of retired members and continued union benefits. A 1987 TUC survey showed that only eight unions had not followed this path (Pratt, 1993a). This commitment translates into resources, for example funding newspapers and campaigning materials at local and national levels.

A more openly committed approach to lobbying led to the founding of the National Pensioners Convention (NPC) in 1979, drawing support from both coalitions: 'pensioner' and 'age'. The initiative was supported by the TUC following a mass demonstration in Trafalgar Square in London. This move towards some form of unity was an attempt to focus and channel the competitive lobbying of the different organisations claiming to speak for older people. The NPC's 'Declaration of Intent' has, over the years since 1979, continued to provide a unifying statement for the disparate organisations which sign up to its clauses.

The NPC was to lose steam following the change of government in 1979 and only re-emerged as a significant voice after the late 1980s (Miles, 1994). Though supported by the TUC until 1990, it has subsequently became independent. Funding for a national pensioner organisation is still elusive. Though the NPC calls an annual Pensioner Parliament with 2,500 delegates, and sends delegates to European assemblies of older people, as an organisation it still has only a modest income and no full time worker. The commitment of Jack Jones, and the retired members' section of his union, has guaranteed organisation and leadership as well as continuity and a London-based office from which to unite strong support from other parts of the country, notably East Anglia, the West Midlands and the North West.

The central role of trade unions has brought many significant gains for pensioner organisations and not only in terms of financial support. It has also guaranteed consistent leadership at a local level. Many of the local organisations are led by men and women who have long been committed to campaigning issues and who have a lifetime's experience in mobilising and leading from the grass-roots. Andrews' study of older left-wing political activists identifies this group as having a 'culture of responding' to 'problems in the environment', with a 'pattern of behaviour that has existed over a protracted period of time (that) has become characteristic of these individuals...they are lifetime activists' (Andrews, 1991: 167-8).

These older campaigners speak a language which thousands of older people have heard over the decades, and which appeals directly to those whose lives have been determined by bread and butter issues of jobs and living standards. The evocation of the struggles of the war years, and of the values of the 1945 post-war settlement, draws on a generational experience and makes a direct link to their current situation as older people. These convictions, born of personal and generational experience and renewed through anxieties about being old in the late twentieth century, are easily transformed into action. National and regional rallies of pensioners were consistently thousands strong in the late 1980s, and have continued into the 1990s, undoubtedly drawing in many who might otherwise describe themselves as 'non-political'.

However, the close relationship between the organised pensioner movement and trade unions has produced a set of structures which, for some people, have not always been as inclusive as their rhetoric might suggest. The issue of women's and men's unequal forms of involvement is one which some feminists have identified. From positions which are critical of both the women's liberation movement for its neglect and exclusion of older women (Macdonald and Rich, 1983; Grant, 1985; Curtis, 1989; Stacey 1989) and of the pensioners' movement (Curtis, 1993), some women point out that leaders consistently fail to acknowledge the particular perspective and contribution of older women. Ginn argues that the neglect of gender and race is a direct result of the strength of the movement's ties with the trade union movement: 'As women, ethnic minorities and disabled people know to their cost, trade unions have often been slow to recognise and respond to their needs' (Ginn, 1993: 41). Nevertheless, as she points out, women participate at all levels in these organisations. Indeed there is a danger in overemphasising the effect of trade union domination of the formal organisation of pensioner action on older women's identities as activists. Traditionally, it was women who led local campaigns for laundry provision, road crossings, libraries, schools and nurseries. Older women are not without organisational and campaigning histories of their own (Campbell, 1984; Rowbotham, 1989).

Until the mid 1990s, at a local and regional level, women chairs and speakers were common but of the national organisations only Pensioners' Voice (as NFRPA became) consistently elected a woman to the top office of president. It could be that this organisation's political independence, and its detachment from trade union structures, has offered some older women at a local level over the decades opportunities to socialise and campaign in ways which offer greater continuity with their life experience.[1]

It is a lack of identification with the particular issues confronting women in old age which Zelda Curtis identifies as a problem for women in the trade union styled pensioners movement. While women form a majority of those out on the streets with placards, gaining signatures for petitions and arguing the case for pensioners, the men tend to hold the positions of power within local and national organisations (Curtis, 1993). However, whilst she also commented that 'the women colluded with the men and accepted roles as minute-taker, tea maker and organiser of jumble sales' (pp. 193–4), she now notes that women are becoming more vocal and are being voted into leading positions (personal communication). Indeed, as the century draws to a close, women are beginning to take over the leadership of the National Pensioners Convention, with its two vice presidents, Joan Hall and Helen Grew, running the Pensioners' Parliament and, with Jack Jones, representing the movement in discussions with the Labour Chancellor.

Zelda Curtis' experience led her to resign as treasurer of the Greater London Pensioners' Assocation to concentrate her efforts into activity with other older women in AGLOW (Association of Greater London Older Women), which campaigns on issues of health, housing, transport and discrimination and generally aims to raise levels of awareness and self-confidence amongst working class women and older women from black and minority ethnic communities. At a national level, organisations of older feminists continue with what seem like separate agendas so far as the broader pensioner movement is concerned. The Older Feminists Network, which began in 1982 as an identity group for older women within the women's liberation movement, has so far made little impact on either 'age' or 'pensions' coalitions. The Growing Old Disgracefully Network, a loose national association inspired by the writing and self-assertion of a small group of older women (Hen Co-op, 1993), tends to take as its focus individual self-fulfilment through the development of mutual support structures, in a language which is far distant to that of the organised pensioner movement. Appeals to unity and a suspicion, by both women and men, of feminist ideas mean that issues for women in old age have been consistently subsumed into a general set of 'pensioner' demands. Despite numerous revisions and rewordings, the National Pensioners Convention's Declaration of Intent still takes a deliberately 'degendered' line in the mid 1990s.

At local and national levels, the two 'coalitions' share memberships and goals, yet their perspectives remain separate. The pensioners' movement, with some exceptions, has adopted a more partisan commitment seeking powerful and sympathetic allies in the Labour party and amongst trade unions, while the age coalition seeks a position of apparent independence. As the century nears its end, each raises the issue of the efficacy of different campaigning forms: the power of the lobbying machine versus the power of older people taking action on their own behalf.

Local and national: divisions as strength?

While the leaders of the 'pensions coalition' may publicly protest the need for unity and undivided support, local strength and the activities of older feminists and other interest groups working at a grassroots level may offer the possibility of strength through diversity (Miles, 1990: 19). Indeed local campaigns, often run through Pensioners' Forums, are more likely to reflect the actual range of older people's interests and concerns. Hospital closure programmes, cost of living indices, transport, standing charges for gas and electricity, privatisation issues in residential care, housing, health care rationing and social care charges have all been the target of groups of older people locally. As Miles points out 'They are a locus where being "old" – even being old, black and female – carries a positive connotation' (1994: 7). Local campaigns and local identities help to keep issues affecting older people in the public eye. Thus for example, North Staffordshire Pensioners' Convention has been able to raise sufficient resources to employ a paid co-ordinator who helps to sustain local activity and publicity. While the national media consistently chooses to ignore major events in the pensioner movement calendar, local newspapers and even local television and radio have shown that they are more likely to feature older people's claims and perspectives.

The Declaration of Intent (see p. 192) takes a broadly undifferentiated position as a national programme. It illustrates the development of the movement away from an almost exclusive focus on incomes and savings in old age, to a more

Declaration of intent

This Convention declares that every pensioner has the right to choice, dignity, independence and security as an integral and valued member of society.

These rights require an adequate State Retirement Pension. Although we seek concessions we adhere to this central aim, an adequate pension to enable pensioners to pay their way.

There must be an immediate commitment to a pension not less than one half of average gross earnings for a married couple and not less than one third of average gross earnings for a single person, to be up-rated at six-monthly intervals by the increase in gross average earnings or the increase in the cost of living, whichever is the greater. There should be an additional flat-rate pension, non-means-tested for those over 75 years of age, and a further payment at the age of 80, to be increased annually in line with the RPI or average earning whichever is the greater. Other benefit levels should be adjusted accordingly. Further, as soon as possible, all elderly people should receive the full basic pension, regardless of sex or marital status.

In addition to an adequate income a pensioner should, as of right:

- live in accommodation which is appropriate to personal need and circumstances with reasonable degree of choice including sheltered housing

- be able to call on the full range of free community and personal social services to give full support as need arises, for example, home care, including domestic help, meals on wheels, chiropody, television and telephone

- in view of the wide disparity in the availability and types of existing travel concessions around the country, have access to a National Scheme which should be introduced involving a levelling up of existing schemes to the level of the best schemes in operation

- have ready access to comprehensive free health care on demand

- be able to maintain a warm and well lit home with additional heating payment for all pensioner households from October to March each year

- have full access to a varied and extensive range of education and leisure facilities

- be paid a tax-free Christmas bonus restored to its 1972 purchasing power and adjusted annually in line with inflation

- be eligible for an adequate retirement pension on ceasing work at any time of his or her own choice after the age of 60 years

- be entitled to an adequate death grant irrespective of age

- be relieved of standing charges on gas, telephones, electricity and water

- have a right to be consulted by central and local government and public utilities over plans which might affect their lives.

broad-reaching platform, representative of a wide range of issues affecting people as they grow older. Nevertheless, on reading through it betrays a conflicting set of identities: that of citizens with equal rights to a basic standard of living and as undifferentiated deserving poor to be rewarded by concessions and benefits according to attainment strictly in terms of years. The lack of acknowledgement of diversity, whether in terms of gender or citizenship, might be seen as inclusivity, yet a refusal to include reference to specific issues facing older women and black and minority ethnic pensioners means that at a national level at least, certain interests and identities are being marginalised or submerged.

The political issues of old age, as expressed in the Declaration of Intent, broadly match the views of 1,005 people over the age of 55 recorded in a poll carried out by MORI for Anchor Housing (Sykes and Leather, 1997). Crime, vandalism and drug abuse ranked with the National Health Service as the three main issues concerning this particular sample. On these and other questions, it appears that older people are expressing anxieties common to many sections of the population, while at the same time focusing on issues which link directly to inequality and concern over access to health and pensions.

Since 1997, the NPC includes amongst its affiliates organisations with a membership not obviously campaigning by nature. One example is the Association of Retired Persons (ARP) which was set up in 1988 to draw support from unaffiliated and better off older people who respond to the label 'retired' in preference to 'pensioner'. Within four years it had over 120,000 members with an average age of 61. ARP is modelled on the successful American Association of Retired Persons and includes among its activities, advocacy for the over-50s, political lobbying, financial discounts for members, sports and leisure activities, campaigning against ageism in the NHS and in employment, and support for private medical insurance. ARP has targeted more affluent over-fifties with local organisations focused on Friendship Centres for couples and singles, and National Companions for single unattached active members. A change in direction in the leadership of the ARP has brought the organisation into closer association with traditional campaigners with the result that the NPC now extends affiliated membership to a wider age group of people who may after all, it seems, find the label 'pensioner' less distasteful.

Another significant constituency amongst NPC affiliates is made up from the industry-based retirement associations with headquarters staff and their own publications. Largest amongst these is the National Federation of Post Office and British Telecom Pensioners. People who once worked for these major UK employers comprise a large group, some of whom are members of branches with 1,000 members. The Civil Service Pensioners' Alliance is a similarly large body with over 60,000 members, a quarterly journal and paid staff. These are people who have a stake in issues relating to retirement and although such associations are not overtly political, tending to focus on welfare activities, legal advice and support networks amongst members, they bring the interests of occupational pensioners to the NPC. So for example, the Post Office and British Telecom Association has campaigned on the issue of pensioner trustees for pension funds and, in the words of their General Secretary, Gay Appleby, have generally become 'more professional' (personal communication).

One thesis, developed around the notion of coalitions, is that organisation by older people has grown in relation to steps taken by the state to provide for its older citizens (Pratt, 1993b: 9). However, Pratt suggests that future governments may back away from large-scale commitments to pensions and health care, and that this may have implications for older people's organisation. Government's questioning of the commitment to pensions, and the substitution of policies which promote private and personal responsibility for financial security in old age, may weaken the bargaining strength of the pensions and age coalitions. Pratt sees the future as possibly seeing 'new interest groups formed and existing groups to some extent transformed [in] an era of enlarged autonomy and independence' (1993a). What he may be ignoring is the strength of local organisation, built around persisting political and social networks, campaigning and continuities in older people's lives. Member organisations, of both coalitions, offer older people more than political representation. These groupings are very much embedded in localities, urban and rural, and in terms of their social structure provide active support and meaning in the lives of their members, men and women.

One way to get some kind of measure of the likelihood of Pratt's prediction is to look at the national political scene, and to seek some means to identify to what extent pensioner organisation translates into effective electoral power.

From local mobilising to national power broking

Given the Conservative government's record during the 1980s, ending the link between pensions and earning, freezing the Christmas bonus, and breaking the consensus in relation to health and social care, it might have been expected that in terms of voting interests, opposition politics and pensioner politics would exactly match, and that older people would vote with one voice. In fact, the opposite was the case, as organisations of older people were to discover to their dismay following the 1992 General Election. After the earlier experience of the 1987 election when 47 per cent of those over 65 voted Conservative and 31 per cent voted Labour (Midwinter and Tester, 1987), the result should not have been unexpected. A post-election survey of 1880 voters carried out by Gallup showed that of the 306 people over 65 who responded, a majority had voted Conservative in 1992 (Bornat, 1994: 67). It seemed as if the pensioner movement was out of step with pensioners generally.

Early analysis of the 1997 General Election, based on the MORI rolling poll of 13,000 voters, showed older people joining in the general trend away from the Conservative party. However, of all the age groups polled, only the over 75s on balance were less inclined to vote Labour. The Anchor survey, carried out in July-August 1996, had suggested that voting intentions in the 1997 election might well be swayed by concern over specific issues. For example, 57 per cent of those surveyed said that they would be more likely to vote for a party which pledged increased financial support for long term care and more local services for older people. Though two thirds of those polled said that they were unlikely to change their vote, a third of older voters suggested that they might switch their allegiance (Sykes and Leather, 1997: 44–45). However, the MORI rolling poll of voters in the month before the election suggested that volatility was least marked amongst older voters surveyed. Conservative voters over 59 remained the most steadfast, with switchers comprising between 9 and 15 per cent, compared to proportions of 20 to 27 per cent amongst voters aged between 24 and 54.

Given the British electoral structure and the general invisibility of older people so far as party political campaigning is concerned, Midwinter (1992) doubts if older people could ever become an active party political force. Indeed, party political style organisations set up in the 1980s, such as the Pensioners' Protection Party, have not acquired any mass appeal. Phillipson's (1996) contention that age may be less of a factor than characteristics linked to home ownership, social class and trade union membership in determining voting patterns may indeed have been borne out by the 1997 election results.

Yet, there are signs that political parties ignore the interests of older people at their peril. So, for example, mass mobilisation around the issue of VAT on fuel bills prevented the level being increased to 17.5 per cent (Walker and Maltby, 1997: 116) and Barbara Castle's attack on the Labour leadership at the party's pre-election annual conference in 1996 successfully divided delegates, making the decline in value of the state pension in relation to average earnings a public political issue. Votes across all age groups may be withdrawn if expectations, life styles and living standards are threatened, and with an awareness of the low ranking of British pensioners' standard of living compared to retired people in most European countries (Walker and Maltby, 1997). Indeed, finer analysis of 1997 voting behaviour suggests that the Conservatives performed particularly badly in areas with high proportions of older and long term ill people. This suggests that reactions to the Conservatives election proposals to privatise the state pension, and to introduce personal saving towards the cost of long term care, were not vote catching policies amongst older people.[2] Older people clearly have political interests of their own. In addition, their ability through campaigning to highlight arguments about health, funding of long term care, access to transport and levels of income in old age undoubtedly played a part in destabilising support for the Conservatives across all age groups.

Conclusion

How much has changed for pensioner organisations in the last fifty years? Clearly the agenda for action is very different if the clauses of the Declaration of Intent are to be taken as a basis for comparison. Pensioners today are, it seems, concerned with a range of different issues connected with health, transport, heating and entertainment, as much as with basic levels of income. Changed issues for a changed society, but have the conditions and context for organisations of older people changed at all? Lobbying targets remain broadly the same and forms of organisation are little different. Yet, within the ranks of the current generation of potential pensioners, there lies the possibility of change. Just as previous generations brought with them into old age the particular experiences and accomplishments of their time, so members of the new generations of pensioners will bring their own cohort histories with them.

   People approaching old age at the end of the twentieth century already have experience of campaigns and affiliations which link them with other, younger groups in society. Environmental issues, neighbourhood and educational campaigns, nuclear weapons, animal rights, countryside access and fear of crime have seen cross generational action over the last thirty years. Similarly, access to transport, the quality of health care, the erosion of family capital as payment for continuing care, heating costs and water charges are all issues which have significance to a broad section of the population. Awareness of these issues raises the possibility of alliances and common cause with younger disabled people, and around other identities: parents, gays and lesbians, greens, transport users, UK citizens. It may also provide the basis for alliances around issues relating to ageing which draw on shared inter-generational experiences, rather than the protection of the interests of a particular generation. The persistence and continued strength and presence of a pensioners' movement at national and local levels is evidence of the claim which ageing issues have on the political life of broad sections of the community. Yet despite this the 'two nations in old age' with different lifestyles and income sources predicted by Titmuss (1958) persist. Now, we can see other divisions of gender, ethnicity and disability each adding their own dimension to the determination of quality of life for older people.

The need to find a compromise between representative and collective strength comes at a time when a new Labour government is apparently distancing itself from claims of rights and equitable treatment in old age. The traditional view of the pension as a just reward for a lifetime's contribution to society's wealth, which has fired the pensioner movement over the years, is being undermined with proposals embedded in notions of individual responsibility and thrift. Where differences amongst older people might in the past have been rolled up in campaigns on behalf of the aged or deserving poor, differences amongst older people at the end of the twentieth century appear to be as wide ranging as those of the rest of society. However, as we enter the twenty-first century, it seems that pensioners are people with allegiances and alliances that link across generations and identity groups. The challenge for the pensioners' movement in the next century will be to recognise and profit from these links, while maintaining a politicised age presence which continues to stir up and equip society to defend the interests of all citizens as they age. A new challenge perhaps, but evocative of the political inclusivity of that earlier generation of 1945, which has done so much to prepare the coming generations for the struggles of the twenty-first century.

Acknowledgement

With thanks to Zelda Curtis (Association of Greater London Older Women), Dave Goodman (North Staffordshire Pensioners' Convention) and Joe Harris (National Pensioners' Convention Research co-ordinator) who gave helpful criticism and advice as I wrote this chapter.

Notes

1 I am grateful to the late Monica Jones of Wellingborough Pensioners' Voice for this insight.

2 I am grateful to Professor Ron Johnston of the Department of Geography, University of Bristol, who provided me with voting data for the 1997 General Election.

References

Age Concern, (1996) 'Pensioner organisations in England', *Briefings*, no 2595, London: Age Concern England.

Andrews, M. (1991) *Lifetimes of Commitment: aging, politics, psychology*, Cambridge: Cambridge University Press.

Blaikie, A. (1990) 'The emerging political power of the elderly in Britain 1908–1948', *Ageing and Society*, 10 (pt 1): 17–39.

Bornat, J. (1994) 'Age as resource', Unit 15 in *An Ageing Society*, Buckingham: Open University Press.

Bourke, J. (1994) *Working Class Cultures in Britain, 1890–1960*, London: Routledge.

Campbell, B. (1984) *Wigan Pier Revisited*, London:Virago.

Curtis, Z. (1989) 'Older women and feminism: don't say sorry', *Feminist Review*, 31 (Spring): 143–7.

Curtis, Z. (1993) 'On being a woman in the pensioners' movement' in Johnson, J. and Slater, R. (eds) *Ageing and Later Life*, London: Sage.

Ginn, J. (1993) 'Grey Power: age based organisations responses to structured inequalities', *Critical Social Policy*, 38 (Autumn): 23–47.

Goodman, D. (1987) *No Thanks to Lloyd George: the forgotten story – how the pension was won*, Newcastle, Staffs: D Goodman.

Grant, L. (1985) 'The selling of old age', *SpareRib*, 154 (May): 6–8.

Jones, J. (1992) Interview with the author for Open University Course, *An Ageing Society*, Open University/BBC.

Labour Research (1993) 'Retired? Your Union needs you', *Labour Research*, October: 19–20.

Laczko, F. and Phillipson, C. (1991) *Changing Work and Retirement*, Buckingham: Open University Press.

Macdonald, B. and Rich, C. (1983), *Look me in the eye*, Minneapolis: Spinsters Ink. Published in the United Kingdom by the Women's Press.

Means, R. and Smith, R. (1985) *The Development of Welfare Services for the Elderly*, London: Croom Helm.

Midwinter, E. (1992) *Citizenship: from ageism to participation*, Carnegie Inquiry into the Third Age, Research Paper no 8, Dunfermline: Carnegie United Kingdom Trust.

Midwinter, E. and Tester, S. (1987) *Polls Apart? Older Voters and the 1987 General Election*, London: Centre for Policy on Ageing.

Miles, J. (1990) 'Towards equality: how pensions campaigns are changing. A study of the Greater London Pensioners Association, 1989–1900', unpublished MSc, University of London.

Miles, J. (1994) 'Slow progress: why a political framework is necessary for the evaluation of pensioners campaigns', *Generations Review*, 4(1): 4–7.

Phillipson, C. (1996) 'Intergenerational conflict and the welfare state: American and British perspectives' in Walker, A. (ed) *The New Generational Contract: intergenerational relations, old age and welfare*, London: University College London Press.

Pratt, H. J. (1993a) 'The emergence of seniors organisations an international perspective', *Ageing International*, 1 (March): 9–12.

Pratt, H. J. (1993b) *Gray Agendas: interest groups and public pensions in Canada, Britain and the United States*, Michigan: University of Michigan Press.

Rowbotham, S. (1989) *The Past is Before Us: feminism in action since the 1960s*, London: Penguin.

Smith, H. J. (1995) 'Gender and the Welfare State: the 1940 Old Age and Widows Pension Act', Historical Association.

Stacey, M. (1989) 'Older women and feminism: a note about my experience of the WLM', *Feminist Review*, 31 (Spring): 140–2.

Sykes, R. and Leather, P. (1997) *Grey Matters: a survey of older people in England*, Oxford: Anchor Trust.

The Hen Co-op (1993) *Growing Old Disgracefully: new ideas for getting the most out of life*, London: Piatkus.

Timmins, N. (1995) *The Five Giants: a biography of the welfare state*, London: Fontana.

Titmuss, R. M. (1958) 'Pension systems and population change' in *Essays on the Welfare State*, London: Allen & Unwin.

Tout, K. (1997) *Towards a Golden Age*, Bishop Auckland: Pentland.

Walker, A. and Maltby, T. (1997) *Ageing Europe*, Buckingham: Open University Press.

12 Advocacy, empowerment and older people

Andrew Dunning

In a period when demographic change is being viewed by governments in a manner close to panic, it is particularly timely that we remember the need to consider the views and interests of those who are part of that change... Old age all too frequently produces marginalisation. There is a need to ensure that the current emphasis upon community care and bringing services to older people in their own homes does not contribute to this... The alternative of residential care has its own problems for individuals attempting to exercise their rights and choices... I can only see a greater need for advocacy.

Helen Grew, National Pensioners' Convention, in Foreword to Dunning (1995) Citizen Advocacy and Older People: a code of good practice, CPA, pp. 6–7

Introduction

Advocacy generally involves people making a case for themselves and advancing their own interests, or representing others and supporting them to secure and exercise their rights on an individual or collective basis. The concept is especially important where people are disadvantaged or discriminated against and are at risk of mistreatment or marginalisation. Advocacy by and for younger disabled people, people with learning difficulties and people with mental health problems has burgeoned in Britain since the 1970s. However, interest in the rights and representation of older people has been a more recent departure. The Centre for Policy on Ageing has been committed to such development and has contributed a number of pieces of work to these areas (Norman, 1987; Wynne-Harley, 1991; Wertheimer, 1993; Dunning, 1995). This chapter is in three parts. It begins with an outline of the developmental and definitional aspects of advocacy with older people. This is followed by a discussion of the location of advocacy as a process of empowerment. Finally, it considers consumerism and citizenship as key approaches to advocacy with older people.

Advocacy in context

Interest in advocacy with older people stems from several interrelated developments and concerns. Six issues are identified here relating to population, legislation, protection, transition, discrimination and participation. Each of these is considered briefly.

First, the ageing of the *population* has been accompanied in some quarters by doomsday scenarios of a 'demographic timebomb' of dependency (see Chapter 1). This is a view that has been strongly challenged (Vincent, 1995). Yet, as we live longer, levels of frailty are subject to increase, and more of us are likely to find ourselves in a vulnerable position when it comes to making our needs known and being heard (Sidell, 1995). A further consequence of demographic change is that some older people may well not have family or friends to act as 'natural advocates', whilst for others conflict within existing relationships could be the main problem (Wertheimer, 1993).

Second, in terms of *legislation*, the Disabled Persons' (Services, Consultation and Representation) Act 1986 includes the statutory right for individuals to appoint a representative regarding local authority social services and other provision. But, the relevant sections which would do so have yet to be implemented. Moreover, the recent reforms in community care and institutional settings ostensibly promote user involvement and choice in the planning and provision of health and social care services (National Health Service and Community Care Act 1990). This has been accompanied by the proliferation of official guidance and charters stating a commitment to rights or entitlements, quality and standards for these services nationally and locally. Such initiatives suggest or make specific reference to the need for advocacy and independent representation, where required (Home Office, 1991; Social Services Inspectorate, 1991a).

Third, the role of advocacy in the *protection* of vulnerable adults generally and older people in particular has been recognised by the Law Commission within both its call for evidence and final recommendations of its review on the law and mental incapacity (Law Commission, 1993; 1995; Dunning, 1997). Surveys of adult abuse guidelines produced by health and social services authorities have also revealed that advocacy is incorporated in most procedural documentation (Bennett and Kingston, 1993). Conversely too, older people can be subjected to paternalistic attitudes and over protection within day to day living, so might require advocacy skills and support to take risks from time to time (Wynne Harley, 1991).

Fourth, changes in care needs or living arrangements can place an older person in a vulnerable position at times of *transition*, when their own views should be of paramount consideration. Such situations include deciding upon admission to residential care, hospital discharge, decisions about hospital treatment and the closure or changes of management of institutional settings (Phillipson, 1990). Advocacy is a means of ensuring that the voice of the older person is heard in the face of the pressure which can be exerted by those with conflicting interests (Ward, 1991). Beyond these points advocacy may be useful in resisting institutionalisation and assaults on personhood which can occur within 'caring' environments (Booth, 1993).

Fifth, ageism means *discrimination* against, and denial of the rights of, classes of people on the basis of chronological age. Social attitudes, policies and services can create and perpetuate negative assumptions and stereotypes which may be internalised by older people themselves (Bytheway and Johnson, 1990). Further, ageism may have a differential impact upon groups of older people on individual and institutional levels according to social divisions such as income and class (Phillipson, 1982), 'race' and ethnicity (Blakemore and Boneham, 1994), gender (Arber and Ginn, 1991), disability (Zarb and Oliver, 1993) and sexuality (Starr and Weiner, 1981). Advocacy presents a way to challenge the multiple oppression and exclusions experienced by many older people.

Finally, it is important to recognise that advocacy has not just grown out of health and social care related issues, but as a means of enabling *participation* in the wider society. This entails having access to a range of substantive and procedural rights as full citizens, of being seen not just as 'service users' but as people with a breadth of identities, ideals and interests (Dunning, 1993). This is a theme which is emphasised in the call for advocacy coming from older people and others within marginalised groups and 'user movements' themselves (Lindow and Morris, 1995).

Forms of advocacy

Having identified the main factors which have influenced interest in the need for advocacy, we shall now consider the various forms of advocacy which have emerged for, and by, older people in Britain. Creating a typology of existing forms of advocacy is problematic given the dynamism, diversity and disputed nature of the field. Several authors have variously aimed to provide definitions and descriptions (Gathercole, 1988; MIND, 1992; UKAN, 1994; Brandon, 1995) and a working party convened by the Centre for Policy on Ageing to devise a code of practice for citizen advocacy with older people has further contributed to this debate (Dunning, 1995). There is now some consensus that three broad categories of advocacy exist. These are professional advocacy, lay advocacy and self advocacy and, from these, flow several other forms, as considered below.

PROFESSIONAL ADVOCACY

In relation to professional advocacy, it is evident that a range of trained professionals and workers are paid to undertake an advocacy function on behalf of older people as a primary or partial element of their roles. Such professional advocacy is carried out by lawyers, ombudsmen, welfare and housing rights workers, health and social care workers, campaign bodies and paid advocates. Legal advocacy is perhaps the most widely known form of professional advocacy, and is undertaken by professionally qualified lawyers on behalf of their clients on a personal basis. The ombudsman system is a similarly well established means of independent representation, and way of seeking redress in relation to maladministration within a variety of areas of public service. The work of welfare and housing rights workers also involves a legalistic or casework relationship in the provision of advice and representation for individuals and groups (Bateman, 1995).

Health and social services professionals can have an advocacy role on behalf of service users. Davies (1994) argues that social workers and care managers may provide advocacy on a personal or structural level where they possess the requisite skills and qualities and have access to resources which can tip the balance of power in favour of service users whose interests would otherwise be ignored. The United Kingdom Central Council (UKCC) Code of Professional Conduct formalises advocacy by nurses:

> expecting practitioners to accept a role as advocate on behalf of their patients, thereby ensuring that they have enough information to exercise control over their own health care, their legal and moral rights are respected, and health care resources are adequate to provide an appropriate quality and quantity of nursing.
>
> *Cahill, 1994: 371*

Despite the positive intentions and actions of health and social services professionals in performing an advocacy role, there are also significant limitations in their ability to do so effectively. Gathercole (in Butler et al, 1988: 13) suggests several conflicts of interest. At an organisational level the survival of the service might outweigh the interests of users; on a professional level, promoting the views of users which challenge the name of a profession might be discouraged; managerial interests might differ from the views of staff working directly with service users at the grass roots; individual staff may have their own personal needs to consider; and service workers may have competing demands on their time from other individuals or groups of service users. Furthermore, it is not always easy for professionals to acknowledge such conflicts and still work in an enabling way to advance the rights and entitlements of users (Brandon, 1995).

Organisations which employ staff to lobby and campaign on behalf of a particular group of people, may be said to engage in public advocacy. They tend to be national voluntary organisations with local networks. Age Concern, for example, has initiated campaigns on a range of issues including the need for wider availability of breast cancer screening for older women, better services for older people living in their own homes, and adequate provision for continuing care. Such organisations often provide direct services themselves as part of their activities. There is a need to recognise that this dual function could throw up conflicts of interest and compromise the independence of the advocacy role (Willis, 1988; Wood, 1991). It is also significant that most of these organisations are not controlled by those they seek to represent, as some have themselves indeed acknowledged:

> But for whom do we really speak? When are we speaking *for* older people and when are we speaking *about* them, but not being their voice? Is there more we could do to ensure that we fully understand the views of older people and present these effectively to the outside world? What other voices do we have?
>
> *Age Concern, 1993: 1*

There are now a growing number of paid advocates who provide a specific advocacy service covering either particular issues such as complaints, or specific client groups. They are more or less independent according to their sources of funding and organisational arrangements. Some are very rooted within the communities they serve, others are inextricably linked to services within which they operate (National Association of Health Authorities and Trusts, 1993). At present paid advocates are perhaps less well known than the professionals and bodies mentioned above. The following case study is drawn from the experiences of Card (1990):

> The Brighton Mental Health Project, a voluntary organisation, agreed to manage an advocacy worker for older people with mental health problems in an initiative funded by Brighton Health Authority. The work concentrated upon taking referrals from an acute hospital and a day care unit. The worker found that before representation could be undertaken it was necessary to spend a good deal of time gaining the confidence and getting to know the needs and wishes of each person referred. The tasks undertaken by the worker included providing support to an individual throughout a Mental Health Review Tribunal, representation at multi disciplinary meetings, securing personal possessions, releasing welfare benefit personal allowances, and pursuing complaints or reporting on poor standards of food, transport and discharge arrangements. The worker also recorded the need to overcome the tendency towards passive acceptance on the part of users to whatever was on offer and the deficits in staff awareness and training to encourage the development of user centred services.

LAY ADVOCACY

As previously suggested, family and friends can be strong advocates or may have interests which conflict with those of the older person in need of support. Citizen advocacy and crisis advocacy have developed as alternative lay responses to the rights and representation of older people. Ivers (in Bernard and Glendenning, 1990: 51) provides a useful definition of such responses based upon the work of the Advocacy with Older People in North Staffordshire Project, established by the Beth Johnson Foundation,

> Advocacy occurs when a private citizen enters into a relationship with and represents the interests of an elderly person who needs assistance to improve his or her quality of life to obtain full rights and entitlements. By providing emotional support through friendship, spokespersonship, opportunities to learn new skills and help in obtaining needed services, volunteers work for the benefit and growth of the elderly person. The advocate maintains complete loyalty to the partner and represents his or her wishes, needs and preferences as if they were their own.

The main principles of citizen advocacy are that it is *independent* of services or others whose interests conflict with those of the partner; the *loyalty* of the advocate is to the partner alone; the advocate is involved on a *voluntary* basis; the advocate is involved with the partner on a *one to one* basis; the partnership has the capacity to develop on a *long term* basis; and that citizen advocacy schemes should ensure a *diversity* of relationships and involve a whole range of people in their activities (Butler et al, 1988). Crisis advocacy shares the same principles as citizen advocacy but, as its name implies, is short term in nature. This tends to be one-off involvement centred upon a specific task or situation such as a housing benefit query or threat of eviction in which a partner needs the support of an advocate.

Citizen advocacy was originally developed during the 1960s in the United States of America where it was associated with ideas around normalisation (Wolfensberger and Zahua, 1973; O'Brien and Wolfensberger, 1977; O'Brien, 1987). It subsequently grew in Canada, Australia and Scandinavia. The first scheme in Britain was established in 1982 by Advocacy Alliance for the residents of three long stay hospitals for people with learning disabilities in South West London (Sang and O'Brien, 1984). Such schemes were initially focused upon younger adults with learning disabilities or mental health problems, but by the late 1980s citizen advocacy projects for older people were being set up (Age Concern England, 1989; Dunning, 1991; Ivers, 1994). In reviewing the scale, status and scope of citizen advocacy with older people, Wertheimer (1993) collated a list of sixteen schemes; while an unpublished mapping exercise of schemes conducted by the Centre for Policy on Ageing in 1997 identified sixty, stretching from Fife to the Isle of Wight. Birmingham Citizen Advocacy, as outlined in the following case study, was one of the earliest of these schemes.

Birmingham Citizen Advocacy was established in 1987. It is a voluntary organisation with an independent management committee which has included representatives from pensioners' organisations and consumer groups of older people. The scheme was a response to the expressed needs of mental health service users through the Birmingham Community Care Special Action Project, a three year initiative in which the local authority and health authorities attempted to develop services based upon the needs and involvement of users and carers. Birmingham Citizen Advocacy initially concentrated upon younger adults with mental health problems but went on to develop part of its work specifically with older people with mental health problems and dementia. The scheme employs a coordinator who is responsible for seeking older people who might need an advocate; recruiting and training advocates; supporting advocacy partnerships; raising awareness about advocacy and initiating project development. The work is centred upon a particular electoral constituency and includes older people with mental health problems and dementia living within community and institutional settings. As well as providing citizen advocacy the scheme has gone on to develop or support other forms of lay and self advocacy. It was recently involved in representing older people with dementia affected by the closure of a local authority residential care home.

Birmingham Citizen Advocacy/Friends of Bourn House, 1996

Advocates may have two broad and sometimes overlapping roles: instrumental and expressive. The instrumental role involves the advocate as a formal representative, spokesperson, troubleshooter, information aide or agent. The expressive role involves the advocate meeting the needs of the partner through compassion and concern, and in being a companion and enabler.

SELF ADVOCACY

Self advocacy, by contrast, is essentially about 'speaking up for yourself'. It involves an individual or group of people making their own choices and decisions, expressing their own needs and concerns, acting on their own behalf and representing their own interests. Most older people are well able to advocate for themselves on an individual basis, but there can sometimes be difficulties in speaking up alone which the benefits of speaking up alongside others on a peer or collective basis can address.

As was the case with the emergence of lay forms of advocacy, the growth of self advocacy has usually been associated with the achievements of younger disabled adults and those with mental health problems (Rogers and Pilgrim, 1991; Flynn and Ward, 1991; Shakespeare, 1993). However, there are longstanding and recent examples of these forms being developed by older people for one another. They have taken a diversity of shapes but are generally underpinned by principles of self help and mutual support.

Peer advocacy takes place where one person advocates for another of similar background and experience. Furthermore:

> Peer advocacy could be an important element in the overall struggle to include rather than exclude people from mainstream society. It involves a form of judo which begins to value those qualities which were until only recently both devalued and dismissed.
>
> *Brandon, 1995: 114*

An early example of such support in the field of mental health is that of John Perceval, a former long stay psychiatric patient who acted as a peer advocate for another patient at the Bethlehem Hospital. Perceval founded the Alleged Lunatics' Friends Society in 1845 which translated peer support into political action (Brandon, 1995). A hundred and fifty years or so later the Beth Johnson Foundation developed a programme of peer health counselling in which older people with an interest and enthusiasm to share knowledge about self health issues were able to do so amongst peers (Ivers and Meade, 1990). Some of the peer health counsellors involved in this initiative went on to become advocates on a one to one basis with other more vulnerable older people (Ivers, 1994). In this sense peer advocacy may be seen to provide a bridge between advocacy on behalf of older people, and advocacy by older people themselves.

Collective or group advocacy entails a self advocacy body which offers mutual support, skill development and a common call for change. This could include national organisations or local forums run for and by older people. Collective advocacy may be said to highlight that the 'personal is political', though such bodies may themselves be more or less explicit in their political agendas. Pensioner membership organisations such as the National Federation of Retirement Pensioners Associations (Pensioners' Voice) began to develop during the 1930s and 1940s, mainly to demands for adequate pension provision. This focus has subsequently widened to encompass a variety of other matters including transport, housing, and health and social care. The National Pensioners Convention was created in 1979 through the collective efforts of elders' organisations to have a coordinated voice for the concerns of older people. The first Pensioners Parliament was held in 1995 and has since become a focus for the pensioners movement to discuss and determine issues to pursue with politicians and policy makers (Thain in Jack, 1995).

At a local level too there has been widespread development of forums to influence public policy, including the Strathclyde Elderly Forum and the West Midlands Pensioners Convention (Carter and Nash, 1993). The Greater London Forum for the Elderly initiated the 'Older Voice in Community Care Planning and Provision' project, which is working with individual members of pensioners forums across London, including representation from local minority ethnic groups and frail service users, to provide the necessary information and skills to participate in community care consultations (Lindow and Morris 1995). Residents' committees, and other groups of users within service settings themselves, can provide a further means of collective organisation and of being heard, subject to the sensitive support of service staff (Elkan and Kelly, 1991). Some organisations have also been established to give voice to particular social groups of older people including the Standing Conference of Ethnic Minority Senior Citizens and the Older Women's Project, a forerunner to the Association of Greater London Older Women, which aimed to help older women, '...gain confidence to speak out and become guerillas in the battle for a brighter future' (Curtis in Jack, 1995: 170).

Conceptualising advocacy and empowerment

Having discussed the emergence and forms of advocacy with older people, we will now explore some of the conceptual issues involved within its development. Despite its apparent pervasiveness and potential, advocacy with older people has largely eluded empirical study (Holly and Webb, 1993; Ivers, 1994; Blaker, 1995; Bull, 1996) and has been subject to little critical analysis (Phillipson, 1990; Wood, 1991; Dunning, 1993; Brandon, 1995). However, advocacy is a process of empowerment (Age Concern England, 1989) and might accordingly be located within debates around this concept. Empowerment has been described as,

> Making it possible for people to exercise power and have more control over their lives. That means having a greater voice in institutions, agencies and situations which affect them. It also means being able to share power or exercise power over someone else, as well as them exercising it over you.
>
> *Beresford and Croft, 1993: 50*

Power and participation are explicit within this definition of empowerment, and each can be further analysed in order to inform our understanding of advocacy.

Lukes' (1974) dimensional analysis of power directly relates to debates around empowerment and advocacy. Lukes suggests that a one dimensional analysis of power highlights explicit conflict and considers whose preferences prevail. The two dimensional view is more subtley involved with the mobilisation of bias by the powerful in their efforts to ensure that rules work in their favour and to strike off the agenda any conflictual issues. The three dimensional view is concerned with the powerless being influenced by the forces of ideology and relations of production to act against their own objective interests through lack of expression or consciousness of their position. Digeser (1992) extends Lukes' analysis by adding a fourth dimension or 'face', in which power operates within all structures of thinking and behaviour, and dictates the discourses which govern our whole

This analysis may be related to the work of Croft and Beresford (1995) who suggest that there are two competing discourses around participation within the arena of community care; the discourse of politicians and professionals on the one hand, and the discourse of disabled people and service users, including older people on the other. There can be common purpose and alliances between individuals and organisations from each of these groups. Indeed, some will have experience of both. Nevertheless, in general there are significant differences in the principles and purposes apparent within these discourses as:

> That of the service providers and their associates is crucially concerned with their agencies and services; how to make them more efficient, cost effective, better managed and responsive. That of disabled people and service users is primarily concerned with their lives, rights, choices and opportunities.
>
> *Croft and Beresford in Jack, 1995: 61*

The picture presented above has profound implications for debates around empowerment and advocacy with older people. In relation to Lukes' third dimension, a number of studies have suggested that older people themselves may not always 'express' or even be 'conscious of their interests' (National Consumer Council, 1982; Allen et al, 1992). Advocacy can provide a means of raising awareness, returning the interests of older people onto the agenda and redressing the imbalance of power. However, advocacy may itself be all too easily subject to the fourth face of power and become colonised or otherwise compromised by politicians, policy makers and professionals (Dowson, 1991; Booth, 1993).

One way of illuminating the true extent to which both empowerment has taken place, and advocacy has been able to flourish is by way of a systematic analysis of levels of citizen or user power. Arnstein (1969) provided an early means of measurement through the following ' ladder of citizen participation':

8 Citizen Control

7 Delegated Power   Degrees of Citizen Power

6 Partnership

5 Placation

4 Consultation   Degrees of Tokenism

3 Informing

2 Therapy

1 Manipulation   Non Participation

This idea is further developed in the context of community care policy in Britain by Taylor et al (1992) in a table of levels of empowerment.

High	Users have the authority to take decisions
	Users have the authority to take some decisions
	Users have an opportunity to influence decisions
	User views are sought before making decisions
	Decisions are publicised and explained before implementation
Low	Information is given about decisions made

Clearly, the higher the level occupied on the ladder or table, the greater the degree of empowerment. At the foot of the ladder of citizen participation older people, individually or collectively, are non-participants who are merely subjects of therapy or manipulation. At its mid-point they might be informed about decisions already taken, consulted without necessarily influencing decisions, or placated with limited access to decision making. Toward the top of the ladder they might operate alongside powerful others in partnership within the decision making process, obtain delegated power to make decisions for themselves, or ultimately control the whole process.

Older people are often seen to occupy the bottom rungs or lower levels of these constructs (Thornton and Tozer, 1994; Goss and Miller, 1995). Thus, advocacy can be a way of redressing the imbalances of power so that disempowered older people may move on up and take control of the decision making processes and services which shape their lives. However, it is apparent that advocacy must be focused upon their interests, and independent of the vested interests of the powerful, if real progress is to be made. Social attitudes, legislative frameworks, sources of funding, organisational arrangements and the involvement of older people themselves, can all play a part in the extent to which advocacy overcomes the more destructive facets of power highlighted by Lukes and Digeser.

A further important element of the empowerment debate with direct relevance to the development of advocacy with older people is that of empowerment strategies. Hirschman (1970) identifies two main strategies for service user empowerment: 'exit' and 'voice'. The exit strategy refers to the power that users may exert over providers by being able to move to other providers if dissatisfied with the service they receive. This strategy supposes that there are a range of options and alternative sources of provision from which to choose, and is related to market or consumerist perspectives on welfare. The voice strategy assumes that users remain with the same service provider but have a say in how that service is delivered. This accords with a democratic or citizenship perspective of welfare in which users may influence the general and specific provision of public services (Hoyes et al, 1993). This strategy might be further extended towards having 'a right or entitlement to a service in the first place' (Hoggett, 1992: 19).

Advocacy with older people can be located within each of these strategies of empowerment. An older person might leave one type of accommodation in preference for another by advocating for themselves or with the support of someone else; a group of older service users might be involved in a local community care forum and advocate for a change or modification in the delivery of services; and a national body of older people might advocate for legislative change which enshrines rights to services or fair treatment.

The consideration of these strategies moves this discussion along from the conceptualisation of advocacy as a process of empowerment, towards the identification of consumerism and citizenship as distinct approaches to advocacy itself. These approaches will now be explored in more detail with regard to policy and practice.

Advocacy and consumerism

The market ideology of the new right and successive Conservative government administrations between 1979 and 1997 gave rise to the notion of consumerism in all things. The National Health Service and Community Care Act 1990 heralded the purchaser/provider split and the contract culture in terms of health and social services. The stated rationale for the reorganisation of these services was the empowerment of users and carers, who were to be placed at the centre of new community care structures and processes. As around half of all NHS and personal social service users are over the age of 65, this has been particularly significant for older people.

The reforms established three separate mechanisms which were said to be aimed at giving people who use services a greater say in the support they receive by means of:

- annual consultation to be conducted by local authorities with users, carers and their local communities with regard to community care plans;
- involvement of users and carers as the central component of the assessment and care management process;
- accessible and comprehensive complaints procedures to be produced by all social services departments in order to enable users and carers to challenge the decisions and actions of service providers.

However, as far as older people are concerned there is longstanding and recent evidence that in themselves these mechanisms will not be sufficient to bring about greater participation, as demonstrated by the findings of two major studies a decade apart:

> The outstanding impression which emerges from this report is that although the elderly have similar concerns to the rest of the population, they are least likely to complain or even to ask for advice and information. Through this report we may hear echoed the voices of people who take pride in 'putting up' with things as they are. The quality is admirably stoic, but it can and does lead to a serious social injustice unless it is watched over solicitously by a society which protects, respects and takes pride in its older citizens.
>
> *National Consumer Council, 1982: 2*

> Few, if any elderly people interviewed had any choice in what went into their package of care and some did not have anything in their package at all. They usually had no choice about the time which the service was delivered, the person who delivered it or how much they received… Choice and participation usually took a negative form, with elderly people refusing services.
>
> *Allen et al, 1992: 325*

Indeed, it would appear that even the most basic requirement for older people to participate in marketised welfare as 'informed' consumers remains unfulfilled. As stressed by the British Pensioners' Federation,

> lack of information is one of the main reasons for elderly people's indecision on many things which affect their lives. One never hears about too much information being given to people…people often do not ask for information and do not understand the system.
>
> *Lindow and Morris, 1995: 35*

Without further forms of support and encouragement it remains difficult for older people to be heard. This is to some extent recognised within the guidance on the community care reforms published by the Social Services Inspectorate (SSI, 1991a). The guidance envisages that care managers will be 'in a better position to act as advocate for the user' by separating out the tasks of assessment and care planning from direct service provision. As well as undertaking such 'professional' advocacy there is acknowledgement that there 'will be circumstances where independent advocacy is considered to be the best option'. In such circumstances the guidance proposes that the user or carer should be given information about such schemes locally, and that they should be 'supported in securing independent representation' if unable to do so for themselves. Moreover, the guidance suggests that managers should support the development of local independent advocacy schemes (including forms lay and self advocacy). The Citizens Charter also fleetingly refers to the idea of 'independent representation or advocacy where necessary' in respect of social services assessment and provision (Home Office, 1991: 21).

Despite these references to independent forms of advocacy, there is little in the way of rigour or vigour in implementation. Simons (1993) comments that the guidance is notable for its passive voice. Who, for example, decides when 'it is clear' that independent advocacy is needed? There is no definition of particular forms of advocacy and no suggestion of who advocates might be or of their specific roles or of their support needs. The official response to funding requirements for advocacy was buried in a written answer to the House of Commons by Virginia Bottomley, the then Minister of Health, who stated that the cost of advocacy for everyone being assessed under the terms of the community care reforms would be prohibitive (Bottomley, V, 1991 written answer – disabled people, Hansard 22 March, 254–55).

Given such ambiguities it is perhaps unsurprising that in a review of assessment procedures developed under the new legislation the Social Services Inspectorate itself found that little was being done by local authorities to encourage a range of independent advocacy, or to enable users to find advocacy. This was especially true of the representation of older people as service users as:

> Departments seemed to think that periodic consultation with groups representing users' interests such as MIND and Age Concern was sufficient.
>
> *SSI, 1991b*

The contract culture has given rise to tensions between purchasers and providers and independent advocacy schemes as to the purpose and performance of advocacy on offer. There has been a tendency for statutory bodies to view advocacy as a 'service' which can be bought in the same way as day care or domiciliary support. This leaves advocacy itself vulnerable to being reinterpreted to fit in with the organisational imperatives of service purchasers and providers, to become a component of quality assurance or even a substitute for good practice, rather than being retained as a community or elders' response to rights and representation. Advocacy projects may be tempted to lose their independence, vociferousness and creativity in order to secure a contract and survive. The evaluation critieria as set down by the statutory authorities issuing contracts may also compromise projects:

> The problem with existing conventional outcome measures is that they are not geared to the underlying principles of advocacy and indeed may undermine them.
>
> *Hunter, 1995:*

In the process of consultation for the *Code of Practice for Citizen Advocacy with Older People* (Dunning, 1995) a number of stories were told of the pressures faced by advocacy organisations to comply with the priorities of statutory authorities who were also funding them. These included that of a project which lost health authority funding because it refused to provide advocates for older people with learning disabilities in a hastily arranged hospital unit closure. Whilst advocacy projects should of course be subject to evaluation and public account-abiity, that need not entail ownership by the statutory authorities who fund or contract.

Ellis (1993) suggests that a major cultural shift is required in terms of both policy and practice if independent forms of advocacy are to be used effectively to advance the interests of the majority of people approaching social services departments for help. Marshall (in Killeen, 1996: 33) echoes this when she states that, 'If real empowerment of people with dementia through advocacy is to be advanced in this country then fundamental changes need to take place in the culture of the caring professions within statutory authorities.' Such concerns are not new, in that paternalistic welfare bureaucracies of the past purported to 'know best', clientise and effectively disempower their users (London Edinburgh Weekend Return Group, 1979). Nevertheless, consumerism may be said to have produced a particularly acute instrumentality and inequality within relationships between statutory authorities and service users and indeed advocacy initiatives.

Advocacy and citizenship

Since the late 1980s there has been a revival of interest in the concept of citizenship (Roche, 1992; Turner, 1993). These debates have emphasised the need for social rights and entitlements (Plant in Coote, 1992). They are also concerned with issues of inclusion, recognition of diversity and the nature of social relations (Taylor, 1996; Barnes, 1997). Age and the status of older people are clearly dimensions within these discussions. A link between citizenship, age and advocacy is made by Phillipson (1990) who suggests that advocacy may be seen as a way of realising human potential as well as rights, increasing power and participation based on citizen action, and enhancing intergenerational relations and the sharing of resources. Consideration will now be given to developments in policy and practice which promote advocacy as a means of securing and exercising the substantive and procedural rights of older people. Particular attention will be given to the implementation of legislation, funding arrangements, raising awareness, building alliances and ensuring social inclusion.

At present, advocacy does not have any legal status in Britain. The non implementation of Sections 1 and 2 of the Disabled Persons (Services, Consultation and Representation) Act 1986 has denied disabled people the right to appoint an independent representative. The representative or advocate would have been able to receive information, attend key meetings, gain access and generally act on behalf of the person in dealing with local authority and other services. Charters may well proclaim the entitlement to such arrangements, but fall short on meeting the obligation in practice.

Whilst this chapter is focused upon advocacy and older people in Britain, it is worth noting that advocacy forms an important part of provision in other jurisdictions including the United States of America, Australia and Canada. In 1992 the Ontario provincial government in particular passed a tranche of legislation which was aimed at clarifying and expanding the rights of health service users. The reforms included the Advocacy Act, Consent to Treatment Act and Substitute Decision Making Act, and led to the establishment of an Advocacy Commission, the majority of whose members were older and disabled people (Wahl, 1994). Legislation alone is of course insufficient in itself to ensure that the interests of older people are protected. It is nonetheless a means of establishing non negotiable rights and a baseline for further gains.

A consequence of the lack of statutory status accorded to advocacy is the lack of available and appropriate funding (Philpot, 1993). This situation is unlikely to change in the foreseeable future if advocacy schemes rely upon cash strapped and reprioritised local authority social services departments (Means and Smith, 1994). A practical manifestation of citizenship, in terms of funding advocacy on a national level, might be direct grants to local projects from central government, thus enhancing the independence of such projects in their dealings with all local services. Such mechanisms are already in place in other areas of social policy. Independent local victim support schemes, for example, have been funded directly by central government. Alternatively, on a local level funding could be allocated to advocacy projects from the office of the local authority chief executive, rather than by social services or health authorities. Again, this provides a greater degree of independence and underlines that those requiring advocacy do so as citizens of that authority, who have the right to the same wide range of services and activities enjoyed by all and are not just users or consumers of a particular health or social service (Dunning, 1993).

Raising awareness and forming alliances, constitute important measures for advocacy on the basis of citizenship from the 'bottom up'. Advocacy projects need to raise awareness about their activities among politicians, professionals, voluntary groups and local communities. One reason that alliances need to be made with caring professionals and workers is that without legislation advocacy can often only be undertaken at their behest (Ivers, 1994). On a more positive note, there is a tradition within the service user movement of identifying 'allies' in services who are supportive of advocacy principles and upholding citizen rights. Moreover, service staff might value these links when they are aware of conflicts of interest within their own role. A number of trade unions and professional associations have also officially recognised the need for independent advocacy beyond the confines of consumerism (Read and Wallcraft, 1994; Carpenter, 1995). In their work on issues of consent and care with older people the British Medical Association and the Royal College of Nursing jointly state that independent advocacy:

> can be invaluable in helping a patient to express his or her views if there are difficulties in communication. As the advocates are neither a relative nor associated with the health care facility, they can offer assistance without being influenced by conflicting interests.
>
> *British Medical Association/Royal College of Nursing, 1995: 38*

Finally, a citizenship rights-based approach also presents some further challenges to the advocacy movement itself with regard to participation and purpose. Amongst the considerations and decisions to be made here are: to what extent do independent advocacy initiatives work on an intergenerational basis or a peer basis; how are both individual and collective approaches incorporated; how are older people with dementia or other severe impairments to be involved; how are issues affecting black and minority ethnic elders addressed; how do the concerns about the rights and representation of older people overlap with those of other social movements?

Conclusion

Despite the limitations and difficulties indentified in the preceding pages, advocacy and empowerment are now clearly on the agenda in social policy terms. This chapter has outlined the emergence and manifestations of advocacy with older people in Britain. Debates around empowerment, including the identification of dimensions of power, competing discourses and degrees of participation, have served to underpin advocacy at a conceptual level. Through the location of advocacy as a process of empowerment it has been possible to highlight two distinct approaches to advocacy itself: consumerism and citizenship. The consumerist perspective may at best reduce older people to being viewed as users of health and social services alone and restrict advocacy to customer care. The citizenship perspective has been shown to offer fresh opportunities and challenges along the way to securing rights and creating a greater level of involvement on the part of marginalised and mistreated individuals and groups, including many older people.

References

Age Concern England (1989) *Guidelines for Setting Up Advocacy Schemes*, Mitcham: Age Concern England.

Age Concern (1993) *Recognising Our Voices*, Belfast, Edinburgh, London and Cardiff: Age Concern Northern Ireland, Scotland, England and Wales.

Allen, I., Hogg, D. and Peace, S. (1992) *Elderly People: choice, participation and satisfaction*, London: Policy Studies Institute.

Arber, S. and Ginn, J. (1991) *Gender and Later Life*, London: Sage.

Arnstein, S. (1969) 'A ladder of citizen participation', *Journal of the American Institute of Planners*, 35(4): 216–24.

Barnes, M. (1997) *Care, Communities and Citizens*, Harlow: Longman.

Bateman, N. (1995) *Advocacy Skills: a handbook for human service professionals*, Aldershot: Arena.

Bennett, G. and Kingston, P. (1993) *Elder Abuse: concepts, theories and interventions*, London: Chapman and Hall.

Beresford, P. and Croft, S. (1993) *Citizen Involvement: a practical guide for change*, London: Macmillan.

Bernard, M. and Glendenning, F. (eds) (1990) *Advocacy, Consumerism and the Older Person*, Stoke on Trent: Beth Johnson Foundation.

Birmingham Citizen Advocacy/ Friends of Bourn House (1996) *Closing A Home For Dementia Sufferers*, Birmingham Citizen Advocacy, Sparkbrook, Birmingham, B12 8LF.

Blakemore, K. and Boneham, M. (1994) *Age, Race and Ethnicity*, Buckingham: Open University Press.

Blaker, V. (1995) *Care Through Empowerment: an evaluation of Age Concern Nottinghamshire's Advocacy Service*, Nottingham: Age Concern Nottinghamshire.

Booth, T. (1993) 'Obstacles to the development of user centred services', in Johnson, J. and Slater, R. (eds) *Ageing and Later Life*, London: Sage.

Brandon, D. (1995) Advocacy: power to people with disabilities, Birmingham: Venture.

British Medical Association/ Royal College of Nursing (1995) *The Older Person: consent and care*, London: British Medical Association.

Bull, A. (1996) *Gwent Befriending and Avocacy Project: evaluation report 1994–1996*, Gwent: Alzheimer's Disease Society.

Butler, K., Carr, S. and Sullivan, F. (1988) *Citizen Advocacy: a powerful partnership*, London: National Citizen Advocacy.

Bytheway, B. and Johnson, J. (1990) 'On defining ageism', *Critical Social Policy*, 10(2): 27–39.

Cahill, J. (1994) 'Are you prepared to be their advocate?', *Professional Nurse*, 9(6): 371–75.

Card, H. (1990) 'Senior citizen advocacy', *Openmind*, 45 (June/July): 17.

Carpenter, M. (1995) *Normality is Hard Work: trade unions and the politics of community care*, London: Lawrence and Wishart.

Carter, A. and Nash, C. (1993) *Pensioners' Forums: an active voice*, University of Surrey, Guildford: Pre Retirement Association.

Coote, A. (ed) (1992) *The Welfare of Citizens: developing new social rights*, London: Rivers Oram Press.

Croft, S. and Beresford, P. (1995) 'Whose empowerment? Equalising the competing discourses in community care', in Jack, R. (ed) *Empowerment in Community Care*, London: Chapman and Hall.

Curtis, Z. (1995) 'Gaining confidence – speaking out, in Jack, R. (ed) *Empowerment in Community Care*, London: Chapman and Hall.

Davies, M. (1994) *The Essential Social Worker*, 3rd edition, Aldershot: Arena.

Digeser, P. (1992) 'The fourth face of power', *Journal of Politics*, 54(4): 977–1007.

Dowson, S. (1991) *Keeping it Safe: self advocacy by people with learning difficulties and the professional response*, London: Values into Action.

Dunning, A. (1991) 'Citizen advocacy', *Midlands Pensioner*, 35 (Winter 1991/1992): 6.

Dunning, A. (1993) *Who Owns Citizen Advocacy?* Paper presented at the European Community Care and Elderly People conference, University of Plymouth.

Dunning, A, (1995) *Citizen Advocacy with Older People: a code of good practice*, London: Centre for Policy on Ageing.

Dunning, A. (1997) 'Advocacy and older people with dementia' in Marshall, M. (ed) *State of the Art in Dementia Care*, London: Centre for Policy on Ageing.

Elkan, R. and Kelly, D. (1991) *A Window in Homes: links between residential care homes and the community*, Surbiton: Social Care Association.

Ellis, K. (1993) *Squaring the Circle: user and carer participation in needs assessment*, York: Joseph Rowntree Foundation.

Estes, C. L. (1979) *The Ageing Enterprise*, San Francisco: Jossey Bass.

Flynn, M. and Ward, L. (1991) 'We can change the future: self and citizen advocacy', in Segal, S. S. and Varma, V. P. (eds), *Prospects for People with Learning Difficulties*, London: David Fulton Publishers.

Gathercole, C. (1988) *Citizens First*, Clitheroe: Citizens First North West.

Goldsmith, M. (1996) *Hearing the Voice of People with Dementia*, London: Jessica Kingsley.

Goss, S. and Miller, C. (1995) *From Margin to Mainstream*, York: Joseph Rowntree Foundation.

Hirschman, A. (1970) *Exit, Voice and Loyalty: responses to the decline in firms, organisations and states*, Harvard: Harvard University Press.

Hoggett, P. (1992) 'The politics of empowerment', *Going Local*, 19: 18–19.

Holly, L. and Webb, B. (1993) *Citizen Advocacy in Practice: the experience of the Scarborough-Rydale-Whitby Advocacy Alliance*, London: The Tavistock Institute.

Home Office (1991) *The Citizen's Charter*, London: HMSO.

Hoyes, L., Jeffers, S., Lart, R., Means, R. and Taylor, M. (1993) *User Empowerment and the Reform of Community Care*, Bristol: School for Advanced Urban Studies.

Hunter, S. (1995) *Safeguarding Advocacy*. Unpublished Paper, Department of Social Administration and Social Work, University of Edinburgh.

Ivers, V. (1990) 'Advocacy with older people in North Staffordshire', in Bernard, M. and Glendenning, F. (eds.) *Advocacy, Consumerism and the Older Person*, Stoke on Trent: Beth Johnson Foundation.

Ivers, V. (1994) *Citizen Advocacy in Action: working with older people*, Stoke on Trent: Beth Johnson Foundation.

Ivers, V. and Meade, K. (1990) *Peer Health Counselling: a new approach to training and development*, Stoke on Trent: Beth Johnson Foundation.

Jack, R. (ed) (1995) *Empowerment in Community Care*, London: Chapman and Hall.

Killeen, J. (1996) *Advocacy and Dementia*, Edinburgh: Alzheimer Scotland Action on Dementia.

Law Commission (1993) *Mentally Incapacitated Adults and Decision Making: an overview*, Law Commission Consultation Paper No. 119, London: HMSO.

Law Commission (1995) *Mental Incapacity*, London: HMSO.

Lindow, V. and Morris, J. (1995) *User Involvement: synthesis of findings and experience in the field of community care*, York: Joseph Rowntree Foundation.

London Edinburgh Weekend Return Group (1979) *In And Against the State*, London: Pluto.

Lukes, S. (1974) *Power: a radical view*, London: Macmillan.

Means, R. and Smith, R. (1994) *Community Care: policy and practice*, London: Macmillan.

MIND (1992) *The MIND Guide to Advocacy: empowerment in action*, London: MIND.

National Association of Health Authorities and Trusts (1993) *Investing in Patients Representatives*, Birmingham: NAHAT.

National Health Service and Community Care Act (1990), London: HMSO.

National Consumer Council (1982) *The Elderly Consumer*, London: National Consumer Council.

Norman, A. (1987) *Rights and Risk: a discussion document on civil liberty in old age*, London: Centre for Policy on Ageing.

O'Brien, J. (1987) *Learning From Citizen Advocacy Programs*, Atlanta: Georgia Advocacy Office.

O'Brien, J. and Wolfensberger, W. (1977) *Standards for Citizen Advocacy Programme Evaluation*, Toronto: CAMR.

Phillipson, C. (1982) *Capitalism and the Construction of Old Age*, London: Macmillan.

Phillipson, C. (1990) 'Approaches to advocacy', in Bernard, M. and Glendenning, F. (eds) *Advocacy, Consumerism and the Older Person*, Stoke on Trent: Beth Johnson Foundation.

Philpot, T (1993) 'Lip service that gags advocacy', *The Guardian*, 17 March.

Plant, R. (1992) 'Citizenship, rights and welfare', in Coote, A. (ed) *The Welfare of Citizens: developing new social rights*, London: Rivers Oram Press.

Read, J. and Wallcraft, J, (1994) *Guidelines in Advocacy for Mental Health Workers*, London: MIND/UNISON.

Roche, M. (1992) *Rethinking Citizenship: welfare, ideology and change in modern society*, Cambridge: Polity Press.

Rogers, A. and Pilgrim, D. (1991) 'Pulling down churches: accounting for the British mental health users movement', *Sociology of Health and Illness*, 13(2): 129–48.

Sang, B. and O'Brien, J. (1984) *Advocacy: the UK and American experience*, King's Fund Project Paper, No. 51, London: King's Fund Centre

Shakespeare, T. (1993) 'Disabled People's Self Organisation: a new social movement?', *Disability, Handicap and Society*, 8(3): 249–64.

Sidell, M. (1995) *Health in Old Age: myth, mystery and management*, Buckingham: Open University Press.

Simons, K. (1993) *Citizen Advocacy: the inside view*, Bristol: Norah Fry Research Centre, University of Bristol.

Social Services Inspectorate (1991a) *Care Management and Assessment: managers' guide*, London: HMSO.

Social Services Inspectorate (1991b) *Assessment Systems and Community Care*, London: HMSO.

Starr, B. D. and Weiner, M. B. (1981) *Report on Sex and Sexuality in the Mature Years*, London: W. H. Allen.

Taylor, D. (ed) (1996) *Critical Social Policy: a reader*, London: Sage.

Taylor, M., Hoyes, L., Lart, R. and Means, R. (1992) *User Empowerment in Community Care: unravelling the issues*, Bristol: School for Advanced Urban Studies, University of Bristol.

Thain, J. (1995) 'Not too "grey" power' in Jack, R. (ed) *Empowerment in Community Care*, London: Chapman and Hall.

Thornton, P. and Tozer, R. (1994) *Involving Older People in Planning and Evaluating Community Care*, York: Social Policy Research Unit, University of York.

Turner, B. S. (1993) *Citizenship and Social Theory*, London: Sage.

UKAN(United Kingdom Advocacy Network) (1994) *Advocacy: a code of practice*, London: NHS Executive Mental Health Task Force User Group/Department of Health.

Vincent, J. A. (1995) *Inequality and Old Age*, London: University College London Press.

Wahl, J. (1994) *An Introduction to the Substitute Decisions Act, Consent to Treatment Act and Advocacy Act*, Toronto, Ontario: Advocacy Centre for the Elderly.

Ward, L. (1991) 'Having a say in community care', *Community Care*, April.

Wertheimer, A. (1993) *Speaking Out: citizen advocacy with older people*, London: Centre for Policy on Ageing.

Willis, E. (1988) *Advocacy: some perspectives for the nineties*, Berkhamstead: The Volunteer Centre UK.

Wolfensberger, W. and Zauha, H. (1973) *Citizen Advocacy and Protective Services for the Impaired and Handicapped*, Toronto: NIMR.

Wood, R. (1991) *Speak Up For Yourself: putting advocacy into practice*, London: Age Concern England.

Wynne-Harley, D. (1991) *Living Dangerously: risk taking, safety and older people*, London: Centre for Policy on Ageing.

Zarb, G. and Oliver, M. (1993) *Ageing with a Disability: what do they expect after all these years?* London: University of Greenwich.

13 The sexual politics of old age

Carole Archibald and Elizabeth Baikie

An elderly man who shows any signs of sexual interest is called 'dirty', and older women who make themselves sexually attractive as 'mutton dressed as lamb'. The author of the 'In England' column in *The Lancet* comments that 'the younger generation, so liberal, so free, so uninhibited by old-fashioned social conventions according to themselves, are often rigid, narrow, puritanical, and censorious when it comes to the behaviour of the older citizens'.

Alison Norman (1987) Aspects of Ageism, CPA, p. 15

Introduction

Fifty years ago social policy with regard to sexuality and older people was characterised by silence and omission, reflecting past and prevailing attitudes towards sexuality and ageing. The situation, with few exceptions, remains largely unchanged today. The stereotyping of older people as asexual and generally powerless has been a constant theme throughout the last half of the century and is in direct contrast to the changing locale of younger people. For the young there has been an increasing politicisation of sexuality from the late 1960s onwards. Until then it would have been unthinkable to link sex and politics (Caplan, 1987). The liberation movements ushered in the growth of sexual permissiveness which ostensibly, with the aid of contraception, allowed sexual freedom for both men and women. This freedom however was double edged and Millett (1969), amongst others, argued forcibly that gender relations and sexuality were about power: sexuality was consequently political. The radical women's movements were instrumental in bringing sex onto the political agenda highlighting, for example, sexual violence, pornography and abortion (Caplan, 1987). The cultural construction of sexuality and the ageism, which permeates some of the sociological literature and society generally, confine many old people to an asexual identity.

Feminists are now deeply divided on the politics of sexuality (Jackson, 1996; see also Rich, 1980; Jeffreys, 1990; Delphy, 1992; Jackson, 1992; Holloway, 1993; Kitzinger and Wilkinson, 1993) and while they have added much to the debate on sexuality and have politicised virtually everything, they have not politicised ageing (Woodward, 1991). Older people are literally written out of the script. The need to 'stay young and "beautiful" if you wanna be loved' has a certain resonance here. Sontag (1975 cited in Woodward 1991) discusses the double marginality of sexism and ageism to which women, in particular, are exposed. In western and other societies, it is a woman's sexual allure which is often seen as her most important 'economic possession' (Woodward, 1991: 16); one that diminishes more rapidly with age in comparison with men.

Gay groups, mainly in the US, have rendered sexuality a potent political issue (Caplan, 1987). They have given voice to people who were seen as marginal; but they have also been youth orientated and have not served the older generation particularly well (McDonald and Rich, 1984). Such negative messages need to be challenged, not least because if we live long enough then 'the subject of aging is one that belongs to all of us' (Woodward, 1991: 23). The politicised and radical movers of the 1960s are themselves now in their fifties and getting older. Ageing is not simply a theoretical construct. Existentially it is happening to everyone. As a consequence issues around sexual needs, identity and desire must be acknowledged and addressed at both a personal and policy level. Examining the relationship between ageism, race, gender and the structural processes at work in society, this chapter seeks to make visible older people including older people with dementia, challenging the myths and stereotypical views with regard to sexuality. It argues that sexuality needs to be seen as an intrinsic part of what makes us what we are as individuals, regardless of whether or not we remain sexually active. Sexuality contributes to that part of what Kitwood and Bredin (1992) refer to as personhood, and thus is fundamental to our being.

Age and ageism

Some (old) people remain sexually active, some choose not to be sexually active and some have that choice taken from them due to death of a partner, ill health or admission to long term care. Some are, or have been gay, lesbian or bi-sexual in their orientation. In societies where homosexuality is still denied or stigmatised, a gay or lesbian identity, Caplan (1987: 47) argues, will inevitably constitute a political choice: 'Identity is not a destiny but a choice.' Bancroft (1989: 185–9) suggests that the heterosexual/homosexual dichotomy, so evident in western societies is, rather, a social construct which operates through the mechanism of cognitive learning. The development of sexual identity is constructed as a complex process involving three stages: the pre-labelling stage; the self labelling stage; and the social labelling stage. He discusses a number of factors which contribute to this sexual learning, sexual preferences and sexual identity and concludes that sexual identity, as a cognitive variable, contributes to sexual preferences and the exclusively human phenomenon of exclusive homosexuality.

Whilst it can be said that sexuality is central to one's identity and sense of self, it is also embedded in, and intrinsic to, a whole set of social relations (Adkins and Merchant, 1996) including ageism, class, gender and race. Some have argued for sexuality to be seen in context as one of many gendered social practices (Jackson, 1996). Power operates on many levels and as a result sexuality needs to be seen as one aspect of life, albeit an important one. This is not disputed, but we need to consider the word 'seen'. Sexuality in later life, rather than being 'seen', is often disregarded by both theorists and practitioners. 'Omission is a powerful statement' (Starr and Weiner, 1981) and indicates how society (dis)regards (old) people as sexual beings. There is often little accommodation made, in a literal and metaphorical sense, to meet for example the sexual needs of older people in residential or hospital care. Hockey and James (1993: 173) point to the 'pervasive cultural strategy of infantilisation' and, in this climate, the sexuality of older people is often deemed inadmissible.

Literature can provide a sense of the subjectivity of ageing (see for example Woodward, 1991), providing some valuable insights. In her book *Love, Again*, Lessing's (1996: 136) main character, a woman of 60 plus years, talks of 'to get old, or even to grow older, is one so cruel...a husk, without colour, without the lustre, the shine'; but the book is essentially that of exploring the sexual, erotic and passionate thoughts and emotions of this older woman in love with two (younger) men. It gives voice to, and allows the possibility of an older woman, albeit an attractive, middle class, white woman, to be sexual.

Old age is a subjective experience, but outward manifestations are also evident. Physiologically there are marked changes in the body, the more obvious being those of skin and muscle changes. The symptoms ascribed to the menopause – irritability, depression and the possibility of painful heterosexual intercourse, place women at odds with 'the representations of the ideal feminine counterpoint to male sexuality' (Harding, 1988: 38) and in effect disqualifies older women as sexual beings. The medical discourse on Hormone Replacement Therapy (HRT) discuss the many benefits it offers women in terms of relief from transitory symptoms and prevention of certain diseases. It also holds out the promise for women to stay young and feminine forever (Wilson, 1966 cited in Harding, 1988) and has been seen as a means of defying the ageing process.

Sexuality and old age

Numerous physical conditions may occur as people age, for example heart disease, diabetes, arthritis and incontinence (Seymour, 1990). These conditions have the potential to affect a person's sexual life but, in themselves, they do not necessarily cause a cessation of sexual activity. Various studies have explored sexuality in later life (Verwoerdt et al, 1969; Pfeiffer and Davis, 1972; Pfeiffer, 1978; Hegelar Mortensen, 1978; White, 1982; Seymour, 1990) and provide helpful insights. Spence (1991: 249–50) furnishes a useful summary of research findings:

- Although sexual interest and activity tend to decrease in later life compared to earlier years, many older people continue to have active and enjoyable sexual relationships.
- Older males tend to show greater levels of sexual interest and activity than older females.
- Sexual activity patterns in old age tend to reflect the person's patterns in earlier years.
- Although physiological changes in sexual responding occur with age, these are insufficient to explain the decrease in sexual interest and activity found amongst many elderly people.
- The physiological changes in sexual responding which occur with age do not on their own result in sexual dysfunction.

Other factors, for example, bereavement, physical illness, relationship problems, the person's own attitude towards sexual activity and body image, can determine whether the person is sexually active in later life, as can societal factors such as the disapproval of others. Older people, when they were younger, were often subjected to repressive (religious) ideas about the expression of sexuality with much shame associated with touching and viewing their bodies, particularly their genitalia. The function of sex was often portrayed as that of procreation with masturbation pilloried and deemed sinful. There is a certain irony and pathos therefore in this age of sexual freedom and liberation, that old people now unwittingly, sometimes wittingly, have these repressive ideas and practices reinforced by younger people.

A major determinant of sexuality in old age seems to be how others view such activity yet having high self esteem, self worth and feeling good about oneself, are determinants of sexual activity in old age, as at any age. Other determinants of sexual activity in later life might include low personal concern about sex and problems in the relationship. Thus if sex has not been important to an individual in younger adulthood it is unlikely to be important later in life. When anger and resentment are present in relationships, this will also affect sexual communication. Unsuitable circumstances, for example lack of privacy, may cause individual couples to feel uncomfortable and inhibited about sexual expression (see Greenwood and Bancroft in Bancroft, 1989). For many younger adults this may result from living in close proximity to young children and teenagers in the home. For older people it may be living in close proximity to other residents in a residential home. Thin walls and poor sound proofing can be a problem at any age. Space and privacy are at a premium in nursing and residential homes and are factors which contribute to the creation of 'sexless' environments experienced by older people (Walz and Blum, 1987 cited in Fairchild et al, 1996).

Gender, class and race

In the study of sexuality, class and gender are intertwined. Discourses in western culture have generally been framed in a white, middle class, male and heterosexual perspective (Jackson, 1996). Issues of class are interpersed in the study of sexuality and as such there is a need to examine ways in which people's class position 'intersects with sexuality' (Richardson, 1996: 3). Social gerontological research, for the most part, has been concerned with white, middle class, non-institutionalised old people (Harding, 1988) and the literature on ageing assumes heterosexuality (Laner, 1978). It has typically meant a consideration of sexual intercourse (Catania and White, 1982) with little mention made of older women. Asexuality is, and has been, one representation of ageing women in feminist discourses (Harding, 1988).

Gender is of issue in the research on sexuality and older people. White (1982) found that older men are more frequently studied than older women, which is interesting given the greater proportion of older women in the population as a whole. This emphasis on older men may be explained by virtue of older men being more sexually active than older women or alternatively, a key consideration might be, as other researchers (Masters and Johnson, 1966; Lowenthal et al, 1975; Starr and Weiner, 1981) have indicated, that the sexual interest and sexual competence of the male is the key factor in sexual activity in older couples.

Earlier revolutionary ideas of sexual liberation have influenced and affected some older people. The emphasis has been on teaching about different sexual techniques. Solnick (1978) advocating such practices for *older couples* as non-demanding pleasuring of each other through massage, vibrators and oral sex could be seen as revolutionary although limited in who would and could, access, and use this information. The target audience seemed to be heterosexual middle class older people who had the health, the confidence and vocabulary with which to articulate their needs, and the wealth to pursue these activities. Sviland (1978) questioned the assumption that older people had an understanding of the sexual anatomy of their bodies. In a chapter that was ahead of its time Sviland (1978), within the context of older married heterosexual couples, provided novel ideas in sex educational material. The aims were several and included: to counter previously taboo ideas, increase the couples' repertoire of sexual ideas and techniques, including sexual fantasy and to encourage the idea that making love is not simply having sex. Thus, sex was good for older people in many ways.

Alongside gender, one can also speculate that sexual knowledge is correlated with a person's class position. People who live in poverty, suffer poor health and poor housing are disadvantaged. The life expectancy of men in the lower socio-economic groups is shorter than that of their 'middle class' counterparts. Older women, as others have noted, are even more disadvantaged (Arber and Ginn, 1997). All this, it can be argued, will impact on the expression of sexuality. If ill health bedevils, then clinically this too will influence sexual expression (Bancroft, 1989 fully discusses the impact of certain diseases on sexual function). According to Seymour (1990) the medical profession has traditionally taken little interest in the subject of sexuality and older people and this is reflected in, for instance, the few referrals for sexual counselling. One study (Opaneye, 1991) showed 75 per cent of the 87 men who attended a genito-urinary clinic were sexually active with 19 showing positive tests for syphilis and 10 reporting two or more partners in the last three months.

The Communicable Diseases Surveillance Centre (1994) pointed to a small but significant number of people over 55 years of age contracting HIV in the UK. There has been a commonly held assumption that HIV and AIDS only affects certain groups in the community for example intravenous drug users and gay men. It is now recognised that this has served to increase the stigma about these groups whilst ignoring the needs of others, including the needs of older people (Rickard, 1995). There are numerous reasons why information about HIV is essential for older people. Rickard (1995) elucidates these and includes such reasons as older peoples' only or preferred sexual outlet might be through paid sex, either through female prostitutes or rent boys. The reasoning for this suggested information giving is based on the premiss that older people are (or potentially are) sexually active and is a positive acknowledgement of their sexuality. In terms of health alone there is no room therefore for ageism. The emphasis on safe sex is equally relevant in later life whatever a person's social class, gender or race.

There has been little discussion of race and sexuality (hooks, 1989), and even less for race, sexuality and age. Some people have broken the silence surrounding this issue (but not with reference to age) and, as in the 'dominant' society, it has been the radicals who have tended to undertake this work. Gender predominates in some of the debates. Almaguer (1991) discussing the research of Lancaster (1987) looks at homosexual identity and behaviour of Chicano men. What is interesting is that although stigma accompanies homosexual activity in Latin cultures 'it does not equally adhere to both partners' (p. 78). The stigma is conferred, in 'gender-coded terms' to the anal-passive, feminine, subservient (cochon or pasivo) partner. The active partner (activo or machista) is seen as just a normal male and treated with a certain indulgence.

Blakemore (1989) argues that we should not lose sight of the interactive influences which age, ethnicity, social class and gender have on each other over time. Many of the issues affecting older white people from the dominant society also affect various ethnic groups, and Blakemore suggests that there is a need for caution when ascribing the triple jeopardy label to people from ethnic minorities. What also needs to be acknowledged is that people from minority ethnic groups, like older people generally, are not homogenous. In the UK, research has mainly centred on services (Bhalla and Blakemore, 1981 cited in Bytheway et al, 1989). What does have some bearing on sexuality and sexual expression is the research on residency patterns. This has shown that the majority of older people from Asian communities live with relatives, though not necessarily close relatives, usually in large households (Bhalla and Blakemore, 1981). This is often extolled as an advantage, and for many it is, but privacy will to some extent be compromised. The greater contact with relatives has many benefits but it may also serve to increase 'surveillance' and to some extent lessen potential opportunities for sexual expression, especially in the case of older women. This not only applies to older people from minority ethnic groups but also older people from the dominant society who live with their family. The status of older people in some minority groups can be low, especially for women and in particular widows, who do not have male relatives to guard their interests (Blakemore, 1989).

Further issues – sexuality and dementia

The expression of sexuality by people with dementia is an area which has been largely neglected by research, yet in practice it appears to be of concern (Archibald, forthcoming). Demographic changes this century will result in an increasing number of older people and thus, by extension, an increasing number of people with dementia. In terms of increased incidence of dementia, the subject of sexuality and dementia needs to be considered and questions posed as to why the subject has suffered such neglect.

The expression of sexuality by people with dementia has been seen, for the most part, as problematic (Cooper, 1987; Zeiss et al, 1990; Nadal and Allgulander, 1993; Haddad and Benbow, 1993a and b; Alexopoulos, 1994). Lichtenberg and Strzepek (1990) explore the difficulties but also examine the ethical principles with regard to the competency to engage in sexual relationships and provide, as a result, practical help and guidance to practitioners. Informed consent is understood to require voluntary participation, mental competence and awareness of risks and benefits. Often the primary concern of staff is whether the person with dementia is able to give informed consent with regard to involvement in a sexual relationship with the issue of exploitation ever present. For staff, the tension is frequently that of allowing autonomy and the consequent risk-taking involved, and the duty to protect and care. The line between care and control is sometimes difficult to ascertain and Lichtenberg and Strzepek (1990) are helpful in their guidance on these ethical issues.

Since the 1980s a great deal of research has been carried out in the US and UK on issues related to aspects of care-giving relationships, in particular carers of people with dementia. Gilhooly et al (1994) have reviewed the literature and conclude that significant levels of stress are experienced by carers. A fairly consistent finding is that male and female carers react differently, with men adopting more of a problem solving approach to caring rather than a high level of emotional involvement. In terms of sexuality and dementia there are a few studies which explore spouses' willingness to continue a sexual relationship (Shapira and Cummings, 1989) and the effect of dementia on a couple's sexual relationship (Litz et al, 1990). From the authors' experience various issues arise which are a possible result of the dementing process. These have an impact on the couple's relationship and include: loss of reciprocity, change in role and role reversal, lack of conversation, loss of interest in sex or conversely increased demand and challenging behaviours of various kinds. Dementia therefore adds another level of complexity to the sexual relationship. Given the putative changes in intimate relationships discussed above, spouses may not be willing in the future to care for a chronically ill spouse, either through mental or physical disability. Current research by Baikie seeks to investigate the relevant changes in the spouse's role as the spouse changes from that of lover to nurse. Often when asked why they give care, spouses often make reference to their marriage vows, i.e. 'till death do us part' but will this still hold in the future given the current divorce rates for younger couples?

Homosexuality

If there has been a failure to acknowledge people with dementia and older people generally in the various discourses on sexuality, older homosexual people, particularly older lesbians, have suffered further marginalisation (Berger, 1982) and have become almost invisible (McDonald and Rich, 1984). Gay sexual expression was illegal until fairly recently, and lesbian sexual expression was unthinkable and certainly marginalised for most of this century with the exception perhaps of the avant-garde group on the Left Bank of Paris in the 1920s and 1930s. Some argue that whilst there is now increasing attention being paid to older people, and to homosexuals as a group now, this has not extended to older homosexuals (Berger, 1982).

Ageism is not only the prerogative of the younger heterosexual or homosexual population. Adelman (1986), in her study of older lesbians, found the taboo of discussing ageing and old age as strong in the lesbian community as in mainstream society. Berger (1982) argues that politically as a group, older homosexuals (in the US) are short-changed with regard to publicly funded social services. There is a presumption that all older people are heterosexual which leaves agencies ill prepared to deal with what he regards as the unique situation of older homosexuals. In the UK, Humberstone (1997) notes that when an older gay man or lesbian woman is admitted to hospital there is a reluctance to see partners as next of kin. She further argues for the development of policies to address this anomaly.

As a group, gay men and lesbians are mostly well adjusted and self accepting and appear to be adjusting well to the ageing process (Friend, 1991). Studies on gay and lesbian older people from the early 1980s challenged previous findings, which simply reinforced negative stereotyping (Rapheal and Robinson, 1980; Gray and Dressel, 1985). These and other studies added to the growing knowledge of ageing homosexuals but, as McDougall (1993) suggests, they do not identify the diversity of life experiences in this group. Older lesbians and gay men, who were young in the 1930s, grew up experiencing a need for concealment prior to the sexual revolution and with it the emergence of the Gay Liberation movement of the 1970s. Adelman (1986) found that without the benefit of the supports that exists for many lesbians today, lesbians were previously rendered unprotected and vulnerable. Marriage was the only socially acceptable and practical option open to many women. The case studies gathered in her study depict sadness but also many 'success' stories; success in adapting to life as a lesbian.

There have been no studies to date which have only focused on lesbian and gay sexuality within nursing homes (Fairchild et al, 1996) and few on sexuality and long term care generally. Mulligan and Palguta (1991) for example found three original research publications on the topic of sexuality and nursing home care in the English language literature between 1975 and 1989 (Wasow and Loeb, 1979; White, 1982; Szasz, 1983). In these studies men are to the fore. The Mulligan and Moss (1991) and the later Bullard-Poe et al (1994) studies focus on the importance of intimacy for male residents in nursing homes and their interest in sex. Mulligan and Palguta (1991), in common with Wasow and Loeb (1979), found that libido persists despite institutionalisation. They also found that the majority of male residents preferred coitus as opposed to hugging, kissing, oral sex or masturbation. These results are interesting when looking at Szasz's (1983) study which reveals that nursing home staff's view of what was appropriate sexual behaviour included only a hug or a kiss on the cheek. Fairchild et al (1996) ask if resident sexuality is assumed by nursing staff to manifest itself as only heterosexual expression and that is considered to be seriously disturbing (Szasz, 1983), how will staff react to homosexual expression in a nursing home?

The future

There is, and has been, a profound ambivalence in our attitude to old people and this is reflected in both the theorising on sexuality and the day to day existence of people's lives with regard to sexual expression. There are now changes in size and in the diversity of the older population which Hudson (1996) suggests is unprecedented. Speaking about the US, but equally pertinent to this country, he reports the variations in economic wellbeing amongst older people in terms of race, gender and age itself. Gibson (1992), for example, considers that new forms of marriage and sexual union may develop in the next century in response to demographic and other changes. After the age of 60, women far outnumber men to an increasing extent and Gibson (1992) states that it is unlikely that this discrepancy will be resolved, at least in the first half of the twenty-first century. He suggests that present sexual behaviour patterns of younger people and their relation to marriage will be relevant in the future. Extra-marital relationships will possibly be more a feature of marriage in the future.

In discussing the alternatives to the institution of marriage in terms of 'love' and achieving sexual fulfilment, Gibson (1992) considers 'the lesbian alternative'. He argues that given the great shortage of available men in the later decades of life, it would be reasonable for older women who do not have a male partner to form lesbian associations with one another, even though they have been exclusively heterosexual in their younger years. In support of his argument, Gibson comments that when men are deprived of female company, it is known that they turn easily to homosexual behaviour (for example, in prisons, the navy and other all male communities) and although a similar phenomenon is observed amongst women (for example, in convents, boarding schools, etc) the tendency is far less pronounced. However, Spence (1991) points out that patterns of sexual activity in old age tend to reflect patterns in earlier years and older women, exclusively heterosexual throughout their lives, may find it difficult or unnecessary to adopt a homosexual pattern of sexual relationships. Bancroft (1989) in his discussion of sexual preferences and girls, observes that women may have the greater facility for enjoying both homosexual and heterosexual relationships, i.e. bisexuality

How sexuality or sexual relationships will manifest themselves in the next fifty years will depend on how society balances the needs for sexual satisfaction, companionship, personal identity and self growth in later life with the potential threats, i.e. AIDS and potential family disharmony, family disunity, lack of social support and lack of filial caring in old age. Hall (1991: 2) suggests that there have been tensions between the ideals set up for men and 'the lived experience as they perceived it'. Will this change with the (potentially) greater demands and expectations placed on men by women for sexual satisfaction? Whether the liberation movements and their legacies will result in all women expecting and achieving more sexual satisfaction from relationships remains questionable. Whether older women's sexual assertiveness, as now, will be affected by factors of race, ageism and their economic position is open to speculation. Cultural differences in sexual behaviour still exist – for example, the practice of female genital mutilation, often perpetuated by grandmothers – and we can predict that in fifty years time further changes, whether subtle or dramatic, will have taken place. In terms of younger people what will be interesting to note is whether, over the next fifty years, they will conform to society's stereotypical, often asexual view of older people as they themselves age, or whether they will be sexually assertive (Archibald, 1997). Will gay men or lesbians be able to acknowledge their relationship freely if, for example, a partner is admitted to residential care? Will there be policies in place?

Policy measures to address the sexual needs of older people now and in the future were discussed at the Newcastle Social Services Department and Age Concern Conference in 1995. They suggested that there was a need for senior managers to acknowledge that sexuality and the sexual health of older people was an appropriate and important area of work for staff. Following on from this was the need to identify current good practice already existing in older people's services and that these should be set out as 'quality standards'. There is a need to address how sexuality and sexual health of older people can be better identified, and then considered, when staff are assessing people as part of the community care assessment process.

What seems encouraging is the suggestion that development work, whilst acknowledging the difficulties pertaining to sexuality and sexual health, should respond in a positive manner. This can be achieved by recognising the rights of older people to have for example, information or appropriate services, to promote sexual health, protection from abuse and an acceptance of the importance of sexuality in the lives of older people in a non-oppressive manner. It has been suggested that the voices of older people should be heard through surveys, and through linking into older people's social networks, and that this would be a way of exploring how older people view their sexual health. The increasing awareness of the sexual needs of older people must therefore be reflected not only in a change of attitude, but also in policy. Residential establishments, by taking account of sexual needs as well as basic needs for comfort and security, may need to reflect this in written policy statements. In Scotland, the Rights and Legal Protection Committee of Alzheimer's Scotland – Action on Dementia, in a positive move, intend to examine the relevant legislation on sexuality and dementia.

The future, in terms of policy, needs to be creative in firstly ending the silences that have surrounded the subject of sexuality and older people. Secondly, there is a need to look at ways in which older people can be empowered to be more fully involved both in discussions and in service provision with regard to their sexual needs, whatever their sexual orientation. As the millennium approaches the subject needs to be on the agenda of all those developing social policy for older people so that discrimination does not occur through omission.

References

Adelman, M. (ed) (1986) *Long Time Passing: lives of older lesbians*, Boston: Alyson Publications.

Adkins, L. and Merchant, V. (1996) *Sexualising the Social*, British Sociological Society, London: Macmillan.

Alexopoulos, P. (1994) 'Management of sexually disinhibited behaviour by a dementia patient', *Australian Journal on Ageing,* 13(3): 119.

Almaguer, T. (1991) 'Chicano men: a cartography of homosexual identity and behaviour', *Differences, A Journal of Feminist Cultural Studies*, 3(2): 75–100.

Arber, S. and Ginn, J. (1997) 'Gender and older age' in *The Social Policy of Old Age*, London: Centre for Policy on Ageing

Archibald, C. (1997) 'Sexuality and dementia' in Marshall, M. (ed) *The State of the Art in Dementia Care*, London: Centre for Policy on Ageing.

Archibald, C. (forthcoming) 'Sexuality, dementia and residential care: managers report and response', *Journal of Health and Social Care in the Community*.

Bancroft, J. (1989) *Human Sexuality and It's Problems*, Edinburgh, London, Melbourne and NY: Churchill Livingstone

Berger, R. M. (1982) *Gay and Gray: the older homosexual man*, Champaign, Illinois: University of Illinois Press.

Bhalla, A. and Blakemore, K. (1981) *Elders of Minority Ethnic Groups. Birmingham: All Faiths for One Race* cited in (Blakemore) Bytheway, B., Keil, T., Allatt, P. and Bryman, A. (eds) (1989) *Becoming and Being Old – Sociological Approaches to Later Life*, London: Sage.

Blakemore, K. (1989) 'Does age really matter? The case of old age in minority ethnic groups' in Bytheway, B., Keil, T., Allatt, P. and Bryman, A. (eds) (1989) *Becoming and Being Old – Sociological Approaches to Later Life*, London: Sage.

Bullard-Poe, L., Powell, C. and Mulligan, T. (1994) 'The importance of intimacy to men living in a nursing home', *Archives of Sexual Behaviour*, 23(2): 231–6.

Caplan, P. (ed) (1987) *The Cultural Construction of Sexuality*, London: Routledge.

Catania, J. A. and White, C. B. (1982) 'Sexuality in an aged care sample: cognitive determinants of masturbation', *Archives of Sexual Behaviour*, 11(3): 237–45.

Centre for Communicable Diseases Surveillance and Communicable Diseases and Environmental Health Unit (Scotland) (1994) Unpublished quarterly surveillance table no 21 (September 1993) table no 20 (Mesmac Tyneside Report 1993/94).

Cooper, A. J. (1987) 'Medroxyprogesterone Acetate (MPA) treatment of sexual acting out in men suffering from dementia', *Journal of Clinical Psychiatry*, 48: 368–70.

Delphy, C. (1992) 'Mother's Union?', *Trouble and Strife*, 24: 12–19.

Fairchild, S. K., Carrino, G. E. and Ramirez, M. (1996) 'Social workers perceptions of staff attitudes toward resident sexuality in a random sample of New York State nursing homes: a pilot study', *Journal of Gerontological Social Work*, 26(1–2): 153–69.

Friend, R. A. (1991) 'Older lesbians and gay people: a theory of successful aging', *Journal of Homosexuality*, 20(3–4): 99–118.

Gibson, H. B. (1992) *The Emotional and Sexual Lives of Older People*, London: Chapman and Hall.

Gilhooly, M., Sweeting, H. N., Whittick, J. E. and McKee, K. (1994) 'Family care of the dementing elderly', *International Review of Psychiatry*, 6: 29–40.

Gray, H. and Dressel, P. (1985) 'Alternative interpretations of aging among gay males', *The Gerontologist*, 25(1): 83–7.

Haddad, P. and Benbow, S. (1993a) 'Sexual problems associated with dementia: Part 2. Aetiology, assessment and treatment', *International Journal of Geriatric Psychiatry*, 8: 631–7.

Haddad, P. and Benbow, S. (1993b) 'Sexual problems associated with dementia: Part 1. Problems and their consequences', *International Journal of Geriatric Psychiatry*, 8: 547–51.

Hall, L. A. (1991) *Hidden Anxieties, Male Sexualities*, Oxford: Polity Press.

Harding, J. (1988) 'Ageing, women and sexuality', *Radical Community Medicine*, Winter: 37–43.

Hegelar Mortensen, M. (1978) 'Sexuality and ageing', *British Journal of Sexual Medicine*, 5(32): 16–19.

Hockey, J. and James, A. (1993) *Growing Up and Growing Old*, London: Sage.

Holloway, W. (1993) 'Theorising heterosexuality: a response', *Feminism and Psychology*, 3(3): 412–17.

hooks, b. (1989) *Talking Back: thinking feminist, thinking black*, Boston: South End.

Hudson, R. B. (1996) 'The changing face of ageing politics', *The Gerontologist*, 36(1): 33–5.

Humberstone, N. (1997) 'Positive strategies for working with older lesbians and gay men', paper given at the PSIGE Annual Conference, Brunel University 9–11 July.

Jackson, S. (1992) 'The amazing deconstructing woman: the perils of Post Modern feminism', *Trouble and Strife*, 2: 25–31.

Jackson, S. (1996) 'Heterosexuality as a problem for feminist theory' in Adkins, L, and Merchant, V. (eds) *Sexualising the Social*, British Sociological Society, London: Macmillan.

Jeffreys, S. (1990) *Anticlimax: a feminist critique of the sexual revolution*, London: The Women's Press.

Kitwood, T. and Bredin, K. (1992) 'Towards a theory of dementia care: personhood and well-being', *Ageing and Society*, 12: 269–87.

Kitzinger, C. and Wilkinson, S. (1993) 'Theorising heterosexuality' in Wilkinson, S. and Kitzinger, C. (eds) *Heterosexuality: a feminism and psychology reader*, London: Sage.

Lancaster, R. N. (1987) 'Subject honor and object shame: the construction of male homosexuality and stigma in Nicaragua', *Ethnology*, 27(2): 11–125.

Laner, M. R. (1978) 'Growing older male: heterosexual and homosexual', *The Gerontologist*, 18(5): 496–501.

Lessing, D. (1996) *Love, Again*, London: Flamingo.

Lichtenberg, P. A. and Strzepek, D. M. (1990) 'Assessments of institutionalised dementia patients competencies to participate in intimate relationships', *The Gerontologist*, 30(1): 117–20.

Litz, B. T., Zeiss, A. M. and Davies, H. D. (1990) 'Sexual concerns of male spouses of female Alzheimer's disease patients', *The Gerontologist*, 3(1): 113–16.

Lowenthal, M. F., Thurner, M. and Chiriboga, D. (1975) *Four Stages of Life*, San Francisco: Jossey-Bass.

MacDonald, B. and Rich, C. (1984) *Look Me in the Eye*, London: The Women's Press.

McDougall, G. J. (1993) 'Therapeutic issues with gay and lesbian elders', *Clinical Gerontology*, 14(1): 45–57.

Masters, W. H. and Johnson, V. E. (1966) *Human Sexual Response*, Boston: Little, Brown.

Millett, K. (1969) *Sexual Politics*, New York: Doubleday.

Mulligan, T. and Moss, C. R. (1991) 'Sexuality and aging in male veterans: a cross sectional study of interest, ability, and activity', *Archives of Sexual Behaviour*, 20(1): 17–25.

Mulligan, T. and Palguta, R. (1991) 'Sexual interest, activity and satisfaction among male nursing home residents, *Archives of Sexual Behaviour*, 20(2): 119–205.

Nadal, M. and Allgulander, S. (1993) 'Normalisation of sexual behaviour in a female with dementia after treatment with Cyproterone', *International Journal of Geriatric Psychiatry*, 8: 265–7.

Opaneye, A. A. (1991) 'Sexuality and sexually transmitted diseases in older men attending the genito-urinary clinic in Birmingham', *Journal of Royal Society of Health*, February.

Pfeiffer, E. (1978) 'Sexuality in the aging individual' in Solnick, R. L. (ed) *Sexuality and Aging*, Ethel Percy Andros Gerontology Centre University of Southern California: California Press.

Pfeiffer, E. and Davis, G. C. (1972) 'Determination of sexual behaviour in middle and old age', *Journal of the American Geriatric Society*, 20: 151–58.

Rapheal, S. M. and Robinson, M. K. (1980) 'The older lesbian', *Alternative Life-styles*, 3(2): 207–29.

Rich, A. (1980) 'Compulsory heterosexuality and lesbian existence', *Signs*, 5(4): 631–60.

Richardson, D. (1996) 'Heterosexuality and social theory' in Richardson, D. (ed) *Theorising Heterosexuality*, Buckingham and Philadelphia: Open University Press.

Rickard, W. (1995) 'HIV/AIDS and older people', *Generations Review*, 5(3), 2–6 September.

Seymour, J. (1990) 'Sexuality in the elderly', *Care of the Elderly*, 8 September 2: 315–16.

Shapira, J. and Cummings, J. L. (1989) 'Alzheimer's disease: changes in sexual behaviour', *Medical Aspects of Human Sexuality*, June 6: 32–6.

Solnick, R. L. (1978) 'Sexual responsiveness, age, and change: facts and potential' in Solnick, R. L. (ed) *Sexuality and Aging*, Ethel Percy Andros Gerontology Centre: University of Southern California Press.

Spence, S. H. (1991) *Psychosexual Therapy: a cognitive behavioural approach*, London: Chapman and Hall.

Starr, B. D. and Weiner, M. B. (1981) *Report on Sex and Sexuality in the Mature Years*, London: WH Allen.

Sviland, M. S. (1978) 'A progam of sexual liberation and growth' in Solnick, R. L. (ed) *Sexuality and Aging*, the Ethel Percy Andros Gerontology Centre: University of Southern California Press.

Szasz, G. (1983) 'Sexual incidents in an extended care unit for aged men', *Journal of the American Geriatric Society*, 31: 407–11.

Verwoerdt, A., Pfeiffer, E. and Wang, H. (1969) 'Sexual behaviour in senescence', *Geriatrics*, 24: 137–54.

Walz, T. H. and Blum, N. S. (1987) *Sexual Health in Later Life*, Washington, DC: Lexington. Cited in Fairchild, S. K., Carrino, G. E. and Ramirez, M. (1996) *Social Workers' Perceptions of Staff Attitudes Toward Resident Sexuality in a Random Sample of New York State Nursing Homes: A Pilot Study.*

Wasow, M. and Loeb, M. E. (1979) 'Sexuality in nursing homes', *Journal of the American Geriatric Society*, 27: 73–9.

White, C. (1982) 'Sexual interest, attitudes, knowledge and sexual history in relation to sexual behaviour in the institutionalised aged', *Archives of Sexual Behaviour*, 11(1): 11–21.

Wilson, R. (1966) *Feminine Forever*, New York: M Evans. Cited in Harding, J. (1988) 'Ageing, women and sexuality', *Radical Community Medicine*, Winter: 37–43.

Woodward, K. (1991) *Aging and It's Discontents*, Bloomington and Indianapolis: Indiana University Press

Zeiss, A. M., Davies, H., Wood, M. and Tinklenberg, J. R. (1990) 'The incidence and correlates of erectile problems in patients with Alzheimer's disease', *Archives of Sexual Behaviour*, 19: 325–32.

Health care rationing, non treatment and euthanasia: ethical dilemmas

Kenneth Howse

Liberty is an elusive concept. No human being has complete freedom of action…
Old people are taken from their homes when domiciliary support and physical treatment
might enable them to stay there; they are subjected in long-stay hospitals and homes to
regimes which deprive them of many basic human dignities; and they are often not
properly consulted about the care or treatment to which they are subjected.

*Alison Norman (1980) Rights and Risks: a discussion document on civil liberty in old age,
NCCOP, p. 7*

Introduction

The last fifty years have seen a great deal of change in medical practice and also in
public views about what should be permitted or required in medical practice.
Hospital medicine has been transformed by new demands and new opportunities.
Before the Second World War most of the patients under the care of hospital
physicians were children, adolescents and younger adults with conditions such as
rheumatic fever and tuberculosis (Isaacs, 1987). With more people living longer
lives, physicians and surgeons now spend a much greater proportion of their time
providing care for elderly people. There is also much more that they are able to
do for them. The repertoire of effective interventions has been expanded
enormously, even for the very old (Jennett, 1995). New and better technologies are
available for saving life (e.g. cardiopulmonary resuscitation), for sustaining life (e.g.
mechanical ventilation and dialysis) and for enhancing life (e.g. coronary bypass
surgery or total hip replacement).

As a result of these new demands and opportunities, difficult questions have
been forced on the medical profession, the courts and the government. The same
questions have also been enthusiastically taken up by academics from various
disciplines (most notably philosophy and law) as well as the popular media. A
doctor from the 1940s would be astounded, and probably shocked, by the extent
to which issues that were previously seen as falling largely within the competence

of the profession, have been opened up to public scrutiny and debate. This reflects and also reinforces changes that have taken place in the quality of the relationship between individual doctor and individual patient. Democratic openness has increasingly taken the place of corporate *hauteur*; and clinical openness has increasingly taken the place of medical paternalism.

Among the various ethical questions connected with the provision of medical care to older people there are three which stand out because of the magnitude of their repercussions on medical practice concerning matters of life and death. The issue which has emerged most recently into public debate – rationing of health care resources – offers an example of a dispute about the relevance of the phenomenon of old age and its typical incidents (such as declining powers or closeness to death or a changing role) to decisions about the rationing or allocation of health care resources. The other two issues – 'non treatment' decisions for older people, especially those who are no longer 'of sound mind', at the end of life – and medical euthanasia – have a somewhat different connection with the phenomenon of old age. Although death may of course occur at any age, it is nowadays much more common in old age than in earlier life. The ethical (and legal) constraints with which we surround the medical management of the passage from life to death have, therefore, a special importance for older people. If changes in these constraints are seen as advantageous to individuals at the end of life, then it is older people who stand to benefit most. And, conversely, if the prospect of change is rightly viewed with anxiety or fear, then it is older people who have most to fear.

This chapter provides an overview of recent developments in the ethical analysis of these major issues. These particular topics have been selected, not only for their intrinsic importance, but also because of the way they illustrate the progress of the idea of the right to autonomy in the ethical and legal framework for the practice of medicine. As far as medical practice is concerned, the progress of this idea is arguably the single most important ethical theme that has been sounded in the period under review.

The right to autonomy

Although the right to autonomy is by no means the only principle to which appeal is made in academic debate about medical ethics (Beauchamp and Childress, 1989), it has acquired a place of preeminence in nearly all such discussions. It owes this position partly to its role in justifying criticisms of the authority and privileges of the medical profession (see, for example, Kennedy, 1981), and partly also to the difficulty of finding a stable solution to problems which are not soluble by its means. Appeals to the right to autonomy are especially attractive when the prevalence of sharply different views about what is good, worthwhile and needful in human life is seen to inhibit social consensus about the solution to our moral perplexities. It offers firm ground, therefore, in an area of debate where there is still considerable theoretical disagreement about the best approach to the ethical analysis of particular practical problems (Gillon, 1994).

By asserting the right to autonomy, individuals lay claim to an exclusive right of control over some aspect of their affairs. In the context of medical practice, the right to autonomy is a right of authorisation and a rejection of paternalism: a medical intervention is authorised by the patient, and not by the doctor's view of the patient's best interests. The increasing recognition of this right in medical practice has been signalled most notably in the recognition of a moral and legal obligation on doctors to enable patients to make *informed* choices about their own medical care.

The transformation which has been effected in medical practice by the extension of the domain in which patient autonomy is exercised, has implications both for categories of patient and for categories of decision previously placed beyond the reach of autonomy. It is now widely accepted, for example, that the right to autonomy of confused elderly patients should not be too readily dismissed on the grounds of incapacity. If there is a duty to help patients make responsible choices about their medical treatment, then this duty extends to these patients also. This chapter is not, however, about the extension of autonomy to a particular category of patient such as confused elderly people. Rather, it is concerned with the controversial or contested extension of autonomy to categories of decision which are of special importance to older people.

Scarce resources and setting priorities for treatment

About fifty years ago geriatric medicine emerged as a distinct specialty, and from the very beginning, it challenged a widespread tendency within the medical profession to underestimate the benefits of medical interventions for older people (see Chapter 7). The specialty has consistently affirmed the importance of securing even small improvements in quality of life for older people, as well as the value of 'caring' when there is no longer much hope of 'curing'. Attention has shifted to the implications of the steady increase in demand that has accompanied this expansion in available interventions. As the pressure to make the best possible use of scarce health care resources has increased, a new and very important debate has emerged about the kind of policy response that should be made to this demand. How should competing claims for health care resources be assessed or ranked? How should the more deserving be distinguished from the less deserving? In such circumstances, *distributive justice* requires that preferential treatment be given to those with the strongest claim. Are the claims of older people therefore weakened because they have reached the final stage or stages of life?

One of the most far-reaching developments in recent years arises from the application, by health economists, of utilitarian thinking to such questions of distributive justice in health care. The thoroughgoing utilitarian will argue that decisions about the allocation of health care resources should be guided, first and foremost, by the requirement to maximise benefit (Williams, 1988). The corollary, that the strength of claims to health care resources should be assessed *solely* in terms of capacity to benefit, has profound implications for older people.

The implications are most clearly seen if we consider the various uses that might be made of the analytical tool closely associated with this approach to decision-making. The 'quality adjusted life year' (QALY) is a unit of measurement of benefit, which takes into account the impact of an intervention on quality of life as well as life expectancy. Interventions may be assessed, and compared, as productive of more or fewer QALYs – and of course according to the cost per QALY. Technical problems aside, it seems not unreasonable to use QALYs to help compare the effectiveness (and cost-effectiveness) of two or more proposed treatments for, say, cancer of the prostate. It is quite a different matter, and much more controversial, to compare treatments across different age-groups in respect of their QALY-efficiency. In any such comparison, QALYs are, as it were, loaded against older people: the capacity to benefit diminishes in line with decreasing life-expectancy, declining functional abilities and diminishing powers of recuperation (Harris, 1988). To protest that such a use of QALYs would be discriminatory is beside the point. It is indeed a *consequence* of the proposal that the interests of older people carry less weight than those of younger people. But, for the QALY theorist, this is as it should be. Age *is* relevant to decisions about the allocation of health resources because of its intimate connection with capacity to benefit.

The real problem at issue, therefore, is the principle which argues for the assessment of the relative strength of claims to health care *solely* in terms of the capacity to benefit. As health economists have themselves recognised, there is more to distributive justice than a principle of efficiency, and more to resource allocation than QALY maximisation (Culyer, 1991). Very often the counterbalance is sought in the language of needs, which is familiar in the context of *clinical* decisions about the priority to be given to different individuals on a single waiting list for treatment. When it comes, however, to making *policy* decisions about the allocation of resources across different spending programmes (cardiology, neonatal intensive care, stroke rehabilitation, etc), it seems that the concepts of 'need' and 'capacity to benefit' are in a sense contesting the same ground. It can certainly be argued that a diminished capacity to benefit from an intervention does not entail that it is needed less.

It is part of the logic of applying a utilitarian calculus to the problems of distributive justice in health care that age should be incorporated into the calculations in such a way as to weaken the claims of older people. In what have come to be known as 'fair innings arguments', the appeal to chronological age as a relevant characteristic in making decisions about the allocation of health care resources is made more directly and explicitly. In its most general form, the argument can be stated as follows: someone who needs medical resources in order to have – or to increase the likelihood of having – a fair innings has a stronger claim on those resources than someone who has already had a fair innings.

One of the most notorious versions of the fair innings argument, certainly in the USA, was developed by Daniel Callahan in *Setting Limits: medical goals in an aging society* (Callahan, 1987). The background to the argument is the view that elderly people in the USA receive an unfairly large share of health expenditure, which is most manifest in the use of expensive life-preserving technologies. Too much is foregone by younger people to warrant the increasing amount of resources (including research expenditure) dedicated to extending the lives of the very old. Callahan appeals to the idea of a 'natural life span' in developing his proposals for redressing the imbalance in expenditure. Individuals who have come to the end of their natural life span ('somewhere between 75 and 85') have much weakened claims on public resources for the purpose of extending life. For this reason – given certain background social conditions – it is not unfair to set a fixed age as an eligibility criterion in decisions about the expenditure of public funds on life-preserving technologies. It is proposed, not merely that Americans should be persuaded to accept the idea of a natural life span and so moderate their demands on the health care system, but that someone who has exceeded the natural life span should be deemed ineligible for life-preserving technology.

Critics of Callahan have fastened on three key points: the view that older people (in the USA and elsewhere) receive an unfairly large share of the cake; the idea of a natural life span; and the use that is made of this idea as an eligibility criterion for life-preserving medical treatment. The kernel of the idea of a natural life span, which rests on 'biography', not biology, is that death does not come prematurely for those who have had a fair opportunity to work out, as best they can, their life's projects. Fair opportunities, of course, do not depend on length of life alone, which has important important implications for the kind of society in which a natural life span can be fairly used in rationing decisions (Callahan, 1994). There is, furthermore, something inherently problematic about the idea of a natural life span (of the biographical kind) in a pluralist society. Even if Callahan's proposal was toned down into an educational project for the recovery of culturally shared assumptions about the proper ends of human life, it would have to face the challenge of liberal individualism ('why should we try to recover a uniformity which is better lost?'). But, as pointed out earlier, Callahan's argument is stronger than this: all individuals over a certain age are to be treated as the same in respect of their diminished entitlement to life-preserving technologies, irrespective of differences in prognoses and widely divergent views about the 'completeness' of their own biographies. To the critic of the fair innings argument, however, it is not chronological age, but these very individual differences which are all-important in determining what is fair in any given case.

The final idea considered here in connection with rationing of health care resources is more speculative analysis than practical proposal (Smith, 1996). Imagine a society in which wealth is more equally distributed than in our own, and in which health care is funded entirely through individually purchased insurance policies. The content, and therefore the pricing, of these policies will reflect the choices that individuals make about how to spend their money on health care. One policy, for example, might offer open heart surgery up to the age of 75 years; another more expensive option would extend the offer to 90 years. Is it possible to devise a set of conditions which would make it fair to hand over decisions about the rationing of health care to individual purchasers of health insurance? And would people in these circumstances choose to restrict their own entitlement to health care in old age? This second question we are to construe not as a piece of hypothetical social forecasting, but as an exercise in prudential reasoning under appropriately specified conditions. What kinds of choice would a rational agent make?

What is significant about this suggestion (the 'prudent insurance principle') is the role it assigns to individual choice. It is argued that a just solution can be found to the rationing problem if social arrangements are made which permit individuals to make their own choices about the health care they want *and* if we suppose that these choices are made rationally. Now this is not an appeal to the right to autonomy as normally understood in the context of medical practice (see above). Nor is it an appeal to autonomy in the sense that failure to institute the appropriate arrangements constitutes a violation of individual autonomy. The idea of autonomy is being proposed rather as a model which helps to solve an otherwise intractable problem.

End of life decisions

The arguments considered in this section all tend in the same direction. They emphasise the threat to autonomy in the constraints that surround the medical management of the transition from life to death, and argue that the violation of the right to autonomy is no trivial injury, especially in a matter of such fundamental personal importance as the way in which life is ended.

TREATMENT REFUSAL AND ADVANCED DIRECTIVES

There is a large measure of ethical consensus, which reflects and is reinforced by the law, about the range of cases in which the presence of a life-threatening condition neither obliges nor entitles doctors to provide life-prolonging treatment to patients against their declared wishes (Skegg, 1984). In such circumstances the doctor's duty of care is to make the patient as comfortable as possible without overriding their wishes.

The last thirty years or so have seen a major shift in the way in which the problem posed by patient refusal of life-prolonging treatment has been conceived. A preoccupation with the distinction between suicide (as something *morally* prohibited) and treatment refusal in circumstances which would foreseeably lead to death (as something occasionally permitted), has been replaced by a preoccupation with the protection of patient autonomy. The attempts of moral theologians to elaborate a moral viewpoint which saw both doctor and patient as bound by common principle and a shared view of the situation (Ramsey, 1970), have been largely swept aside by acceptance of an ethical framework which sees the assessment of the benefits and burdens of treatment as a task for the patient. The ethical crux of the matter is now seen to lie in the resolution of the conflict which may arise when doctor and patient are not bound by common principle and a shared view of the situation.

The increasing recognition of the coercive potential of new life-preserving technologies has been of great importance in effecting this shift of moral focus. Patients may find themselves 'trapped' in artificial life support machines with no way out except through medical compliance with their request to discontinue treatment. It is easy to see the coercion involved in the use of physical restraint or sedation on an unwilling patient. It has taken quite a few years to establish the principle that medical reluctance to discontinue life-preserving treatment may be equally coercive. The reluctance of principle has been exacerbated – especially in the litigious USA – by medical fears of the legal consequences of non-treatment. Where courts have been required to adjudicate between the respective claims of doctors and patients in such cases, they have tended to come down on the side of patient self-determination and have set firm limits to the medical obligation to preserve life.

The patient's right to autonomy is largely uncontested *if* the patient is 'of sound mind', and what is at issue is the authorisation of invasive medical treatment. The fact that non treatment will lead to death is neither here nor there. (The kinds of case in which the right is contested usually concern younger patients e.g. a Jehovah's witness who is a mother with dependent children refuses a blood transfusion.) In recent years this same right has been extended to patients who are no longer of sound mind, provided that they have made some sort of anticipatory treatment refusal – i.e. a 'living will' or 'advanced directive'. By means of such a document an individual may inform future medical attendants of a *present* decision in case of future incompetence (Age Concern Institute of Gerontology, 1988).

If we suppose that the right to autonomy is extinguished when the capacity to exercise it is absent, then the impairment of this capacity is certain, in some circumstances, to present doctors with serious problems about the use of life-prolonging interventions. What is the doctor's duty of care if an acute and life-threatening crisis supervenes against a background of continuing deterioration? It is widely agreed that doctors should not view the situation simply as an opportunity for them and/or the relatives to escape from the burdens of caring for the patient. It is also widely agreed that there is no duty to intervene if all that is achieved is a prolongation of the process of dying. Such consensus does not prevent difficulties from arising, however, over treatment decisions for demented patients in acute crises. Does doctor or relative decide that this is an opportunity for *the patient* to be relieved of the burdens or indignities of his or her condition? And how does the doctor or patient evaluate the burdens and indignities of the condition to decide whether they are sufficient to warrant non intervention? The advanced directive is a way of avoiding these problems. No-one is *obliged* to decide what to do for the patient because the patient has already made the decision. By extending the right of autonomy to the situation, the force of the advanced directive is strengthened: no-one is *entitled* to decide what to do for the patient because the patient has already made the decision.

In some countries, for example the USA, Canada and Australia, advanced directives have received legal recognition through statute (Kennedy and Grubb, 1989). To what extent the force and scope of advanced directives should be governed by statute is a disputed matter. In the UK, the House of Lords Select Committee on Medical Ethics (1994) took the view that legislation was unnecessary as a means of affording legal protection (against criminal prosecution or civil action) to doctors who honour advanced directives; and undesirable because it ties the hand of doctors too tightly and might deprive patients of the benefits of interventions which had become available since the advanced directive was signed. The Select Committee therefore recommended that 'the colleges and faculties of all the health-care professions should jointly develop a code of practice to guide their members' and suggested that the British Medical Association (1992) Statement on Advanced Directives could usefully form the basis of such a code. The Law Commission (1995), in its more recent report on mental incapacity, has disagreed with the Select Committee in its recommendation for legislation on anticipatory refusals of treatment as part of a new mental incapacity bill.

The extension of the principle of autonomy to cover the anticipatory refusal of treatment in advanced directives has had (and still has) opponents (see, for example, Gormally, 1992). The 'idea' of advanced directives is uncontroversial, not in the sense that there has been no controversy – but in the sense that the controversy (or at least its ethical dimension) may be taken, for all practical purposes, as settled. The consensus may be illustrated by a recent editorial in the *British Medical Journal* (Doyal, 1995). The ethical case for honouring an advanced directive is taken for granted, and attention is shifted to the personal obligation on each citizen to make provision for future incompetence.

Agreement about the application to advanced directives of the principle of the right to autonomy does not mean, however, that the justification by this principle of the obligation to honour advanced directives is uncontested in *all* circumstances, irrespective of the content of the directive and the condition of the patient. There are situations in which the force of the principle is seriously questioned as, for example, when a doctor has to decide whether to respect a prior refusal of life-sustaining treatment by someone who now has advanced dementia and yet appears to be relatively untroubled by the condition. The patient's present contentment lends colour to the contention that it is not in the best interests of the patient to honour the directive. And since the patient is no longer capable of making decisions about present interests, someone else should make the decision on his or her behalf. Dworkin (1993), on the other hand, urges us to reject any such arguments and hold fast to the now incompetent patient's previous exercise of autonomy.

PROXY DECISION-MAKING FOR INCOMPETENT PATIENTS

Although the condition which has become known as persistent vegetative state (PVS) is much less prevalent than dementia (and also is more likely to occur in younger age groups), the difficulty of decisions about the discontinuation of life-preserving measures (especially artificial nutrition and hydration) for PVS patients has prompted a great deal of debate relevant to the care of demented elderly people. For the PVS patient there is no longer any possibility of experiencing the benefits or burdens of medical care because there is no longer any possibility of experiencing anything (Jennett and Dyer, 1991). This irrecoverable loss of consciousness can be argued to place the PVS patient at the extreme end of a continuum of intellectual impairment where are to be found the much larger number of patients with dementia.

It is the very extremeness of PVS which raises in a stark fashion hard questions about the value of human life. What reasons are to be advanced for continuing or discontinuing treatment in such cases? Continuing intervention will preserve a life which has been diminished to the farthest conceivable limit, distinguishable from death by physiological function only (and in some eyes indistinguishable from death). The question of the value of the kind of life preserved in the PVS patient by continuing intervention, appears to be inescapable because there is no other discernible gain from intervention. What is uncomfortable about this line of thought is the suggestion that someone, other than the patient whose life is at stake, may be empowered to decide that a human life is no longer worth living and therefore no longer worth preserving (see, for example, Kuhse and Singer, 1983; and Post, 1990). A great deal depends, however, on how we make use of this sort of 'quality of life' judgement. It is one thing to argue that a human life may be so bereft of those distinctively human qualities which make it valuable that it ceases to exercise any claim on our charity; and quite another matter to argue that the benefit of treatment is too small to warrant the burdens and risks associated with an invasive intervention (Linacre Centre, 1982). An argument which *forbids* intervention because in some way or another it offends against the patient is different from, and more acceptable than, an argument which *absolves* us from the duty to intervene because of what the patient has become. The distinction is important, but the central problem remains. A judgement about the value of the benefit conferred by intervention still has to be made – and in the case of the PVS patient the only conceivable benefit is the continuation of a life which no longer has any value for the person living it.

As pointed out above, advanced directives relieve us from the necessity of making this kind of judgement. The issue is settled by appealing to the right of autonomy. But in the absence of an advanced directive someone else has to take up the burden of decision, and advanced directives are still relatively rare. This is so even in the USA, where the 1991 Patient Self-determination Act required all hospitals receiving federal funds to inform patients about the advanced directive legislation in their state and of their right to refuse treatment. Recourse to the courts in these circumstances is common, especially in the USA, where they have proved themselves willing to give very detailed guidance on decision-making in such difficult cases.

Bolstered by the reports of such influential bodies as the President's Commission on Bioethics (1983), the US courts have favoured an approach to decisions about life-preserving treatment for incompetent patients which relies heavily on an appeal to the right to autonomy. They have taken the view that the right to autonomy is extinguished neither by the mischance of present incapacity, nor by a prior failure to exercise autonomy in an advanced directive. It is sometimes possible of course to ascertain the patient's declared wishes on this kind of treatment decision, even though there is no advanced directive. A reported conversation may be as informative in this respect as a properly witnessed document. If, however, the issue of medical treatment in the patient's present condition has not been explicitly addressed by the patient at all, then the courts will recognise proxy decision makers as a means of affording protection to the patient's threatened right of autonomy. The task of the proxy is to substitute his or her judgement for that of the patient, in order to determine what kind of treatment decision the patient *would have* made. The proxy is empowered to refuse treatment on the patient's behalf by saying to the doctor 'you should not do this because she would not have wanted it'.

English courts have been reluctant to adopt this kind of approach to proxy decision-making, preferring instead 'the best interests of the patient' as a legal standard for guiding decisions about patients who cannot decide for themselves. The preference for a 'best interests standard' goes hand in hand with the belief that, in these circumstances, responsibility for decisions about medical treatment at the end life is usually best left with the medical practitioner (House of Lords Select Committee, 1994). This should not, however, be construed as a licence to doctors to ignore the views of close relatives. Nor does it exclude the view, advanced for example by the Law Commission (1995), that the problem of determining what is in the patient's best interests will often resolve itself into the problem of determining what the patient would have wanted.

But, as Lord Mustill pointed out in Airedale NHS Trust v Bland (1993), there are circumstances in which the attempted application of a 'best interests standards' runs into serious problems. Does a patient who is no longer sentient have 'best interests' of any kind? The justification of proxy decision-making as a form of protection for the right of autonomy may seem, therefore, to solve an otherwise difficult problem. We want to deal with these cases by arguing that unwanted interventions are in some sense an offence against the patient; and an appeal to the right to autonomy enables us to do precisely this in cases where an appeal to the best interests of the patient seems flimsy. But is it not paradoxical to claim that one person may exercise the right to autonomy on behalf of another? It is precisely this sense of paradox in the extension of protection for autonomy to patients who are no longer capable of its exercise which recent philosophical work on advanced directives and proxy decision-making seeks to dispel (Erin and Harris, 1994).

THE CASE FOR A RIGHT TO DIE

In 1994 the arguments for reforming the law in relation to medical euthanasia (and also in relation to non medical mercy killing) were dismissed by the House of Lords Select Committee on Medical Ethics, which concluded that there was no reason 'to weaken society's prohibition against intentional killing'. It is evident that the Select Committee addressed the issue because it saw that there was a case to answer – as indeed there is. The last ten years or so have seen growing pressure for reform and in some countries the pressure has brought about changes in the law.

In Holland, in 1985, the Supreme Court recognised a specifically medical defence against a charge of mercy killing (a separate offence from murder in the Dutch Penal Code, but not in English law): it accepted the argument of the Royal Dutch Medical Association (KNMG) that, under certain circumstances, the intentional killing of a patient by a doctor might reasonably be regarded as good medical practice and declared that doctors who broke the law out of a sense of professional duty should not be convicted. In 1990 this guidance was codified in an agreement between the Dutch government and the KNMG: the actions of doctors who followed the relevant guidelines (e.g. the request for euthanasia should come from the patient and be free and voluntary; the patient should be experiencing intolerable suffering; a second opinion should always be sought) would not be investigated by the public prosecutor. More recently this agreement has achieved legal status through an amendment of the regulations for death certification, though the prohibition of mercy killing in the penal code remains unchanged.

In the USA and Australia the pressure for change has taken a somewhat different turn. The focus of the debate has switched from the permissibility of intentional killing by a doctor, to the permissibility of medical assistance with suicide (also unlawful). In the USA the debate has been carried along by a succession of court rulings on the constitutionality of measures to prohibit (as in Michigan), or permit (as in Oregon) physician-assisted suicide. The constitutionality of state legislation prohibiting physician-assisted suicide is now being considered by the US Supreme Court (Lemmens, 1996). And, in the Northern Territory of Australia in 1995, a private member's bill to secure the Rights of the Terminally Ill was introduced into the territorial parliament. The bill, which permits physician-assisted suicide in certain circumstances, was enacted in May of the same year and came into force into July 1996. The measure, vigorously opposed from the first by the Australian Medical Association, was recently overturned (amidst much argument about the constitutional rights of the territorial parliament) by the federal legislature in Canberra.

From the point of view of the ethics of medical practice, where we are concerned with determining the doctor's duty of care, the relevance of the right to autonomy to the issue of euthanasia is far from obvious. What is a doctor's duty of care to a patient of sound mind who declares a fixed desire to die and asks the doctor to help – either by lethal injection or by procuring the means for suicide? Most proponents of medical euthanasia will say that, granted the seriousness and voluntariness of the request, it depends on the patient's condition. How close is death anyway? What is the likelihood of remission or improvement? How severe and intractable is the patient's suffering? In some circumstances, so it is argued, the doctor may 'discern a duty' to help the patient to an easeful death, and will be justified in granting the request (Institute of Medical Ethics, 1990). Opponents of medical euthanasia argue to the contrary that it cannot be part of good medical practice to agree to such a request.

What appears to be at issue here is first, the scope and force of the doctor's duty to relieve suffering; and second, the scope and force of the moral prohibition against the deliberate taking of human life. On one side it is argued that the medical duty to relieve suffering may justify an intervention by the doctor which breaches the moral prohibition against 'deliberate taking of innocent life'. On the other side it is argued that this same duty, which includes a duty to mitigate the pains of dying, should never lead to a decision to end life (Church of England, 1975; Linacre Centre, 1982; BMA, 1988). Expressed in this way we can see why the issue has been of such importance to those concerned with palliative care, many of whom argue that good palliative care can eliminate what is more often than not only an *apparent* conflict between these two duties (Donovan, 1996).

The relevance of the right to autonomy to this particular debate about the medical duty of care at the end of life is far from obvious. No-one argues that respect for the right to autonomy *obliges* doctors to help patients to easier or more dignified deaths. The appeal to the right to autonomy is not made, however, in order to articulate the obligations of the doctor in these situations; it is made in order to criticise the interference of the state in a particularly important transaction between doctor and patient. From this point of view, the determination of the doctor's duty of care is really a secondary issue. That is to say, euthanasia is primarily an issue of public rather than professional morality. The question of the recognition by the state of a right to self-determination in the matter of death is distinct from, *and prior to*, the question of the duties of a doctor when faced with someone wishing to exercise this right. It is perfectly consistent to argue that the state should recognise a right to self-determination in the matter of death; and that the medical profession should never act as 'executioners'.

In Holland, the USA and Australia, the debate about euthanasia and physician-assisted suicide debate has been transformed, so that it is no longer seen as a debate about a doctor's duty of care. In spite of the inevitably close involvement of the medical profession (as both opponents and proponents of reform), the rhetorical heart of the debate is now the disputed right of patients to choose the timing and manner of their own death. If this right is granted, equality would appear to require that individuals who are not able to exercise this right without assistance should lawfully be able to receive such assistance.

There is, however, something to be put in the balance against the acceptance of this requirement. Grant that there are individual cases in which a doctor may justifiably help a patient exercise a right of self-determination in the manner and timing of death. Will it be possible to contain the practice within the limits represented by these kinds of paradigm case? It is with this question in mind that so much attention has been directed in the last few years to the 'Dutch experiment' (Van der Maas, 1991; Pijnenborg et al, 1993; Van der Wal, 1994; Keown, 1995).

Conclusion and issues for the future

The theme of this chapter has been the preeminence of the right to autonomy among the various principles to which appeal is made in current discussions of the ethics of medical practice. Advanced directives and proxy decision-making have extended this right into areas where, not so long ago, it was thought to be inapplicable – when decisions have to be made about medical treatment at the end of life for patients who are no longer of sound mind. Liberal political theorists argue that it reaches even farther than this, and should guide policy responses to the growing pressure to reform the law on medical euthanasia and physician-assisted suicide. Under a somewhat different guise, it is suggested that it points towards a solution to the difficult and increasingly important problem of health care rationing.

Appeals to the right to autonomy are most powerful over ground where there is no social consensus about the solution to our moral perplexities, where sharply different views flourish about what is good and worthwhile and needful in human life. Answers to precisely this kind of question are presupposed by the opponents of the extension of autonomy to what can be called the contested ground. This indeed is what makes it so difficult to reach agreement on the answers, and what makes the appeal to autonomy so attractive.

It seems certain that debate about the rights and wrongs of medical euthanasia will intensify in the face of growing pressure for legal reform. The issue is rapidly acquiring the status of a moral landmark in social policy. The logic of liberalism pulls in one direction as the weight of a social morality, still deeply coloured by religious values, leans in the other. Between these two pressures, the moral consensus of the medical profession appears to be slowly dissolving.

Debate about the ethics of rationing in medical care and the requirements of distributive justice in the allocation of health care resources, also seems set to intensify rather than die away over the next few years. In view of the connection between age and capacity to benefit, it is important that explicit consideration be given to the claims of older people on health care resources. Although it seems unlikely that any proposal to implement age-based rationing in an explicit and thoroughgoing fashion would command widespread support, either within the medical profession or outside it, it seems not at all unlikely that the connection between age and capacity to benefit will make itself felt in a wide variety of proposals and decisions about the allocation of health care resources between various services and programmes.

References

Age Concern Institute of Gerontology (1988) *The Living Will: consent to treatment at the end of life*. A report by the Age Concern Institute of Gerontology and the Centre for Medical Law and Ethics, London.

Airedale NHS Trust v. Bland (1993) Butterworth Medico-Legal Reports 1993: 64–143.

Beauchamp, T. L. and Childress, J. F. (1989) *The Principles of Biomedical Ethics*, Third edition, Oxford: Oxford University Press.

British Medical Association (1988) *Euthanasia*. Report of the working party to review the British Medical Association's guidance on euthanasia, London: BMA.

British Medical Association (1992) *BMA Statement on Advanced Directives*, London: BMA.

Callahan, D. (1987) *Setting Limits: medical goals in an aging society*, New York: Simon and Schuster.

Callahan, D. (1994) 'Setting limits: a response', *Gerontologist*, 34: 933–38.

Church of England General Synod Board for Social Responsibility (1975) *On Dying Well: an Anglican contribution to the debate on euthanasia*, London.

Culyer, A. J. (1991) 'The promise of a reformed NHS: an economist's angle', *British Medical Journal*, 302: 1253–6.

Donovan, C. (1996) 'General practitioners and voluntary euthanasia' in Dunstan, G. R. and Lachmann, P. J. (eds) *Euthansia: death, dying and the medical duty*, London: Royal Society of Medicine.

Doyal, L. (1995) 'Advanced directives: like a will, everone should have one', *British Medical Journal*, 310: 612–13.

Dworkin, R. (1993) *Life's Dominion: an argument about abortion and euthanasia*, London: Harper Collins.

Erin, C. and Harris, J. (1994) 'Living wills: anticipatory decisions and advanced directives', *Reviews in Clinical Gerontology*, 4: 269–75.

Gillon, R. (1994) *The Four Principles*, London: Routledge.

Gormally, L. (1992) 'Living wills' in *The Dependent Elderly: autonomy, justice and quality of care*, Cambridge: Cambridge University Press.

Harris, J. (1988) 'EQALYty' in Byrne, P. *Health , Rights and Resources*, London: Kings College.

House of Lords Select Committee on Medical Ethics (1994) *Report for Session 1993–94*, Volume 1, (HL Paper 21–1), London: HMSO.

Institute of Medical Ethics (1990) 'Assisted death. Report of a working party on the ethics of prolonging life and assisting death', *Lancet*, 336: 610–12.

Isaacs, B. (1987) 'Introduction to ethical dilemmas in geriatric medicine' in Elford, R. J. (ed) *Medical Ethics and Elderly People*, Edinburgh: Churchill Livingstone.

Jennett, B. (1995) 'High technology therapies and older people', *Ageing and Society*, 15: 185–98.

Jennett, B. and Dyer, C. (1991) 'Persistent vegetative state and the right to die: the United States and Britain', *British Medical Journal*, 302: 1256–8.

Kennedy, I. (1981) *The Unmasking of Medicine*, London: George Allen and Unwin.

Kennedy, I. and Grubb, A. (1989) *Medical Law*, London: Butterworths.

Keown, J. (1995) 'Euthanasia in the Netherlands: sliding down the slippery slope', in Keown, J. (ed) *Euthanasia Examined*, Cambridge: Cambridge University Press.

Kuhse, H. and Singer, P. (1983) *Should the Baby Live? The problem of handicapped infants*, Oxford: Oxford University Press.

Law Commission (1995) *Mental incapacity: item 9 of the fourth programme of law reform: mentally incapacitated adults*, London: HMSO.

Lemmens, T. (1996) 'Towards the right to be killed: treatment refusal, assisted suicide and euthanasia in the United States and Canada', in Dunstan G. R. and Lachmann, P. J. (eds) *Euthanasia: death, dying and the medical duty*, London: Royal Society of Medicine.

Linacre Centre (1982) *Euthanasia and clinical practice: trends, principles and alternatives.* The report of a working party, London.

Pijnenborg, L. et al (1993) 'Life terminating acts without explicit request of patient', *Lancet*, 341: 1196–9.

Post, S. (1990) 'Infanticide and geronticide', *Ageing and Society*, 10: 317–28.

President's Commission for the Study of Ethical Problems in Medical and Biomedical and Behavioural Research (1983) *Report on deciding to forego life sustaining treatment*, Washington.

Ramsey, P. (1970) *The Patient as Person*, New Haven, CT: Yale University Press.

Royal College of Physicians (1994) *Ensuring Equity and Quality of Care for Older People*, London: RCP.

Skegg, P. (1984) *Law, Ethics and Medicine*, Oxford: Clarendon Press.

Smith, R. (1996) 'Being creative about rationing', *British Medical Journal*, 312: 391–2.

Van der Maas, P. J. (1991) 'Euthanasia and other medical decisions at the end of life', *Lancet*, 338: 669–74.

Van der Wal, G. (1994) 'Euthanasia in the Netherlands', *British Medical Journal*, 308: 1346–9.

Williams, A. (1988) 'Ethics and efficiency in the provision of health care' in Bell, J. M. and Mendus, S. (eds) *Philosophy and Medical Welfare*, Cambridge: Cambridge University Press.

5 The politics of ageing

Margaret Simey

The findings of this study point properly and remorselessly in the direction of a greater politicisation of the entire nation about older age. However, neither politicians nor public seem ready to understand or address the basic issue of older age. They stand on the wrong side of the chasm between what old age is thought to be and what it actually is in reality or prospect... The aim must be to make older age a 'universal' theme, applicable to everyone (as indeed it is) in all its aspects, positive as well as negative.

The raising of national consciousness onto a higher plateau of comprehension, and thus, one hopes, of more serious action, concerns the political culture as much as the political machinery. It is about the determination of an ethos.

Eric Midwinter and Susan Tester (1987) Polls Apart? Older voters and the 1987 general election, CPA, p.51

Introduction

On first contemplating the content of this chapter, I was surprised to be told by many who operate in the field of services for the ageing that I need not bother to argue the case for change in our social policy: we know all that, I was assured. There seems to be a general grasp of the fact that the lives of older people in our society cannot escape from the whirlwind of change that engulfs us all. In particular, there can be no avoidance of the fact that the centre of gravity in the population has shifted dramatically during the past decades as a consequence of the huge increase in the number of older people and the accompanying decrease in the numbers potentially able to support them. There can be no evasion of the consequences. Change in our policy regarding those we call the aged is inevitable.

All this is common ground between us. What took me by surprise was the difference between our respective responses. To those actively engaged in the field, the focus of attention was either the detached study of the process of ageing, or the provision of services for its amelioration. Their dedication cannot be questioned and the progress made in the understanding of the needs of those affected and the range of support offered is impressive: the focus of their attention is the individual. Whereas to me, a product of the women's movement and a lifelong student of society, the issue is essentially that of the relationship between the community and those of its members we categorise as aged. Given all the remarkable advance in understanding of the process of ageing and the progress made in improving the delivery of support services, it is evident that political policy has not kept pace.

The problem for the policy makers of today is that of how to translate increased understanding of what is needed into a practical and affordable programme for action. Yet, I have never been more acutely aware of the gulf between social reality and social policy. The two seem to be right out of touch with each other. The needs of the ageing multiply and change with uncontrollable rapidity; by comparison, policy-making seems to be static, stuck in a rut of custom and convention. Whether this is because of an aversion to all things political, or from a lack of politeracy – the know-how of managing our common affairs – the only policy to emerge is a despairing 'do-as-you-did-before only do it better'. Is that really the best we can do? My purpose here is to explore what alternatives, if any, are available to us and what their implications would be.

The case for change

It is always wise to look back before planning the future, but in this case it is peculiarly relevant to do so because current policy so closely reflects the past. In the industrial society of the nineteenth century, those who were no longer able to make an active contribution to the economy by reason of age or infirmity were regarded as objects of pity, victims of fate or of their own inadequacies. Old age in such circumstances was seen as an on-going struggle by the poor against deprivation and ill health, ending all too often in the workhouse. The prolific output of the classic Victorian novelists, and the stark statistics of the social historians, have ensured that the association of old age with poverty and ill health continues to be deeply embedded in our social thinking.

Though these old ideas persist, they are overlaid by changes which are specifically related to the circumstances of more recent years. Significantly, ageism, the justification of the injustice of the prejudice against older people, is a twentieth century phenomenon. Why this should be so is too complex a subject to be pursued here; in any case it is the outcome with which policy today must be concerned. It is an ugly reflection of the current takeover of social policy making by economic values that the old are effectively treated as a waste product of the market economy. They are seen accordingly as a separate category of persons, a category to which they are arbitrarily allocated at the age of 60 for women and 65 for men, in accordance with the financial requirements of the pension scheme. The increase in their numbers means that their care has become an end in itself, and this in turn perpetuates the assumption that elderly people are a burden and a problem. The cost is prohibitive.

Inevitably, this allocation of elderly people to an inferior status implies an assertion of control by those set in authority over them. And this inevitably, even in the best intended of societies, results in what has been aptly described as a peculiar form of social oppression (Bytheway, 1995). This is all the more unacceptable because it is negative, a framework of prohibition rather than a compulsion to action. Control breeds contempt for the controlled; it provokes bullying of the weak by the strong. The old are never allowed to forget their inferior status. They are given special concessions and free bus passes because they are assumed to be poor and frail. They are referred to as old girls and old boys. Their lives are subject to all manner of constrictions as to what work they may do and where they may live. The old age ghettos of the South Coast and the inner cities are equally repugnant as demonstrations of exclusion.

Those subjected to this treatment react exactly as might be expected. The majority accept their dependent status as of right, though many resent their exclusion from membership of ordinary society and find compulsory retirement a bitter and unrewarding experience. Some find solace in voluntary work of some sort. Others flee to Spain or escape into their own ill health as their major interest. Their relationship with younger generations subtly changes. We know a lot about biological ageing but little thought is given to the consequences of social ageing either for the individual or for the community in general. They are in fact disinherited citizens (Simey, 1996).

So to speak provokes a fury of rebuttal. The gallant grey movement, the regiment of committed older workers in the field of voluntary service, the spirited pursuit of the development of a wide variety of unsuspected talents, are all rightly quoted as evidence of the effective participation by older people in the life of the community in which they live and of their enjoyment of retirement. Nor can it be denied that the onset of decrepitude brings with it an undeniable need for support on the part of those growing old, to whom increasing dependence is an inescapable fact of life.

Nevertheless the stubborn fact remains that set in the context of the approaching millennium, current policy is increasingly recognised as being neither viable nor sustainable: it is not only irrelevant to the circumstances of today but constitutes an actual obstacle to forward thinking and planning. The slow disintegration of the safety net of the public sector, the massive disruption of the customary pattern of a life focused on 'work' as we have known it, the onset of a climate of insecurity, all these force the conclusion that change in social policy regarding the older members of our society is inescapably upon us.

Change – to what end?

Though there is consensus as to the need for change in the policy concerning older people, there is none whatsoever as to what change it is that should be made. The invariable answer is that it is all a matter of resources knowing, even as we speak, that there is little prospect of any increase in funding that will be adequate to the rising demand. Policy is geared accordingly; it is resource-led and we must resign ourselves to operating in a cycle of chronic crisis. Hence the frenzy of effort that goes into devising schemes for reconstruction and prioritising, targeting and rationing, all of which add up to no more than tinkering with the status quo. Clearly it is the assumption that social policy must necessarily be money-led that is the basic issue that must be challenged. It is the belief that money is the answer to social need, which results in the fatal mismatch between economic values and social policy that so grievously nullifies effort today. That is where change could, should and must be achieved.

To change from a money-led to a socially oriented policy would mean, in effect, that the focus would no longer be on money but on what we do with such money. This pinpoints the major difference between the two approaches. Policy making on an economic model requires a straightforward contract between those who provide services and those who use them. Their respective obligations are distinct. Under a social model, the public are not only users but also providers, not only customers but also responsible citizens, which gives rise to a situation of great complexity. In their capacity as representatives of the users, the public must do their best to protect the interests of those users: as providers of public services, their task is to balance the needs of particular groups against those of the community as a whole. They must act as a fulcrum where a balance is struck between conflicting demands. It is for them, for example, to determine whether or not to push for an increase in old age pensions if the outcome will be to cripple services for abused children. This calls for a completely different system of management and a vastly more sophisticated understanding on the part of all concerned with the working of the political machinery.

Moreover, the decision as to what needs are to be given priority is essentially a political, and not an economic, responsibility. This is not something that can be delegated to an executive. It must remain with the community, because it concerns the terms of the relationship between individuals and the society of which they are members. There can be no question of the exclusion of any single person, no second class citizens. No one can be denied their right to share in what is a common responsibility. If older people require special services to enable them to get by, these must be provided and authority delegated to appropriate agencies to provide them, but the responsibility for the original decision to act cannot be off-loaded. It is vested in the community and must remain so. This will have far-reaching implications for the relationship between management and older people. The habitual distinction between 'Us' and 'Them' will have to be replaced by a system in which the ageing are fully integrated into the process of policy and decision making on equal terms, a startling thought to all those born and bred in the habits of bureaucratic tradition.

The implications of all this for the status of the senior sector of the population will be fundamental. Instead of being the recipients of such provision, as the state of the economy permits and popular opinion approves, the ageing themselves will become active partners in the determination of social policy concerning their needs. And since social policy must reflect the social values of the community and not those of an accountant, the role of the elders of the tribe in formulating and transmitting those values becomes of crucial importance. By denying those entering upon the Third Age the obligations, as well as the benefits, of membership – as we often do – we deprive both them and our society of an essential element of governance. In the correction of the injustice of ageism, and the recognition of the period other than retirement from 'work' as the Third Age and the peak of a life cycle, lies the way ahead.

Appreciation of the potential of mature people as workers in the market economy is gathering ground, but little recognition is as yet paid to the essential nature of the contribution of older citizens to the quality of the life of the community as a whole. Politicians and administrators hopelessly underestimate the vital nature of the role of older people as a stabilising influence on both family life and that of a society. Our elders are the vital storehouse of the inherited memories and values which should constitute the launching pad for future policy, and for lack of which the same old mistakes are repeated over and over again. 'We never learn' is a common complaint amongst those of long experience. Housing policy provides a perfect illustration. Families are ruthlessly torn apart by clearance schemes even as we weep over the decline in family values which it is the particular responsibility of older generations to preserve. 'Get on your bike' is an outright contradiction of any plans for the regeneration of disintegrated communities.

It is a matter of common observation that freedom from the stresses of working life often seems to set free the development of capacities that have never been suspected. That there's more to life than work is a truism that is discovered with delighted surprise by the numbers of retired people who exclaim that they can't imagine how they ever found time to go to work. The realisation that retirement can bring its own compensations is, however, regarded as entirely a matter for the individual. Little thought is ever given as to how the community can cash in on the experience of long years of life and labour of an older person. The idea that older members of society should be active participants, because of their age and not in spite of it, ill accords with the stereotype of ageing as a process of decay. In fact, it is argued, that the opportunity to make a contribution on the basis of life experience can lead to the development of an ability to take a comprehensive view that should be an acquisition for any society. Seen in this light, a pension becomes less a reward for past efforts and instead represents an investment in the future (Walker, 1996).

The prime target for change in social policy making thus becomes the abolition of discrimination on the grounds of chronological age. Only on that basis will it be possible to explore the immense potential of the contribution that could and should be made to the promotion of our common welfare by the senior sector of our society. Here is new territory for us to explore. Here there is room for manoeuvre, scope for change. Here lies that hope for the future after which we so desperately yearn.

Practical politics of the Third Age

If this vision of the Third Age as an indispensable sector of the political structure is to add up to anything more than fodder for party propaganda, a drastic review of the working relationship between older people and the establishment will be an absolute essential. It will be futile to dream dreams unless the machinery for their implementation is adequate to the demands that will be made upon it. Good management should reflect purpose: in real life purpose is all too often dictated by management. If the purpose is changed to one that requires the integration of old people, the system of management must be geared accordingly.

The widespread use of the word participation in connection with services for old people is revealing. It presumes a system under which one group that has acquired authority – no doubt quite legitimately – invites others who are outside the pale to share in their activities, on terms dictated by those in control. In contrast, a policy dedicated to the principle of public responsibility for a public service, whether carried out by statutory or voluntary agencies, must of necessity be all-inclusive and machinery will have to be devised for this purpose. What will be required will be a system that will recognise that senior citizens have a role to play in initiating policy that is complementary to that of the administration: merely to consult people about plans that have already been drafted is a guaranteed source of frustration, and a waste of valuable social insight. In place of the customary 'Them' and 'Us' encounter for consultation after the event, the whole process of policy making will have to start with joint discussion of whatever is an issue of mutual concern. This will provide the basis on which precise policies can be determined and their implementation monitored. For this process Professor

John Stewart has coined the apt phrase of public discourse (Ranson and Stewart, 1994).

The experience of the habit of 'public discourse' is familiar enough to all who live and work in the inner areas or the outer estates. Our oft-denigrated planners were the first to give it official recognition, but consultation is now accepted as desirable practice in the housing and planning services and to a growing extent by general medical practitioners, the police and the health services. By and large, however, the social services have been slow to follow their example, especially in so far as community care is concerned. Efforts to stimulate active participation by the Third Age are common enough, but the sights are set on little more than encouraging voluntary service in a handmaiden capacity. That social change comes from below is a maxim whose soundness is demonstrated over and over again by those who live and work in deprived areas. It is a sentiment trumpeted with enthusiasm by politicians but any attempt to put principle into practice, so far as the over-sixties are concerned, is consistently resisted. They, meaning the citizenry, aren't ready for it yet, is the cry which, sadly, is often echoed by the outcast breed of old age pensioners.

The approach to the making of social policy advocated by Stewart is, of course, of general import; it stands for a recipe for making government by consent a reality. Its particular relevance to policy making in regard to ageing is obvious. The nub of the demand for change in policy is the fact that older people are categorised as a burden and a species apart. Conversely, it is precisely because they are so regarded that they are denied the opportunity to exercise responsibility. We seem to be trapped in a self-perpetuating downward spiral.

A learning society

Where do we go from here? Commentators on 'the state we're in', prominent amongst them Hutton (1996) and Rifkin (1995), argue with vigour that only a society prepared to abandon its old accustomed habits of thought and to devote itself to learning how to live in the post-industrial revolution world can hope to survive into the next century. The ability to adapt to situations so stupendously different from those we are familiar with, can only come about through a programme of learning at its most comprehensive. A change of mind and the thinking of new thoughts, call for the cultivation of a receptive attitude to learning on the part of the entire population.

The catch phrase about education being a life-long process from cradle to grave acquires a hugely greater significance seen in this light. To put it into operation will require the provision of an on-going and all-inclusive programme of education that extends not only to every individual but, even more urgently, to the society which they jointly constitute. The careful channelling of such educational resources as are allocated to elderly people into the provision of innocuous opportunities designed to keep them amused, bear an unwelcome resemblance to those for young children in a play centre.

The learning needs of those moving into the Third Age are two-fold. First, they have to understand and adjust to their role as senior members of the family in the new circumstances of the changing world. Concern for the rearing of the young is fundamental to the survival of any society, but its traditional expression is often no longer a practical possibility given the dispersal of succeeding generations and the break-up of the pattern of commitment to life-long partnerships. (I know of one grandmother who, defeated by the recurrent appearance of a new 'daughter-in-law', calls each one of them by the same first name of Marjorie.) The ensuing tangle of relationships is further complicated by the fact that many of the current generation of grandparents no longer fit the stereotype, and encounter their offspring in their capacity as colleagues and workers in the world outside the domestic. The young, having known nothing else, cope remarkably well though the long-term consequences are only just beginning to reveal themselves. Nevertheless it is a bewildering experience for all concerned to which past traditions seem irrelevant. Old dogs are having to learn new tricks if they are to survive.

It is, however, in regard to their role as 'elders of the tribe' that the necessity for education is most urgent. If the over-sixties who are at present excluded from social responsibility are to respond to the exciting opportunities of the coming century, training for their integration into the life of the community will be an absolute essential. Recognition of the change in their status from mere recipients of public philanthropy to active partners in the process of determining and implementing social policy, will have to be accompanied by a genuine appreciation of all that such a partnership involves. Education for the continuing exercise of their rights and duties in that capacity will be vital to the success of the change in status from dependency to partnership.

As for those who query the willingness of older people to respond to such an approach, the answer lies in the instinctive need of human beings to 'belong' to some group of people. This is an asset that should be carefully cultivated. It is all too often limited to passing opportunities such as protest marches or bingo clubs. The reluctance of elderly people to embark on what is unfamiliar, and therefore unwelcome, will best be overcome by experience of what is involved. The appetite for responsibility grows by what it feeds on. Action education is the best remedy for so-called apathy.

Much more elusive, because it is something we have not previously attempted to do, will be the promotion of a programme for learning on the part of the community in general, so far as attitudes to ageing are concerned. As a society, individualism has come to dominate our thinking; we have to learn to think communally so that we are able to set the self-interest of the Third Age in the context of society as a whole. The syllabus for such a learning programme will have to include the development of new skills for the management of our common affairs in a democratic society. New machinery for a system in which citizens will have an effective role can only be produced by inventive and educated minds. The level of 'politeracy' will have to be greatly enhanced.

Not least of the social skills to be acquired will be that of learning to articulate the code of social values which embody the lessons of experience. It is accepted wisdom that law and order depend as much on the self-discipline of the community as on its police, but this implies consensus as to what is desirable behaviour. Moral sensibilities can only be achieved as a result of the cultivation of what might perhaps be called 'moralicity', by which is meant the skill of expressing experience in moral terms. The importance of the contribution to be made to this process by the 'elders of the tribe' is self evident.

Indulgence in dreaming of what ought to be is only justified as providing the clear sense of purpose on which policy making must depend. The obstacles to be overcome, if the far-reaching programme for change which I have outlined is to be translated into reality, will obviously be formidable. It is beyond the scope of this chapter to consider policy making for the ageing in the context of the ebb and flow of political policy or economic circumstance in general. Instead, it may be more useful to concentrate on factors over which policy makers might hope to have some influence. What then are the obstacles likely to be encountered by the emergent Third Age?

The way ahead

If emancipation of the over-sixties from the stultifying grip of the stereotype with which they are lumbered is to be accomplished, everything will depend on the reaction of those who presently exercise authority in whatever capacity. However well intentioned they may be, the sheer force of the habit of deference to those in authority, combined with professional tradition will make it difficult for them to accept the mere idea of the sharing of responsibility, let alone display the requisite humility of mind. In their experience as administrators, the aged are dependent clients (to their credit many refuse to call them customers), and the relationship with them is based on the clear distinction between providers and users. They will have to grapple with the difficult concept of themselves as servants of the people, and not the patrons of services they exist to dispense. The habit of superiority will be difficult to dislodge, particularly in regard to older people (Wilding, 1982).

It may seem unjustified to point the finger at a corps of people of whom many have dedicated their entire lives to the care of the ageing, but the fact is that the very intensity of their devotion can make it difficult for them to hand over their responsibilities. Nominally, those who manage, whether in a paid or a voluntary capacity, may lack the legal power to take decisions but, in practice, their control over the decision-making process is all the more powerful because it escapes attention. The supply of information to committees, public gatherings or the media, the advice that accompanies it, the training and selection of staff and the preparation of the budget, are all opportunities for the exercise of control over the making of policy by those who will be responsible for its implementation. This is all the more crucial since the disintegration of the system of local government, and the institution of government by quango, has largely undermined the practice of accountability.

The impetus to challenge such paternalism might be expected to come from the voluntary sector. Their traditional role is to act as the voice of the social conscience, and to initiate and advocate change accordingly. However, unease about the current trend amongst charitable bodies towards becoming agents of the government under contract to supply certain specified services has provoked close examination of their ability to fulfil that role in modern times. (I have actually heard a government spokesperson advise a national conference that the voluntary movement representatives there must grasp the fact that they are now a business, and not a charity, and must conduct themselves accordingly.) In such circumstances, their proud claim to autonomy, and their effectiveness as advocates on behalf of those in need, become exceedingly thin.

There is yet another factor which mitigates against the integration of the Third Age into the process of policy making. The wholesale adoption by voluntary agencies of the management ethos has resulted in a take-over of control by the executive staff at the expense of those supposedly responsible for policy. With surprising gullibility, the numerous inquiries into the governance of voluntary bodies take for granted the traditional assumption that responsibility for their activities is in the hands of committee members who are themselves volunteers. The reality is that as in a business, control is necessarily a matter for the chief executive.

This is of particular relevance so far as provision for elderly people is concerned, in view of the threatened hand-over of responsibility for such services to the private sector. The voice of those on the receiving end of whatever is provided is becoming increasing inaudible. The focus is on the business of providing care for elderly people and not on the wellbeing of the beneficiaries. The harsh reality is that social services and voluntary bodies alike are so hampered by their unquestioning allegiance to the cast-iron barrier of the rigid age of retirement that they no longer speak on behalf of the people.

It is rare indeed to find, even in the ranks of the sturdy 'grey' movements, any confrontation of the injustice of discrimination by age. The Centre for Policy on Ageing has trod a lonely path in its gallant efforts to stimulate discussion of the whole unseemly topic of ageism (Midwinter, 1985). There are all too few who share the approach of organisations such as the Refer to Relatives Association, which campaigns for the ongoing integration of voluntary carers into the provision made for those who eventually have to seek the shelter of a Home. Efforts to restore dignity to the frail inhabitants of a Home by inviting them to contribute to its management are laudable in the extreme, but they fall far short of the target of the integration of the entire cohort of elderly people into the community as a whole.

These are primarily management issues. The wider implications of a policy directed to the promotion of the Third Age as a serious player in the making of social policy are equally important. Thus, the abolition of discrimination on the grounds of age and, by implication, of a policy tied to a fixed age of retirement, immediately raises the whole thorny issue of the urgent need for a review of the pensions system, a subject to which Frank Field has recently made a notable contribution (Field, 1996). This debate is already underway in the wake of the critical questioning to which the entire system of state welfare is now being subjected.

A parallel issue is that of the effects on the economy of the application of a ban on discrimination on grounds of age. In the climate of the times, merely to let loose a horde of unemployed elderly people on an already over-loaded market place would be catastrophic. A recent contribution to this debate comes from the Third Age Challenge movement, but the title is deceptive since it is directed to the reabsorption into the market place of those trapped in the redundancy of the fifties and earlier. The object is valuable, but the choice of title blurs the concept of the Third Age as a specific alternative to a policy determined by an economic purpose. Finally, there remains the tricky question of whether we as a society can afford to adopt the drastic changes advocated by reformers. Even those who most earnestly advocate change admit that money does matter. Various alternatives to an economic wage are already being aired such as that for a social wage of some kind though, as ever, little thought is given to those whose working life has ended. The work of the Centre for Local Economic Strategies on the possibility of grafing new opportunities for employment onto the existing benefit system, instead of making it an either/or matter, suggests the potential of a scheme that would enable pensioners to seek for alternative occupation on an alternative financial basis (Finn, 1996). Field's proposals for putting the provision for pensions on an entirely new footing are yet another indication of the thinking that is being directed to the question of the financial underwriting of the requirements of ageing.

One and all, consideration of the merits of such proposals is invariably thwarted by those who play the financial card. The clue to the way out of the ensuing deadlock would seem to lie in reversing the question. What we ought to be considering is not whether we can afford to make changes, but whether we can afford not to do so. This shifts attention to the question of the means by which we measure the value of what we get for our money. The customary practice of relying on a purely financial audit as a measure of value for money is a classic example of the mismatch of economic values and social policy. As pioneered by Traidcraft, the Third World trading organisation, for example, what is involved is a system that sets against the account of income received, an equally professional evaluation of the consequential outcome. This entails the abandonment of the existing method of short-term accounting for a system that would permit the long-term benefits to be taken into account. This would release policy making from the stringencies imposed by the false restrictions of an audit covering only a single year, and enable the long-term benefits to be taken into account.

Applied to ageing, a social audit would take account of the actual savings accruing from a policy which promoted the active contribution of the older sector and reduced their dependence on support services. The value to the life of the community of a regiment of the Third Age would be presented in the shape of performance indicators specifically designed for that purpose. This might seem a difficult task because of its novelty, but experience of the imaginative use of the factual material provided by the Chartered Institute of Public Finance Accountants (CIPFA) in regard to policing, convinces me of its feasibility. Only a statement of the value of active citizenship in terms of hard cash will convince the financial experts who see no economic gain in the integration of elderly tenants into housing management, for example.

These are undeniably difficult issues, all the more so because they interlock one with another and together set off a domino chain of repercussions throughout the existing structure. Tackled piecemeal, and always in the context of the dominance of economics over social policy, there would seem to be no hope of doing anything more than tinker with the old banger of a system that we already have. The only escape route is to go boldly for the basic change from economic to social values.

The time is surely ripe for a totally fresh approach to the role and responsibilities of the older sector of our society. There is urgent need for a new emancipation movement that will set the elders of our community free to play their part in the challenging world of the technological revolution. Our mission as a society – for once, business speak is appropriate – must be to bring the ageing in out of the cold of dependency into the warmth of mainstream life in the community to our mutual benefit. Only the most comprehensive and far-sighted programme of learning will enable us as individuals to respond to such a change.

What of the future?

One thing is clear. There can be no going back to the fantasy world of those who dream of the communitarianism of the past. That's all gone, along with the Merrie England of the romanticists. Nor can we stand still; in a climate of constant change and turbulence, there can be no question of stopping the world so that we can get off. Even doing nothing is not an option in these circumstances; there is reason to fear that the working population is beginning to resent the increasing numbers of elderly people as constituting too heavy a burden to be borne. Conflict between the generations is an ugly, but a very real, threat. At the end of the day, whether we regard the future as being no more than making the best of a bad job or look forward to it with courage and excitement, we have no choice but to start from the acceptance of the fact that we are sitting on a time bomb. It's up to us to decide what our response will be, but respond we must.

Is all this just day-dreaming, the vapourising of an aged idealist that does not have the remotest connection with the realities of the new future of the twenty-first century? I set out in this chapter to pursue the idea that there is an alternative to the doom and gloom of social policy today. I have tried to anchor theorising in the solid ground of the practicalities of putting my ideas into operation. But what hope is there that any single shred of the whole programme I have outlined – or, indeed, of any other of equal magnitude – will ever come about?

Dark and difficult though the times may be, I believe that there are grounds for optimism. That social change comes from below is an accepted maxim. Change in social policy can only come about if it is impelled by energy drawn from some deep well of common feeling that is fed by common experience. It was because Beveridge's plan tapped an unsuspected source of emotional energy that it won widespread support in spite of outright opposition by Churchill, then Prime Minister.

Hope lies in the fact that there is ample evidence that such a source of energy lies at the disposal of those who now seek to bring about change in the policy concerning our elders; the unanimity of opinion on the need for change was my starting point in embarking on this chapter. All the talk of community, of family values, of social cohesion, arises out of a deep sense of unease about things as they are, and a longing for a way of life that is not dominated by selfishness and materialism even while we enjoy the benefits of the new technology. Inarticulate though it may be and inspired by a complexity of reasons, the tide of public opinion is on the move. It is for the policy makers to see to it that older citizens are not once more excluded from participation in that common purpose.

The attitude to ageing is so entrenched that, of all the injustices that disgrace our society, ageism will perhaps prove to be the most difficult to eradicate. It will require tremendous courage and conviction to overcome it; only total commitment to a clear vision of what the Third Age could and should be will suffice. It is quite simply for lack of a vision that the people perish. Those who denigrate the dream of a caring community and scorn the essential contribution to be made to it by those entering upon their Third Age, totally fail to grasp the vital importance in policy making of a sense of purpose. When Charles Booth, in his other guise as ship-owner, organised 1,000-mile trips up the Amazon, he counselled passengers that to avoid seasickness they should keep their eyes on the horizon. Sound advice; it is because we have lost the vision that we falter. Given that vision, we will survive, and in so doing, not only survive, but – who knows – actually achieve one more step forward, however small, in 'the great historical project of human emancipation' (Meacher, 1992).

References

Bytheway, B. (1995) *Ageism*, Buckingham: Open University Press.

Field, F. (1996) *How to Pay*, London: Institute of Community Studies.

Finn, D. (1996) *Making Benefits Work*, Centre for Local Economic Strategies.

Hutton, W. (1996) *The State We're In*, London: Vintage.

Meacher, M. (1992) *Diffusing Power*, London: Pluto

Midwinter, E. (1985) *The Age of Retirement: the case for a new pensions policy*, London: Centre for Policy on Ageing.

Ranson, S. and Stewart, J. (1994) *Management for the Public Domain*, New York: St Martins Press.

Rifkin, J. (1995) *The End of Work*, New York: Putnam

Simey, M. (1996) *The Disinherited Society*, Liverpool: Liverpool University Press.

Walker, A. (ed.) (1996) *The New Generational Contract*, London: UCL Press.

Wilding, P. (1982) *Professional Power and Social Welfare*, London: Routledge.

6 Great expectations: social policy and the new millennium elders

Maria Evandrou

Many now believe it is necessary to redefine old age in a more dynamic and positive manner, switching the mood and style imaginatively to make the most of this unprecedented opportunity for millions of older citizens to enjoy happy and constructive lives. The waste of experience and other human resources is tragic and the relegation of many old people to second-class citizenship is shaming.

Eric Midwinter and Susan Tester (1987) Polls Apart? Older voters and the 1987 general election, CPA, p. 53

Introduction

This chapter discusses how the different experiences of current generations impact upon the chances of securing a preferable retirement and frame their expectations of the future. The experience of wider educational opportunities, flexible labour markets, consumerism, technological change within the home and workplace, will all act to shape the expectations of future generations of older people.

Will membership of occupational and private pension schemes and greater home ownership mean that the new millennium elders will be wealthier, no longer dependent on the state for income in retirement? Will they be healthier and fitter, placing fewer demands on health and community services? Or will these 'children of the welfare state', with their better education and higher expectations, be more informed about their 'rights' and more vocal in their demands? Will they be far more knowledgeable and discerning consumers in the market place? What role will information technology take in their lives? What new calls will be placed on services, and the family, and how can and should policy makers begin to plan?

Older people in the new millennium will expect to have healthy, active retirements, *not* in poverty and *not* in work. This chapter discusses the extent to which older people will have their expectations met. How should social policy develop in order to respond to these expectations? Moving from a fifth to a third of the electorate, older people in the next century will represent a greater political force. How they direct that potential will be in their hands. Key issues for future social policy development are outlined, locating the debates and highlighting important empirical evidence.

Table 16.1 The new millennium elders: demographic and life course events for selected birth cohorts, England and Wales

	Birth cohort			
	1916–20	1931–35	1946–50	1961–65
Representative cohort year	1920	1931	1947	1964
Size of cohorts in UK at ages 60–64 (millions)[1]	2.9 (1980)	2.8 (1995)	3.8 (2010)	4.4 (2025)
Age in 1997	77	62	50	33
Age in 2027	107	92	80	63
Expectation of life at birth[2]				
men	50.9	59.2	65.2	68.1
women	55.4	63.3	69.8	74.1
Expectation of life at age 60[3]				
men	16.4	17.7	20.7*	21.9*
women	20.9	21.9	24.6*	25.8*
Proportion remaining unmarried at age 30[4]				
men	31	19.1	17.1	45.9
women	24	11.1	8.3	32.1
Proportion of women remaining childless at age 30[5]	30	22	19	39
Proportion who have ever divorced by at age 35[3]				
men	–	3.5	13.7	–
women	–	4.4	16.2	–

Sources:
1 OPCS Population Trends. Projections using 1992-based national population projections (OPCS, 1995a)
2 Case, R., et al (1962)
3 Government Actuary's Department
4 OPCS (1995b)
5 OPCS (1995c)
* From 1994-based population projections.

Table 16.1 shows four distinct cohorts reaching their sixties in different decades of the twenty-first century. Marked differences are to be expected between these generations, particularly when comparing the 1960s baby boom cohort with elderly people today – that is the 1920s and 1930s cohorts – because they were born into, and grew up in, very different economic, social and technological climates. It is their different experiences that will shape their expectations of retirement.

Before examining how social policy might adapt in the future it is useful to detail how future cohorts of elderly persons in 2030 or even 2050 will differ from previous generations of elders.

Changing living arrangements: the rise of 'solo living'

'Solo living' will take on greater relevance in the new millennium. A number of factors will contribute to a rise in the proportion living alone. Firstly, fewer future elderly persons will have married or entered into a co-habiting union than is the case today. If current trends continue, it is predicted that 12 per cent of women and 18 per cent of men from the 1960s cohort will not have formed a marital or co-habiting union by the time they reach the age of 50 (Evandrou and Falkingham, 1997). This compares with 5 and 9 per cent respectively of persons born in 1947.

Secondly, among those who have married, a greater proportion will also have experienced divorce or separation. In fact, 18 per cent of women and 15 per cent of men born in 1961 have already witnessed the break-up of their marriage or union before the age of 30 (OPCS, 1995b). On the other hand, with increasing longevity fewer will have experienced the break-up of their union through death. This will not, however, be sufficient to offset the rise in divorce. The net effect will be an increase in the proportion not living in a union, of between 10 per cent (for women) and 15 per cent (for men) for those born in 1961, as compared to those born in 1931.

Figure 16.1 Proportion living alone at age 60 and 75 (by birth cohort)

Cohort 1916–20   13.5 / 37.3

Cohort 1931–35   14.6 / 37.6*

Cohort 1946–50   20* / 40.8*

Cohort 1961–65   25.5*

■ 60
▨ 75

*Projection

Source: Falkingham (1997)

The marked shift to later and fewer marriages interacts with rising divorce to increase the propensity to live alone. Figure 16.1 shows that over two in every five persons amongst those born in the late 1940s will be living alone by age 75. Moreover, it is predicted that a quarter of the 1960s cohort will already be lone householders at age 60. These different demographic trajectories will have important implications for health and social care in 2030, particularly with regard to the availability of co-residential kin, and in particular spouses.

The proportion of women from different cohorts who have never had a child by a particular age can be compared in Figure 16.2. By age 25 only 37 per cent of the 1947 cohort women had not given birth, whereas 60 per cent of the 1964 cohort were still childless at the same age. Women from the 1920 cohort have experienced the highest levels of childlessness of any cohort this century, with 21 per cent still childless at age 45. Looking at the shape of the trajectory to date for women in the 1964 cohort it is likely that they will exceed this level of childlessness. Similar trends have been found elsewhere in Europe; in the Netherlands 18 per cent of women were still childless by their mid thirties in 1992, and the proportions rise to 20 per cent in Austria and 21 per cent in Switzerland (Coleman, 1996). Assuming this trend continues, over one fifth (21 per cent) of the new millennium elders from the

Figure 16.2 Proportion of women remaining childless (by birth cohort)

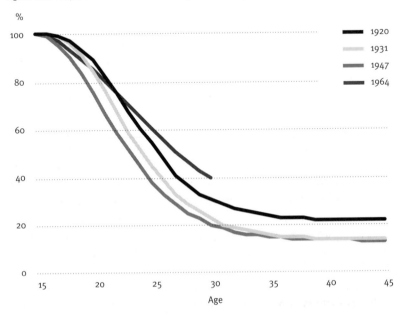

Figure 16.3 Percentage of women childless at age 30 and 40 (by birth cohort)

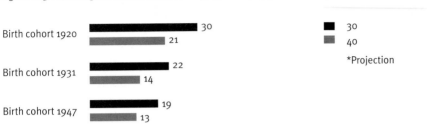

Source: *Evandrou and Falkingham (1997).*

1960s generation, will remain childless throughout their lives (Figure 16.3). On the basis of this, therefore, it is likely that we will see a decline in the potential supply of informal care from (adult) children.

Higher proportions of the 1960s generation will have experienced periods of lone parenthood and step-parenthood. Little is known about how divorce may affect family ties and feelings of inter-generational obligation. Will children of divorced parents, and in particular of fathers who failed to maintain regular contact with them, show the same willingness to care? Similarly, will ex-daughter-in-laws be prepared to offer care to their ex-mother and father-in-law?

Alternative family relationships may assume greater relevance. Traditionally the caring relationship has been that of parent/child. Now the role of grandparent/grandchild is beginning to attract increasing attention. As Jerrome (1996) points out, given increased life expectancy this relationship can now last for many decades, perhaps even as long as fifty years. At present adult grandchildren are not reported as playing a significant role in the care of their grandparents (Qureshi, 1996), but with the growing proportion of grandchildren who will have experienced the divorce of their parents, this may change in the future. Given increased childlessness, relations with nephews and nieces may also assume greater primacy. Similarly, friendship networks will be more important among the twenty-first century elders, be they neighbours or 'virtual' friends on the internet.

Certainly, we are seeing the emergence of increasingly complex family structures, and new forms of family ties. Janet Finch concludes that family responsibilities today are based upon 'individual "commitments" rather than on "fixed obligations" associated with a genealogical link...this means that filial responsibilities cannot be relied upon as the basis for the [future] provision of care' (1995: 61).

What then will be the preferred sources of support among future elderly cohorts? How do changes in social attitudes regarding expectations of family care provision impact? Although there is no doubt that there will be more persons, in terms of absolute numbers, requiring support in 2030 than today, it is less clear who will provide it and what mix of care older people themselves will prefer.

Co-residence with adult children in later life has not been popular historically (Thompson and West, 1984; Qureshi, 1996) and is often linked to an event or crisis. It is unlikely that future cohorts of older people will be any more inclined than previous cohorts to share their homes with their children. Studies on family obligations report that significant proportions (a third of the respondents) thought that children did not have an obligation to look after their parents (Finch, 1995). There is also evidence that elderly people would often prefer to rely on state services than on their children, particularly for some tasks (Sixsmith, 1986; Siim, 1990).

Evidence from Norway indicates that between 1967 and 1989 there was a move away from relatives and towards formal agents as the preferred sources of support among elderly persons (Daatland, 1990). Even if future generations of elders continue to favour formal rather than informal mechanisms for social care and support, the key question is whether the level and range of such support will be available, and if so, whether they will be expected to, or even able to, pay for such services.

Demand for social care will also depend upon future trends in health and dependency.

Healthy and active vs illness and dependency?

Older people in the new millennium will expect to have healthy, active retirements. Will they be disappointed? It could be argued that, having benefited from the NHS and having experienced improved living conditions in their youth and middle age, the post war baby boom cohorts will go on to 'age healthily'. But Dunnell (1995) in a survey of trends in mortality, morbidity and health risk behaviour, found that although almost universal improvements in mortality rates and increasing life expectancy might suggest that we are indeed healthier, trends in self-reported health status suggest there is *no* comparable general improvement in health. Life expectancy in old age has risen, however the extent to which these gains are disability free is the subject of ongoing debate (Grundy, 1992; Robine et al, 1992). Research indicates that as life expectancy increases, there will be a rise in the proportion of people experiencing light to moderate disabilities, but a fall in those with severe disabilities (Bone et al, 1995).

Health in later life will be affected by quality of life during working years. Those who paid attention to health education campaigns, taking regular exercise, having a healthy diet, and who avoided smoking may escape today's major killers: strokes, lung cancer, and heart attacks (Dalley, 1997). On the other hand, new threats such as stress, pollution, food contamination, etc. can lead to the onset of yet unknown health problems in later life.

Trends in limiting long-standing illness suggest that younger cohorts, such as the 1940s and 1960s cohorts, report slightly *higher* levels of limiting long-standing illness than the previous cohort at the same age. However, the good news is that in terms of health risk behaviour, younger cohorts show lower levels of smoking than earlier cohorts (Evandrou and Falkingham, 1997) (Figures 16.4–6). Smoking has been found to be the single largest factor accounting for the ill health of older people today (Evans et al, 1992). Given that smoking is known to be related to a wide variety of illnesses and health states, evidence of decreased prevalence amongst members of the younger cohorts, suggests that future elderly people will be healthier than today's generation of elders.

Figure 16.4 Proportion of women reporting limiting long-standing illness (by birth cohort – 3 year moving averages)

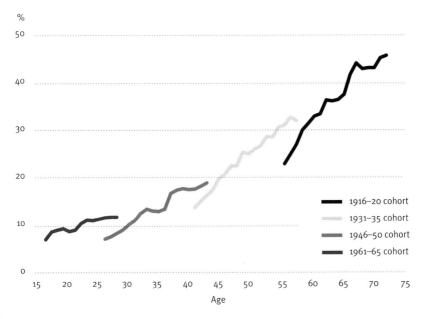

Source: Evandrou and Falkingham (1997).

Figure 16.5 Proportion of men reporting limiting long-standing illness
(by birth cohort – 3 year moving averages)

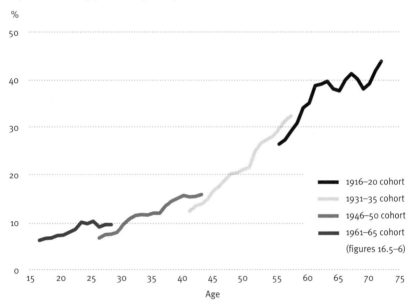

Figure 16.6 Proportion of women currently smoking (by birth cohort)

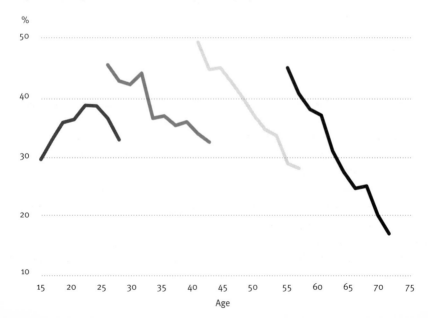

Another influence upon health is the level of stress faced within the workplace. Britain's workers work the longest hours in Europe (CSO, 1996). Moreover, 30 per cent of British workers reported that they found their work stressful and 44 per cent reported that they 'often or always' came home from work 'exhausted' (Curtice, 1993). Pseudo-cohort analysis of the General Household Survey (GHS) data indicates that men from the 1960s cohort have experienced longer working weeks, at earlier stages in their life course, than the preceding cohorts (Evandrou and Falkingham, 1997). By age 30, 20 per cent of men in employment in the 1961–65 cohort reported working fifty or more hours per week, compared with 13 per cent of men in the 1946–50 cohort at the same age. Longer hours worked at younger ages may adversely affect health, directly or indirectly, both now and in later life. Further evidence for increased stress and feelings of dislocation from society amongst the 1960s boomer cohort is provided by the rise in suicide rates among them, particularly males (Charlton et al, 1993; Dunnell, 1995).

Evidence of a growing divide between rich and poor has also been documented. This is likely to manifest itself in health terms in the new millennium (Benzeval et al, 1995; Joseph Rowntree Foundation, 1995). Smoking prevalence increases with indicators of disadvantage (Marsh and Makay, 1994); evidence shows that nearly three quarters of lone parents with low incomes, no educational qualifications, from manual occupations and living in public sector housing, smoked regularly. Health inequalities among lower socio-economic groups, residents living in the north and Scotland, or in inner cities, indicate that these groups may well face a less fortunate and more morbid retirement in the next century (Drever and Whitehead, 1997).

In addition, the new millennium elders will reflect greater ethnic diversity (Table 16.2). The health status of minority ethnic groups varies significantly, both across and between ethnic groups (Smaje, 1995; Evandrou, 1997; Modood et al, 1997; Nazroo, 1997). Caribbeans, Pakistanis and Bangladeshis report worse health than whites, while Indians, African Asians and Chinese share similar levels of health as whites. All minority ethnic groups, with the exception of the Chinese, are more likely to consult their GP and also visit hospital Accident and Emergency and outpatient services, than their white counterparts. However this was not the case with use of hospital inpatient services, suggesting a lower referral rate from primary to secondary care for patients from minority ethnic communities. These findings, based upon large scale survey data (Modood et al, 1997), have far-reaching implications for the health and dependency of older people in 2040 and beyond, and demand for health and social care which is adequate and culturally sensitive.

Table 16.2 Ethnic composition of selected birth cohorts, 1991 Great Britain

	Birth cohort			
	1916–20	1931–35	1946–50	1961–65
Representative cohort year	1920	1931	1947	1964
Ethnicity:				
Men				
White	98.6	95.6	96.0	93.3
Black[1]	0.5	1.6	0.8	2.6
South Asian[2]	0.7	2.2	2.1	2.5
Other groups[3]	0.3	0.7	1.1	1.6
Women				
White	99.0	96.6	95.5	92.7
Black[1]	0.3	1.3	1.0	3.0
South Asian[2]	0.4	1.6	2.2	2.8
Other groups[3]	0.2	0.6	1.3	1.6

1 Black includes Black Caribbean, Black African and Black other.
2 South Asian includes Indian, Pakistani and Bangladeshi.
3 Other groups includes Chinese, Asian and others.
Source: 1991 Census; note that age-sex ethnic groups were weighted by published weighting factors to correct for estimated undercoverage of each group in 1991 enumeration.

In summary, the evidence on the health of future elders is somewhat mixed. Thus it is premature to assume that tomorrow's elderly people will be healthier than today's. Trends in smoking provide one indication that younger generations will be healthier in later life than current generations of elderly people. However, the proportion reporting limiting long-standing illness suggests the opposite; with younger cohorts reporting slightly *higher* levels than previous cohorts at the same age. Furthermore, the 1960s cohort has experienced higher levels of unemployment, and longer working weeks for those in work, at earlier stages in their life course than the 1940s cohort. Increased levels of work-related stress may manifest themselves in poorer health in older ages. Whether future elders will be healthier than today's elders may also depend upon the impact of factors as yet unknown. Greater use of pesticides, genetic engineering in animal farming, and advances in food technology may manifest themselves in better or worse health in later life (Bone et al, 1995).

The world of work

Post-war industrial change has resulted in the emergence of alternative working practices, reflected in the growth of part-time working and self-employment (Phillipson, 1997). For some, this has brought with it greater flexibility, allowing people to combine multiple responsibilities such as child care, elder care and paid employment. For others, this has resulted in a lack of long-term security and fewer employment related benefits such as occupational pensions, maternity leave and holiday entitlements. The 'traditional' life course, with defined periods of education, work and retirement, is being replaced by one where there is significantly more fluidity and movement between states, especially in the labour market. The notion of a *lifelong* career has all but disappeared. Rather, temporary and transitional jobs will become a permanent feature of the employment experiences of some sections of the second 1960s baby boomers.

Table 16.3 Employment characteristics of selected birth cohorts, England and Wales

	Birth cohort			
	1916–20	1931–35	1946–50	1961–65
Representative cohort year	1920	1931	1947	1964
Percentage of cohort economically active at age 15–19 yrs				
men	85[1]	84	74	51
women	71[1]	78	56	49
Percentage of cohort economically active at age 25–29 yrs				
men	98	98	97	95
women	35	40	43	63
Percentage of cohort economically active at age 55–59 yrs				
men	95	81	74	–
women	52	55	56	–
Percentage of cohort economically active at age 65–69 yrs				
men	14	13	–	–
women	3	3	–	–

1 aged 14–20

Source: CSO Historical Labour Force Statistics 1881–1961; Department of Employment Gazette; British Labour Force Projections 1997–2006.

Changes in the labour market have affected men and women differently. Younger cohorts of men both enter the labour market later and leave earlier, and have *lower* overall participation rates at any given age (Table 16.3). In contrast, women from the 1960s cohort experience *higher* rates of participation at any given age (and higher full-time rather than part-time employment), than the earlier cohorts of the 1940s and 1930s. Both of these trends have implications for the level of resources in later life. More women have longer working lives, spending more time in full-time employment, enhancing their potential for accumulating pension entitlement in their own right. The shorter working lives of men, however, will tend to have the opposite impact reducing overall pension entitlements. This may be exacerbated by the fact that the proportion of the 1960s baby boomers who had experienced unemployment by the age of 35, was very much higher than for any previous generation (Evandrou and Falkingham, 1997; Hancock, 1997). Once more, particular groups *within* these cohorts may be disproportionately affected by economic change. For any given age, male unemployment rates have been found to be higher among all minority ethnic groups, except the Chinese (Karn, 1997; Modood, 1997). This will have implications for resources in later life.

Resources in retirement

The value of the basic state pension relative to average earnings has decreased. As Falkingham points out in Chapter 6, if it continues to be uprated in line with prices rather than earnings, the state pension is expected to be worth only 9 per cent of male average earnings by 2030. Most young people no longer expect to have an adequate state pension in later life.

Pensions from non-state sources will become of increasing importance. There has been a substantial rise in membership of occupational pension schemes across time within the cohorts, especially amongst women. Fewer of the 1960s boomer men are members of occupational pensions schemes than previous cohorts. But, both 1960s generation men and women are more likely to have personal pensions. For the younger boomer generation, at least, the certainty of occupational pensions, with a defined benefit,[1] has been transformed into the uncertainty of private pensions, where the final pay-out depends on the 'lottery of the money markets' (Atkinson, 1991).

More of the 1960s cohort will have access to housing wealth, both through their own tenure and through inheritance, than previous generations. Between three quarters and four fifths of the 1940s cohort and an even greater proportion of the 1960s baby boomers will enter retirement owning their own homes. Rising membership of pension schemes, and greater levels of owner occupation, both point to the baby boomers being better off in retirement than today's elderly people (Hancock, 1997). However, any complacency concerning the retirement incomes of the new millennium elders is premature.

In addition to those with better pensions there will also be a group of people who have been unable to accumulate pension rights to a second tier pension, either because of interrupted earnings' histories or low income. Greater reliance on earnings related private pensions will mean that inequalities in working life are perpetuated into retirement.

Increasing polarisation within future cohorts of elderly people, will be a key facet of twenty-first century ageing. Inequalities will persist between those who will experience full work histories, acquired pension rights and housing wealth, and those who will not. The 1960s baby boom cohort, in particular, faced high unemployment levels when they first began to enter the labour market. Some of this group have never had a full-time job and thus the opportunity to accumulate resources and participate actively in society. Others, however, benefited from the Thatcher era, such as the school leavers who entered the city trading, giving rise to the 1980s 'Yuppie'.

The recession of the 1980s also hit the 1940s cohort. Many of those who lost their jobs in their mid forties, face particular difficulties in re-entering the labour market during a period of technological change. Early retirement for this group has often not been through choice but circumstance. Interrupted work histories will perpetuate the inequalities stemming from unemployment and low income into old age.

Older people in the twenty-first century will have higher rates of owner-occupation than previous generations of older persons. However, the combined effect of middle-management shake-outs in the 1990s, later marriages, later child-bearing and higher divorce rates, will mean that significant numbers of older people in the future will enter later life with continuing mortgage commitments (Means, 1997). Many will face difficult financial circumstances.

Differences in inheritance of housing wealth will further reinforce the trend towards polarisation. Holmans and Frosztega (1994) found that a higher proportion of local authority tenant couples than owner-occupier couples, do *not* have owner-occupiers as parents on either side, lending support to the contention that inheritances of house property will go, in the most part, to individuals who are themselves owner-occupiers and already able to accumulate wealth. Intergenerational transmission of wealth reinforces the notion that the rich get richer whilst the poor remain the same – further contributing to 'two nations in retirement' (Titmuss, 1955).

Community care

Polarisation in terms of financial resources will also lead to inequalities in access to health and social care through changes in the financing mechanism of health and social care services. Private health insurance has risen in the last decade and some companies are offering social insurance policies. Those with uneven employment histories are unlikely to be in a position to contribute to either private pensions or private health insurance. Yet, given that employment in turn is related to health status, these groups may be in most need of health care.

We are already witnessing the explicit rationing of publicly funded health care, free at the point of use (Maynard, 1993; New and Le Grand, 1996). Age discrimination already seems to be operating in relation to a variety of treatments and care (Whitaker, 1992; Seymour, 1993; Dalley, 1997) and in times of greater pressures on financial resources, this may continue to grow. Cases such as that which occurred in Hillingdon Hospital where, in October 1996, it was announced that all persons aged 75 and over referred by their GP for emergency treatment would be refused due to a lack of available beds, may become more widespread (Hunt, 1996). Other examples of rationing of health care include no physiotherapy for those aged 65 plus in a hospital in a south-eastern coastal town. If the current trends towards a two tier health service continue, by 2020 those poorly resourced elderly people, who are unable to purchase services outside the NHS, may find themselves dependent on a residualised publicly funded service where exclusion from particular treatments, on the grounds of age, is commonplace.

Charging for social care services has become more widespread. The Department of Health expected that on average one tenth of the cost of direct service provision in 1996–97 would be met through charges to users (Neate, 1996). By 2020 it is likely that local authorities will be required to raise charges such that they recover the full economic cost of the services they offer. Those who are uninsured, and with low or no private pension income, are unlikely to be in a position to meet such charges.

Thus, the new millennium elders at the bottom of the income distribution may find themselves multiply disadvantaged; without the resources to actively participate in society, without the income to exercise choice over formal and informal sources of social care and possibly excluded from certain medical care.

Of course, trends towards increasing privatisation of health and social care may not continue in the future. Before considering a policy framework for the twenty-first century, however, it is also important to acknowledge the role of technological innovation in shaping options in the future. Technology has permeated all spheres of our lives and will continue to change the face of daily living in the twenty-first century: both through innovation in consumer durables and other goods, and through enhanced communication and access to information. The key question is how will these developments impact upon the quality of life and well-being of elderly people in the next century.

Technology: facilitating and empowering or a new axis of disadvantage?

Computers, and the rapidly expanding use of the internet, are revolutionising the exchange of information. In the future it is not unrealistic to envisage that most homes, or at the very least every public library or advice centre, will have access to the information super-highway via the internet. Already hospital trusts are 'publishing' waiting lists for different specialties in electronic form and, by 2020, it will be the norm that every social services department will have their own 'home page' and consumers will have immediate access to information concerning what services are available, at what price, and by which agency.

Information technology may also facilitate greater participation amongst older people themselves: for example, using the network offers opportunities to access debates and policy discussions, as well as providing feedback to trusts and other organisations regarding the quality of services used. Physical incapacity will no longer be a barrier to accessing such technology through the use of voice or sensory activated computers. Similarly, translation filters will facilitate cross-cultural communication where language remains a barrier. Access to the internet via the TV will bring virtual meeting rooms, art galleries, museums and even holidays in exotic locations, directly into your own living room. Interactive cable networks will offer a wide use of public services, advice lines, transactions from home, entertainment and library services, home security, service metering and itemised billing may all facilitate the everyday life activities of all citizens in the next century. Technology can thus empower people as citizens and consumers.

Technological innovation may also enhance the independence and quality of daily living of older people. As well as providing access to information, new products will facilitate the lives of people with disabilities through smart technology. For example, there are already trials being conducted of community alarms where sensors within an older person's home, locally processed via a neural network, can help to identify unusual behaviour, such as the elderly person becoming unconscious or having a fall (Sixsmith and Sharples, 1996). This then triggers the alarm for help. Smart technology will provide greater environmental control, such as hand held controls to open windows or voice activated systems to boil the kettle. A 'smart house system' could facilitate persons in the early stages of dementia to remain within their own home. The key issues in 2020 will not be the availability of such systems, but rather their affordability and portability. Will systems be easily transferable when people move home? Will they be sensitive to the dynamic nature of dependency and changing needs?

Another sphere where technological advances will impact upon the lives of the ageing boomers is medical care. Telemedicine, where medical advice or care will be administered within one's own home through a communications link, e.g. a videophone, will become more commonplace. Such technologies give rise to new implications for the 'rights' of individuals; e.g. with telemedicine, the person can switch off the machine and put a halt to any further medical care or advice; a response which is not so easy in a hospital environment where you would have little control (Fisk, 1996). Telecommunications may also replace low skill community services such as monitoring people, and make existing services more efficient and cost effective. Such community care technologies can enhance people's independence and facilitate older people to remain independent within the community for longer. Furthermore, by facilitating greater opportunities for home working and flexible employment, individuals with multiple responsibilities may be better placed to combine paid work with family care.

Smart medicine, such as spinal implants that enhance mobility, and medical breakthrough in areas such as Alzheimer's disease, may impact enormously on the quality of life to be expected among the new millennium elders. Reports on the isolation of the Alzheimer's gene has raised expectations of a cure in the future. However, just as the infectious diseases of the nineteenth century have been replaced by the degenerative diseases of the twentieth century, so too, may the twenty-first century produce its own new diseases. The effects of environmental pollution and synthetic chemicals have yet to be fully determined.

That technological innovation will play a much bigger role in the lives of the elderly boomers in the twenty-first century is not contentious in my view. However, that it will *necessarily* enhance their well-being, that it will manifest itself into affordable, portable and transferable aids or services, is far from axiomatic. A critical approach to new technology, and how it affects people's lives, has yet to be adequately developed. Will 'smart housing' and community care technologies be race and culture sensitive? What about technological overload or the potential for 'over-care'? How do we ensure design is user-driven rather than technologically pushed? The involvement of a wide range of users, carers and older persons more generally, in the design of such products and services is essential. Critically, will the benefits of technology be accessible to a wide range of groups or will lack of access to, for example, the internet be another dimension of inequality? Will the 'connected' and 'not connected' be the 'haves' and the 'have nots' of the future? This will depend on the shape of future policy.

Empowerment and the 'grey vote'

Politicians may have to take on board the views and demands of the baby boomers, as electorally they will constitute a significant minority to be reckoned with. In 1991 the total potential electorate in Great Britain constituted 44.7 million people aged 18 years and over, of whom nearly a quarter (10.6 million) were aged 60/65 plus. By 2021, the size of this age group will have risen to just under 18 million, increasing the share of the 'grey vote' from a quarter (23.7 per cent) to one third (33.7 per cent). Furthermore, policies which relate to ageing issues are also the interests and concerns of individuals in middle-age groups. Persons aged 45 and over will constitute over half of those eligible to vote in 2021. Some may argue that it is too simplistic to assume that people will vote according to the age group they represent.

However age-based politics is already much more progressed in the United States, with groups such as the Gray Panthers and Americans for Generational Equity (AGE) constituting powerful lobby groups (Johnson and Falkingham, 1992). Single issue voting has also taken on greater resonance in the late twentieth century and may take centre stage in the next. Technology may facilitate becoming more informed in political and policy issues at home, as well as voting on the internet from your living room. Electoral turnout would take on a different meaning.

Great expectations?

The 1960s baby boomers are better educated than previous generations and have become sophisticated consumers. The notion of retirement is taken for granted and there are clear expectations associated with it. Most see it as a period of leisure in return for a lifetime of work and expect to have a period of active and relatively healthy old age, 'not in work and not in poverty'. Two thirds of elderly people today are healthy and live independently without requiring support from family or formal agencies. One third of informal carers are elderly themselves. Older people have become the focus of market researchers as private enterprise chases after the 'grey pound'. Increasingly, older people are remaining active participants in social and economic life, as well as taking up new ventures.

The new millennium elders are likely to be more discerning consumers, both of leisure activities and of health and welfare services. They will display distinct ideas concerning the welfare state and what they can expect from it as a right, especially with regard to health care and pension provision. Although there is growing scepticism about the continuance of a Beveridgean state pension in their retirement, people nevertheless still expect the government to take responsibility for the core areas of welfare provision (Jowell et al, 1994; Hancock et al, 1995). Social care agencies, purchasing authorities and Trusts in 2030 will be faced with clients as customers who will expect to be involved more fully in the development of services.

Twenty-first century social policy framework

Many of the elderly boomers in the next century will be 'well-resourced' in old age and able to purchase health and social care services outside the public sector, and as such will have many of their expectations met. However, a significant minority will not be so fortunate, as they will not have accumulated adequate resources across their working life. In the 1990s generally, the poor got poorer whilst the rich became richer (Joseph Rowntree Foundation, 1995). This may have longer term implications, in particular for the 1960s baby boomers. The gap between the resourced and under-resourced is likely to be wider in 2020 and beyond: between those who experienced unemployment, endured longer periods of it and diminishing state provision, and those in work, who reaped benefits of higher wages, and lower (direct) taxes.

A policy framework for the twenty-first century needs to be *coherent, involve long-term planning* and be *socially inclusive* in nature. The policy framework Box 16.1 below highlights five overarching principles to be encompassed within future public policy, and advocates strategies in three key areas: income and social security, health and social care, and employment. Planning ahead for the retirement of future generations of elderly people requires a long-term view. Nowhere is this more applicable than in the case of income in retirement and pension provision. Changes in the rules of pension schemes today will impact upon the likely returns tomorrow. However, long-term planning does not fit well within the five year electoral cycle, and difficult decisions concerning the future costs of the ageing baby boomers are all too easily set aside in favour of short-term political gain. Indeed an advisor to Ronald Reagan in the late 1980s questioned why any government of the day would be prepared to 'mortgage their political reputation for tomorrow's agenda'. But it could also be argued that it is in everyone's interests that government does begin to plan to ensure structures are in place to minimise the numbers in poverty and social exclusion.

Social policy planning in the twenty-first century should be coherent, both across policy areas and within the individual's life. At present there is little or no coherent strategy recognising the interlinkages between income support, housing, transport, health and social care. Changes in one sector, for example the introduction of a charge for a service which was previously supplied free of charge, will impact upon another sector – benefit recipients will require a higher income to maintain the same standard of living. Lack of integrated planning can give rise to the emergence of perverse incentives, such as those created by changes in the

Box 16.1 Twenty-first century policy framework

Principles

1 Provide for ethnic diversity

2 Combat ageist and sexist practices

3 Recognise diversity of preferred lifestyles

4 Facilitate greater user involvement and advocacy

5 Value elders as a resource

Policy strategies

1 Income and social security

(i) maximise an individual's potential through positive employment and training policies

(ii) provide a safety net which minimises stigma

2 Health and social care

(i) provide a choice of flexible, appropriate and responsive services tailored to people's needs

(ii) improve preventative services, health promotion and screening

3 Employment policies

(i) encourage the retention of older workers

(ii) facilitate training of successors by older workers and of older workers

(iii) incorporate planning for phased and flexible retirement

(iv) be flexible, offering family friendly practices

social security rules regarding housing support and payments for nursing homes in 1980, which resulted in local authorities relying upon DHSS payments to support elderly people in private residential care rather than provide such care themselves within the local authority sector (Evandrou et al, 1990). Social policy should also reflect experience *over* the life course (Evandrou and Falkingham, 1993).

Policy should aim to foster social inclusion and recognise the social rights of individuals; ensuring equality of opportunity to participate in the social and economic systems of society, regardless of gender, age, ethnicity, social class, whether urban or rural populations, able-bodied or those with handicap. Charities, such as the Centre for Policy on Ageing, and other voluntary organisations will continue to play an important role within this policy process, working *with* and *for* older people to help bring about preferable retirements and improvement in every day living.

Acknowledgement

I am indebted to the ESRC Data Archive, University of Essex, and to the Office of National Statistics for making the General Household Survey data available for analysis.

This chapter contains an edited version of material also contained in 'Building a future retirement: towards a policy agenda' in Evandrou, M. (1997) *Baby Boomers: ageing in the 21st century*, London: Age Concern, 165–80.

Notes

1   With pension payments based on a proportion of final salary.

References

Arber, S. and Ginn, J. (eds) (1995) *Connecting Gender and Ageing: a sociological approach*, Buckingham: Open University Press.

Atkinson, A. B. (1991) 'The development of state pensions in the United Kingdom' in Schmahl, W. (ed) *The Future of Basic and Supplementary Pension Schemes in the European Community in 1992 and Beyond*, Baden-Baden: Nomos Verlagsgesellschaft.

Benzeval, M., Judge, K. and Whitehead, M. (1995) *Tackling Inequalities: an agenda for action*, London: King's Fund.

Bone, M., Bebbington, A., Jagger, C., Morgan, K. and Nicolaas, G. (1995) *Health Expectancy and its Uses*, London: HMSO.

Case, R. et al (1962) *Serial Abridged Life Tables for England and Wales, 1841–1960*.

Central Statistical Office (1996) *Social Trends 1996*, London: HMSO.

Charlton, J., Kelly, S., Dunnell, K., Evans, B., Jenkins, R. (1993) 'Suicide deaths in England and Wales: trends in factors associated with suicide deaths', *Population Trends,* 71 (Spring): 34–42.

Coleman, D. (1996) 'New patterns and trends in Europeanfertility' in Coleman, D. (ed) *Europe's Population in the 1990s*, Oxford: OUP, 1–61.

Curtice, J. (1993) 'Satisfying work – if you can get it' in Jowell, R. et al (eds) *International Social Attitudes: the 10th British Social Attitudes Report*, London: SCPR.

Daatland, S. (1990) 'What are families for? On family solidarity and preference for help', *Ageing and Society,* 10:1–15.

Dalley, G. (1997) 'Health and health care' in Evandrou, M. (ed) *Baby Boomers: ageing in the 21st century*, London: Age Concern, 86–105.

Drever, F. and Whitehead, M. (1997) (eds) *Health Inequalities*, Office of National Statistics Series DS no. 15, London: The Stationary Office.

Dunnell, K. (1995) 'Population review: (2) are we healthier?', *Population Trends* 82 (Winter): 12–18.

Evandrou, M. (1997) 'Health status and health care utilisation amongst elderly persons in Britain'. Background Briefing Paper to the King's Fund London Commission, London: King's Fund.

Evandrou, M. and Falkingham, J. (1993) 'Social security and the life course: developing sensitive policy alternatives', in Arber, S. and Evandrou, M. (eds) *Ageing, Independence and the Life Course*, London: Jessica Kingsley, 201–23.

Evandrou, M. and Falkingham, J. (1997) 'Growing old in twenty-first century Britain: the experience of four cohorts 1974–1993'. Welfare State Programme Discussion Paper, London: London School of Economics.

Evandrou, M., Falkingham, J. and Glennerster, H. (1990) 'The personal social services: everyone's poor relative but nobody's baby' in Hills, J. (ed) *The State of Welfare: the welfare state in Britain since 1974*, Oxford: Oxford University Press, 206 –73.

Evans, J., Goldacre, M., Hodkinson, M., Lamb, S. and Savory, M (1992) *Health: abilities and well-being in the third age*, The Carnegie Enquiry into the Third Age, Dunfermline: The Carnegie United Kingdom Trust.

Finch, J. (1995) 'Responsibilities, obligations and commitments' in Allen, I. and Perkins, E. (eds) *The Future of Family Care for Older People*, London: HMSO, 51–64.

Fisk, M. J. (1996) 'Elderly people and independent living: the implications of smart house technologies', paper presented at the British Society of Gerontology Annual Conference, University of Liverpool, 20–22 September 1996.

Grundy, E. (1992) 'Socio-demographic change' in Department of Health *The Health of Elderly People: an epidemiological overview*, Companion Papers, London: HMSO, 1–9.

Hancock, R. (1997) 'Financial resources in later life' in Evandrou, M. (ed) *Baby Boomers: ageing in the 21st century*, London: Age Concern, 59–85.

Hancock, R., Jarvis, C. and Mueller, G. (1995) *The Outlook for Incomes in Retirement: social trends and attitudes*, London: ACIOG.

Holmans, A. and Frosztega, M. (1994) *House Property and Inheritance in the UK*, London: HMSO.

Hunt, L .(1996) 'Hospital puts ban on elderly patients', *Independent*, 15 October.

Jerrome, D. (1996) 'Ties that bind' in Walker, A. (ed) *The New Generational Contract*, London: University College London Press, 81–99.

Johnson, P. and Falkingham, J. (1992) *Ageing and Economic Welfare*, London: Sage.

Joseph Rowntree Foundation (1995) *Income and Wealth. Report of the Joseph Rowntree Foundation Inquiry Group*, York: JRF.

Jowell, R., Curtice, J., Brook, L. and D. Ahrendt (1994) *British Social Attitudes Survey*, SCPR, Aldershot: Dartmouth.

Karn, V. (ed) (1997) *Employment, Education and Housing Among Ethnic Minorities in Britain*, London: The Stationary Office.

Marsh, A. and Makay, S. (1994) *Poor Smokers*, London: Policy Studies Institute.

Maynard, A. (1993) 'Intergenerational solidarity in health care: principles and practice', *Uniting Generations*, London: Age Concern England.

Means, R .(1997) 'Housing options in 2020: a suitable home for all?' in Evandrou, M. (ed) *Baby Boomers: ageing in the 21st century*, London: Age Concern, 142–164.

Modood, T. (1997) 'Employment' in Modood, T. et al *Ethnic Minorities in Britain: diversity and disadvantage*, London: Policy Studies Institute, 83–149.

Modood, T. et al (eds) (1997) *Ethnic minorities in Britain: diversity and disadvantage*, London: Policy Studies Institute.

Nazroo, J. (1997) *The Health of Britain's Ethnic Minorities*, London: Policy Studies Institute.

Neate, P. (1996) 'Strapped for cash', *Community Care*, 1–7 August 1996.

New, B. and Le Grand, J. (1996) *Rationing in the NHS: principles and pragmatism*, London: King's Fund.

OPCS (1995a) *1992-based National Population Projections*, Series PP2 no. 19, London: HMSO.

OPCS (1995b) *Marriage and Divorce Statistics*, Series FM2 no. 21, London: HMSO.

OPCS (1995c) *Birth Statistics*, Series FM1 no. 22, London: HMSO.

Phillipson, C. (1997) 'Employment and training: planning for 2020 and beyond' in Evandrou, M. (ed) *Baby Boomers: ageing in the 21st century*, London: Age Concern, 41–58.

Qureshi, H. (1996) 'Obligations and support within families' in Walker, A. (ed) *The New Generational Contract*, London: UCL Press, 100–19.

Robine, J., Blanchet, M. and Dowd, J. (1992) (eds) *Health Expectancy: First Workshop of the International Health Life Expectancy Network (REVES)*, London: HMSO.

Seymour, D. G. (1993) 'The aging surgical patient: a selective review of areas of recent clinical and research interest', *Reviews in Clinical Gerontology,* 3: 231–44.

Siim, B. (1990) 'Women and the welfare state' in Ungerson, C. (ed) *Gender and Caring: work and welfare in Britain and Scandinavia*, Hemel Hempstead: Harvester Wheatsheaf, 80–109.

Sixsmith, A. (1986) 'Independence and home in later life' in Phillipson, C., Bernard, M. and Strang, P. (eds) *Dependency and Interdependency in Old Age*. London: Croom Helm, 338–47.

Sixsmith, A. and Sharples , P. (1996) 'Community care technologies: user needs research on the intelligent community alarm', paper presented at the British Society of Gerontology Annual Conference, University of Liverpool, 20–22 September 1996.

Smaje, C. (1995) *Health, Race and Ethnicity: making sense of the evidence*, King's Fund, London.

Thompson, C. and West, P. (1984) 'The public appeal of sheltered housing', *Ageing and Society*, 4: 305–26.

Titmuss, R. M. (1955) 'Pension systems and population change', *Political Quarterly*, 16: 152–66.

Wardsworth, S., Donaldson, C. and Scott, A. (1996) *Can We Afford the NHS?* London: IPPR.

Whitaker, P. (1992) 'Rationing, ageism and the new look NHS', *Geriatric Medicine,* 22(1).

Ageing in tomorrow's Britain

Miriam Bernard and Judith Phillips

The popular concept of 'old age', and the conventional response to it, is now so woefully behind the reality of the phenomenon of 'age' as to require drastic action. One alternative might be to invite government to consider the establishment and maintenance of a permanent council or commission on older age, designed to guarantee that this all-embracing aspect of national life is kept constantly in the public and political eye.

Eric Midwinter and Susan Tester (1987) Polls Apart? Older voters and the 1987 general election, CPA, p. 53

Introduction

On our way to and from the University, we pass daily a huge advertising hoarding which, in metre-high azure blue letters on a startling sunshine yellow background, poses the question: 'The difference between the past and the future?'...and then proceeds to answer with the phrase: 'You can't change the past.'

In essence, this simple question and answer encapsulates both what we have tried to do in this book as well as providing a clue to the tenor of our concluding thoughts and observations. Whilst we certainly cannot 'change the past', the contributions in the preceding pages have revisited Britain's past history, specifically as it relates to the development of social policy and its impact on the lives of older people during the last fifty years. By combining historical descriptions with critical and questioning analyses, the authors in Part One have mapped out for us the origins of the British welfare state and the traditional policy areas with which we are all now very familiar. In Part Two, our contributors have taken these analyses forward by reviewing some of the ways in which social policy in more recent years has come to address, and be informed by, new ways of looking at old age which take us beyond these conventional issues. Finally, Part Three casts an eye to the future in an attempt to debate and discuss what form, or forms, social policy might take in the next century.

The discussions in the present chapter are premised on the belief that the kind of society we might wish to see in the next century, and the social policies which that society promotes and espouses, are for us all to shape and mould. Policies and societies are formulated and constructed by the people who live in them and are, therefore, changeable by those selfsame people. In other words, we are arguing for a proactive role in the creation of future social policy and, moreover, one in which we all, regardless of age, have the potential to be involved. Nor is the irony lost on us that the advertising hoarding which assails us every day is, in fact, for Cable and Wireless and thus, about the abilities of people to communicate with one another.

This chapter, therefore, is our attempt to communicate and discuss the main issues which we regard as important in the development of a social policy for ageing in tomorrow's Britain. It is not our intention to present alternative 'academic' scenarios which address both 'pessimistic' and 'optimistic' visions of the future. Rather, we set out our stall at the beginning and call unequivocally for *an integrated social policy* which addresses the broad needs of an ageing society, as opposed to narrow age-based interests, or the interests of specific problematised or stigmatised groups. In so doing, we shall provide a rationale for why we feel that such an integrated approach is long overdue. We then go on to discuss the values and philosophy which underlie and inform this approach. This is followed by a consideration of three key areas we regard as crucial to the establishment of this new policy agenda for the next century. Finally, we return to the organisation whose creation fifty years ago led to the commissioning of this celebratory book, and who now, as we noted in the opening chapter, stand at the confluence of social policy and social gerontology. What, we ask, will be its role in shaping our view of 'ageing in tomorrow's Britain'?

The views we articulate here are our own, informed by debate, discussion and research over the years we have both been working in this field and, of course, by some of the ideas and views written about in the preceding chapters. They should not though be taken to 'represent' the views either of the authors of these chapters, nor indeed of the Centre for Policy on Ageing.

An integrated social policy of ageing

For far too long, social policy in Britain has been bedevilled by piecemeal and ad hoc approaches. Each traditional policy area identified by the contributors to Part One has blithely trod its own path with scarcely a glance at related areas. Moreover, 'policy' aimed specifically at addressing the needs of older people has suffered – and indeed still suffers – from being very narrowly conceived. Some twenty years ago, just before the advent of the 'Thatcher Years', Nicholas Bosanquet (1978: 77) described the situation thus:

In the past, a policy for old age was seen mainly in terms of a policy for pensions. All other aspects were either secondary or taken for granted. However, in the new situation a policy for old age has to be much more than a policy for pensions. It has to be a policy which will give the most help to retired people in their attempts to find a new way of life.

Whilst we would not take issue with these sentiments, it seems to us that Britain once again faces a 'new situation', but a situation which in our view calls not for a policy 'which will give the most help to retired people', but for one which addresses the diversity of needs of *an ageing society*. This, we would suggest, is a rather different kind of policy orientation from one that targets those whom we label 'old' or 'retired'. It is an orientation which attempts to move us away from traditional views that conceived of older people as the 'deserving poor' in need of a safety net of social protection, and later came to perceive them as a burden on, and cause of, the potential impoverishment of other groups (see Chapter 1). Rather, it attempts to recognise the inter-dependence of individuals one on another, whilst at the same time acknowledging that we all, irrespective of our chronological age, have a common purpose in fashioning an integrated social policy which has less to do with branding people as 'ex' this or that, and more to do with supporting all of us to live in an ageing society.

Eric Midwinter, the Director of the Centre for Policy on Ageing during the 1980s, has recently – albeit in the context of a book about retirement and income – described the need for such a policy re-orientation in these terms:

> In other words, the debate must, in all political propriety, assume a civic character as well as an economic one. It is about the political bottom line being not subsistence, but participation. It is about joining in rather than getting by.
>
> *Midwinter, 1997: 98*

Later, in the same discussion about older age in the twenty-first century, he goes on to reinforce this by saying that 'the argument is a civic, social and political one, rather than just an economic one' (p. 103).

This view is fundamental to our own call for an integrated social policy of ageing, and we can identify three sets of reasons which lead us to this conclusion. The first has to do with the continuing impact of demographic change in general, and population ageing in particular. The second concerns the coming together of demographic imperatives with the economic, social and political realities of life in late twentieth century Britain. The third set of reasons involves what is now referred to as post-modernism and globalisation. Consequently, a word or two about each of these is appropriate at this juncture.

Demographic imperatives

In terms of the *demographic imperatives*, readers will undoubtedly be familiar with the facts and figures of demographic change this century. Briefly, it is important to remind ourselves that never before have we been such an 'old' society (Laslett, 1996), and that alongside increasing life expectancy, ageing is also a progressively gendered experience.

Whilst we have more old people in our population than ever before, what seems to be less appreciated (at least in the public mind) is that this population is itself ageing. The total number of people over pensionable age is projected to grow fairly slowly for the foreseeable future, picking up slightly over the first decade of the next millennium with a rise of 9 per cent (an additional one million people of pensionable age) (OPCS, 1997). However, it is the numbers of people aged 75 and over, and 85 and over which will increase most markedly – the former being predicted to double in size by the middle of next century, and the latter to triple. In fact, percentage increases are greater, the older the age group one considers. In 1994 for example, 8,000 people in the United Kingdom (7,000 women and 1,000 men) were aged 100 years or older (OPCS, 1997). By 2031, it is estimated that 28,000 women and 6,000 men will be this old: a 425 per cent increase over today's figures.

Although Britain's population will continue to age in the next millennium, the last three decades of this century have, in fact, witnessed the most rapid ageing of our population. In some sense then, it is possible to argue that demography, whilst still important, may be less so in the coming decades in terms of its impact on social policy formulation. Indeed, we would contend that it is the conjunction of these demographic trends with changes to *the social, economic and political circumstances* of our ageing population, which is likely to have the greatest influence.

Social, economic and political realities

Many of the contributors to this book have made reference to the situations in which older people today find themselves. We know, for example, that the alteration in the structure of our population has been accompanied by profound changes to the size and composition of the family, as the effects of lowered fertility and increasing divorce begin to make their impact felt on the older generations. Changes to living arrangements, the increasing numbers of widows and widowers in old age, and the rise of solo living have all become more prominent. Women's increased labour market participation and the rise in membership of occupational and private pension schemes, will likewise have the greatest impact as we move into the next century. Health status too is an increasingly important area of debate with, as yet, inconclusive evidence about whether we shall live out our longer lives in better, or worsening, health.

The reality then, at the end of the twentieth century, is a mixture of certainties and uncertainties: the certainties are that we all of us (younger and older generations alike) currently live in a very diverse set of circumstances. The uncertainties concern whether, and in what ways, these circumstances may change in the future. Some of this is predictable as Maria Evandrou has shown in the previous chapter; much more though is unpredictable. However, one inescapable certainty is that we also now live in a post-modern society which has much more extensive links with the wider world and with all that that brings.

POST-MODERNISM AND GLOBALISATION

Post-modernism and globalisation is likely not only to impact on the way we all live in the next millennium, but raises implications for our current considerations about developing a social policy of ageing. It suggests that whereas today we may be primarily concerned with policy at national and local levels, the 'boundaries' of future policy may in fact be much wider than this: today Britain, but tomorrow's Britain in a European and world-wide context.

This move towards globalisation and post-modern lifestyles has also been accompanied in recent years by a much wider appreciation of the diversity and difference which exists amongst the population. Thus, again as our contributors have demonstrated, issues pertaining to dimensions such as one's sexual orientation, gender, race and ethnicity have all assumed greater salience in policy discussions and debates. Growing pressures associated with the rise of consumerism and the mobilisation of citizenship rights through grassroots developments such as the disability and advocacy movements, are paving the way for the voices of previously marginalised and excluded groups to be heard in the policy-making process.

Together then, these three sets of reasons suggest to us that the case for an integrated social policy of ageing, whilst it may not be profoundly new or radical (see Norton et al, 1986), is stronger now than it has ever been. This obviously begs the question about what the framework for such a social policy might be? However, before attempting to answer this, we first outline the values and philosophy which underlie this framework.

A 'value-added' social policy

Policy, like most things, is not plucked from thin air but is the outcome of competing ideologies, values and interests. Thus, in order to shape and give form to a social policy of ageing for tomorrow's Britain, it is important to spell out the value base on which we see this approach to policy being developed. Whilst some readers may well disagree and take issue with us over the details of such a value base, we believe it to be a crucial first step before we can move on to look at how we might plan for, implement, and evaluate an integrated policy framework.

The values we espouse are inter-dependent, and revolve around our commitment to six key areas:

- an intergenerational life course perspective;
- a pluralistic, positive and preventive view of ageing;
- the importance of combating all forms of discrimination;
- notions of empowerment, citizenship and rights;
- enabling the voices of 'ordinary' people to be heard;
- critical commentary in combination with action.

THROUGH THE LIFE COURSE AND ACROSS THE GENERATIONS

It is evident that our belief in the need for an *intergenerational life course perspective* is shared by many of our contributors. Indeed, there are numerous examples from the previous discussions about the need for social policy to be underpinned by just such a viewpoint. Gillian Dalley acknowledges the pressures towards increased fragmentation of the contemporary life course. The concept of a lifelong career is fast vanishing, along with earlier certainties about such things as there being a fixed time for retirement. This means that we need much greater flexibility in how we view the life course, a view echoed by Sheila Peace and Julia Johnson in their call for the long term planning of 'lifetime homes'. Authors such as Joanna Bornat, Andrew Dunning, Eric Midwinter and Julia Twigg, also make strong cases for links across the generations. This, we would suggest, is imperative if we are to combat what Margaret Simey notes as the possibilities for intergenerational conflict as opposed to collaboration.

To this we would add our own concern that it is 'ageing' as opposed to 'old age' or 'old people', that should form a key concept around which to construct social policy. For too long we have exhorted the general populace that they should be interested in old age because, barring any major catastrophe, we will all eventually become 'old'. To propose this notion is immediately, in our experience, to be met with a kind of collective dissonance in which, ostrich-like, people metaphorically bury their heads in the sand. Old age and being old, is something that happens to other people, not to us. It is something to be pushed to one side and considered, if at all, as and when we get there.

Within an intergenerational life course perspective, 'ageing' therefore seems to us to have more potential than focusing on old age or old people. It is not simply a question of semantics, but an issue which goes to the heart of the other values on which we believe policy should be constructed. In other words, it begins to move us away from the idea that there is somehow a separate and distinct group we can all clearly identify as 'old'. Language, and the use we make of it, is important: it has the ability to convey – and at times betray – our value base. In this context too, we would also argue for the need to rid ourselves of what we see as the divisiveness of the increasingly prevalent use of the terms 'third' and 'fourth' age. The 'Third Age', associated as it is with ideas of a healthy, active and poverty-free time in the life course has gradually seeped, uncritically, into the public consciousness. This, we would suggest, provides yet a further way in which it is possible for even greater distancing and polarisation to occur between people in this so-called phase, and those who find themselves ill, sick, impoverished and dependent in the 'Fourth Age' (or growing up in the 'First Age' and raising families and working in the 'Second Age').

PLURALISTIC, POSITIVE AND PREVENTIVE AGEING

We need, then, for a new social policy of ageing to be underpinned by a commitment to *a pluralistic, positive and preventive view of ageing*. Essentially, what we mean by this is that policy, rather than beginning from the premise that what it should be doing is addressing 'problems', ought to recognise, and be built upon, a belief that we can identify a range of 'needs' which cut across generations, and across different sectors. Such a recognition is, we would suggest, a prerequisite to discussions and debates about how we collectively and individually meet these needs, and what the appropriate balance might be between the state and other providers.

This set of values also requires that we regard older people, like younger people, as potential resources. Again, this helps to move us away from seeing particular groups simply as burdens on the state, or as 'problems to be solved'. It has long been observed that much policy and provision is geared to the incompetencies of people, as opposed to building on the positive elements of what people are more than capable of doing for themselves, and for each other. This, in turn, is inextricably linked with a preventive orientation: an orientation which is applicable far beyond its conventional associations with health, and which we take up again below.

COMBATING DISCRIMINATION

Closely allied to a positive, pluralistic and intergenerational life course approach to policy-making, is the undoubted importance of *combating all forms of discrimination*. The insidious impact of ageism, together with the more familiar forms of discrimination such as that linked with race and ethnicity, with gender, with sexual orientation and with physical and mental disability, is something which still needs to be countered at every available opportunity. We live in a society in which, despite the inroads made by legislation and codes of practice over recent decades, is still at bottom riddled with inequalities and with hostile and discriminatory attitudes and practices (McEwen, 1990; Bytheway, 1995). Policy formulation is not exempt from this and, indeed, it is not unusual for the observation to be made that policy, rather than addressing discrimination, actually reinforces it in certain instances. We are tempted to ask here whether, should it ever be possible to truly create a social policy of ageing, this would in fact render discrimination a thing of the past?

EMPOWERMENT, CITIZENSHIP AND RIGHTS

Progress along this road has to be accompanied by a belief in the value of, and a firm commitment to, notions of *empowerment, citizenship and rights.* Whilst there is not the space here to enter into long discussions about these concepts, we would again observe that many of the book's contributors uphold these values in the arguments they put forward. Andrew Dunning argues that advocacy and empowerment has now come onto the policy agenda. At the same time he questions how far such values take us in addressing the needs of, for example, older people with dementia.

What we seem to be witnessing at this point is the coming together of various pressures: pressure from older people themselves to be regarded as active consumers; pressures from professional groups such as those discussed by Jim Ogg and colleagues to reorient their practices, critically question their professional autonomy and to find new ways of working 'with', as opposed to just 'for', older people and other client groups; and political pressures which, as Joanna Bornat shows, are stimulating older people to take action on their own behalf in the defence of their rights and interests as they age. This latter point is also reinforced by Chris Phillipson in his discussion about people's rights to employment and to a secure and fulfilling retirement.

Some might argue that this kind of principled stand is unrealistic, but there is now a growing body of evidence which attests to the importance and efficacy of such an approach, particularly when bolstered and reinforced by proper levels of practical support and access (see for example, Croft and Beresford, 1990; Walker and Warren, 1996; Bernard, forthcoming). Indeed, Alan Walker (1997), amongst others, regards the creation and promotion of what he calls a 'culture of empowerment', as crucial to current and future policy-making and provision.

HEARING ORDINARY PEOPLE

One further essential element of such an approach has to do with *enabling the voices of 'ordinary' people to be heard.* Recent developments on these fronts concern not only the participation of people in terms of political action, but also their commentaries on existing policies and provisions, and their involvement in conducting policy-relevant research (Cooper et al, 1994; Tozer and Thornton, 1995). Through the growth of the kinds of grass-roots Pensioner Action Groups charted by Joanna Bornat, the activities of organisations such as the National Pensioners' Convention and the impact which the election of a new Labour government earlier this year might have, we can foresee increasing opportunities for the voices of ordinary people to be heard in the policy-making process.

However, the situation in Britain contrasts in a number of ways with what happens both in Europe and in North America. In Europe, many countries actively support hearing the voice of older people through advisory boards at local authority level, and through representatives of these boards at national level (Walker and Maltby, 1997). France, Spain, Holland and Ireland all operate such systems. In the United States, where the state welfare system is much less prominent and where there is a longer-standing and more pluralistic political system, older people's interests and voices have been heard much more loudly. Mass membership organisations such as the fifty million strong American Association of Retired Persons, and the Gray Panthers, together with advocacy groups like the Older Women's League, press tirelessly for the integration of older people into the mainstream of society and take an active interest in the development of public policy (Bernard et al, 1993; Older Women's League, 1997). Quite whether this level and intensity of involvement will come about in a British context is, of course, open to speculation although the signs, as we have already intimated, are positive.

CRITIQUE AND ACTION

We come finally, then, to a consideration of our last set of values: to a belief that underlying policy formulation should be the means to develop a *critical commentary* on what is happening, *in combination with action*. The recent British Society of Gerontology's Annual Conference was organised around the theme of 'Elder Power in the 21st Century' and, in the closing plenary session, Professor Peter Townsend expressed the view that researchers, academics and those working in the social policy field need to recognise that they cannot stay aloof from involvement in social change. We would endorse this view wholeheartedly. We ourselves are fortunate to be working in an *Applied* Social Studies Department. Our own backgrounds are also located in practice: in social work and in work with older people in the voluntary sector. We therefore try actively to maintain links with those whom we research and write about, as well as ensuring that the research we undertake can be used to inform both policy formation and the provision of services.

This principle: about the links between a critique of policy, action arising from it and the making explicit of one's value base, can also be applied to a consideration of the 'think tanks', policy organisations and institutes which have sprung up over recent decades. We would question just how far any of these can be truly 'independent' as they often claim. The people who work in and for them, write and research from a particular value base, and we would argue strongly for this to be made explicit.

In social gerontology too, the making explicit of one's value base has come together in what is now labelled the 'critical gerontology' movement: a movement in which we, and many of this book's contributors, are active. On both sides of the Atlantic, publications couched within this perspective have appeared regularly during the 1990s (see for example, Minkler and Estes, 1991, 1997; Moody, 1992; Cole et al, 1993; Vincent, 1995; Jamieson et al, 1997). Essentially, this viewpoint is about ensuring, in the words of Meredith Minkler (1996: 470) that our approach is one which 'puts a human face – and a human body and spirit – on ageing and growing old'. It alerts us not only to the importance of critically examining social policy as a means to providing answers and meeting the needs of people, but also to look at it as part of the problem both now, and for the future. Should our academic critique of policy remain simply at the level of ideas (or even just at passing on information from what we have learnt), then it is our belief that this will not get any of us very far down the road to the goal of generating an integrated social policy of ageing.

Having laid out these six sets of values, which we believe should underpin and inform any attempt to shape an integrated social policy for tomorrow's Britain, we move now to a consideration of what this might begin to look like at local and national levels. We look first at these 'levels' before offering some observations on the wider European context. Finally, we go on to discuss a number of areas which we regard as crucial to the movement towards an integrated social policy of ageing.

Towards a social policy of ageing

Beginning at the national level, and mindful of the possibilities which a change of government earlier this year may herald, it is our belief that the time is now ripe to press for first, a National Commission on 'integrated strategies for a social policy of ageing', to be followed, eventually perhaps, by the creation of a Ministry of Ageing.

For the past fifty years, governments of all complexions have sponsored a variety of major surveys and inquiries. In 1954, for example, The Phillips Report (Chancellor of the Exchequer, 1954) focused on how Britain was going to meet the needs of growing numbers of older people. It made startlingly accurate demographic forecasts at the time, and drew attention to the ways in which needs, and policy responses, had to be seen as inter-related. Since then, there have been numerous such inquiries including, for example, the recent Carnegie Enquiry into the Third Age (1993) and the report on older women produced by the Women's National Commission (1992). Our suggestion is that we now need to go further than these kinds of reports whose recommendations were only 'advisory' and largely applicable to service providers as opposed to policy makers. Thus, our call is now for a large-scale government initiative, to bring together cross-generational, cross-sectoral, cross-departmental and cross-party interests in the future of our ageing population.

Feeding into this national level, we would envisage something which is structurally similar to some of the initiatives already noted to exist in Europe. In particular, we would draw attention to the need to create policy-making boards or councils at local authority level. Unlike some of the European structures, however, our suggestion is that, as at national level, these consist not simply of older people, but of people of all ages and from a variety of local 'constituencies' who are concerned about these issues.

This is not to suggest that inroads have not already been made in these directions – far from it. Earlier this decade, for example, one of us was involved with members of the Local Authorities Research Consortium at the Local Government Centre at Warwick University, to develop work in precisely this area. Headed by Professor John Benington, the Consortium is an attempt to bring together academic researchers, policy makers and managers around structural changes and strategic issuesfacing local government. One stream of work has been concerned with evolving a Research and Development Programme on 'local inter-agency strategies for an ageing population'. Since 1994, this has involved three phases of activity: the first consisted of a survey of local authorities to identify whether or not there were moves to create corporate interdepartmental strategies; second, other agencies in the areas served by the authorities have been asked to complete a postal questionnaire about the ways they are responding to ageing; and third, the findings were presented in June 1997 at a conference in Nottingham which called for a programme to pilot inter-agency strategies for an ageing population.

These three years of work are now bearing fruit. Following the change of government in May, the Cabinet Office began to express an interest in these ideas. Plans are now being developed between the Cabinet Office, the Warwick University Local Authorities Research Consortium, Age Concern England and Anchor Housing, for a modest two to three year action research programme. A budget of approximately a quarter of a million pounds per year, will fund twelve pilot areas to move forward their work on inter-agency strategies from 1 April 1998. This development will complement the government's own 'Best Value' Programme, which will itself also be evaluated by Warwick University. Whilst these kinds of locally based endeavours are important it is not enough, in our view, for them to remain simply at a local project level. Mechanisms need to be developed so that the lessons learnt from these kinds of projects can be fed into a wider-ranging overview of how we move towards an integrated social policy of ageing. In addition, these kinds of local strategies, where different departments get together to discuss ageing as a mutual concern, ought to be mirrored at inter-governmental office level.

Beyond these suggestions about how we see a policy framework developing through national and local strategies, it is also important to reflect too on the ways in which the 'boundaries' of policy are changing, and will continue to change, as we move into the next century. Our primary concern in this book has been with the situation in Britain, at both a national policy level and at local level. We are though, part of the European Community, so that anything we advocate in terms of our policy developments has also to be viewed in this context. In some quarters, it is argued that this inevitably means a shift in the locus of policy-making away from national and local interests towards Brussels, and towards the regions, and that this in turn means we must look to a different policy-making process than the traditional hierarchical one with which we have been accustomed to operate in Britain (Benington and Taylor, 1993). The emergence of a European model of policy-making undertaken through inter-locking 'spheres' (Baine et al, 1992), in combination with the more familiar 'tiers' of government, is something which the development of a social policy of ageing will have to come to terms with.

Having made this call for a national commission and related developments at local authority level, and drawn attention to the European context, we move now to consider three additional areas. These areas are not intended to form a comprehensive social policy agenda. Rather, we see them as crucial to the creation of a new social policy of ageing which moves away from what Michael Cahill (1994) amongst others, regards as an overly narrow conceptualisation of social policy in the past. It is also important to note that we have made a deliberate decision here not to discuss in detail either pensions or health and social welfare. We take it as axiomatic that these areas will continue to hold, if not centre stage in debates about the social policy of ageing, at least a persistent and prominent place.

With respect to pensions, it is our belief that if the present arrangements continue, then the inequalities which have become glaringly apparent over the last decade will be further exacerbated in the next century. Claims that we need state pensions less and less because two thirds of elderly people are in receipt of non-state pensions, are patently untrue: two thirds of men may be in this position, but three quarters of women are not (Ginn and Arber, 1996). Nor do the prospects for younger cohorts look much brighter, with less than a quarter of women between the ages of 40 and 59 belonging to occupational pension schemes, and with over three quarters of women still interrupting their working lives because of children.

In terms of health and social care, the radical alterations to funding over the Thatcher years have, we would suggest, irrevocably changed the face of British welfare. The increasing privatisation of welfare with its accompaniments of charging for services and the rationing (explicitly or otherwise) of publicly funded health care in particular, is also likely to lead to further inequalities in access. Moreover, it is patently clear that the kinds of health and social care we may see in the next century will be fundamentally linked to the political choices we make. Whilst there is no evidence to suggest that we will not be able to afford a welfare state, the issue is more to do with what kind of welfare state we wish to have: one based, as Eamonn Butler (1994) has proposed, on the increasing development of alternatives to state provided services, or one, as Malcolm Wicks (1994) desires, built around the notion of an 'active society'?

Consequently, building on the value base outlined above, we would suggest that the creation of an integrated social policy of ageing will need to focus on three additional areas. It must be:

- educationally-minded;
- technologically-minded; and
- spatially-minded.

AN EDUCATIONALLY-MINDED SOCIAL POLICY OF AGEING

By focusing on what we term an educationally-minded orientation to social policy creation, we do not solely mean it to imply that our concern is with some narrow conception of education for the early years of life. There are in fact two facets to this issue we wish to highlight. Our concern with education is first of all about its role as a *lifelong process*, but secondly too about its interrelationship with work and leisure (including retirement). We are interested in the ways these areas of our lives are currently constituted, and how this balance might alter in the future.

An educationally-minded social policy, in our view, needs first to question critically the conventional definitions of education, work, leisure and retirement before it can begin to reformulate what impact this might have on future policy. Education, as Eric Midwinter has shown in his chapter, is not just about equipping children and young people for the world of work. It is a lifelong undertaking. However, children do need, we would suggest, to be 'educated' early in life about the dimensions of ageing. For the most part, this is abysmally addressed in many of our schools and colleges. Personal and social education seems to consist largely of unimaginative and traditional, community-service type activities whereby our children are encouraged to do things *for* older people, rather than *with* them – collecting and then distributing Harvest Festival hampers comes immediately to mind, as does 'singing for the old people' at Christmas and other similar events.

There are again signs, albeit piecemeal ones, that this is not the case in every school or college up and down the land. The 1990s have witnessed some pioneering projects in, for example, areas such as oral history and the mentoring by older people of children with particular difficulties: projects led primarily by voluntary organisations such as the Beth Johnson Foundation and Age Concern (see too O'Connor, 1993). Yet, British developments lag behind what is happening in places such as North America where there is a much more substantive body of work concerned with bringing the generations together in mutually beneficial school-based projects designed to impact on mainstream curriculum development (Newman and Marks, 1980; Carstensen et al, 1982; Lyons et al, 1984; Aday et al, 1991; Newman et al, 1997). Much is still to be learnt from developments such as these because, in the British case, these initiatives are poorly evaluated if at all. They seem to us to be a necessary prerequisite if we are to begin the process of changing attitudes towards ageing and older people, and inculcating a sense that 'ageing' concerns all of us.

This must also carry through into other sectors of our education system. We, and others, have remarked on the paucity of teaching which goes on about ageing at undergraduate level, or in the training of many professionals (Bernard et al, 1993). What has become alarmingly evident over recent years is that the inroads which were being made through the creation and expansion of programmes at certificate, diploma, post-graduate and post-qualifying levels and, indeed through the distance learning opportunities through the Open University, seem now to be suffering cut-backs as students find it ever more difficult to get even partial funding for such studies. This situation is all the more lamentable given what we have already said about the demographic changes which are happening in concert with social, political and economic transformations.

Work and retirement too have been radically transformed and we would suggest that hard questions need to be asked both about what it is we understand by these concepts, and whether it is ever going to be realistic, in policy terms, to underpin society with the goal of full employment. Even granted that 'full employment' today is not the same thing as envisaged by Beveridge, it is still a very conventional and male-oriented basis around which to organise discussion about the creation of new social policy. Moreover, work and retirement seem to us to be outmoded terms, especially given the variety of forms that 'work' now takes, and the inapplicability of the notion of 'retirement' to many people today. Far better, we would argue, to orient discussions around the needs of those not in paid employment: to look at these people as resources, be they children, informal carers, older people or whatever, and examine how best to value and support these contributors to society. Ironically, it is precisely many of these people who undertake, as Malcolm Wicks (1994) argues, some of the most important 'work': child rearing, domestic activities, care of disabled people and of older people. Policy then should be flexible enough to place these kinds of issues centre-stage, helping us all to determine what sort of balances we might want individually, and collectively, between paid work, education and training, unpaid work, and leisure and how these might be balanced with other lifetime commitments to, for example, the family.

If the worlds of education, work and retirement have undergone major changes over the last fifty years, and look set to continue to change in the future, then one of the forces behind this has been the impact of technological developments.

A TECHNOLOGICALLY-MINDED SOCIAL POLICY OF AGEING

As Maria Evandrou observed in the last chapter, technology is not something we can ignore in the next century. We too would argue that technology should be at the heart of social policy for several reasons. First, it is *intergenerational* in the sense that technology has the ability to improve the situation and quality of life for *all* people. We have already witnessed the brilliance that people such as Stephen Hawkins can produce with the aid of technology. Such technology has enabled him and countless others, to continue to teach, research and publish rather than be 'pensioned off'. But technology is not just about gadgets to assist daily living. Secondly, therefore, technology is important to a social policy of ageing because it pervades *every aspect of life* and has the potential for assisting with many of the traditional problems associated with ageing. Communications, clothing, house design, shopping and medicine are areas all now influenced by technology. The concept of 'lifetime' or 'lifelong' homes could be copied in many other spheres of life. Designing with ageing in mind at home, at work, or in the supermarket will benefit younger as well as older people.

The Dutch, Design for Ageing Network (DAN), has taken a lead in this area. Their aim is to incorporate the ideas of older people into the heart of thinking about new products and services in the home, such as kitchen use or accessibility at the airport, believing that: 'Design has an important new role to play in turning policy concepts into ideas or stories that can inspire people to act' (Netherlands Design Institute, 1997: 3).

As already remarked, the transformation of work and social life is moving on apace. Flexibility in the workplace, enhanced through computerisation and tele working, has enabled some people to work at home or, if they are working carers, to feel confident that while at work, their relative is safe at home. Thirdly, then, technology is *pluralistic and preventative.* It is also about facilitating communication which can enable people, of whatever race, age or gender, to participate as citizens in decision making and can empower people as they shop, vote and seek expert help on line in all areas of policy. Technology can assist us to overcome some of the barriers already noted between conventional policy areas such as housing, health and social services, education and work, in order to help create what Sir Roy Griffiths termed a 'seamless' service (Griffiths, 1988).

All areas of social policy are potentially affected by technological change. In particular, the technological revolution has altered the relationship between the individual and the spaces and places within which we live out our lives. Finally, we turn to a brief discussion of the spatial aspects of a social policy of ageing.

A SPATIALLY-MINDED SOCIAL POLICY OF AGEING

Here, we are arguing for a much closer relationship between the social and spatial aspects of ageing. To date, the spatial dimensions of ageing have been neglected in social policy terms. Yet, as many of our contributors show, ageing and old age is associated with particular places and spaces be they the day centre, a retirement home, or one's own home. Most existing discussions concentrate on the traditional aspects of location and proximity. Recently, for example, Joseph and Hallman (1996), examined proximity and the impact of the geographical separation of home and workplace, on a range of job and caregiving situations in Canada. In Britain, too, long distance caregiving is beginning to receive some attention as it has in the United States (Phillips, 1996; Neal, 1997). Likewise, territorial inequalities in mortality, and the differential access which people have to a whole range of goods and services, has been debated extensively in policy terms (Townsend and Davidson, 1986; Whitehead, 1987; Dorling, 1997).

More recently, however, increasing attention has been paid to the psychological aspects of space. Glenda Laws (1997) describes age specific locations in the US and argues that identities in old age are created and maintained by older peoples' location. She draws on the example of Sun City, where the spatial segregation of older people is considered alongside the promotion of a positive, healthy image. Similar examples of housing communities are growing in Britain and there is a need therefore to consider the impact of space on ageing.

Beyond location, proximity and territorial inequalities what we argue for is a broader conception of the spatial dimension in social policy. Components of such a policy orientation might include examination of other developments that impact on people's sense of space and place, such as transportation, traffic planning, land use management, architecture and design. One innovative example of where social and spatial policy have come together can be seen in the Anderslöv community in Sweden. Here, the *life care idea,* based on the concepts of security, participation and fellowship at an individual and community level, has been operationalised by architects, planners, politicians, older and younger residents, and local organisat-ions working together. The group set out to enhance every aspect of life for older people in Anderslöv, with the main focus being on housing, transportat-ion and the establishment of a 'knowledge bank' (Åhlund, forthcoming).

One further example is that of transportation. Technology has greatly reduced distance, both in a metaphorical sense, and in terms of travelling time and modes of communication. Yet, transport has also become a 'generator' of inequalities as public transportation has declined and access becomes a major problem for younger and older people alike. Again, we can look to Sweden where an integrative policy of public transportation is in place. Here, the planning and design of public transport proceeds from an holistic perspective and presupposes that people have different needs and desires when travelling. Consequently high journey frequency, efficiency and good information about travel options, combined with a high level of service, accessible outdoor environments with short distances to bus stops and train terminals, are the basis on which the policy operates (Ståhl, forthcoming). To achieve full integration the entire chain of events when travelling is taken into consideration, from the design of the vehicle – low floor buses – to the quality of the pavements that people walk on. Moreover, the recognition that a variety of solutions are needed, has led to what is now called *community-responsive public transport* for urban areas, with specific attention being paid to the needs of older people. Service routes have been developed using smaller buses which tour the residential area, making the trip from home to the bus shorter. Special transport-ation is available, by law, for those who are seriously handicapped and need door to door personal assistance. With the new Labour government's emphasis on public transport and pollution reduction, a similar policy could work here.

In our view, a spatial framework for social policy can no longer be ignored, especially as people become more mobile, markets become global and technology assists in linking people, whatever their age, with identifiable places and spaces.

In summary, a social policy of ageing for tomorrow's Britain needs to rest, in our view, on three dimensions. First, as we have argued, it must make explicit the value base on which it is to be constructed. Secondly, and arising from this, action is needed at national and local levels. At the same time, we have to recognise that British social policy needs to pay attention to the European (and, indeed, global) context. Thirdly, we suggest that these values and practical recommendations have also to take into account educational, technological and spatial aspects, if we are to create a social policy of ageing which will move us forward into the next century. Malcolm Wicks (1994: 288) has observed that: 'It was the historic role of the Labour government of 1945 to serve as midwife to modern social policy.' Now, in 1997, another Labour government has the opportunity to fashion a new social policy of ageing which will address the interests and concerns of *all* citizens. Finally then, it remains for us to briefly consider what role the Centre for Policy on Ageing might play in this future.

Conclusion: CPA's role in a social policy of ageing

During the last fifty years, the Centre for Policy on Ageing has striven to promote a positive view of ageing alongside its concerns for traditional policy areas. What though might the next fifty years hold?

It seems to us that CPA is uniquely placed to be at the vanguard of developing a new integrated social policy of ageing in the twenty-first century. The fundamental changes, which all the contributors to this book have detailed, have ushered in a new era which provides opportunities as well as formidable challenges. We hope that the work of CPA in the coming decades might lead it to become equally well known as the 'Centre for Positive Ageing', or indeed, the 'Centre for Promoting Anti-ageist Ageing', if such a thing is possible.

In order to achieve this, the organisation, building on its past reputation for work in fields such as residential care, and the championing of new lifestyles, may now benefit from a more sharply defined social policy agenda. To begin with, we would see it as taking a pivotal role in setting the framework for any Commission on 'integrated strategies for a social policy of ageing', through two main mechanisms. First, through the organising and commissioning of a series of 'state of the art' policy reviews, to be undertaken either by small ad hoc working groups, or appointed individuals with expertise in a given area. These we would see, not as full-blown research reports, but as position papers designed to stimulate and provoke discussion and debate. Second, we would see CPA convening a full plenary session/national conference at which these reviews could be presented and discussed as a prelude to firming up final recommendations to go forward to both national and local government. A series of 'road shows' could take these recommendations out into the regions, cities and towns of Britain.

These policy position papers might, in turn, be the launch-pad for a new CPA policy series. These would differ from the existing Reports and Policy Studies series, in both their focus and scope. Again, we would reiterate here the need for this work to provide critiques of policy and visions for the future which are independent of whatever strategy the current or future governments might adopt. Unlike some of the other well known 'ageing' organisations, CPA is not involved in providing or promoting particular kinds of services and projects, and therefore is in a position to adopt much more of an advocacy role where ageing issues are concerned.

Alongside this, we would see an expanded and enhanced role for CPA's library and information services. The CPA collection is unique in Britain, and whilst it is now accessible through the development of *AgeInfo*, there are still many individuals and organisations beyond those working just with older people, who would undoubtedly benefit from knowing about such a resource. There is scope too, we believe, for it to widen its remit and take in resources with an explicit life course focus and which involve intergenerational work. The dissemination of these sources, together with the collection and collation of related information into relevant directories of research and course information, is also one of CPA's continuing objectives. Again, we would suggest that they are well placed to progress this kind of work with renewed vigour in the next century.

In conclusion, policy formulation and information dissemination are likely to continue to go hand-in-hand in terms of CPA's future role. The first fifty years of the organisation's life saw it develop these twin roles to great effect. We would expect and hope, along with all the contributors to this book, that the next fifty years will prove equally, if not more, productive in this respect and that CPA will perform a pivotal role in moving the social policy of ageing into the twenty-first century.

References

Aday, R. H., Sims, C. R. and Evans, E. (1991) 'Youth's attitudes toward the elderly: the impact of intergenerational partners', *Journal of Applied Gerontology*, 10(3): 372–84.

Åhlund, O. (forthcoming) 'Planning integrated services in a municipality: a collaborative approach' in Means, R. and Phillips, J. (eds) *A Broader Vision of Community Care*, Oxford: Anchor Publications.

Baine, S. Benington, J. and Russell, J. (1992) *Changing Europe: challenges facing the voluntary and community sectors in the 1990s*, London: NCVO.

Benington, J. and Taylor, M. (1993) 'Changes and challenges facing the UK welfare state in the Europe of the 1990s', *Policy and Politics*, 21(2): 121–34.

Bernard, M. (forthcoming) *Promoting Health in Old Age: critical issues in self health care*, Buckingham: Open University Press.

Bernard, M., Meade, K. and Tinker, A. (1993) 'Women come of age', pp. 167–90 in Bernard, M. and Meade, K. (eds) *Women Come of Age: perspectives on the lives of older women*, London: Edward Arnold.

Bosanquet, N. (1978) *A Future for Old Age*, London: Temple Smith/New Society.

Butler, E. (1994) 'Markets and the future of welfare', pp. 241–64 in Gladstone, D. (ed) *British Social Welfare – past, present and future*, London: UCL Press.

Bytheway, B. (1995) *Ageism*, Buckingham: Open University Press.

Cahill, M. (1994) *The New Social Policy*, Oxford: Blackwell.

Carnegie Enquiry (1993) *Carnegie Enquiry into the Third Age – Final Report*, Folkestone: Bailey Management Services.

Carstensen, L., Mason, S. E. and Caldwell, E. C. (1982) 'Children's attitudes toward the elderly: an intergenerational technique for change', *Educational Gerontology*, 8(3): 291–99.

Chancellor of the Exchequer (1954) *Report of the Committee on the Economic and Financial Problems of the Provision for Old Age* (Phillips Report), London: HMSO.

Cole, T., Achenbaum, W. A., Jakobi, P. L. and Kastenbaum, R. (eds) (1993) *Voices and Visions of Aging: toward a critical gerontology*, New York: Springer.

Cooper, M., Sidell, M. and the Lewisham Older Women's Health Survey Project (1994) *Lewisham Older Women's Health Survey*, London: EdROP The City Lit.

Croft, S. and Beresford, P. (1990) *From Paternalism to Participation: involving people in social services*, London: Open Services Project and Joseph Rowntree Foundation.

Dorling, D. (1997) *Death in Britain: how local mortality rates have changed – 1950s to 1990s*, York: Joseph Rowntree Foundation.

Ginn, J. and Arber, S. (1996) 'Patterns of employment, gender and pensions: the effect of work history on older women's non-state pensions', *Work, Employment and Society*, 10(3): 469–90.

Griffiths, R. (1988) *Community Care. Agenda for Action*, London: HMSO.

Jamieson, A., Harper, S. and Victor, C. (eds) (1997) *Critical Approaches to Ageing and Later Life*, Buckingham: Open University Press.

Joseph, A. and Hallman, B. (1996) 'Caught in the triangle: the influence of home, work and elder location on work-family balance', *Canadian Journal on Aging*, 15(3): 393–413.

Laslett, P. (1996) *A Fresh Map of Life*, second edition, Basingstoke: Macmillan.

Laws, G. (1997) 'Spatiality and age relations', pp. 90–101 in Jamieson, A., Harper, S. and Victor, C. (eds) *Critical Approaches to Ageing and Later Life*, Buckingham: Open University Press.

Lyons, C. W., Newman, S. and Vasudev, J. (1984) 'Impact of a curriculum on aging on elementary school students', *Gerontology and Geriatrics Education*, 4(4): 51–63.

McEwen, E. (ed) (1990) *Age: the unrecognised discrimination*, London: Age Concern England.

Midwinter, E. (1997) *Pensioned Off: retirement and income examined*, Buckingham: Open University Press.

Minkler, M. (1996) 'Critical perspectives on ageing: new challenges for gerontology', *Ageing and Society*, 16(4): 467–87.

Minkler, M. and Estes, C. L. (eds) (1991) *Critical Perspectives on Aging: the political and moral economy of growing old*, New York: Baywood Publishing Company.

Minkler, M. and Estes, C. L. (eds) (1997) *Critical Gerontology: perspectives from political and moral economy*, New York: Baywood Publishing Company.

Moody, H. (1992) *Ethics in an Aging Society*, Baltimore: The Johns Hopkins University Press.

Neal, M. (1997) *Long Distance Caring*. Paper presented to the Gerontological Society of America Annual Conference, Cincinnati, November.

Netherlands Design Institute (1997) *Second Activity Report 97*. Amsterdam: Netherlands Design Institute.

Newman, S., Faux, R. and Larimer, B. (1997) 'Children's views on aging: their attitudes and values', *The Gerontologist*, 37(3): 412–17.

Newman, S. and Marks, R. (1980) *Intergenerational Classroom Teaching Teams: the effect of elderly volunteers, teachers and children*, Denver: Association for Gerontology in Higher Education.

Norton, A., Stoten, B. and Taylor, H. (1986) *Councils of Care: planning a local government strategy for older people*, Policy Studies in Ageing No 5, London: Centre for Policy on Ageing.

Older Women's League (1997) 'The path to poverty: an analysis of women's retirement income', in Minkler, M. and Estes, C. L. (eds) *Critical Gerontology: perspectives from political and moral economy*, New York: Baywood Publishing Company.

OPCS (1997) *1994-based National Population Projections*, London: HMSO.

O Connor, M. (1993) *Generation to Generation: linking schools with older people*, London: Cassell.

Phillips, J. (1992) 'The future of social work with older people', *Generations Review*, 2(4): 12–15.

Phillips, J. (ed) (1996) *Working Carers: international perspectives on caring and working for older people*, Aldershot: Avebury.

Ståhl, A. (forthcoming) 'Planning for a community responsive public transport system: the Swedish model' in Means, R. and Phillips, J. (eds) *A Broader Vision of Community Care*, Oxford: Anchor Publications.

Townsend, P. and Davidson, N. (eds) (1986) *Inequalities in Health: The Black Report*, Harmondsworth: Penguin.

Tozer, R. and Thornton, P. (1995) *A Meeting of Minds: older people as research advisers*, Social Policy Reports No 3, York University: Social Policy Research Unit.

Vincent, J. A. (1995) *Inequality and Old Age*, London: UCL Press.

Walker, A. (1997) 'Speaking For Themselves – the new politics of old age in Europe', Beth Johnson Foundation Silver Jubilee Lecture, October 7th.

Walker, A. and Maltby, T. (1997) *Ageing Europe*, Buckingham: Open University Press.

Walker, A. and Warren, L. (1996) *Changing Services for Older People: the Neighbourhood Support Units innovation*, Buckingham: Open University Press.

Whitehead, M. (1987) *The Health Divide*, Harmondsworth: Penguin.

Wicks, M. (1994) 'Social policy and the active society', pp. 265–88 in Gladstone, D. (ed) *British Social Welfare: past, present and future*, London: UCL Press.

Women's National Commission (1992) *Older Women, Myths and Strategies: an agenda for action*, London: The Women's National Commission.

Appendix 1

NCCOP publications and reports

1948   NCCOP *System of accounting for a home for old people.*

1951   NCCOP *A report on almshouses in two counties.*

1951   NCCOP *Homes for old people: notes on buying and converting property.*

1951   NCCOP *The care of the elderly living at home.*

1952   NCCOP *Club premises for old people: notes on design and construction of new buildings.*

1957   NCCOP *Report of an investigation of psychological, electro-encephalographic, clinical and social data from a group of normal old people: 1955–57.*

1959   NCCOP *Boarding out old people.*

1959   NCCOP *A chiropody service for old people: a study of present needs.*

1960   NCCOP *Chiropody for the elderly: a three year study of 120 voluntary schemes.*

1961   Harris, A.I. *Meals on wheels for old people: a report of an inquiry by the Government Social Survey.*

1961   NCCOP *Outlines of a survey on the meals on wheels service: summary of a report by the Government Social Survey.*

1961   Woodroffe, C. and Townsend, P. *Nursing homes in England and Wales: a study of responsibility.*

1962   Exton-Smith, A. N., Norton, D. and McLaren, R. *An investigation of geriatric nursing problems in hospital.*

1963   Miller, H.C. *The ageing countryman: a socio-medical report on old age in a country practice.*

1963   NCCOP *Accommodation for the mentally infirm aged: a report on needs and methods of provision.*

1964   NCCOP *Old age: a register of social research, 1955–1964.*

1964   NCCOP *Not too old at sixty: an experiment in the employment of women of pensionable age by the Over Forty Associaton for Women.*

1967   NCCOP *Private homes for old people: a discussion of their role and standards.*

1967   Leatham, P. E. *Old people's use of the telephone.*

1968   Harris, A.I. with Clausen, R. (for NCCOP) *Social welfare for the elderly: a study in 13 local authority areas in England, Wales and Scotland, vols 1 and 2.* Published by HMSO.

1971   Page, D. and Muir, T. *New housing for the elderly.*

1971   NCCOP *Telephones for the elderly.*

1972   NCCOP *Services for the elderly at home: a review of current needs and problems.*

1972   NCCOP *Old age: a register of social research, 1964–1972.*

1973   NCCOP *Housing in retirement: some pointers for social policy.*

1974   Loughborough University of Technology (for NCCOP) *Evaluation of alarm systems for the elderly and disabled.*

1975   NCCOP/Age Concern England *Health needs of the elderly.*

1975   NCCOP *Services for the elderly: a brief guide.*

1976   Bradshaw, J. (for NCCOP) *Found dead. A study of older people dying alone in York.*

1976   NCCOP *Old age: a register for social research, 1972 onwards.*

1976   NCCOP *Fire precautions in old people's homes.* Homes Advice Broadsheets no 1.

1976   British Council for Ageing (for NCCOP) *Research in gerontology: problems and prospects.*

1976   NCCOP *Day care for the elderly: the role of residential homes.* Homes Advice Broadsheets NO 2.

1977   NCCOP *New literature on old age.* Periodical 6 issues annually.

1977   NCCOP and Age Concern *Extra care? A report on care provided in voluntary organisations' establishments for the elderly.*

1977   NCCOP, Age Concern and Help the Aged *Three organisations, one cause.*

1977   Karn, V.A. (for NCCOP) *Retiring to the seaside.*

1977   Levin, E. *Services for confused elderly people.*

1977   Norman, A. *Transport and the elderly: problems and possible action.*

1977   Todd, H. (ed.) *Old age: a register of social research 1976–77.*

1978   Norman, A. *Outpatient ambulance transport.* NCCOP Conference Report.

1978   Loughborough University of Technology (for NCCOP) *Selecting aids for disabled people.*

1978   Abrams, M. *The elderly: an overview of current British social research.* Published by NCCOP and Age Concern England.

1978   Rose, E.A. (for NCCOP) *Housing for the Aged.*

1978   NCCOP *Finance and old people's homes.* Homes Advice Broadsheets no 3.

1978   Todd, H. (ed.) *Old age: a register of social research 1977–78.*

1979–83 Homes Advice Newsletter Nos 1–15.

1979   NCCOP *Organising aftercare.*

1979   NCCOP *Nutrition and catering in old people's homes.* Homes Advice Broadsheets no 4.

1979   NCCOP *Contact and activity: the linking of neighbourhood and homes for the elderly.* Homes Advice Broadsheets no 5.

1979   Todd, H. (ed.) *Old age: a register of social research 1978–79.*

1980   NCCOP *Mental health and illness in old people's homes.* Homes Advice Broadsheets no 6.

1980   Norman, A. J. *Rights and risk: a discussion document on civil liberty in old age.*

CPA publications and reports

1980   Todd, H. (ed.) *Old age: a register of social research, 1979–80.*

1981   CPA *Keeping elderly people moving in old people's homes.* Homes Advice Broadsheets no 7.

1981   CPA *'Endowed in perpetuity': a feasibility study on the future use of Rye Street Hospital, Bishop's Stortford.*

1982   Todd, H. (ed.) *Old age: a register of social research 1980–81.*

1982   Hedley, R. and Norman, A. *Home help: key issues in service provision.* CPA Reports 1.

1982   Norman, A. *Mental illness in old age: meeting the challenge.* Policy Studies in Ageing 1.

1982   CPA *Out of sight – out of mind: a study of the interface between social services departments and ethnic elderly people.*

1982   Midwinter, E. *Age is opportunity: education and older people.* Policy Studies in Ageing 2.

1983   Midwinter, E. *Ten million people.* Document to accompany the series of five BBC 1 programmes on the position of elderly people in Britain today, conceived and presented by Eric Midwinter.

1983   Taylor, H. *The hospice movement in Britain: its role and future.* CPA Reports 2.

1983   Hearnden, D. *Continuing care communities: a viable option in Britain?* CPA Reports 3.

1984   Norman, A. *Bricks and mortals: design and lifestyle in old people's homes.* CPA Reports 4.

1984   Hedley, R. and Norman, A. *Going places: two experiments in voluntary transport.* CPA Reports 5.

1984   CPA *Home life: a code of practice for residential care.* Sponsored by the Department of Health and Social Security.

1984   Hearnden, D. *Co-ordinating housing and social services: from good intentions to good practice.* CPA Reports 6.

1984   Hooper, B. *Home ground: how to select and get the best out of staff.*

1984   Norton, D. *Leisure and elderly people in Lewisham.*

1984   Meredith, B. (ed.) *Selected bibliographies on ageing: social planning for the elderly.*

1985   Hooper, B. and Jackson, W. *Caring for older people: selected list of audio visual items and training material.*

1985   Todd, H. (ed.) *Old age: a register of social research 1982–84.*

1985   Midwinter, E. *Future imponderable: the issue of private domiciliary care.*

1985   Wynne-Harley, D. *Third age radio*

1985   Walsh, B. and Midwinter, E. '*The Pickwick Papers*'. U3A study materials.

1985   Midwinter, E. and Wynne-Harley, D. *Toynbee's tomorrow's people: a survey of the present work of Toynbee Hall with older people and a strategy for the future.*

1985   Norman, A. *Triple jeopardy: growing old in a second homeland.* Policy Studies in Ageing 3.

1985   Midwinter, E. *The wage of retirement: the case for a new pensions policy.* Policy Studies in Ageing 4.

1986   Norton, A., Stoten, B. and Taylor, H. *Councils of care: planning a local government strategy for older people.* Policy Studies in Ageing 5.

1986   Donovan, T. and Wynne-Harley, D. *Not a nine-to-five job: staffing and management in private and voluntary residential care homes.* CPA Reports 7.

1986   Midwinter, E. *Caring for cash: the issue of private domiciliary care.* CPA Reports 8.

1986   CPA *London homes for the elderly.*

1986   CPA *The Hayward Fund 1974–1985: improving residential care homes.*

1986   Midwinter, E. *Old age: the emergence of a distinctive style.* First CPA/Niccol annual lecture.

1986   Armstrong, J. *Gardens for people: the Newstead experience.*

1986   CPA *Activities in residential homes – dance – drama – music.* CPA Seminar 18 November 1986.

1986   Taylor, H. *Day care under scrutiny.* Report to Lewisham and North Southwark Health Authority.

1987   Taylor, H. *Growing old together: elderly owner-occupiers and their housing.* Policy Studies in Ageing 6.

1987   Norman, A. *Severe dementia: the provision of longstay care.* Policy Studies in Ageing 7.

1987   Jefferys, M. *An ageing Britain: what is its future?* The 1987 CPA/Niccol lecture.

1987   Norman, A. *Aspects of ageism: a discussion paper.*

1987   Armstrong, J., Midwinter, E. and Wynne-Harley, D. *Retired leisure: four ventures in post-work activity.* CPA Reports 9.

1987   Midwinter, E. *Redefining old age: a review of CPA's recent contributions to social policy.*

1987   Midwinter, E. and Tester, S. *Polls apart? Older voters and the 1987 general election.* CPA Reports 10.

1987   Dunn, D. *Food, glorious food: a review of meals services for older people.*
        CPA Reports 11.

1987   Armstrong, J. *Staying active: a positive approach to residential homes.*
        CPA Reports 12.

1987   Norton, D. (ed.) *Selected bibliographies on ageing: education and older people.*

1987   CPA *The Hayward Fund 1984 garden scheme: report – Winter 1986/87.*

1987   Midwinter, E. and Wynne-Harley, D. *Retirement security and its recreational needs: an introduction.*

1988   Midwinter, E. *New design for old: function, style and older people.*
        CPA Reports 13.

1988   Hodgkinson, J. *Home work: meeting the needs of older people in residential homes.* Nine booklets.

1988   Wynne-Harley, D. *Life and work at Libury Hall. I and II.*

1988   Wynne-Harley, D. '*A model of its kind': an evaluation of the role and future status of the Lady Nuffield Home, Oxford.*

1988   Midwinter, E. and Wynne-Harley, D. *Clubability: a resources centre briefing for Help the Aged UK Division.*

1988   Millard, P. H. *Ageing: the antidote to fear is knowledge.* The 1988 CPA/Niccol Lecture.

1988   Dunn, D. *Being at home: a report on the Housing Division of Help the Aged.*

1988   Midwinter, E. *An education in itself: a report on the Education and Research Department of Help the Aged.*

1989   Jackson, W. *Understanding the needs of older people: selected list of audio visual items and training material.*

1989   Johnson, M. *From generation to generation: conflict of the old, the young and the state.* The 1989 CPA/Niccol Lecture.

1989   Dunn, D. *Meals matter: a report on the Broxbourne meals service.*

1989   Tester, S. *Caring by day: a study of day care services for older people.* Policy Studies in Ageing 8.

1989   Crosby, G. *CPA world directory of old age,* Harlow: Longman.

1989   CPA '*My only outing': a review of day care and allied services in Milton Keynes.*

1989   CPA *Inventory of UK courses in gerontology.*

1989   Wynne-Harley, D. '*A place like home'.* For the British Refugee Council.

1989   Quinn, C. *Honouring memories.* For the Age Exchange Reminiscence Project.

1990   Midwinter, E. *Creating chances: arts by older people.* CPA Reports 14.

1990   Bernard, M. '*Beyond our present imagination': leisure and lifestyle in later life.* The 1990 CPA/Niccol Lecture.

1990   CPA *Health and welfare services for older people: an information pack for the Cripplegate Foundation Area.*

1990   CPA *Community life: a code of practice for community care.*

1990   Midwinter, E. *The old order: crime and elderly people.* CPA in association with Help the Aged. CPA Reports 15.

1990   Lodge, K. *Directory of services for elderly people in the UK.* Joint Longman/CPA publication. Second edition 1991.

1991   Wynne-Harley, D. *Living dangerously: risk-taking, safety and older people.* CPA Reports 16.

1991   Midwinter, E. *The Rhubarb People: a childhood memoir.* The 1991 CPA/Niccol Lecture.

1991   Crosby, G. *Old age: a register of social research 1985–90.*

1991   Tester, S. *Health and welfare services for older people: an information pack for the Cripplegate Foundation area.*

1991   *Working with older people: a career guide.* Prepared and presented as a joint venture by Age Concern England, Help the Aged and the Centre for Policy on Ageing.

1991   Wynne-Harley, D. *Homelands: 'the old people's home'.*

1991   Midwinter, E. *Out of focus: old age, the press and broadcasting.* CPA Reports 17.

1992   Age Concern England, Centre for Policy on Ageing, Chief Leisure Officers Association, Help the Aged *Leisure life: a local authority code of practice for the effective provision of leisure to older people.*

1992   Midwinter, E. *Leisure: new opportunities in the third age.* CPA for the Carnegie Inquiry into the Third Age.

1992   Midwinter, E. *Citizenship: from ageism to participation.* CPA for the Carnegie Inquiry into the Third Age.

1992   Wynne-Harley, D. *Changing images: grandparents in fiction and fact.* The 1992 CPA/Niccol Lecture.

1992   Jackson, W. (ed.) *Selected bibliographies on ageing: risk-taking, safety and older people.*

1992   Jackson, W. (ed.) *Understanding the needs of older people: selected list of audio-visual items and training material.*

1992   Tester, S. *Common knowledge: a coordinated approach to information-giving.* CPA Reports 18.

1993   Wertheimer, A. *Speaking out: citizen advocacy and older people.* CPA Reports 19.

1993   Crosby, G. *European directory of older age: information and organisations concerned with older people in the twelve EC member states.*

1993   *Older people in the European Community: fact sheet.* CPA and the Family Policy Studies Centre.

1994   McGlone, F. and Cronin, N. *A crisis in care? the future of family and state care for older people in the European Union.* CPA and the Family Policy Studies Centre.

1995   CPA *Age Info CD ROM.* Issued quarterly.

1995   CPA *Age Info CD ROM User Guide.* (Revised edition, 1997).

1995   Dunning, A. *Citizen advocacy with older people: a code of good practice.*

1995   CPA *Health service needs of members of ethnic communities in Riverside.* Report to Riverside Community Healthcare NHS Trust.

1995   Dalley, G., Peretz-Brown, S. and Seal, H. *Homeshare in Sutton: a report of an evaluation study.* CPA with Age Concern Sutton Borough.

1995   CPA *Leisure activities for people over 50.* Report to Dacorum Borough Council.

1996   CPA *A better home life: a code of good practice for residential and nursing home care.*

1996   CPA *A framework for promoting the health of older people.* Report to the Health Education Authority.

1996   CPA *Older people assessing standards of care.* Report to Health Services Accreditation.

1996   CPA with MTW Limited *Review of day care services for older people with functional mental health needs.* Report to the London Borough of Richmond upon Thames.

1996   Dalley, G. and Howse, K. *A review of health and social care provision for older people in London.* Report to the King's Fund London Commission.

1997   CPA *Achieving a better home life: establishing and maintaining quality in continuing care for older people.* CPA Reports 20.

1997   Marshall, M. *State of the art in dementia care.* CPA 50th anniversary volume.

1997   CPA with MTW Limited *Review of day care services.* A report to the Metropolitan Borough of Sandwell.

1997   Dalley, G. *100 at 100.* A study of centenarians commissioned by DGAA Home Life.

1997   Dalley, G. and Denniss, M. *Patient satisfaction: older people discharged from hospital,* CPA Reports 21.

1997   Qureshi, T. *Living in Britain – growing old in Britain: a study of Bangladeshi elders in London,* CPA Reports 22.

1997   Killoran, A., Howse, K. and Dalley, G. *Promoting the health of older people: a compendium.* CPA with the Health Education Authority.

1997   CPA *Estimating the demand for personal social services for older people.* A report to the Department of Health, CPA in association with the Centre for Health Economics, York University.

1997   CPA *Briefings Nos 1–12*. Subjects covered: advocacy, day services, minority
        ethnic communities, residential care, health care, leisure, centenarians, health
        promotion, role of local government and voluntary sector, social services, deaths
        of older people alone and learning difficulties.

1997   CPA *Findings No 1 – Deaths of people alone.*

1997   CPA *Findings No 2 – Living in Britain – growing old in Britain: a study of the
        lives of Bangladeshi elders living in the London Borough of Camden*

1997   CPA *Review of voluntary sector services for older people.* A report to the London
        Borough of Lewisham.

1997   Howse, K. *Deaths of people alone.* CPA Reports 23. CPA with Help the Aged.

1997   Bernard, M. and Phillips, J. *The social policy of old age: moving into the 21st
        century.* CPA 50th anniversary volume.

About the authors

Sara Arber is Professor of Sociology at the University of Surrey. Her research interests include older women's financial resources and health, the provision of informal care and inequalities in women's health. She is co-editor (with Jay Ginn) of *Connecting Gender and Ageing: a sociological approach* and (with Maria Evandrou) of *Ageing, Independence and the Life Course.*

Karl Atkin is Senior Research Fellow at the Ethnic and Social Policy Research Unit (ESPR), Department of Social and Economic Studies, University of Bradford. He is co-editor (with Waqar Ahmad) of *'Race' and Community Care*, and co-author (with Julia Twigg) of *Carers Perceived: policy and practice in informal care.*

Carole Archibald is Senior Fieldworker at the Dementia Services Development Centre, University of Stirling and has worked in the field of dementia for twelve years. Her interests include activities for people with dementia, respite care, specialist dementia units and sexuality.

Elizabeth Baikie is a Clinical Psychologist at the Royal Victoria Hospital in Edinburgh, specialising in work with older adults. She is currently researching into issues relating to intimacy, sexuality and dementia. For a number of years she has been involved in the training and supervision of bereavement counsellors, marriage counsellors and sex therapists.

Miriam Bernard is Gerontology Course Director and Reader in the Department of Applied Social Studies at Keele University. She has researched and written on a wide range of issues relating to older people, first as Research Officer at the Beth Johnson Foundation and subsequently at Keele. She is currently completing, with colleagues, a three year research project looking at 'Older People and Family Life', and she is also engaged in research examining the lives of older people living in retirement communities. Her other research interests are around health education and promotion, women and ageing, and informal care.

Joanna Bornat is Senior Lecturer in the School of Health and Social Welfare at the Open University. Her research interests include the contribution of reminiscence and biography to work with older people, family reconstitution and older people, and pensioners' organisations. She edited *Reminiscence Reviewed: perspectives, evaluations, achievements* and she is co-editor of the journal *Oral History.*

Gillian Dalley is Director of the Centre for Policy on Ageing. Before joining the Centre she was a senior manager in the NHS working for a regional health authority. Her academic training is in anthropology, and she has worked for the Policy Studies Institute and the King's Fund on health services research. She is the author of *Ideologies of Caring: rethinking community and collectivism.*

Andrew Dunning is a Policy Officer at the Centre for Policy on Ageing. He has previously worked as a lecturer, social worker and co-ordinator of a citizen advocacy project. He is the author of *Citizen Advocacy with Older People: a code of good practice* (CPA).

Maria Evandrou is a Fellow in Health Policy Analysis at the King's Fund Policy Institute, and Associate Research Fellow on the Welfare State Programme, London School of Economics. She is the editor of *Baby Boomers: what future when we retire?* Dr Evandrou is a Governor of the Centre for Policy on Ageing.

Jane Falkingham is a Lecturer in Population Studies in the Department of Social Policy and Administration at the London School of Economics, and Research Fellow on the Welfare State Programme, also at the LSE. She is co-author (with Paul Johnson) of *Ageing and Economic Welfare* and co-editor (with John Hills) of *The Dynamic of Welfare.*

Jay Ginn is a Research Fellow in the Department of Sociology at the University of Surrey. She was previously a researcher at the National Institute for Social Work. Her research interests include older people's incomes and material assets, including gender and class differences, the implications of the changing balance between public and private pensions and international comparison of pension systems' treatment of women. She is co-editor (with Sara Arber) of *Connecting Gender and Ageing: a sociological approach* and co-author (with Sara Arber) of *Gender and Later Life.*

Kenneth Howse is a Policy Officer at the Centre for Policy on Ageing. He was previously a Research Fellow in the Department of Psychiatry of Addictive Behaviour at St George's Hospital Medical School. His research interests include medical ethics, health promotion and addictions.

Julia Johnson is a Lecturer in the School of Health and Social Welfare at the Open University. She is co-editor (with Bill Bytheway) of *Welfare and the Ageing Experience* and (with Robert Slater) of *Ageing and Later Life.*

Eric Midwinter is Visiting Professor of Education at the University of Exeter and Chairman of the Community Education Development Centre. He was Director of the Centre for Policy on Ageing from 1980–1991 and vigorously promoted the interests of older people on the broad fronts of education, leisure, pensions, design, crime, the media and politics. He is particularly associated with the University of the Third Age and is author of the recently published *Pensioned Off*, a history of retirement and income maintenance in old age.

Jim Ogg is a researcher in gerontology. He worked as a social worker with Waltham Forest from 1987–1991, and before that he had several years in residential work. From 1994–1997 he worked as a Research Fellow in the Centre for Social Gerontology at Keele, on the 'Older People and Family Life' project.

Sheila Peace is Sub-dean (Research) in the School of Health and Social Welfare at the Open University. A social geographer by discipline, she has written widely on many gerontological issues including environment and ageing, residential care and the quality of life of older women. She is co-author of *Re-evaluating Residential Care; Private Lives in Public Place* (with Leonie Kellaher and Dianne Willcocks); *Elderly People: choice, satisfaction and participation* (with Isobel Allen and Deborah Hogg) as well as editor of *Researching Social Gerontology* and co-editor of *Ageing in Society* (with John Bond and Peter Coleman).

Judith Phillips is a Lecturer in Social Work and Gerontology at Keele University. Her research interests include work and family issues, private residential care and community care. She is author of *Working Carers* and is currently working with colleagues on research on the family life of older people.

Chris Phillipson is Professor of Applied Social Studies and Social Gerontology, and Director of the Centre for Social Gerontology, Keele University. His research interests include social theory and ageing, social change and the family, and work and retirement. He is the author of *Capitalism and the Construction of Old Age* and co-author of *The Sociology of Old Age, Changing Work and Retirement,* and *Elder Abuse in Perspective.* His most recent book is *Reconstructing Old Age: new agendas for social theory and social practice* (to be published by Sage in 1998).

Julia Twigg is Reader in Social Policy at the University of Kent. She was formerly at the Social Policy Research Unit, University of York. A sociologist by training, she has written extensively on carers and service support. She is co-author (with Karl Atkin) of *Carers Perceived: policy and practice in informal care.* Her current research interests are on the provision and acceptance of personal care, with a particular focus on bathing.

Margaret Simey was the first student to take the degree in social science pioneered by the Liverpool University. She was awarded a D.Litt (Hon) by the University and is now a Senior Research Fellow (Hon) in the Department of Sociology, Social Policy and Social Studies at the University. She has been actively involved in community politics all her life, and served as Deputy Chair of the Social Services throughout the initiation and implementation of the Seebohm Report. Publications include *Democracy Rediscovered, The Disinherited Society* and *Charity Rediscovered.*

Index